CANADIAN WATER POLITICS

Canadian Water Politics

Conflicts and Institutions

EDITED BY
MARK SPROULE-JONES, CAROLYN JOHNS,
AND B. TIMOTHY HEINMILLER

McGill-Queen's University Press
Montreal & Kingston · London · Ithaca

© McGill-Queen's University Press 2008
ISBN 978-0-7735-3468-1 (cloth)
ISBN 978-0-7735-3469-8 (paper)

Legal deposit fourth quarter 2008
Bibliothèque nationale du Québec

Printed in Canada on acid-free paper that is 100% ancient forest free
(100% post-consumer recycled), processed chlorine free.

McGill-Queen's University Press acknowledges the support of the Canada
Council for the Arts for our publishing program. We also acknowledge
the financial support of the Government of Canada through the Book
Publishing Industry Development Program (BPIDP) for our publishing
activities.

Library and Archives Canada Cataloguing in Publication

Canadian water politics: conflicts and institutions/edited by Mark
Sproule-Jones, Carolyn Johns, and B. Timothy Heinmiller.

Includes bibliographical references and index.
ISBN 978-0-7735-3468-1 (bound)
ISBN 978-0-7735-3469-8 (pbk)

1. Water – Canada.   2. Water – Government policy – Canada.   3. Water
use – Canada.   4. Water conservation – Canada.   5. Water-supply – Canada.
6. Water – Management.   7. Water rights – Canada.   I. Sproule-
Jones, Mark, 1941–   II. Johns, Carolyn M., 1967–   III. Heinmiller, B.
Timothy, 1975–

HD1696.C2C284 2008   333.9100971   C2008-904152-6

This book was typeset by Interscript in 10.5/13 Sabon.

Contents

Tables and Figures

TABLES

FIGURES

Preface

MARK SPROULE-JONES AND CAROLYN JOHNS

The purpose of this book is to explore the nature of water conflicts and the operation of water management institutions in the Canadian context. It is designed to help analysts and students in the social sciences, environmental studies, and policy studies explore water resource conflicts and the roles that governments and others play in mediating, amplifying, reducing, or exacerbating these disputes. The book was written for both teaching and research purposes. On the teaching side, it fills a big gap in policy and political studies on water in Canada. We have sought in this volume to use a basic and varied institutional approach to policy analysis that is accessible to students in many different disciplines. We do so by presenting overview chapters on the nature of water and water politics, together with various chapters highlighting specific water policy issues and conflicts in different parts of Canada.

The work includes research by a number of contributors on water resource management across Canada. The unifying concern is with institutional analysis and design to improve water policy and governance. The focus on conflicts related to multiple uses of water is a key element in the growing body of work on common property resources, water conflict, and water policy internationally. For the purposes of this book, all authors assume that institutional arrangements evolve, are adaptable, and can be redesigned and improved. The individual chapters illustrate the diversity and complexity of water resource issues and policies in Canada and highlight the enduring and future challenges policy-makers face in trying to govern and manage Canada's waters.

The editors wish to acknowledge the help and support of our home universities: McMaster, Ryerson, and Brock. Our funders include the National Centre of Excellence, the Canadian Water Network, the City of Hamilton, and the Economic Policy Research Institute at the University of Western Ontario.

Contributors

KEITH BROWNSEY teaches political science at Mount Royal College in Calgary. He has written extensively on provincial politics and government and resource policy issues. His books include *Executive Styles in Canada: Cabinet Structures and Leadership Practices in Canadian Government* (2005), edited with Michael Howlett and Luc Bernier. He is also a frequent media commentator on both provincial and national issues.

PETER CLANCY is a professor of political science at St Francis Xavier University. He is co-author of *Against the Grain: Foresters and Politics in Nova Scotia* (2000) and *The Savage Years: the Perils of Reinventing Government in Nova Scotia* (2000) and author of *Micropolitics and Canadian Business: Paper, Steel and the Airlines* (2004). He is currently completing a study of offshore petroleum governance on the Scotian Shelf.

JOHN K. GRANT is a PhD candidate in his final year at McMaster University. His major fields include public policy, public administration, and comparative politics in advance industrial democracies. He is a senior policy analyst with a Hamilton-based consulting company and currently holds a position as an external researcher with the York Centre for International and Security Studies.

B. TIMOTHY HEINMILLER is an assistant professor in the Department of Political Science at Brock University, where he researches and teaches in the areas of public policy and public administration, focusing specifically on environmental and resource management policy. He has done extensive research in water and natural resources governance in Canada, Australia, and the United States, and his articles have been published in such journals as *Canadian Public Administration*, *Governance*, and *Natural Resources Journal*. Professor Heinmiller is currently working on an SSHRC-funded research project on the evolution of resource rights in Canada and Australia.

CAROLYN JOHNS is associate professor in the Department of Politics and Public Administration at Ryerson University. Her research interests include comparative environmental policy, water policy, intergovernmental relations, and policy capacity issues in the public sector. She is presently working on a co-authored book with Dr Gregory J. Inwood and Dr Patricia L. O'Reilly entitled "A Comparative Analysis of Intergovernmental Policy Capacity in Finance, Trade, Environment and Health" and a sole authored book entitled "Walkerton, Water Pollution and Water Policy in Canada."

KEN RASMUSSEN is director of the Johnson-Shoyama Graduate School of Public Policy at the University of Regina. He is the author of numerous articles on public management reform, provincial politics, and public policy. Professor Rasmussen recently published *Defending a Contested Ideal: Merit and the Public Service Commission, 1908–2008*, co-authored with Luc Julliet. With David Siegel, he co-edited *Professionalism and Public Service: Essays in Honour of Kenneth Kernaghan* (2008).

RICHARD SCHWINDT holds a joint appointment in the Department of Economics and the Faculty of Business Administration at Simon Fraser University. His research focuses on the industrial organization and public policy for renewable resources. His publications dealing the salmon fishery include a cost-benefit analysis, written with Aidan Vining and Steven Globerman, that appeared in the *Journal of Policy Analysis and Management* in 2000.

MARK SPROULE-JONES is emeritus professor of political science and Victor K. Copps Professor of Urban Studies at McMaster University. He has published eleven books on institutional analysis and design. His work on water resources governance includes *The Real World of Pollution Control* (1982), *Governments at Work* (1993), and *The Restoration of the Great Lakes* (2002).

KAREN THOMAS holds a doctoral degree in comparative public policy from McMaster University, where her research focused on understanding the effectiveness of voluntary policy instruments in managing toxic substances in Canada and the United States. She spent five years as a senior adviser for the Ontario Ministry of the Environment and worked in policy areas such as children's environmental health, source water protection, and air quality. Dr Thomas is currently a senior writer with the Agricultural Sustainability Institute at the University of California, Davis.

AIDAN R. VINING is the CNABS Professor of Business and Government Relations in the Segal Graduate School of Business at Simon Fraser University. He obtained his PhD from the University of California, Berkeley, and also holds an LLB from King's College, London, and an MBA and an MPP. He researches in the areas of public policy, policy analysis, and business strategy and has published many books and articles on public policy issues dealing with public-sector efficiencies, organizational choices, and human capital.

Abbreviations

ACA	Alberta Conservation Association
ANSI	area of natural or scientific interest
AOC	area of concern
BAIT	Bay Area Implementation Team (Hamilton)
BARC	Bay Area Restoration Council (Hamilton)
BMP	best management practice
BOD	biochemical oxygen demand
CAFSAC	Canadian Atlantic Fisheries Scientific Advisory Committee
CCME	Canadian Council of Ministers of the Environment
CCPA	Canadian Chemical Producers Association
CEAA	Canadian Environmental Assessment Act
CEPA	Canadian Environmental Protection Act
CIELP	Canadian Institute for Environmental Law and Policy
CPR	common-pool resources
CSO	combined sewage overflow
CUFTA	Canada–US Free Trade Agreement
CWA	Canada Water Act
DFO	Department of Fisheries and Oceans (federal)
DOE	Department of the Environment (federal)
EC	Environment Canada
EFP	environmental farm plan
EFR	environmental fiscal reform
EPA	environmental performance agreement
	Environmental Protection Act (Ontario)
	Environmental Protection Agency (US)
EPP	Environmental Farm Plan (Ontario)
ESA	environmentally sensitive area

FWF	Federal Water Framework
FWP	Federal Water Policy
GATT	General Agreement on Tariffs and Trade
HPA	Hamilton Port Authority
ICNAF	International Commission for Northwest Atlantic Fisheries
IFAW	International Fund for Animal Welfare
IJC	International Joint Commission
ITQ	individual transferable quota
INAC	Indian and Northern Affairs Canada
MAA	Master Agreement on Apportionment (Alberta)
MAFRA	Ministry of Agriculture, Food and Rural Affairs (Ontario)
MISA	Municipal-Industrial Strategy for Abatement
MNR	Ministry of Natural Resources (Ontario)
MOE	Ministry of the Environment (Ontario)
MOU	memorandum of understanding
NAFTA	North American Free Trade Agreement
NMA	Nutrient Management Act
NMP	nutrient management plan
NMS	nutrient management strategy
NPRI	National Pollutant Release Inventory (Canada)
NPS	non-point source
NRTEE	National Round Table on the Environment and the Economy
OECD	Organisation for Economic Co-operation and Development
OP	official plan (Ontario Planning Act)
OWRA	Ontario Water Resources Act
PAH	polyaromatic hydrocarbons
PCB	polychlorine biphenyl
POP	persistent organic pollutant
PPWB	Prairie Provinces Water Board
PRI	Policy Research Initiative
RAP	remedial action plan
ROP	regional official plan (Ontario Planning Act)
SPA	source-protection authority
SPC	source-protection committee
SPP	source-protection plan
STP	sewage-treatment plant
TAC	total allowable catch
TDML	total daily maximum load

TPM   total phosphorus management
TRI   Toxic Release Inventory (US)
WQT   water quality trading
WTO   World Trade Organization

CANADIAN WATER POLITICS

Introduction

CAROLYN JOHNS

Water is essential to life. It is a vital resource, required for all environmental and societal processes (Gleick, 1993). It makes up two-thirds of the human body. A person can live without food for more than a month but without water for only a few days (Canada, Environment Canada, 2005b). Although water is essential for survival and increasingly valuable as a resource, many countries have used and exploited it to such a degree that freshwater supplies have decreased and pollution levels are unsustainable. Globally, the two biggest stresses on water systems are population growth and economic development (Averill and Whelan, 2000). Competition for water between various uses has strained the supply and quality of fresh water. Internationally, water use has been growing at more than double the rate of the population (Canada, Environment Canada, 1998a), and humans are now using over half the available freshwater supply and polluting the waters they leave behind (Averill and Whelan, 2000). According to the World Health Organization, 1.5 billion people do not have a safe supply of drinking water, and 1.7 billion people do not have adequate sanitation facilities (Miller, 2004). As a result of these inadequate conditions, 5 million deaths a year worldwide are attributed to polluted drinking water (Clarke, 2003). As the world's population continues to grow and development increases, even those countries with an abundant supply of available water such as Canada need to consider the multiple, competing uses of water to manage water sustainability. However, conflicts over the use of water have historically presented many challenges to policy-makers and will continue to do so in the future.

Water helps to define Canada. Indeed, it is part of Canadian identity. Some 25 per cent of the world's fresh surface waters are within Canadian boundaries. In a national poll, 97 per cent of Canadians expressed their support for water being recognized as a human right (Ipsos Reid, 2004). Many Canadians consider water part of their national identity but have become so accustomed to living in an environment which boasts a large water supply that they have taken it for granted. This abundance creates a policy environment in which there are many stakeholders in the management of water resources, yet it remains undervalued in many instances. The relative abundance of water varies throughout the country. In most places there is a myth of overabundance, regardless of how much water is actually available for use. Despite Canada's vast water resources, many communities face shortages, and such shortages already hamper uses in some regions of the country. Recent reports indicate these problems will likely become worse as a result of climate change (Canada, Natural Resources Canada, 2004; Environment Canada, 2008b).

There have been increasing calls from many different stakeholders for new approaches and institutional arrangements to govern Canada's waters. Policy debates about the quantity and quality of water resources in Canada are increasingly on the agendas of all levels of government in both urban and rural communities across the country. With multiple and competing uses of water, there are an increasing number of stakeholders with claims related to water governance, and the policy landscape is home to numerous conflicts. Hydroelectric dams and logging operations have seen protests from fishers and recreationists in the West, and the irrigation of farm lands in the southern prairies has resulted in conflicts between farmers, fishers, and Aboriginals. In the Great Lakes, most commercial stocks of fish have been exhausted or are so polluted that they constitute a health threat if eaten regularly. Some 57 million tonnes of liquid wastes are poured into the Great Lakes annually by the 33 million basin inhabitants, their industries, and municipalities (Colborn et al., 1990, 64). Thousands of commercial ships use the lakes and the St Lawrence Seaway and River to transport goods, resulting in dredging and other alterations as lake levels continue to decline. The Atlantic cod story is well-known in East Coast waters, and Aboriginals and other fishers fight over dwindling stocks in other basins. Conflict and competition are defining characteristics of water resource use in Canada. In these circumstances, people turn to governments or the courts, or they take their own collective actions to find solutions.

As outlined in the preface, the purpose of this book is to examine and analyze the nature of water conflicts and the operation of water

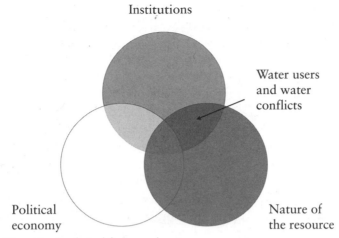

Figure I.1 Analytical framework.

management institutions in Canada. This volume is designed to help analysts and students in the social sciences, environmental studies, and policy studies explore water resource conflicts and the roles that governments and others play in mediating, amplifying, reducing, or exacerbating these disputes. The unifying concern is with institutional analysis and design to improve water policy and governance. The book assembles several case studies in which drama and conflict over the use of water resources feature in order to illustrate and examine a variety of water governance institutions. The analytical framework of the volume emphasizes four key variables in water-use conflicts: users, the nature of water resources, management institutions, and the broader political economy. As figure I.1 demonstrates, water users and conflicts between them are at the centre of this framework, the context for these disputes being significantly determined by the other three variables. Although this conceptualization simplifies the complexity of water politics, conflicts, and institutions, it allows for the examination of the wide range of interconnected water governance institutions in each of the case studies.

WATER USERS

Given the extreme diversity of economic, anthropological, and ecological uses related to water, the potential for conflict between different types of water users is particularly acute. Consider for a moment that a water resource can simultaneously serve any or all of the following purposes: a habitat, a transportation route, a waste disposal outlet, a source of renewable energy, a recreational area, a source of food and water, a climatic component, an aesthetic backdrop, and a venue of spirituality. The potential for competition and conflict between these uses is self-evident.

Water also attracts unusually large and diverse groups of users because of its fugitive and cross-medium characteristics. It has the propensity to be in continuous motion and interconnected with the other two media – air and land – in hydrological systems that often extend across vast geographic areas. This characteristic is further compounded by the fact that people sharing a single water resource may be separated by vast geographic, cultural, and political spaces, making it difficult for them even to recognize their hydrological interdependence and the implications of their use for other users. In short, the user groups for many water resources are quite large and heterogeneous, so that it is hard for them to cooperate in the management of their shared resource and the management institutions required can be quite complex. This is particularly the case if the user group is fragmented among a number of sovereign jurisdictions and water management becomes an issue of international or domestic intergovernmental negotiation.

In terms of policy actors, therefore, there are users and those actors involved directly or indirectly in trying to manage multiple uses in different water bodies across the country. In most of the cases in this book, the users and actors are domestic, but increasingly, transboundary and international users and actors have a role in water resource conflicts and collective actions.

THE NATURE OF WATER RESOURCES

In many ways, water is a deceptively complex resource. It is often grouped with a number of other natural resources known as "common pool" resources. Common pools are distinctive because they are inherently shared and "subtractible" – if one person removes or degrades part of a common pool, there is less available to the others who share it. Resources of this type are vulnerable to destruction through overuse, over-consumption, and over-pollution because sustainable management of common pools usually requires cooperation and trust among those who use and share the resource, and such collaboration can be very difficult to achieve. In the absence of cooperation, unrestrained competition among resource users can result in accelerated resource use and, eventually, a "tragedy of the commons" in which the resource is completely depleted or degraded, to the detriment of all (Hardin, 1968). A voluminous literature exists on managing water as a common-pool or common-property resource. Social scientists have studied it as a common-pool resource for some time, mostly in an effort to determine what types of institutions are most effective in avoiding a tragedy of the commons (Ostrom, 1990).

Equally important is the simple fact that the quantity and quality of water available for human use is generally variable over time and space, resulting in situations that differ quite vastly in terms of water abundance and scarcity. The relative abundance or scarcity of water resources significantly impacts on how people use water and the institutions they create to manage it. The property rights in the water-scarce Canadian prairies, for instance, are much different from those in the water-abundant Canadian east. The importance of water abundance/scarcity is particularly evident when a resource becomes scarcer over time. Water-use practices and water management institutions that are acceptable in situations of abundance may be entirely dysfunctional in circumstances of scarcity, highlighting the importance of both institutional design and institutional change.

INSTITUTIONS

Institutions are the primary focus of this book because, of the four elements in our analytical framework, they are the most subject to human agency. In most cases, water management institutions are created and designed by communities, stakeholders, and governments to manage water uses and water-use conflicts. They do so by establishing configurations of water-use and water management rules that influence and routinize behaviour and conflict resolution. Water management institutions can range from informal arrangements and practices between various water users to more formal legal mechanisms such as property rights, regulations, statutory laws designed by federal, provincial, and local legislative bodies, and constitutional laws. They can also range from simple single-level, single-use governance designs to very complex multi-level, multi-use forms, depending on the water-use situation. Small-scale, single-use, homogenous user groups with a history of cooperation were at one time a feature in watersheds across Canada. However, most watersheds are now characterized by multiple uses and heterogeneous user groups and policy actors with limited interaction and varying interests and powers to collectively protect and manage the resource.

As indicated above, a growing social science literature exists concerning institutional designs for water management. On the basis of work done by Elinor Ostrom and others, a set of general institutional design principles has been posited for the management of common-pool resources, but much of the more recent literature, including Ostrom's own work, recognizes that resource management institutions in multiple-use contexts must be adapted to local and international exigencies if they are to have any hope of effective and sustainable resource management. Analysis at multiple scales and recognition of the presence of multiple institutions are required. These concerns mean that the study of any single institution may not provide an accurate and complete picture of the political processes involved in most water policy issues. In some of the recent common-pool literature, scholars have grappled with this problem and the institutional and political complexity inherent in it by focusing attention on the phenomenon of "institutional interplay." In this book, institutional interplay refers to the connections and interaction effects that result from the presence of multiple institutions involved in a water governance system. In terms of scale, these include institutions at multiple levels, from local watersheds to rivers and estuaries to lakes to coastal waters.

Institutional interplay and the issue of effective institutional design are a major theme of this book. A central line of inquiry is to examine the role of institutions in addressing various water-use conflicts in order ultimately to consider how communities and policy-makers can design institutions to get many different users of water resources, most of who do not know one another and who use water for very different uses, to come together to manage water quantity and quality for the benefit of all. The case studies in this book are used to illustrate the complexity of water resource governance, identify shortcomings, and highlight various institutional design solutions. Whether these suggestions are feasible and achievable is another – and equally important – question, one that is heavily reliant on the prevailing political economy.

POLITICAL ECONOMY

The political economy of water use refers to the larger social, political, and economic forces at work which determine, at any given point in time, those uses and users that are likely to be most prevalent and most powerful in the management of a given water resource. For example, the fact that a heavily industrialized economy emerged in the Great

Lakes Basin while a predominantly agricultural economy evolved in the South Saskatchewan Basin was in large part determined by the presence of water and had a formative impact on both the water users and the water management institutions that eventually emerged in these respective basins. In turn, the entrenchment of institutions favouring industrial and agricultural uses had a similarly formative impact on later water-use conflicts in these basins, as new potential uses emerged to challenge the existing entrenched ones.

Though most water management institutions have been designed to deal with conflicts, it is also a historical truth that they create conflict by privileging certain uses and users over others. Generally, the privileged users are those whose claims to water are recognized by governments first, and the main power dynamic of many water-use conflicts is defined by the fortuitous circumstance of which agricultural, industrial, or commercial water users were the first to have their water claims institutionalized in law. As a result, efforts to reform established institutions and displace existing uses are usually pitched as uphill battles, with established users occupying the institutional high ground. This is a second major theme running through all the case studies in this book, and it is important because it places considerations of institutional design in a more dynamic historical context.

APPLICATION OF THE FRAMEWORK

Figure I.1 depicts water users and conflicts at the centre of analysis for each of the case study chapters. As outlined above, the framework presents overlapping circles, indicating that the nature of the resource, institutions, and political economy interact in different ways in each of the case studies. For example, political economy and the nature of water as a resource can act as broader constraining factors that impact on the design of water management institutions and thus on prospects for conflict resolution. Government is the conflict-resolver or mediator between various water users and therefore is at the centre of the figure, where these interests intersect. The cases illustrate the need for better integration of environmental concerns in all three spheres; a better understanding of the nature of water as a resource and its multiple uses, the historical privilege of various water users, and the ways in which institutions embed these historical and current realities; and the implications these factors have for future success in water resource management, in order for governments and stakeholders to do a better job in managing multiple uses.

Finally, we should note that water resource conflicts are endemic in all communities. As illustrated in all the cases in this book, situations change. Climate can be a bigger factor in affecting water quantities than any human withdrawals or diversions, for example. Technological and scientific innovations can change water uses; for example, the use of new technologies in sewage treatment plants can radically reduce discharges into lakes or rivers, with various benefits for ecosystems. Environmental and human health crises, new water uses, and new rights to water domestically and, increasingly, internationally all have the potential to change the nature of water uses and conflicts in basins across Canada.

ORGANIZATION OF THE BOOK

Part One of this book provides further background and detail concerning the four main elements of the analytical framework, with particular emphasis on the multiple uses and users of water as a resource in Canada. Chapter 1 outlines how the character of water as a multiple-use resource underpins the conflicts in subsequent chapters and the broad policy and institutional framework in which water politics has developed in Canada. This chapter presents an overview of the principles of water itself and how these set the stage for conflict, water governance challenges, and collective action. The chapter focuses on the defining scientific, social, cultural, and economic features of water and the multiple applications that underpin political conflict over different types of water uses: withdrawal, consumptive, pollution, and in-stream. It is based on the assumption that in order for policy-makers and analysts to design institutional arrangements and policy instruments to ensure sustainable water resource governance, a fundamental understanding of the properties of water as a resource is required.

Part Two focuses on the institutions, instruments, and property rights that have evolved to manage water resources in Canada. This section lays the institutional foundation for the case studies that follow. It highlights how institutions for water quantity and quality management have developed, the variations in policies for surface and groundwater, and the wide range of options available to policy-makers in designing policy instruments and institutions to address water resource conflicts. This section also outlines how the politics of water varies in terms of withdrawals, water pollution, and in-stream uses.

Chapter 2 provides an overview of the historical and current political landscape related to water resource management in Canada, including an account of how federalism, intergovernmental management, Aboriginal rights, and other state and non-state factors interact to structure water policy institutions. This chapter provides the broad institutional context for all the case-study chapters. It also outlines the basis for various authorities in Canada, setting the foundation for the instruments and implementation options covered in chapter 3.

Chapter 3 outlines the wide variety of policy instruments and institutional arrangements used to address a range of water-use conflicts in Canada. Four broad types of instruments are discussed: regulatory, financial and market-based, voluntary, and information-based. Examples of different policy instruments in each of these categories are reviewed to demonstrate the range of instruments being implemented under the various institutional arrangements described in the case-study chapters. The diversity of instruments presented also reveals how institutional arrangements determine preferences for certain choices over time and how and why some instruments from the toolbox are not used at all in the Canadian context.

Chapter 4 outlines the importance of property rights and the ways in which they underpin institutional arrangements. Property rights are important because they significantly influence the power dynamics of any water-use situation. Those with recognized water rights enjoy a privileged legal position in relation to those without such rights. In this chapter, historical property rights are examined in relation to different water uses and users, how rights concerned with water have evolved, and how many of the rights are held in common or held by a government (acting in legal terms on behalf of the Crown).

Parts Three, Four, and Five build on this background by examining a variety of water use and water conflict case studies from across Canada. The case-study chapters build upon and draw from the context provided in Part Two by analyzing a wide range of actual water-use conflicts in Canada in order to determine how the existing water management institutions have functioned in practice. In each of the chapters in these sections, the issues of institutional design, interplay, and change are the primary focus of analysis. The case studies were selected to illustrate a variety of water-use conflicts from all regions of the country, reflecting the great diversity of water resource governance challenges in Canada. They also highlight the need to map and design institutional arrangements for water governance on various scales, from local to international, and they all have a common concern with competing uses, the role of government agencies, and the involvement of stakeholders in water resource management. All the cases demonstrate how networks of water users and government actors are increasingly important in understanding and redesigning institutions for sustainable and responsible water resource use (Bressers et al., 1995; Rydin and Falleth, 2006).

In general, the cases are presented on the basis of the broad type of water-use conflict involved: quantity, quality, and in-stream. They demonstrate the institutions of Canadian water management in action and provide empirical evidence with which to explore the themes of institutional design and change in order to address water-use conflicts and better manage water resources in the future. The cases were also sequenced to illustrate various institutional approaches, but all use historical institutionalism to highlight how political economy and user rights have evolved and are embedded in current institutional arrangements and conflicts among various users.

Part Three presents the cases of water withdrawal issues in Alberta and the water export debate in the Great Lakes Basin to examine the complexity of water withdrawal institutions and policies. In chapter 5 Keith Brownsey analyzes the water management institutions of Alberta, showing how agricultural users, mainly irrigators, have successfully laid claim to most of the water in one of the most water-scarce regions of Canada, simply because their rights were institutionalized first. After outlining the state of water resources in Alberta, he examines the various uses in the province and outlines how new uses and demands are putting pressure on institutions, resulting in recent policy reforms. He describes how existing policy structures and processes reaffirm long-standing institutions governing water use in Alberta, and he questions whether fragmented institutional arrangements for different users will meet the water policy challenges in this province.

In chapter 6 John Grant also analyzes water institutions in a water quantity case. In contrast to the previous cases, which examine the institutions involved in managing long-standing water uses and related conflicts, this chapter covers a relatively recent water-use conflict related to water quantity. Although an issue since the 1960s, the potential bulk export of Canadian water has been particularly contentious politically since Canada entered the North American Free Trade Agreement. Through an analysis of the pan-Canadian issue of bulk water exports, Grant argues that institutional fragmentation is centrally important in understanding the continuing inability of Canadian governments to develop a comprehensive policy banning bulk water exports, despite overwhelming support for such a policy among the Canadian public.

Part Four uses the cases of Hamilton Harbour and the Walkerton water pollution tragedy in Ontario to examine institutions and policies for water pollution management. In chapter 7 Mark Sproule-Jones analyzes the multiple uses of the Great Lakes that have contributed to water pollution, particularly deployment of the lakes as a depository for waste. He examines the long-standing efforts to remediate the pollution problem in Hamilton Harbour and identifies a number of institutional, political and economic factors that continue to obstruct the cleanup process. This case study presents an example of a conscious effort to design institutions for stakeholder involvement on the Great Lakes and outlines the institutional reasons why these community-based institutions have produced very limited outcomes in terms of remedial action and pollution prevention.

Chapter 8, by Carolyn Johns, then explores the Walkerton water contamination tragedy, using this incident to highlight the complexities of non-point source pollution problems, the neglect of policy-makers to acknowledge these pollution sources, and the challenges involved in devising institutions to regulate them. This case also highlights the difficulties of institutional change in the context of the existing institutional arrangements and hierarchy of uses, even under extreme public pressure and political commitment to change. At the same time, it outlines some important policy and institutional innovations that have resulted across Ontario and in other provinces since Walkerton related to drinking-water management and watershed-based institutions.

The set of cases presented in Part Five investigate how long-standing in-stream users such as commercial shippers and fishers have institutionalized their rights over time and yet, more recently, have been challenged by new water users, technological developments, and new knowledge about water quantity and quality in Canada.

In chapter 9 Timothy Heinmiller examines the St Lawrence River and its evolution from a river into a main shipping route. He highlights how the long-standing deployment of this waterway for shipping and hydro-electricity production has resulted in a hierarchy of rights that are embedded in the political institutions governing the St Lawrence. His case study also outlines the significance of bi-national institutions and the role they have played in managing the various competing uses, both economic and environmental, in this intensively employed water source. This case also highlights how, over time, water uses and users change, how institutions are being challenged, and how an uphill battle is still being fought to alter institutional arrangements in favour of environmental protection.

In chapters 10 and 11, one of the oldest in-stream uses of water resources, that of fisheries, is examined. Fisheries rights are well entrenched at the pinnacle of water uses in many inland and coastal areas, partially because of their local and economic significance and partially because of government involvement through a powerful federal agency that predates Confederation yet still interfaces with local community-based knowledge and management traditions.

Chapter 10, by Peter Clancy, explores the plethora of fisheries management problems and conflicts that have plagued the East Coast in recent years, providing insight into some of the institutional and political economic factors at their root. His chapter highlights how even within the commercial fishery, multiple users and institutional arrangements exist for different species of fish and the seal hunt. Overlaid on these uses are other important uses and users, such as First Nations and environmental groups, which challenge the existing institutional dominance of commercial fisheries uses and the federal Department of Fisheries and Oceans.

In chapter 11 Richard Schwindt and Aidan Vining provide a detailed analysis of the institutional underpinnings of British Columbia's salmon fishery. They outline how long-standing institutions designed to manage wild salmon in inland and coastal waters have been altered by governments in response to cyclical economic and ecological crises and technological change in the salmon fishery in the past fifty years. They note there are three main threats to the wild salmon fishery: over-harvesting, farmed salmon, and degradation of salmon habitat. The two authors outline how, as in the East Coast fisheries, institutional arrangements have had to be altered in response to new challenges, such as the farmed salmon industry and First Nations rights. In the last part of their chapter Schwindt and Vining explore a number of policy options and possible institutional reforms for improving the efficiency, equity, and sustainability of this key resource and industry. Like Clancy's, their chapter highlights the significance and power of the federal government and the DFO and the important role that knowledge, science, and technology play in institutions for water governance. Their chapter also demonstrates that institutional redesign does have costs and that fisheries policy is broadening beyond economic policy goals to incorporate environmental concerns and, more broadly, issues related to other users of water resources. Yet, ultimately, Schwindt and Vining show that fishers still have limited institutional incentives to practise conservation and stewardship of the fishery or water habitat.

Finally, the concluding chapter provides a summary of the common water governance challenges in Canada, as well as the implications of current institutional arrangements for future water governance. The chapter is organized according to five themes – the nature of water, its multiple uses, and the issues these present in terms of a governance challenge; institutional interplay; property rights and the importance of laying claim; state managerialism and community involvement; and learning processes and the policy process – each theme suggesting a number of propositions and principles that can further both our theoretical and our empirical understanding of Canadian water governance. The conclusion pulls issues and institutions together, summarizing observations and lessons from the case studies, future challenges, and areas for further debate and research. A number of significant challenges seem to be looming on the horizon, and the future politics of Canadian water may centre on how well the current water management institutions are able to adapt to meet these changes.

CONCLUSION

There have been many calls for policy-makers to pay greater attention to water policy in Canada. These include demands for new policy approaches that address surface- and groundwater challenges, water quantity and quality interactions, point source and non–point source pollution, cross-medium interactions, ecosystem- and watershed-based dynamics, and water conservation and protection. Institutionally, these issues are reflected in calls for more comprehensive or integrated water policy frameworks, more networked and multi-stakeholder institutions, and at the same time, a stronger federal role but more decentralized participatory governance models.

In this book we argue that new water policy approaches must be well grounded in an understanding of the multiple uses of Canada's waters, the political economy that underpins current policies, how institutions play a critical role in perpetuating existing approaches, and how important institutional interplay is to future approaches that attempt to move toward greater balance between different water uses, particularly for environmental sustainability.

PART ONE
Background

1

Water as a Multiple-Use Resource and Source of Political Conflict

CAROLYN JOHNS, MARK SPROULE-JONES,

AND B. TIMOTHY HEINMILLER

This chapter outlines how the character of water as a multiple-use resource underpins the conflicts in subsequent chapters and the broad policy and institutional framework in which water politics has developed in Canada. It presents an overview of the principles of water itself and how these set the stage for conflict, water governance challenges, and collective action. The chapter focuses on the defining scientific, social, cultural, and economic features of water and the multiple applications that underpin political conflict over different types of water uses: withdrawal, consumptive, pollution, and in-stream.

INTRODUCTION

Water as a natural resource has its own distinctive scientific and natural principles which make its governance a challenge. Because it is interconnected to land, air, and the broader environment, its governance is particularly complex. These defining features of water underpin the conflicts and institutions designed to govern water resources in Canada. This chapter presents an overview of the natural properties of water itself and its multiple uses in Canada, which set the stage for conflict, water governance challenges, and collective-action dilemmas. The chapter is based on

The authors thank Kate Stiefelmeyer and Andrew Smart, whose research assistance laid the groundwork for this chapter.

the assumption that in order for policy-makers and analysts to design institutional arrangements and policy instruments to ensure sustainable water resource governance, a fundamental understanding of the properties of water and its multiple uses in the Canadian context is required.

THE NATURAL PROPERTIES OF WATER

Water is vital to all living things. Human and plant life depend on it for survival. Other essential nutrients are dissolved and transferred by water (Canada, Environment Canada, 2003a). It is the physical and chemical properties of water that make it so necessary for biological processes. Water is also remarkable because it can be found and used in all three states: liquid, solid, and gas. Water in the environment can be transformed into all three states as a result of seasonal and atmospheric temperatures, and it is constantly changing and moving. The constant movement and change of water is called the hydrologic cycle. During this process water moves, changes forms, and is taken up by plants and animals, but never disappears (Laycock, 1987). The amount of water moving through this cycle is thought to remain fairly consistent on a global scale, but it varies between regions and within regions over time (Laycock, 1987).

Water's cyclical movement from the earth to the atmosphere and back to the earth again is carried out by the five transportation processes of the cycle: precipitation, infiltration, runoff, evaporation or transpiration, and condensation. All five processes seen in figure 1.1 occur simultaneously and continuously, except precipitation, which occurs in bouts. The hydrologic cycle also involves the interaction of flows between surface waters and groundwater. While the term is somewhat self-explanatory, *surface waters* are those waters that run on and over the earth's surface. Surface water and precipitation can infiltrate or percolate through soil macropores, cracks, and fissures until it reaches groundwater aquifers. The classic definition of *groundwater* is the subsurface water that occurs beneath the water table in soils and in geologic formations that are fully saturated (Stamp, 1999). Groundwater accumulates from precipitation and is stored beneath the surface, filling cracks, pores, and crevices of underground materials and creating aquifers (Ontario and Canada, 1998b). *Aquifers* are large formations of rock or other material that contain groundwater (Vonhof, 1985). They can vary in size from a few hectares to thousands of hectares and can be found within a few meters from the surface or a few hundred meters from the surface (Canada, Environment

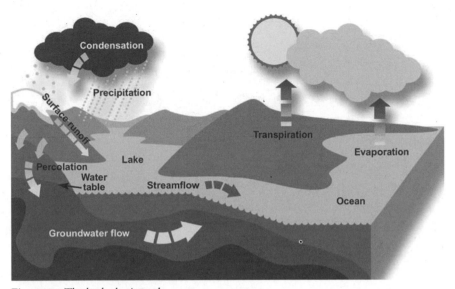

Figure 1.1 The hydrologic cycle.
SOURCE: Canada, Environment Canada, 2004a.

Canada, 2003a). Aquifers are not confined to a number of open channels or depressions but are found virtually everywhere underground (Canada, Environment Canada, 2003a).

Groundwater flows down slope through aquifers towards surface waters, including streams, lakes, rivers, and oceans (figure 1.2). This circulation and movement of groundwater ensures that it remains a part of the hydrologic cycle. When precipitation occurs, some water runs into surface waters, some is quickly evaporated back into the atmosphere, and some infiltrates the soil and finds its way to the water table. This process of water percolation is called *recharge* because the groundwater supplies are being recharged with a fresh supply of water. Oppositely, when water is removed from aquifers through flow into surface water sources or through the pumping of wells, this process is called *discharge* because the water is being discharged back to the surface (Canada, Environment Canada, 2003a).

Water can remain in underground aquifers for long periods of time, even thousands of years, before it re-enters a surface water system. Precipitation can also be carried into water sources through overland *runoff* if infiltration does not occur. The rate of infiltration through the soil will depend on a number of factors, including soil type, vegetation, topography, and soil moisture content. In Canada, when precipitation

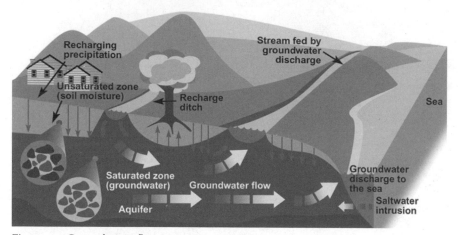

Figure 1.2 Groundwater flow source.
SOURCE: Canada, Environment Canada, 2003a.

occurs in the winter months, it remains on the surface in the form of snow or ice, and as temperatures warm in the spring, it melts and runs off into the nearest lakes and rivers, which take it back to the ocean by way of stream-flow. It is the surface runoff portion of the hydrologic cycle that is the primary source of fresh water used to satisfy human water needs (Gleick, 1993, 15).

CANADA'S WATER RESOURCES

Canada is a water-rich nation. Its water resources consist of both *salt water* and *fresh water*. Canada's wealth in water resources is evident in terms of coastal water and inland water resources (surface waters, wetlands, and groundwater). As outlined in table 1.1, the *coastal waters* of the Atlantic, Pacific, and Arctic oceans comprise the longest coastline in the world and constitute Canada's primary saltwater stocks.

Canada's Freshwater and Surface-Water Resources

Canada boasts 9 per cent of the world's available freshwater supply (surface water and groundwater) and 24 per cent of the world's wetlands (Canada, Environment Canada, 2003a). It houses less than 2 per cent of the world's population but contains 23 per cent of its fresh water, compared to Asia, which is home to 60 per cent of the world's population and has access to less than 37 per cent of global freshwater

Table 1.1
World distribution of water stocks

	Total water (%)	Fresh water (%)
SALTWATER STOCKS		
Oceans	96.5	
Saline groundwater	0.93	
Saltwater lakes	0.006	
Total saltwater stocks	97.44	
FRESHWATER STOCKS		
Glaciers, snow-cover	1.74	68.7
Fresh groundwater	0.76	30.06
Ground ice, permafrost	0.022	0.86
Total frozen and underground fresh water	2.522	99.62
Freshwater lakes	0.007	0.26
Soil moisture	0.001	0.05
Atmospheric water vapour	0.001	0.04
Marshes, wetlands	0.001	0.03
Rivers	0.0002	0.006
Incorporated in biota	0.0001	0.003
Total not frozen or underground fresh water	0.0103	0.389
Total freshwater stocks	2.5323	100
Total water on earth	100	

SOURCE: Gleick, 2000.

supplies (United Nations, 2003). Canada also ranks ninth in the world in available water per capita at 98 353 cubic metres per person per year, compared to Kuwait (10 cubic metres per capita per year), which has ranked as the poorest country in terms of water availability (United Nations, 2003).

In terms of *inland waters*, approximately 8 per cent of Canada is covered by fresh water in lakes and rivers (*Canadian Atlas Online*). It has more freshwater lakes than any other country in the world. There are approximately 2 million lakes in Canada, 563 of them greater than 100 square kilometres (Canada, Statistics Canada, 2003). Canada is home to six of the top ten largest lakes in the world (Gleick, 1993), and together, lakes and rivers cover 755 000 square kilometres (*Canadian Atlas Online*). However, table 1.1 also shows that the greatest source of fresh water, in the form of ice and accounting for 68 per cent of all fresh water, is unavailable for human use. Once groundwater is added, over 99 per cent of freshwater supplies are accounted for. The remaining fresh water, including all lakes, rivers, and streams, accounts for less than 1 per cent of the total supply.

Water is not distributed evenly throughout the country. Approximately 60 per cent of Canada's fresh water drains to the north, while 85 per cent of the population lives along the southern border with the United States (Canada, Environment Canada, 2005b). Despite Canada's abundant supply, there are areas of the country that at times are incredibly dry and desert-like, such as parts of British Columbia's interior and the prairies. These regions have severe soil moisture deficits during most summers and can suffer from long-term drought conditions. Combined, these areas make up 1 million hectares (10 000 square kilometres) of irrigated cropland in Canada, with Alberta alone accounting for 60 per cent (Canada, Environment Canada, 2005b). In contrast, other regions on the east and west coasts receive a large amount of rain annually.

The amount of water found in various areas of Canada helps to distinguish the various ecosystems of the country. *Ecosystems* are distinctive groupings of plant, animal, and micro-organism communities and their non-living environment interacting as a functional unit (United Nations, 2003; Canada, Statistics Canada, 2002). They vary in size and have no fixed boundaries. Canada is so vast that it contains a number of differing ecosystems. Because ecosystems represent common biophysical characteristics, they are used as areas to monitor the health of the environment, including human impacts on water resources (Canada, Statistics Canada, 2002), and do not correspond with political boundaries. Measures of water health include water quality indicators, the monitoring of hydrology, and the monitoring of biodiversity within an ecosystem (United Nations, 2003). Many of these monitoring activities take place at different scales. Some are undertaken on a small scale in individual lakes, streams, and rivers in Canada or on a large drainage-basin scale.

The 2 million lakes within Canada discharge approximately 105 000 cubic metres per second (Canada, Environment Canada, 2005b) into one of five large ocean drainage basins (figure 1.3). A *drainage basin* is an area that drains all precipitation received as either runoff or base flow (groundwater sources) into a particular river or set of rivers. The boundary of a drainage basin is defined as the ridge beyond which water flows in the opposite direction. A drainage basin is also known as a catchment area or a watershed (Canada, Environment Canada, 2003a).

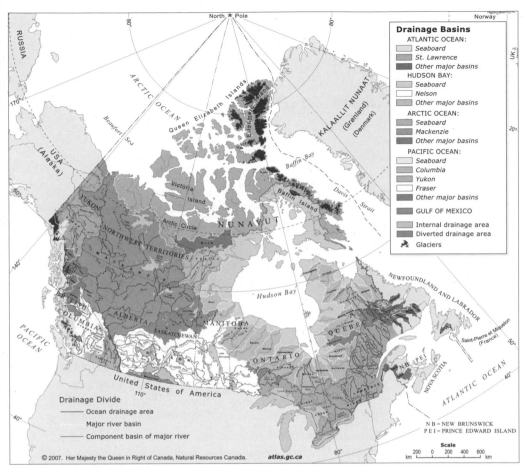

Figure 1.3 Drainage basins of Canada. The figure gives a rough idea of the number of drainage basins. A colour version can be found at http://atlas.ncan.gc.ca/site/English/ maps/environment/hydrology/drainagebasins.
SOURCE: Canada, Natural Resources Canada, 2003.

The term *watershed* is also used at various scales to include all the creeks and streams that drain into a major river or lake. Watersheds themselves contain sub-watersheds.

Canada has five major drainage basins: the Atlantic (including the Great Lakes and the St Lawrence River), the Hudson Bay, the Pacific, the Arctic, and the Gulf of Mexico, the last of which covers only a small area of southern Alberta and Saskatchewan (Canada, Environment Canada, 2002a). Parts of Saskatchewan and Alberta also contain internal drainage areas, in which some river systems do not drain into an ocean (Canada, Environment Canada, 2003a). The case-study chapters in this book outline the multiple uses of water and political conflicts in several of these basins and watersheds. The cases highlight the fact that the major basins in Canada are governed by numerous orders of government: federal, provincial, Aboriginal, territorial, and municipal.

Canada's Wetlands

In addition to lakes and rivers, Canada contains 25 per cent of the world's wetlands (Canada, Environment Canada, 2003a; *Canadian Atlas Online*). *Wetlands* are areas of water that can be natural or artificial, permanent or temporary, with fresh or salt water (Stuip et al., 2002). There are four primary types of wetlands – coasts, estuaries, flood plains, and marshes or swamps – each of which is distinct (Stuip et al., 2002). *Coasts* are areas between the land and oceans that are not at all influenced by the flow of rivers; these include shorelines, beaches, mangroves, and coral reefs (Stuip et al., 2002). *Estuaries* are wetlands that are situated where rivers flow into the sea and water changes from fresh to salt, including deltas, mud flats, salt marshes, and mangroves (Stuip et al., 2002). *Flood plains* are lands situated next to the permanent course of a river that are periodically flooded during heavy flow periods (Stuip et al., 2002). The most commonly thought-of wetland type consists of *marshes* or *swamps*. These wetlands are constructed of land where water permanently sits at the surface and causes saturation of the soils (Stuip et al., 2002). Examples of marshes include wooded swamps, bogs, fens, and peatlands.

Globally, wetlands cover 6 per cent of the earth's surface (Stuip et al., 2002), and they account for approximately 14 per cent of the land area in Canada (Canada, Environment Canada, 2005b). Canada's wetlands are concentrated in the central provinces (Canada, Statistics Canada, 2003). All types of wetlands perform important ecosystem functions. They are particularly valuable because of their biodiversity. A variety of species of plants and animals depend on wetlands to survive. The value of wetlands also derives from a number of other important functions that they perform. One of the most valuable of these is the treatment of runoff or waste water through absorption by plants and through filtering sediments and toxic substances, including plant nutrients, nitrogen and phosphorus, and inorganic contaminants (Peterson, 1998; Lilley and Labatiuk, 2001). Another valuable function of wetlands is groundwater recharge. As well, wetlands provide protection against flooding because they can hold excess amounts of water from rising water bodies in times of high water levels, such as during spring snowmelt (Stuip et al., 2002). Like other water sources, wetlands also hold high social, cultural, and recreational significance. Many are used for recreational purposes such as canoeing, fishing, duck hunting, and bird watching, and many communities, individuals, and environmental groups such as Ducks Unlimited place high values on the existence of wetlands and work to maintain them for cultural or historical purposes (Stuip et al., 2002). Wetlands are also valuable for economic reasons. Some are used for small resource industries that harvest peat, reeds, fish, or lumber. In Canada it is estimated that they generate between $5 and 10 billion annually (Canada, Environment Canada, 1994a).

Although these wetlands are one of Canada's and the world's most valuable resources, over 50 per cent of the world's wetlands have been lost since 1900 (Stuip et al., 2002; United Nations, 2003). Significant wetland loss has taken place in many regions of Canada. Over the past two hundred years, about 14 per cent (20 million hectares) of wetlands have disappeared from the Canadian landscape (Linton, 1997). Conversion of land for agricultural purposes is considered the principal cause of disappearance worldwide (Stuip et al., 2002). Some analysts argue that the significant loss and degradation of wetlands over the past one hundred years may have resulted from the insufficiently defined role of governments in the protection and management of these systems (Averill and Whelan, 2000). Regional statistics suggest that 70 per cent of original wetland area in the central prairies has been converted and that 65 per cent of the Atlantic salt marshes have been destroyed (Canada, Statistics Canada, 2000). Of the original Pacific estuarine marshes, 70 per cent have been converted, and 70–80 per cent of wetlands located along the shorelines of southern Ontario and the St Lawrence valley have also been converted to other land uses (Canada, Statistics Canada, 2000). Approximately 8100 hectares per year of wetlands around the Great Lakes disappear (Canada, Environment Canada, 1994a), and two-thirds of original wetlands in the lower Great Lakes Basin have been lost (Canada, Environment Canada, 2000c), with an estimated 1000 hectares lost per year in southern Ontario (Canada, Environment Canada, 2000c).

Canada's Groundwater Resources

Globally, groundwater is two hundred times more abundant than surface water and makes up two-thirds of the entire world's freshwater supply (Karvinen and McAllister, 1994). Although we picture Canada with an abundance of lakes and rivers (surface water), there is substantially more water held underground. Of all the fresh water in Canada, groundwater makes up 95 per cent; the remaining comes from lakes, rivers, and wetlands (Ontario and Canada, 1998b). Although groundwater is more abundant, the natural replacement period is so long that the supply actually available each year is smaller than the amount of water available in river and lakes (Healy and Wallace, 1987).

Canadian groundwater supplies that are available for human use may also seem much smaller than might be indicated by the country's area because of the location of much of the land and because of the climate in certain areas. First, much of the northern part of Canada experiences permafrost year-round, inhibiting the groundwater supply (Healy and Wallace, 1987). Secondly, low annual rainfall in the prairie region limits the supply of natural groundwater (Healy and Wallace, 1987). And lastly, the large rocks in the Canadian Shield, the Western Cordillera, and the Appalachians have very low porosity (Healy and Wallace, 1987) and therefore contain small reserves of groundwater. Other areas, however, have vast supplies of groundwater and use them extensively.

In contrast to surface waters, the main users of groundwater sources are municipalities at 31 per cent, industry at 22 per cent, agriculture at 20 per cent, and rural residents at 19 per cent (Karvinen and McAllsiter, 1994). As shown in table 1.2, groundwater is the primary water resource for almost one-quarter of all Canadians, and almost 9 million Canadians rely on groundwater for domestic use (Canada, Environment Canada, 2003a), the majority being rural residents. Many large urban centres in Canada are situated at or near surface water sources and are therefore not as dependent on groundwater supplies. Many areas that utilize groundwater employ it for both domestic and industrial use, and many municipal systems are solely dependent on groundwater supplies. Some 142 municipal systems in Quebec are reliant on groundwater, and 1.3 million of Ontario's population are dependent on groundwater (Rutherford, 2005). Other areas that rely heavily on groundwater supplies include Prince Edward Island and the Prince George area in British Columbia. Approximately 38 500 new water wells are drilled each year in Canada; of those, 15 000–20 000 are installed in Ontario (Ontario and Canada, 1998b).

Protecting and supplying groundwater sources has historically received little attention from policy-makers because groundwater tends to be "out of sight, out of mind" (Nolan, 2007). In Canada, water management has traditionally focused more intently on surface waters, an emphasis that

Table 1.2
Groundwater use in Canada, 1996

Province/territory	Population reliant on groundwater (%)[1]	Municipal systems reliant on groundwater (%)[2]
Newfoundland and Labrador	33.9	23.5
Prince Edward Island	100	100
Nova Scotia	45.8	41.2
New Brunswick	66.5	72.7
Quebec	27.7	36.7
Ontario	28.5	42.7
Manitoba	30.2	50
Saskatchewan	42.8	65.7
Alberta	23.1	29
British Columbia	28.5	45.3
Yukon Territory	47.9	100
Northwest Territories	28.1	—
Canada	30.3	41.2

SOURCE: Canada, Statistics Canada, 2000.
1 It is assumed that the population not covered by the Municipal Water Use Database is rural and that 90 per cent of this population is groundwater-reliant.
2 Including population and municipal water systems that are reliant on groundwater alone and those that are reliant on groundwater and surface water.

may be due to the fact that the highly populated areas of the country have an abundant supply of surface water (Vonhof, 1985). The neglect of groundwater policy is an important issue that requires attention from all levels of government (Canada, Policy Research Initiative, 2006b). As discussed in chapter 8, it is important to protect groundwater sources as much as surface water sources since they are essentially one source and are linked through the hydrologic cycle. The protection of groundwater supplies is also a much safer and less expensive alternative than the high cost of mitigating groundwater contamination.

THE MULTIPLE USES AND USERS OF WATER IN CANADA

In addition to the biophysical functions outlined above, water has a number of human and non-human uses. Given the vastness of Canada's water resources, it is not surprising that the human uses of water are numerous and varied. The country's freshwater resources help to drive the nation's economy, contributing directly to its agriculture, forestry, inland fisheries, hydroelectricity production, mining, hydrocarbon extraction, and transportation, as well as recreation and tourism. Primary industries that use water in production accounted for nearly 6 per cent of the GDP in 2000, generating over $45 billion and employing more than 650 000 people (Canada, Environment Canada, 2005b)

Many of these economic, social, cultural, and environmental uses tend to be centred on harbours, bays, and rivers, in part because human settlements cluster around these geographic sites (Sproule-Jones, 2002). These uses frequently impinge on one another, creating "negative interdependencies" between water users (Sproule-Jones, 2002). In any given water body, too much of any single use can reduce the availability of the resource for others and also reduce the availability of the site for future use, creating a potential for conflict and a challenge for policy-makers.

Generally speaking, all water uses can be categorized as consumptive, withdrawal, or in-stream uses.

Consumptive uses: water taken is greater than water returned. Consumption removes water from a water system and makes it unavailable for other uses. The irrigation of crops is by far the largest consumptive use, although some of this water returns to water basins in the form of runoff. Other consumptive uses include water export and water bottling, and there are quality and environmental dimensions to these uses as well.

Withdrawal uses: water taken and water returned are roughly equivalent. Domestic and municipal water use, thermal power generation, industrial use, and various agricultural uses are examples of withdrawal uses. Although the quantities of water taken and returned are roughly equivalent, the quality of water is often the source of conflict, as many withdrawal uses return water in a degraded state.

In-stream uses: water is used at its source. Many uses of water do not require the transportation of water from its source to another location. Such activities use water at its source and are called in situ or in-stream uses. These activities use water within or close to its natural source. The primary in-stream water uses in Canada are commercial fishing, commercial shipping, hydroelectricity generation, recreation, and waste disposal. Flow rates and water levels have very important impacts on

Table 1.3
Volumes of water use in Canada, by region (millions of cubic metres)

Region	Water intake	Consumption	Gross water use	Recirculation	Discharge
Atlantic	2 884	139	3 849	965	2 475
Quebec	4 252	435	7 346	3 094	3 817
Ontario	21 230	589	25 352	4 122	20 641
Prairies	5 363	2 256	10 038	4 675	3 107
British Columbia	3 789	487	6 851	3 062	3 302
Canada	37 518	3 906	53 436	15 918	33 342

in-stream uses. When these conditions are changed by a dam or in terms of quality, for example, it is easy for conflicts to arise.

Consumptive, withdrawal, and in-stream water uses are all widely evident in Canada, with specific configurations of uses varying according to local ecological and socio-economic conditions. All three of these types of uses have environmental impacts. For the purposes of this book, the case studies reflect the broad uses.

As outlined in table 1.3, the uses of water also vary by region and province. Figure 1.4 lists some of the most significant water uses in Canada along with the water sources upon which these uses are dependent. Each of these human uses is described in greater detail in the sections below.

Commercial Fishing

Commercial fishing is one of the oldest uses of water resources in Canada. Salt- and freshwater fish provided an abundant food source for Aboriginal communities and a sustainable trade item for European settlers. By the early 1800s a commercial fishery was established in the Great Lakes (Sproule-Jones, 2002). The historic treatment of fish as an open-access resource was gradually replaced with voluntary restrictions adopted by fishers to avoid overfishing and subsequently intervention by governments trying to manage stocks and fishing conflicts. There are three primary fishing sectors in Canada: the Atlantic fisheries, the West Coast fisheries, and the freshwater inland fisheries. The book contains case studies on the two coastal fisheries.

Although relatively small compared to the coastal fisheries, the inland freshwater commercial fisheries of Canada are the largest in the world (Linton, 1997). The freshwater fisheries hold particular importance in

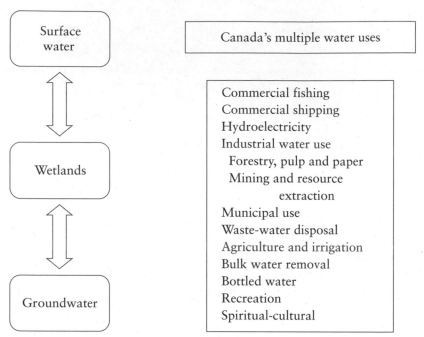

Figure 1.4 Water and its uses.
SOURCE: Canada, Environment Canada, 2003a.

terms of foreign trade to Japan, Europe, and the United States (Healy and Wallace, 1987). In 1997 the freshwater fishing industry employed roughly 3500 people and contributed $71 million to Canada's gross domestic product (Canada, Statistics Canada, 2000). The Great Lakes are home to a large part of the industry, but collectively, Manitoba lakes are almost as significant in terms of the freshwater fishery. The inland fishing industry has also had some setbacks as a result of overfishing and the degradation of the Great Lakes Basin, where a number of lake species stocks have disappeared. It is important to note, however, that it is the recreational fishing industry that has landed most of the catch in the last decade – more than two and a half times that of the commercial industry (Linton, 1997).

As outlined in chapters 10 and 11, Canada's coastal fishing industry has fallen on hard times in the past few decades because of a decline in a number of fish stocks, particularly in the 1980s and 1990s. This has resulted in a decreasing contribution to Canada's gross domestic product (Canada, Statistics Canada, 2000) and significant political turmoil and conflict. Although its contribution to the GDP has decreased, the fishing industry's importance remains high as a water use, particularly in some communities. As outlined in the case studies, in order to maintain a healthy fishing industry and continued harvesting, complex institutional arrangements have developed to manage conflicts, and the industry is closely monitored through the use of quotas and licences. In order to fish commercially, a fisher must hold a valid licence, and quotas have been set on the basis of scientifically determined stock numbers and health, so that the overfishing that was experienced in the 1980s and 1990s will not occur again.

The other fish industry that has evolved into a user of water resources is the Canadian aquaculture industry, which has been growing rapidly as a result of the decline in wild fishing stocks and an increasing demand for aquatic products. In 2000 Canada's aquaculture industry contributed $665 million to the gross domestic product and produced 123 924 tonnes of farmed fish. The most common cultured species are Atlantic salmon, rainbow trout, and various shellfish. The industry is most predominant in the coastal regions: British Columbia and New Brunswick are the major aquaculture producing provinces. As the case studies in chapter 10 and 11 illustrate, this industry presents important challenges for existing water resource management institutions.

Commercial Shipping

The other long-standing use of water resources in Canada is commercial shipping. Inland waterways and surface water were important elements of early colonization and economic prosperity, first during the fur trade and later when timber exports dominated Canada's economy (Innis, 1930). Likewise, the east-west navigation of waterways in Canada allowed for the creation of a link across the entire country that served as a check against the north-south flow of commerce and the prospect of greater continental ties to the United States (Creighton, 1956). Historically in Canada, human exploration and settlement were intimately related to the transportation uses of water. The movement of goods and people via waterways eventually led to a natural and manmade network of navigable waters used for commercial and military purposes. By the nineteenth century, ship and shipbuilding technologies were driving economic development in many areas of Canada. Lakes and rivers were used as navigation and transportation channels, and commercial shipping became a major use by the twentieth century.

Commercial shipping remains the most economical means of moving bulky cargo and raw materials great distances (Canada, Environment Canada, 2002a). In 1996, marine transport moved 309 billion tonnes of exports, including wheat, pulp, lumber, and minerals (Canada, Statistics Canada, 2000). Container shipping of other goods has also contributed to the shipping use of water resources in Canada. The transshipment of goods by water remains the core of economic activity in many Canadian cities (Sproule-Jones, 1993). Three main transport routes are deployed in Canada: the Mackenzie River, which is the link to the north; the Lower Fraser River, which links to the Pacific; and the St Lawrence–Great Lakes Basin, otherwise known as the St Lawrence Seaway, which is one of the largest inland navigable waterways in world and the subject of analysis in chapter 9. The six busiest shipping ports in Canada are Vancouver, Sept-Îles, Montreal, Halifax, Port-Cartier, and Thunder Bay. Although commercial shipping has declined in recent decades as a result of the development of rail, road, and air transportation options, it remains an important use in many areas of Canada. As outlined in chapter 8, commercial shipping is still the dominant use of some water resources, significantly affecting other important uses.

Hydroelectricity

Internationally, Canada ranks number one in terms of the amount of water that has been redirected for use in another location (Healy, 1987). The primary purpose of redirecting water resources via diversions and dams in Canada is for hydroelectricity generation. *Diversions* consolidate water from two or more sources, usually two rivers, into one source, in order to increase the security and quality of flow through the source (Canada, Statistics Canada, 2000). Diversions have generally been constructed to increase water flow in order to support hydroelectric projects, to increase water supplies in dry areas, or to direct water away from flood-prone areas (Canada, Statistics Canada, 2000). *Dams*, in contrast, retain water in its drainage basin (or reservoir) and store it for use at another time. They fundamentally alter rivers and manipulate the resource so that benefits derived from the resource are reallocated from their original location (World Commission on Dams, 2000).

Canada's development of hydroelectricity projects has led to its ranking by the United Nations as the world's largest producer. In 1995 it was estimated that Canada contributed 14 per cent of the global output (Canada, Environment Canada, 2000c). Hydroelectricity constituted 64

Table 1.4
Number of large dams in Canada, by region

Prince Edward Island	0
Yukon Territory	3
Northwest Territory	3
New Brunswick	16
Manitoba	34
Nova Scotia	35
Saskatchewan	38
Alberta	51
Newfoundland and Labrador	80
Ontario	80
British Columbia	89
Quebec	189

SOURCE: Canada, Environment Canada, 1994a.

per cent of the power generated in Canada in 1999, compared to 10 per cent in the United States. The Niagara Falls power-generating plant is probably the most famous in North America and is the largest producer of hydroelectricity in the world. About 3000 cubic metres per second flow over Niagara Falls, and about half this water is redirected to produce hydroelectricity (Canada, Environment Canada, 2000c).

Canada is also one of the world's leading dam builders (Averill and Whelan, 2000) and is home to many of its largest dams. The World Commission on Dams (2000) defines a large dam as one that is 15 metres high or greater from its foundation or a dam that is 5–15 metres in height with reservoirs greater than 3 million cubic metres. Canada has 600 dams with a height greater than 10 metres (Averill and Whelan, 2000), 53 dams that have the capacity to hold 1 billion cubic metres, and over 100 dams that store a capacity of greater than 100 million cubic metres (Linton, 1997; table 1.4). Canada is home to an estimated 10 000 dams when hundreds of small and medium-sized dams are included (Prowse et al., 2003).

The most recent diversions have been some of the largest to date, including the James Bay Project in northern Quebec, the Churchill–Nelson River diversion in northern Manitoba, and the Churchill Falls project in Labrador (Quinn and Edstrom, 2000). These three projects contain seven diversions and constitute two-thirds of all the diverted water in Canada (Quinn and Edstrom, 2000). Manitoba, British Columbia, and

Table 1.5
Hydroelectric power generation as a percentage of total
power generated, by province and territory, 1997

Newfoundland and Labrador	96.2
Prince Edward Island	—
Nova Scotia	9.3
New Brunswick	14.1
Quebec	96.8
Ontario	27.2
Manitoba	99.2
Saskatchewan	23.6
Alberta	4.0
British Columbia	92.1
Yukon Territory	68.7
Northwest Territories	36.4

SOURCE: Canada, Environment Canada, 2000.

Quebec and British Columbia produce almost all of their power through hydroelectric projects, as shown in table 1.5. Prince Edward Island has no rivers that would have a flow large enough for producing power and is the only province in Canada that does not generate hydroelectricity.

Dam construction in Canada has decreased in recent decades for a number of reasons. First, so many dams already exist in Canada's waterways that not many suitable locations remain undeveloped. Second, public opposition to dam construction has grown, given both the large costs of hydro projects and the growing concerns with environmental and habitat damage wrought by dams (Quinn and Edstrom, 2000). Between 1984 and 1991 only six large dams were constructed in Canada, and a number of other planned projects were cancelled (Linton, 1997).

The environmental damage caused by dams is now much better understood than in the past. The flooding that can occur behind dams has often displaced people, destroyed the use of valuable land, and disrupted the migration of spawning fish (World Commission on Dams, 2000). The construction of dams and canals to divert large amounts of water can directly or cumulatively disrupt the health of a drainage basin if not properly engineered or monitored (Canada, Environment Canada, 1992). The environmental impacts of dam construction are virtually irreversible and include changing a river's seasonal flow, water temperature, and dissolved oxygen levels and increasing nutrient and sediment

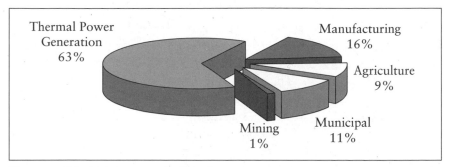

Figure 1.5 Principal water uses in Canada, 2000.
SOURCE: Canada, Environment Canada, 2002a.

transport (Postel, 2000). Alterations in flora and fauna around dam sites have also occurred as a result of the physical and chemical changes a river endures after it is blocked or its water flows altered. Many First Nation communities have been displaced because of the construction of diversion projects. The Churchill–Nelson River diversion project affected a number of Cree communities that lived downstream from the project in Split Lake and York Landing (Hertlein, 1999). Several Native bands are currently being compensated for their losses in the James Bay hydroelectric project, as a result of which the James Bay and Northern Quebec Agreement was signed in 1975 (Quinn and Edstrom, 2000).

In addition to hydroelectricity generated from dams, thermal power generation is an important source of electricity in Canada. It is the largest industrial user of water in the country. As outlined in figure 1.5, thermal power generation used 64 per cent of total water intake in 2000. Other than fuels, water is the most important material used in thermal power generation (Canada, Environment Canada, 2003a). Water power meets about two-thirds of the nation's electrical needs (Canada, Environment Canada, 2005c). The greatest amount of water use in this activity occurs in the Lake Ontario and Lake Huron basins, where Ontario's major nuclear generating plants are located (Ontario, Ministry of Natural Resources, 1984), the Darlington Nuclear Generating Station on Lake Ontario and the Bruce Nuclear Power Plant on Lake Huron. Although the cooling of thermal electric generators requires a large withdrawal of water, this process returns nearly all of the water back to its source (Linton, 1997). However, the water discharged from thermal power generation is higher in temperature after it has been used in the power-generation process, and this is an important environmental concern for aquatic ecosystems.

Industrial Water Use

Globally, industrial use of water constitutes 59 per cent of all water used, and on average, this amount increases in countries with higher incomes (United Nations, 2003). The manufacturing sector is the second largest user of water in Canada, accounting for approximately 20 per cent of total water used. Overall, it draws twice as much water as agriculture (Karvinen and McAllister, 1994). In addition to thermal power generation, the large industrial users of water are primary metals manufacturers, allied products, and chemical manufacturers (Canada, Environment Canada, 2003a).

Water is used for a number of purposes in manufacturing: as a coolant, a solvent, a raw material, or a transport medium (Canada, Statistics Canada, 2003). The largest industrial water use in Canada is in Ontario, at 45 per cent (Canada, Environment Canada, 1994a). Quebec is the next largest provincial user of water, but still uses less than half the amount that Ontario does (Canada, Environment Canada, 1994a). Of the various manufacturing sectors, the pulp and paper industry, the primary metals manufacturers, and the chemical manufacturers require the greatest amount of water for their processes (Coote and Gingerich, 2000; Canada, Environment Canada, 2002a). For example, it takes 295 000 litres of water to produce 910 kilograms of paper (Canada, Environment Canada, 1994a), and approximately 120 000 litres of water are required in the manufacturing of one car (80 000 litres to produce one tonne of steel and 40 000 litres of water in the fabrication process) (Canada, Environment Canada, 2002a).

Although industry withdraws such a large amount of water, only about 7 per cent of it is consumed (Coote and Gingerich, 2000). The majority of industries develop their own water supply systems (Coote and Gingerich, 2000), which explains why so much industrial development takes place adjacent to water sources. Most of the water is returned to the original source after it is used. More recently, some industrial users have developed water-recycling facilities, decreasing the demands for a continuous source. Of the major water users, both the mining and manufacturing sectors have decreased their water withdrawals in the last decade as a result of technological and design improvements that recycle their waste waters (Linton, 1997).

Forestry and the Pulp and Paper Industry

The forestry industry has long had major impacts on the use of water resources for several reasons: the logging of lands in close proximity to water resources, the use of water resources to transport logs to mills downstream, and the processing of forest products at pulp and paper mills, often located next to water sources. The third dimension of the use in this sector is now the most contentious. The pulp and paper industry is an infamous industrial user of water because it remains the largest producer of waste water of all manufacturing industries (Marsalek et al., 2002). Pulp and paper mills discharge approximately 50 cubic metres of process water for every tonne of pulp processed, although this amount can vary depending on the type of paper that is being produced.

Water is required in the pulp and paper industry for a number of reasons. First, as in many other manufacturing areas, water is used extensively to maintain mechanical equipment, including cooling, sealing, lubricating, and cleaning the equipment to maintain its optimum functionality (Lindholm, 2000). But the most important use of water in the pulp and paper mills is as the "universal solvent" to separate fibres from the rest of the plant material; this is the most fundamental process in pulp and paper production (Lindholm, 2000). An indirect impact that pulp and paper mills have had on water sources in Canada is the need for electrical energy, which has resulted in the development of numerous dams adjacent to mills (Linton, 1997).

The pulp and paper industry has attempted to improve its environmental performance and reduce its water demands through "cleaner production" designs and processes. It has reduced its use of water by more than two-thirds in the last two decades through water reuse and recycling programs (Averill and Whelan, 2000). The use of biological treatments has increased water recycling in plants because they effectively degrade slime in waste waters and produce water that is clean enough water to be recycled back into the production process, rather than being discharged after just one circulation (Lindholm, 2000).

Mining and Resource Extraction

Mining has always been an integral part of the Canadian economy, employing a large part of the labour force during the early part of the century. Canada is known around the world as a country rich in mineral resources and is now one of the largest exporters of mineral products. In 1995, 558 mines and quarries were in active production across Canada (Canada, Natural Resources Canada, 2003); of these, approximately 60 per cent contained primary materials such as sand and gravel. Canada is the world's largest producer of potash and uranium and is ranked second in the world in terms of nickel and asbestos production. Water is used in the extraction processes for many minerals as well as for oil.

Compared to other industrial and agricultural uses, mining is one of the smallest users of water, employing approximately 10 per cent of the amount that agriculture uses (Coote and Gingerich, 2000). It withdraws so little water because most mining operations are "closed systems" and recirculate intake water more than any other water user (Canada, Statistics Canada, 2000). Although water discharges are low, the waste water being released is often loaded with toxic contaminants such as heavy metals and acids, as well as suspended sediments (Coote and Gingerich, 2000). Mining operations use water to separate the metal from the waste rock, as a coolant for drills, to wash and dry the ore, and as a transport medium (Canada, Statistics Canada, 2000). A single ore plant may use up to 15 million litres of water per day (Linton, 1997).

Although the issue is largely regional, there has been concern recently over the amount of water used in the oil and gas industry, particularly in Alberta. Water is used for oil production and for oil sands mining. In Alberta in 2004, over 7 per cent of total water allocations (surface water and groundwater) were for the production of oil and gas. The proportion of groundwater allocations is far higher, at 37 per cent. The demand for water by the oil industry is growing. Large volumes of water are used to extract oil from bitumen in the oil sands, and it expected that the demand for water in northern Alberta will increase rapidly with the planned expansion of the oil sands (Griffiths et al., 2006). As outlined in chapter 8, this industry presents new policy and institutional challenges when considered alongside the other major use of water in Alberta and Saskatchewan – irrigation.

In terms of mining's relationship with water, it is not the uses of water but the impacts that have been substantial. The gold rushes, for example, were extremely harsh on water sources. Diamond mining is also very destructive to water sources since many lakes and rivers have been excavated in the search for these gems. The environmental and flow impacts of oil and gas production and mining on surface water and groundwater in Canada are only now being revealed.

Municipal Water Use

Although municipal water use is a small portion of Canada's total water use, it is probably the most common and the most visible for Canadians because municipal use constitutes the water supplied to all

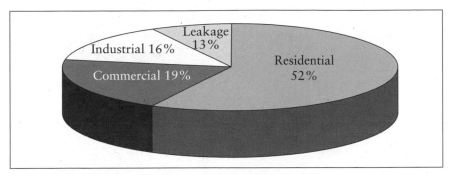

Figure 1.6 Canadian municipal water use by sector, 1999.
SOURCE: Canada, Environment Canada, 2002a.

residents, businesses, and industries by a municipality (Canada, Natural Resources Canada, 2003). Most municipal water is used by residences, followed by commercial uses and industry (see figure 1.6). Leakage of pipes and faulty infrastructure throughout municipal systems is so substantial that it takes up roughly 13 per cent of all water used. Commercial use involves all water distributed to institutions and businesses, such as schools, universities, hospitals, and large office buildings (Canada, Natural Resources Canada, 2003).

In Canada more than 24 million residents are supplied with municipal drinking water, and 22 million are served by municipal sewage systems (Wood, 2002), including 80 per cent of rural residents (Coote and Gingerich, 2000). Overall, there are approximately 4000 plants that treat water and make it safe for drinking-water purposes (Wood, 2002). Most of the water-treatment plants pump their water supply directly from surface water sources; only 12 per cent utilize groundwater sources (Canada, Natural Resources Canada, 2003). A municipal supply system is usually made up of a network of pipes and sewers across an urban area, together with a plant that consists of an intake, storage, treatment, and distribution centre.

Residents not served by municipal systems receive their water through private groundwater supplies. In communities in the far north, some water is trucked in because groundwater supplies are frozen when they are too shallow (Canada, Natural Resources Canada, 2003). In other regions covered in permafrost, water is trucked in because, if underground piping systems were constructed, they would generate heat that would cause the permafrost to melt and areas of the ground would be susceptible to caving in (Canada, Natural Resources, 2003). In some

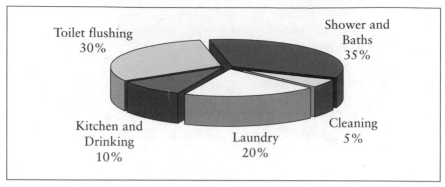

Figure 1.7 Average Canadian water use in the home, 1999.
SOURCE: Canada, Environment Canada, 2002a.

of these communities, above-ground distribution systems have been installed that are insulated and heated (Canada, Natural Resources Canada, 2003).

Of total domestic use, less than 5 per cent of treated water is actually used for drinking, and a major portion is employed for flushing toilets and other aspects of personal hygiene (figure 1.7). Bathing and showering account for more than 30 per cent of all domestic water use. A five-minute shower with a standard head uses approximately 100 litres of water (Wood, 2002). Canadians rank second behind only residents of the United States in terms of per capita domestic use per year. The average Canadian uses 395 litres of water per day (Canada, Environment Canada, 1998a), twice as much as the average person from France or Germany (Boyd, 2001). Rural residents are slightly more conservative water users than urban residents; the average rural resident uses only 160 litres of water per day (Canada, Environment Canada, 1998a). Domestic water use peaks in the spring and summer months when homeowners are watering their lawns and gardens.

Although Canadians are among the highest per capita users of water in the world, they pay the lowest consumer prices for water and wastewater services in the developed world (Schaefer and Hurst, 1997). Canadian households pay, on average, $28 per month and use approximately 30 000 litres of water for domestic purposes only. Prices do vary across the provinces, with the lowest prices being in Quebec, Newfoundland, and British Columbia (Canada, Natural Resources Canada, 2003). The Prairie provinces and northern Canada pay the highest monthly bills on average (Canada, Natural Resources Canada, 2003).

In addition to the fact that the prices Canadians pay for water are too low to cover the costs of providing it, approximately 50 per cent of residential water connections are not metered (Rollins et al., 1997). As a result, consumers feel no pressure to change their over-consuming behaviour (Averill and Whelan, 2000). Charging fair value for providing water and treatment services might create incentives for Canadians to conserve, encourage industry to develop more efficient technologies and water-recycling systems, and also provide cash-strapped municipalities with revenue that could be reinvested in delivery and treatment systems (Canada, Environment Canada, 1998a; Averill and Whelan, 2000; Clarke, 2003).

Waste-Water Disposal

Historically, human and industrial wastes have been dumped into bodies of water, using these water bodies as disposal systems. On a small scale, water bodies are able to filter and digest the waste, but their ability to absorb or filter contaminants can become limited when the waste loads become too large. During the nineteenth century, urban centres grew too fast to accommodate their waste, and water sources were overloaded (Linton, 1997). Once water has been used by residences and industry, it is either discharged directly into a water source or, preferably, returned to the sewer system and transported to the waste-water treatment plant; at this stage it is referred to as sewage. About 3000 municipal waste-water treatment plants in Canada combat the loads of contaminants in used water by treating the water and returning it to its source (Wood, 2002). Approximately 0.6 per cent of the mean annual flow leaving Ontario through the St Lawrence River is water that has been returned to the source by these plants (Ontario, Ministry of Natural Resources, 1984).

Water-treatment plants utilize a multi-stage approach to render sewage as clean as possible before returning it to water sources. A number of contaminants must be removed, including nutrients, solids, organic matter, chemicals, and disease-causing organisms from human excrement, to name a few. Primary treatment comprises settling the water to generate sedimentation of the remaining solids and to remove greases and oils from the top layer of the waste water (Mancl, 1996). Secondary treatment usually involves biological processes to remove organic matter that has been dissolved in the water (Mancl, 1996). Many treatment plants use micro-organisms to ingest the organic matter by adding them directly to water or by directing the water over barriers to which the micro-organisms are attached (Mancl, 1996). Tertiary treatment processes involve the removal of disease-causing organisms that are commonly found in human wastes (Mancl, 1996). Approaches used for their removal include high levels of chlorination or ultraviolet light. Many of Canada's water systems feature combined sewer overflows (csos) in which discharges of untreated sewage and stormwater are released directly into rivers and lakes during heavy rainfall, when sewers have reached their capacity. Although the sewage in csos is greatly diluted by stormwater, both csos and stormwater may be harmful to public health and aquatic life because they carry chemicals and disease-causing pathogens. As a result, holding tanks and other measures have been designed to improve these systems, a process that is critical as the systems expand to serve more users.

Over the past twenty years, Canada has improved in terms of the number of people who are served by sewage treatment plants. In 1997, 78 per cent of the population was served by public sewage treatment, up from 64 per cent in 1980 (Sierra Legal Defence Fund, 2006). However, Victoria, Halifax, and St John's are among the approximately 90 municipalities (accounting for 12 per cent of the population) that continue to dump raw sewage into their water sources (Boyd, 2001), resulting in more than 1 trillion litres of untreated sewage being dumped every year (Wood, 2002). The rest of the population is not served by any network of sewage and instead utilizes private underground septic tanks (Boyd, 2001).

Agricultural and Irrigation Uses

Agriculture is the largest consumer of water globally and requires a reliable supply of water for a variety of activities, including livestock watering, growing crops, cleaning equipment, and diluting manure (Coote and Gingerich, 2000; Averill and Whelan, 2000). In Canada, agriculture accounts for 8.5 per cent of total water used (Coote and Gingerich; Averill and Whelan, 2000), and although this is a relatively low amount, most water used in agriculture is consumed; agriculture returns less than 30 per cent of the water it uses (Canada, Environment Canada, 2000c). Water for irrigation consumes approximately 70 per cent of the water used for agriculture (Canada, Environment Canada, 2000c), and approximately 856 000 hectares of agricultural land is irrigated (Canada, Environment Canada, 2000c). Some 75 per cent of all water

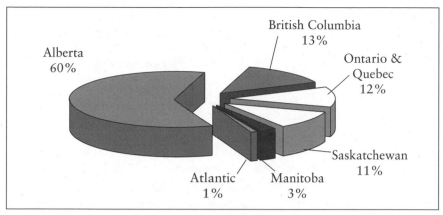

Figure 1.8 Distribution of irrigated land in Canada, 2000.
SOURCE: Canada, Environment Canada, 2002a.

used for agriculture in Canada is withdrawn by the Prairie provinces (Coote and Gingerich, 2000) because of the extensive irrigation projects that have been constructed in those provinces. The majority of irrigation users are in southern Alberta and Saskatchewan (Linton, 1997; figure 1.8), with two-thirds of Canada's irrigated farmlands found in Alberta alone (*Canadian Atlas Online*).

In Ontario, irrigation constitutes 54 per cent of total annual agricultural water use (de Loe et al., 2001), and drains have a significant impact on natural flow. The Maritimes periodically experience drought-like conditions during the summer growing season, similar to those experienced on the prairies, and utilize irrigation to compensate for natural precipitation and to prevent crop stress from drought (Nova Scotia, Department of Agriculture and Fisheries, 2002).

Irrigation is extensive on the prairies because of the climate of the region; generally, levels of irrigation are negatively related to the amount of natural precipitation (de Loe et al., 2001). Rates of precipitation on the southern prairies are not adequate for optimal crop yields. Irrigation began as small diversion projects by individual ranchers and farmers, who constructed dams to divert stream flow closer to their croplands. Today, irrigation projects occur on a large scale and usually involve a group of farmers, ranchers, or other investors who put substantial amounts of money into the irrigation of large expanses of irrigated land (Mitchell and de Loe, 1997). Between 1951 and 1987 the area of land on the prairies covered by irrigation grew by over 400 per cent, and water intake increased in proportion (Linton, 1997). Currently, in southern

Alberta alone, more than 10 000 kilometres of irrigation channels exist (Linton, 1997). Many provinces issue licences for using water in large irrigation schemes; the licenses are essentially quotas for water withdrawals and are employed to control the amount of water taken from a single source and to minimize conflicts among users within one irrigation scheme (Coote and Gingerich, 2000). This issue in the case of Alberta is explored in chapter 5.

One of the benefits of irrigation, as shown above, is that it provides a constant water supply for crops. During times of low precipitation or in climates with low precipitation, it increases the stability of production (Canada, Natural Resources Canada, 2003). Another benefit is that it allows agricultural operations to produce a wider variety of crops, including higher-value crops (Canada, Natural Resources Canada, 2003). Although there are many benefits to the irrigation of croplands, such as the production of a higher yield, it can also have a number of impacts on water levels and aquatic ecosystems, including the high levels of water that it consumes. Irrigation results in the loss of water as a result of high levels of evaporation; some water becomes polluted by the large concentrations of nutrients and pesticides in agricultural land, so that it is rendered unsuitable for irrigation purposes (Howell, 2001); increases in sedimentation in water bodies also occurs resulting in reduced aquatic habitat (Howell, 2001); and irrigation can greatly alter the hydrologic regime of the water source when the cumulative withdrawals are too much for the source to sustain. Salinity, rising water tables, and waterlogging are other negative environmental impacts of irrigation. Reservoirs built for irrigation have been developed on every major water system in the southern prairies (Linton, 1997), and they have had a major impact on river and stream flows in the area. For example, during times of low precipitation, when withdrawals are high, flow through the South Saskatchewan River has dropped by one-half (Linton, 1997).

Other than irrigation, there are a number of other ways that the agricultural industry has impacted on water resources. Erosion from cultivated land has increased sediment loads in nearby water sources; the application of fertilizers, pesticides, livestock wastes, and biosolids have resulted in surface water and groundwater contamination; and the access by livestock to waterways has impaired shoreline habitats and can also result in direct fecal contamination of these waterways. Lastly, the development of agricultural land in Canada, especially in Ontario, has resulted in the disappearance of a large number of valuable wetland ecosystems.

Bulk Water Removal

Bulk water removal refers to the transfer and removal of water out of its basin not only by manmade diversions but also by tanker ships, trucks, or pipelines (Canada, Environment Canada, 2006a). This use is not currently permitted in Canada, but its potential has sparked great political debate (as outlined in chapter 6). The controversy relates to trade and water scarcity. The gap between the existing available freshwater supply and projected water demands is growing across all parts of the globe (Brown, 1997). World water use has tripled in the last fifty years (Brown, 2001), and demands will continue to rise with both increased population and industrial growth.

Because of Canada's abundant supply of water and the anticipated increase in water scarcity in other parts of the world, the country may feel growing pressure to export water in bulk. While water demands are increasing and water is being inefficiently used, the total amount of fresh water supplied through the hydrologic cycle remains finite (Postel, 2000; Brown, 2001). Water scarcity can be seen in all areas of the world, in rivers whose stream flow has been significantly reduced by water withdrawals. The Colorado River, for example, no longer flows out to sea during dry periods of the year because it has been so extensively manipulated for the purposes of irrigation in the American Southwest (Brown, 2001). Similarly, China's Yellow River, which was once the lifeblood of much of the population, has been drying up frequently for the last twenty-five years, and the trend has recently increased to at least once a year. The severely low water levels have been attributed to the over-extraction of water by large-scale irrigation projects, and the populations living in the lower river valley are now facing severe shortages. With China's decision to import most of its grains, the situation will, it is hoped, turn around. While technology may hold the solution to increased demands, the export of fresh water may be an important issue in the future. Water is currently bottled for export on a smaller scale, and this use has also seen its share of political conflict.

The Bottled Water Industry

Across the country, Canadian exporters have the right, through permits and licences, to extract over 30 billion litres of water for bottling per year (Averill and Whelan, 2000). Of this amount, Clearly Canadian, a large bottled water manufacturer, has a permit to extract 400 million litres per year alone. Clearly Canadian extracts the water from wells in southern Ontario and then trucks it in bulk form to bottling plants in Michigan and New York (Quinn and Edstrom, 2000). Overall, the total exports of bottled water in 1998, amounting to 274 million litres, would not have filled one medium-sized tanker ship if it had been transported in bulk rather than in bottles (Quinn and Edstrom, 2000). This statistic shows why bottled water is not part of the debate over the export of Canadian water in bulk and why this type of use is not included in bulk-water policy. Instead, in terms of trade, bottled water is considered a food product under the federal Food and Drugs Act, regardless of where it goes, and all bottled water sold in Canada (locally sourced or imported) is supposed to meet quality standards and labelling requirements. Also, some very big companies, such as Coke and Pepsi, use municipal water supplies, not groundwater, and constitute a significant and growing market share in terms of withdrawals.

The bottled water industry has been growing strongly throughout North America; it increased by at least 10 per cent a year in the 1990s (Quinn and Edstrom, 2000). Despite the abundant, and cheaper, sources of water provided by water-treatment plants and municipalities, the average Canadian consumed 21.4 litres of bottled water in 1997 (Wood, 2002), with the highest per capita consumption being in Quebec (Quinn and Edstrom, 2000).

Canada's bottled water industry is a net exporter, meaning the country exports more bottled water than it imports. The rate of exports is over four times that of imports (Canada, Industry Canada, 2002). Canada's exports of bottled water have more than doubled since 1994, with revenues exceeding $230 million in 2001 (Canada, Industry Canada, 2002). The largest importers of Canadian bottled water are the United States (which imported more than 90 per cent of all exports), Japan, the United Kingdom, and Taiwan (Canada, Industry Canada, 2002). The amount of bottled water that Canada exports to the United States is over 100 times what it imports from that country (Quinn and Edstrom, 2000). In terms of total beverages exported, bottled water represented 33 per cent of all beverage exports in 1998, compared to beer at 44 per cent and soft drinks at 19 per cent (Quinn and Edstrom, 2000).

Recreational Water Use

Tourism and recreation in Canada is largely based around the country's abundant water resources. In terms of recreation, water sources are

Table 1.6
Percentage of Canadians participating in water-based activities, by region, 1996

Region	Swimming/ beach activities	Canoeing/ kayaking/sailing	Boating	Fishing
Canada	23.7	9.9	9.3	17.7
Newfoundland and Labrador	24.1	9.0	7.4	30.6
Prince Edward Island	27.0	5.2	4.3	12.5
Nova Scotia	27.5	10.2	4.8	14.9
New Brunswick	23.0	10.2	5.5	17.0
Quebec	16.4	8.6	6.5	17.6
Ontario	26.1	11.4	10.1	17.2
Manitoba	32.2	10.1	14.4	19.8
Saskatchewan	28.8	9.3	16.7	22.6
Alberta	22.7	8.6	9.5	16.9
British Columbia	26.6	9.3	10.7	17.5
Yukon Territory	16.7	10.3	10.4	32.2

SOURCE: Canada, Environment Canada, 2002a.

highly valued, although putting a monetary value on them is virtually impossible. Canadians and tourists take part in a number of water-related recreational activities each year, such as water skiing, windsurfing, swimming, beaching, fishing, boating, sailing, canoeing, and birdwatching. Other recreational activities such as camping, biking, and hiking are also enhanced by Canada's water sources. More than one-third of Canadians take part in a water-related activity at least once a year (Canada, Environment Canada, 2002a); participation by region is shown in table 1.6. Recreational fishing is the second most popular water-related activity in Canada and an important tourist industry in its own right. In 1996 more than 1.1 million Americans came to fish in Canada's waters (Canada, Environment Canada, 1996). Nature-based tourism contributes $12 billion to Canada's gross domestic product (Canada, Environment Canada, 2003a), and most of this revenue comes from water-based activities; $4.9 billion was spent on recreational fishing alone (Canada, Statistics Canada, 2000).

All of these recreational uses of Canada's water sources depend highly on unpolluted, clean waters, yet some of them can also contribute to pollution. Recreational factors that can cause water pollution include power boats that leak oil and gas and the increased waste in and around water sources where recreational activities take place. The use of power boats not only degrades the water quality through oil and gas leaks but can also alter the shoreline habitat through increased water movement and the construction of marinas, boat slips, and docks. It is estimated that 400 000 recreational powerboats operate on Lake Michigan every year and that during the 1980s and 1990s, 1000 new boat slips were built per year (Great Lakes National Program Office, 2000).

Although the overall quality of Canada's waters used for recreation is high, some people have become exposed to contaminants in some areas. Bathing areas and beaches, especially at or around larger metropolitan areas, are monitored regularly for indicator organisms such as fecal coliforms and *Escherichia coli* (E. coli) for microbiological contamination. These contaminants can come from a variety of sources, including wildlife, agricultural runoff, shoddy waste-disposal systems on recreational boats, and sewage treatment plants. If microbial pollutants are too high, health authorities will shut down beaches and swimming areas to ensure public safety. Unfortunately, when waters are contaminated, Canadians lose out, not only from lost revenue but also from the enjoyment of these waters that they might otherwise have.

Cultural and Spiritual Uses

Most uses of water in Canada derive from a Western perspective on water as part of the physical environment whereby its uniqueness is attributed to its physical and chemical properties as part of the ecosystem, rather than to its spiritual properties and uses (Blackstock, 2001, 12). Aboriginal peoples, however, have long viewed water as primarily cultural and spiritual. For them, it is the basis of all life. Canada's Aboriginal populations are profoundly linked to water and waterways for both physical and spiritual health. At the beginning of time, the Creator gave instructions to them to respect water by keeping it pure. These instructions are reflected in Aboriginal culture, beliefs, values, and uses of water *(Canadian Atlas Online)*.

For First Nations peoples, water is a source of power, and most importantly, it has a spirit that underlies their ecological perspective (Blackstock, 2001, 5). They use water in many of their spiritual ceremonies (Blackstock, 2001), and they consider many places close to water to be sacred *(Canadian Atlas Online)*. The core principle is one of respect, and a primary use is spiritual as well as economic. Cultural perspectives provide a rich arena in which to examine management issues. Understanding and identifying cultural practices and traditional ecological knowledge is for some an important first step in collaborative resource management between different user groups to prevent and resolve conflict (Flanagan and Laituri, 2004). Water is a part of Canadian identity, culture, and art (Canada, Environment Canada, 2006a). It is a central theme in Canadian art, particularly art related to our national identity. Water is a national symbol. As outlined in the case studies, particularly the water export case in chapter 6, this symbolic character of water underpins important institutions, debates, and conflicts related to water governance. Although the cultural and spiritual uses of water are hard to quantify, they are reflected in both political culture and political institutions, and they are also related to intrinsic environmental uses. Water is thus valued as part of Canadian identity, but it is also undervalued as a resource, in terms of both quantity and quality.

Water Use and the Problem of Pollution

Many of the properties of water, the functioning of ecosystems, and the various human uses of water can be significantly compromised and impaired through pollution. There are essentially two types of pollution that can degrade water quality: point source pollution and non-point source pollution. *Point source pollution* enters water directly from a specific point: for example, a pipe or a ditch. This type of pollution occurs at specific locations such as factories or mines and is easily identified; therefore it can readily be monitored and regulated (Miller, 2004, 486). *Non-point source pollution*, on the other hand, is not as easy to monitor because it is ill-defined. It is generated from a diffuse source and generally occurs over a broad area. Often, non-point sources of pollution are a function of land use (Averill and Whelan, 2000) and can include agricultural runoff, urban runoff, stormwater runoff, atmospheric deposition, and the effects of forestry on aquatic ecosystems.

Water pollution is determined by the nature of pollutants that have caused the contamination and the assimilative capacity of the receiving water. Pollutants can be divided into two major categories: persistent and non-persistent contaminants. *Persistent pollutants* are non-degradable or degrade very slowly when in the environment, leading to irreparable damage. These types of pollutants are becoming more and more common as result of the increased use of inorganic substances in many manufacturing processes. *Persistent pollutants* include such contaminants as water-soluble inorganic chemicals, organic chemicals, sediments, and suspended matter. Water-soluble inorganic chemicals include acids, salts, toxic metals such as mercury and lead, and dioxins. The presence of these chemicals is harmful to human health if found in food and drinking water. They can also cause damage to fish and other aquatic organisms and, if used on crops as irrigation water, can result in crop failure or depressed crop yields. Persistent organic pollutants (POPs) are also very harmful to aquatic plants and animals and are known to bioaccumulate in the food chain. Some POPs are considered carcinogenic to humans and animals when ingested and are known to cause negative health effects such as kidney disorders and birth defects. Environment Canada estimates that the total tonnage of toxics released into water increases by some 40 per cent per year (Canada, Environment Canada, 2004c).

Sediments are the most widespread cause of water pollution. Sediment pollution is also considered a persistent pollutant because its mitigation can be difficult. It results from agricultural runoff, soil erosion, logging, mining, and development. Some sediments are flushed into sewage treatment plants. This kind of pollution can be minimized through the use of vegetated buffer strips, control of livestock from stream banks, and proper engineering of development and construction. Sediments are most harmful to fish populations in water sources because they can clog their gills and deprive them of oxygen. Sediments also cause water to become so murky that species cannot see their prey. As well, sediments require oxygen to be broken down; therefore they compete with fish for needed oxygen, and fish populations are killed off. Sediments also bind to many persistent pollutants and become relatively persistent sources of pollution.

Many types of pollutants are non-persistent and are degradable in water sources. These can be broken down through chemical reactions or by the biological interactions of bacteria into other non-polluting forms or reduced to acceptable levels (Miller, 2004, 55). Non-persistent pollutants include disease-causing agents such as E. coli, other bacteria, protozoa, and fecal coliforms, as well as organic wastes and nutrients.

The primary source of nutrient loadings today is farm runoff of manure and fertilizer. Nutrient-containing laundry detergents were another source in the past. The effects of oxygen-demanding wastes and inorganic plant nutrients on water sources are similar; both types of pollutants eventually cause the depletion of dissolved oxygen levels. Oxygen-demanding wastes are decomposed in aquatic environments by aerobic bacteria that use the oxygen in the degradation process. These bacteria utilize the oxygen in the water, keeping it from other aquatic life. Nutrients such as nitrate and phosphorus stimulate excessive algae growth. The growth of and reproduction of aquatic flora is called eutrophication, and this process is stimulated in the presence of excessive levels of nutrients. If growth becomes exponential, death and decay will result, which will horde the oxygen from fish and aquatic plants because it will be used during the decaying process. Eventually this cycle kills all life in the water body. Fortunately, this type of damage is reversible if nutrient loadings are decreased and controlled.

Groundwater pollution is distinctive because it is not visible and therefore can go unnoticed for long periods of time. The principal sources of groundwater pollution are leaky underground storage tanks, seepage from landfill sites, hazardous waste dumps, livestock wastes, septic tank leakage, road salt, application of fertilizers and pesticides on agricultural land, and storage lagoons, to name a few (Karvinen and McAllister, 1994; Miller, 2004, 493). Groundwater pollution is also very expensive to mitigate, compared to surface water pollution; therefore preventing it is the best way to protect groundwater sources (Miller, 2004, 495). It can be a serious human health threat to many rural residents who utilize private groundwater supplies, especially if regular monitoring is not conducted. A Canadian survey conducted on the quality of drinking water from wells found that 10 per cent of all wells were contaminated with common industrial chemicals, and fecal coliforms and nitrates were even more common (Linton, 1997).

CONCLUSION

This chapter has outlined the basic scientific properties of water, the significance of water resources in Canada, and the multiple uses of water. The basic chemical, physical, and biological features define the potential uses of water in any given ecosystem or drainage basin. Although Canada is a comparatively water-rich nation, water is not distributed evenly throughout the country. The uses and conflicts stemming from different uses therefore vary by region, province, and jurisdiction. Polluted waters heighten the potential for conflict, given that uses are impaired or lost. Water pollution in the form of the degradation of habitat for fish and other species is a critical problem in Canada. Many of the properties of water and the functioning of ecosystems can be compromised if human and non-human uses are impaired as a result of water pollution.

Many different uses and users of water exist in Canada. From the earliest deployment of water for shipping, navigation, agriculture, and human settlements to the more recent uses for industry, electricity generation, recreation, and bottling, there has been a gradual increase. The use of cheap and abundant water resources for agricultural and industrial development of hydroelectric projects, for pulp and paper mills, and for mining and oil extraction continue to point to the fact that for most of Canada's history, the institutional arrangements have been designed to manage the quantity of water available for economic development, rather than the quality of water available for Canadian citizens and ecosystem health.

In many areas there are additional competing uses and impacts from neighbouring US users. Congestion and competition over the uses of water as a natural resource can occur in any water body – rivers, lakes, and coastal waters. Economic, social, cultural, and environmental uses and human users are found in virtually every watershed in Canada. All of the three general types of uses – withdrawal, consumptive, and in-stream – have the potential to generate political conflicts. It is clear from this chapter that multiple uses of water make political conflict inevitable and sustainable management increasingly important.

Given the number and variety of uses of water outlined in this chapter, it is not surprising that political conflicts over who, what, when, where, and how water can be used by different individuals and groups have sprung up. There are several key aspects of water as a resource that tend to engender political conflict. The primacy of large-scale, industrial, commercial, and agricultural uses; the high and increasing per capita residential and urban uses; the low price placed on water; the reliance on and degradation of surface water and groundwater; and finally, the lack of knowledge about the state of water resources and their use in Canada all set the stage for a number of different, concurrent, and enduring water conflicts in Canada.

The next three chapters in Part One provide the context in which institutions have evolved to address water-use conflicts in Canada. Chapter 2 follows with an overview of the institutional arrangements designed to manage water-use conflicts and the various federal, provincial, municipal, and Aboriginal actors involved in water governance in the Canadian federal system. Chapter 3 provides an overview of the policy instruments used in Canada to implement water policies and manage water-use conflicts. And chapter 4 reviews the property rights that underpin water use and access in Canada. Collectively, these chapters provide the backdrop for a closer examination of water institutions in action in the cases analyzed in Part Two.

PART TWO

Institutions, Instruments, and Property Rights for Water Resource Management in Canada

2

Institutions for Water Resource Management in Canada

CAROLYN JOHNS AND KEN RASMUSSEN

In this chapter we provide an overview of the historical and current political landscape related to water resource management in Canada, including an account of how federalism, intergovernmental management, Aboriginal rights, and other state and non-state factors interact to structure water policy institutions. The chapter provides the broad institutional context for all the case-study chapters. It also outlines the basis for various authorities in Canada, setting the foundation for the instruments and implementation options covered in chapter 3.

INTRODUCTION

As outlined in chapter 1, the multiple uses and users of Canada's water resources have the potential to lead to numerous and persistent conflicts at the local, provincial, and national levels. This chapter provides an overview of institutional arrangements at various levels in the Canadian federal system based on the fundamental assumption that it is critical to understand the historical development and evolution of Canada's water management institutions in order to analyze the current policy context and political conflicts related to multiple water uses across the country.

Chapter 1 highlighted the unique and multi-purpose properties of water as a natural resource and public good which make it distinctly challenging to manage. Historically, various institutional arrangements have been designed to resolve enduring conflicts between those with water rights and those without. The power dynamics of many water-use conflicts have been defined by which water users were first to have their rights recognized in law. As a result, the pattern of institutions designed to foster economic-development uses of Canada's vast water resources were well-established by the mid to late nineteenth century, and they continue to define many of the institutional arrangements that endure to this day.

Also as outlined in chapter 1, water has been a fundamental economic resource in Canada since before Confederation. Water policy has evolved for both water quality and quantity (Boyd, 2003) and can be analyzed over two interrelated periods – the common-law period and the public-law period (Brooks, 2003). In terms of institutional arrangements, common law or "riparian rights" form the foundation of water rights, use, and access in Canada. Common law does not apply in Quebec, but civil water rights are similar in substance to common-law rules in other provinces. Common law in the eastern Canadian provinces provided that riparians – those holding land adjacent to or under a stream, lake, or harbour – have legally enforceable rights to the quantity and quality of water they use. As detailed in chapter 4, the basic principle is that every riparian is entitled to the water of his or her stream in its natural flow without sensible alteration to its character or quality (Canada, Environment Canada, 1975). This legal right means that if an individual or owner upstream changes the quality or level of water flowing past his or her land to the detriment of those downstream, he or she may be liable to a suit in civil court (Estrin and Swaigen, 1993). Although constitutional and statutory laws override common law, many water governance institutions in Canada trace their roots to common-law and property rights principles. Water governance and management must therefore be understood in this evolutionary legal context.

Historically in Canada, many disputes between users were addressed through private litigation. However, from the earliest days of colonial rule, public authority has played a role in water management. Public authority has traditionally served to ensure an adequate supply of water for economic development and to address disputes between those with competing property rights. Occasionally, boundary issues between Canada and the United States emerged as something of an irritant, but these were still primarily issues of access and quantity (Waterfield, 1970).

Thus the early governance regime of common law predicated on property rights, with rules being determined by the courts, has increasingly been supplemented and further defined by statutory law under the authority of the Canadian constitution. Under the constitution, Canadian federalism divides responsibility for water management and regulation between two or more levels of government. On the surface there is what appears to be a tidy division of authorities and responsibilities stemming from the constitution, but in reality a complex layering of legislation, authorities, and agreements exists to manage water resources in Canada.

Jurisdictional complexity is also related to the physical nature of water resources. As many scholars have observed, the multi-jurisdictional scale and fugitive or transitory nature of water and its many interrelated uses make it hard to fit neatly within well-defined categories of property rights that are recognized under common law (Lucas, 1986; Barton, 1986; Kennett, 1992; Sproule-Jones, 2002). Hence "the legal character of water [has] made it more difficult than other resources to fit into the constitutional division of powers" (Lucas, 1986, 42).

The institutional arrangements for the management of water in Canada are complex and involve a large array of federal government departments, agencies, and authorities, multiple provincial and territorial government departments and agencies, local governments and authorities, and a number of Aboriginal band governments. On top of all this, Canada also has numerous bilateral agreements with the United States concerning the Great Lakes and other freshwater resources that flow across the border between the two countries (Bloomfield and Fitzgerald, 1958). Thus a complex network of policy actors and institutions is involved in all aspects of water management.

Conflicts exist between Aboriginal people and both the federal and provincial governments; between various categories of agriculture and residential users; between competing visions of who "owns" the water and how it should be priced; and between those who wish to encourage more private-sector involvement in water resource management and those who wish it to remain a public resource under complete public management. There are also numerous conflicts between provinces and the federal government and even among individual provinces that share common borders. Most of these conflicts, however, take place within an institutional structure established with different purposes in mind, and those new institutions that have been established, such as environmental assessment and protection legislation and related bureaucratic agencies, must now compete with existing and powerfully entrenched systems of power.

Only recently have governments attempted to balance the economic uses of water resources with other social, cultural, and environmental uses. As outlined later in this chapter, infrastructure development and public concerns related to public health were the primary reason provincial and local governments began legislating concerning water quality.

Issues of water quality related to environmental concerns were late arrivals on the policy agenda and emerged in an institutional context that was very well-established. Indeed, most water management institutions were formed to support a different set of public policy problems in the nineteenth century.

Environmental concerns, especially those associated with water quality, have continued to move up the policy agenda. Such concerns, among elites and the population at large, have created a host of environmental groups and spawned a new generation of environmental agencies (Parson, 2001a). New actors and events have brought the complexity of water resource governance to the fore. The recent shocking event known as the Walkerton tragedy, in which seven residents of a small town in Ontario died after drinking water tainted with E. coli bacteria from animal waste that had leached into the groundwater (O'Connor, 2002), pushed the issues surrounding water management and responsibility for it to the very top of the political agenda and made Canadians question their complacency about how this resource was governed (Burke, 2001). As the case study in chapter 8 highlights, the inquiry that was held into this incident exposed the complex set of institutions and legislation involved in the governance of water. This case clearly indicates how water uses are intimately interlinked, and it also highlights the fact that governments in Canada have not been very effective in establishing institutions capable of dealing with these multiple-use challenges. The reason for the gap between an ability to identify the problem and an ability to act can be found in the historical development of Canada's institutional arrangements concerning the management of water (Lee and Perl, 2003).

Canadian governments have not been exceptionally innovative protectors of our water resources, and the explanation lies in the various governments' historic relationships with politically powerful resource industries (Barlow and Clark, 2002). Proponents of this argument make the observation that institutional arrangements for water management clearly reflect the dominant role that natural resource industries have played in economic development in most provinces and that, combined with the pull of globalization and decentralization that characterizes the Canadian federal system, consistently allows economic uses to trump other uses, such as environmental protection, both historically and at the present time. Others argue that the complex governance regimes for water management have blurred responsibility for managing this important resource, resulted in buck-passing, and reduced the overall capacity to manage this national resource.

What is clear from this volume is that institutional arrangements for water develop and change over time, but earlier decisions and rules set limits on what can happen later. The key to this kind of institutional analysis is to focus on government as the establisher of the rules of the game, which means that it can open or close off access for various groups with different needs, values, and stakes in access to water. In many diverse aspects of Canadian water governance, early interests (pre- and post-Confederation) have succeeded in entrenching their power in Canadian water management institutions, which have proved resistant to change despite the emergence of new interests and uses. The ability to empirically assess the validity of this argument is based on a detailed understanding of the evolution of institutions for water resource management in Canada. This chapter thus lays the foundation on which institutions can be analyzed in the case studies presented in Part Two. It is important to note, however, that the case studies in this book clearly indicate that the governance of water resources in Canada is not as tidy, hierarchical, and compartmentalized as the organization of this chapter might suggest. The following sections review institutional arrangements for water governance at all levels in the federal system, highlighting the intergovernmental character and institutional interplay between these various levels of authority.

FEDERAL INSTITUTIONS

At the national level, the federal government derives its power with regard to water resource management from a number of sections in the Canadian constitution. First, section 108 assigns ownership of public land to the federal government. Federal lands include harbours, national parks, northern lands, armed forces bases, and other such territory. Secondly, section 91 of the British North America Act (BNA Act; later the Constitution Act, 1982)* gives the federal government legislative authority in a number of areas relevant to water resource management. "Navigation and shipping" powers (section 91.10) provide Parliament with broad powers over works and operations that affect navigable waters. "Sea Coast and Inland Fisheries" (section 91.12) allows the federal government to pass regulations pertaining to fisheries and restrict the pollution of fishing waters. Another critical legislative strength of the federal

---

* Section 1 of the Constitution Act, 1982, replaced the reference to the Canadian constitution as the British North America Act, 1867.

government lies in its criminal law powers and its jurisdiction over works and undertakings connecting a province with one or more other provinces or extending beyond the limits of a province (section 91.29 and section 92.10c). Finally, the residual or general power to pass laws for the "peace, order and good government of Canada" gives the federal government some legislative leeway on issues of national and international concern. Other constitutional areas of federal jurisdiction that can affect water policy include trade and commerce, interprovincial waters, taxation, and Aboriginal lands and peoples.

Federal navigation power has been a key source of federal involvement in Canadian water issues historically. The Navigable Waters Protection Act was first passed in 1882, although the courts had recognized its principles in common law much earlier. Navigation powers have played a central role in Canada's economic development and have given the federal government involvement in many water issues. For example, every time the provinces want to build a dam on a navigable river, they have had to get a federal permit to do so.

The other constitutional and legislative area where the federal government has derived authority related to water resource management has been in the management of fisheries. The powers of the federal government in this area derive from section 91 of the BNA Act, which assigned responsibility for inland fisheries and oceans to the federal government. Under this authority, the federal government passed the first Fisheries Act in 1868. Constitutional powers and court decisions have subsequently resulted in federal reliance on the federal Fisheries Act (and its amendments) as an important statute and rationale for involvement in water quality management. Section 35.1 of the Fisheries Act (1991) makes it an offence for any person "to carry on any work or undertaking that results in the harmful alteration, disruption or destruction of fish habitat." Section 36.3 prohibits deposition of deleterious substances into waters frequented by fish. This legislation is viewed by some as the most powerful weapon in protecting the environment and water resources.

Another area where the federal government has exercised its powers related to water resource management has been under its international treaty–making authority. This includes global agreements related to international waters, biodiversity, trade, and climate-change conventions. Canada is a signatory to several bilateral treaties and agreements with the United States dealing with fisheries, wildlife, and water quantity and quality issues that stem from the massive border waters between Canada and the United States. These include various treaties such as the Boundary Waters Treaty (1909), the Niagara River Water Diversion Treaty (1950), and the Columbia River Treaty (1961, 1964) and agreements such as the St Lawrence Seaway Project (1952) and the Great Lakes Water Quality Agreement (1972, 1978, 1987).

The Boundary Waters Treaty of 1909 established the International Joint Commission (IJC) and set the basic principles guiding boundary water relations between Canada and the United States. The IJC is supported by the federal government in its task of addressing disputes related to water use and movement and its investigative, monitoring, research, and policy functions. Although this institution primarily focuses on the Great Lakes, it also has responsibility for and is involved in the management of other water sources that cut across the Canada–US, border, including the Souris River in Manitoba, Saskatchewan, and North Dakota and the larger Columbia River further west. Early involvement by the federal government related to the IJC's mandate related to monitoring levels and flows, especially in relation to the generation of electricity by water power. Early responsibilities of the IJC included authorizing water uses and approving projects such as dams or canals. Although water pollution was being studied by the IJC as early as 1912, it was not until the signing of the 1972 Great Lakes Water Quality Agreement that the commission had a mandate to investigate a wide range of issues related to water uses and pursue common water quality objectives. The international treaty–making authority of the federal government also resulted in other international agreements related to water, such as those concerned with acid rain, but it was not until the trade agreements of the late 1980s and early 1990s (discussed below) that these authorities had broader impacts on federal powers related to water resource management.

Although the federal government has various aspects of water management under its jurisdiction, historically, it only has been active in quality dimensions of water resource management since the early 1970s. It was not until the 1970 Canada Water Act (CWA) that the federal government passed its first piece of legislation explicitly related to water resource management. The overall objective of the legislation was to encourage the use of fresh water in an efficient and equitable manner consistent with the social, economic, and environmental needs of present and future generations. This legislation was "enabling" rather than "regulatory" as it articulated the federal government's authority in this policy area, enabled the establishment of institutional arrangements, and empowered the federal government to reach agreements with the provinces and industry to address water pollution problems (Doern and Conway, 1994, 22). The CWA explicitly articulated that the approach to water quality management would be based on consultation (part I, section 4) and negotiated agreements with the provinces (part I, sections 5–8).

The CWA and other pieces of legislation around the same time did, however, lead to the building of the federal government's bureaucratic capacity regarding water resource management. The Government Organization Act and the Department of the Environment Act in 1970–71 set out the authority and responsibility of the DOE and departmental officials. The department brought together several units of other departments into seven service-based divisions, including the Water Management Service. The department underwent several "mandate debates" and reorganizations in its formative years (Doern and Conway, 1994, 17). The focus during this period was on the implementation of the Canada Water Act. Eventually, the scientific, technical, and operational capacities of the DOE were predominantly located in the Inland Waters Directorate. The DOE (now Environment Canada) remains the key federal institution with legislative authority over water resource and water quality management. However, ongoing internal struggles over water resources management plagued the DOE during the 1970s. The department lacked a unifying role and mandate that could integrate the Lands Directorate and the Wildlife Service. In many ways the DOE remained a "house divided," and weak statutory capacity contributed to its ineffective role in water pollution management (Doern and Conway, 1994, 32–7).

Separate fisheries management responsibilities were granted to the Department of Fisheries and Oceans (DFO) in 1979. The DFO operates under a variety of statutes such as the Fisheries Act, the Navigable Waters Protection Act, and the Fishing and Recreational Harbours Act. Combined, these acts give it a mandate for the management and control of the fisheries; the conservation, protection, restoration, and enhancement of fish and fish habitat; prevention, preparedness, and response to pollution incidents; search-and-rescue, recreational boating, marine communications, and traffic services; icebreaking; the establishment of marine aids to navigation; protection of navigable waters; and provision of public harbour infrastructure in support of commercial fishing and transient boating. The legislation and bureaucratic capacity of the DFO has provided the federal government with significant powers related to fisheries protection in both inland and coastal waters.

Another area where the federal government has attempted to assert a role in water management is through financial support for the construction and upgrading of sewage treatment plants in municipalities across Canada. Early on, primarily through its spending powers, it worked with provinces and municipalities on joint resource planning and water-related infrastructure projects. With urbanization and population growth, the construction and maintenance of water treatment and distribution systems for industrial and domestic uses have remained a critical part of Canada's water management system. The federal government's spending powers have resulted in its involvement in this area.

In the 1970s the federal government also began regulating toxic substance under part III of the CWA and the Environmental Contaminants Act. Its role remained passive in terms of implementation, however, since it relied predominantly on bilateral monitoring and implementation agreements with the provinces. The federal government during this time exhibited ambivalence "and rejected the notion of national standards altogether," in large part because of opposition on constitutional grounds to federal unilateralism from four of the most populous provinces (Harrison, 2000).

It was not until 1984 that the federal minister of the environment established the Inquiry on Federal Water Policy, led by Dr Peter Pearse, to examine the federal government's role in water resource management and protection. Using commissioned research papers, public hearings, and a comprehensive consultation on water in Canada, the inquiry gathered information and generated a report that was reviewed by and generally endorsed by the provinces. The cooperative approach and regional flexibility recommended by the report made it a sound starting point for further federal policy development. The federal government then established an Interdepartmental Water Policy Task Force, which examined the recommendations in the Pearse report and developed a federal water policy for consideration by the new Conservative government (Filyk and Cote, 1992, 75). The result was the 1987 Federal Water Policy (FWP).

The FWP set out the goals and actions by which the federal government intended to contribute to water quality objectives through its own and cooperative programs, the development of information and expertise, technological development and transfer, and promotion of public awareness. Although a proposal to further develop water policy into comprehensive legislation, as recommended by the Pearse report, was approved by cabinet, ultimately the FWP merely reconfirmed the federal government's commitment to water quality research and a waste-water infrastructure support role. As articulated in five broad strategies and specific policy statements, the approach to water management continued to reflect the recognition of the provinces' proprietary rights over land and water resources (Canada, Environment Canada, 1987). The proposed legislation, the Canada Water Preservation Bill, focused on regulation of water exports, which at the time had become a controversial subject in connection with the free trade debate (Filyk and Cote, 1992, 76), and the legislation died when the 1988 election was called.

Until 1988, the CWA, the Fisheries Act, and the FWP formed the foundation of the federal government's policy authority in the area of water resource management. The Canadian Environmental Protection Act (CEPA) passed that year emphasized pollution prevention, an ecosystem approach, and toxic substances management. It superseded the Clean Air Act, the Environmental Contaminants Act, the Ocean Dumping Control Act, and part III of the Clean Water Act. This new legislation emphasized the federal government's focus on toxic substance regulation as central to its water quality mandate. The Supreme Court decision in *R v. Crown Zellerbach* (1988) reinforced the federal government's constitutional authority in an ocean-dumping case under the peace, order, and good government clause of the constitution.

The federal government's powers related to water management and trade also became a key issue in the free trade debate in 1988. Before the introduction of free trade, the only significant institutional constraint on Canadian governments' policy actions in water export was the constitutional division of powers. For Canadians, the debate about whether to include water in the Canada–US Free Trade Agreement (CUFTA) and, later, the North American Free Trade Agreement (NAFTA) was an acrimonious and emotional one. In the end, "[w]aters, including natural or artificial mineral waters and aerated waters, not containing sugar or other sweetening matter," were included under heading 22.01 of the CUFTA's schedule of "goods" slated for trade liberalization. When NAFTA superseded the CUFTA in 1994, it retained the regime of trade rules for water established under the CUFTA with only a few modifications. Yet controversy about NAFTA's competence over trade in water remained because there was some uncertainty about whether water could accurately be described as a tradable "good." In 1993 the governments of Canada, Mexico, and the United States issued a joint statement on this matter, noting that "[u]nless water, in any form has entered into commerce and become a good or product, it is not covered by the provisions of any trade agreement including the NAFTA ... Water in its natural state in lakes, rivers, reservoirs, aquifers, water basins and the like is not a good or product, is not traded, and therefore is not and never has been subject to the terms of any trade agreement" (Canadian Council of Ministers of the Environment, 1999b, 4).

In sum, the joint statement confirmed that Canadian water resources in "a natural state" are not subject to NAFTA trade rules; however, this clarification does not prevent Canadian water from being taken from its natural state, being put into containers, and made into a "good" fully subject to NAFTA rules. In fact, in the case of bottled water, this is exactly what has happened. As outlined in chapter 2, the introduction of free trade brought a series of new institutional constraints that have changed the way Canadian governments relate to one another in water export policy and concerns about the future powers of the federal government in this area. In addition, new institutions were established, such as the North American Commission for Environmental Cooperation, which has powers to make recommendations on environmental issues, including water pollution, in any of the three countries in NAFTA and not just related to the Great Lakes, like the IJC.

In 1990 the Conservative government made a significant investment in environmental initiatives. However, the $3 billion federal Green Plan, which was implemented between 1990 and 1995, did not result in any significant changes in terms of federal powers and water policy except for an investment in water-related research capacity and funding to clean up polluted waters. The plan contained very little in the way of federal incentives to develop national water quality standards and avoided confrontation with the provinces by focusing on research partnerships (Hoberg and Harrison, 1994).

This issue of water quality was increasingly becoming a source of major conflict between the federal and provincial governments, particularly by 1995, with the passage of the Canadian Environmental Assessment Act (CEAA). This act was passed in response to a number of court challenges raised by environmental groups and others about the construction of dams in two provinces. When the federal courts began to assert their authority over these issues related to the environment, the federal government felt it needed to get more involved. The act that emerged as a result, no matter how sensible and administrative, did have the capacity to reduce provincial discretion, particularly those aspects of the act that compel the federal government to order an environmental review of a project that might have serious adverse environmental affects in another province or country.

Naturally, the Canadian Environmental Assessment Act was opposed by some provinces, which argued that they were already doing a very good job and that the federal government was simply interested in "cherry-picking" by getting itself involved in only those high-profile cases where it could claim some political credit. Some provinces preferred the existing Federal Environmental Assessment and Review Office, which involved the federal government and ministerial coordination without the need for a federal statute. The CEAA also challenged the ability of provinces to manage their own Crown resources, and provinces that had fought hard for control of these resources were not about to have the federal government enter the process through the back door. The provinces were especially concerned that environmental groups would use the environmental assessment regulations to block dozens of major projects within their jurisdiction. As one close observed noted, "The provinces' shared desire to control the pace and direction of economic development within their jurisdictions spurred them to present a common front in opposition to federal proposals" (Harrison, 1996, 137). Thus a major institutional transformation that would see any meaningful authority transferred to the federal government was unlikely in the face of persistent and unified provincial opposition.

One area related to water resource management where the CEAA did have an immediate impact was regarding the federal government's own land uses that would impact on water. In addition to its constitutional and legislative powers related to water resource management, the federal government is also a major landowner. Some 41 per cent of all lands in Canada are federally owned Crown lands. Provinces own 48 per cent of the available land, and only 11 per cent of the country's total land mass is privately owned (*Canadian Encyclopedia*, 2000, 601). However, federally owned lands are mostly in the remote northern areas of Canada, and Ottawa owns only a very small portion of land within provincial borders, primarily federal parks, wildlife preserves, and military bases. The provinces own most of the land within their jurisdiction, but the proportion varies from province to province, with Newfoundland owning 95 per cent of the land within its borders and Prince Edward Island owning less than 2 per cent of all land. Despite its ability to use the CEAA and other legislation related to management of its own lands in proximity to waters, federal powers related to fisheries, navigation, and environmental protection have continually come into conflict with provincial powers over natural resources. Many of these conflicts ended up in the courts. A second area where the CEAA has had an impact is related to the federal government's fidiciary responsibilities for Aboriginal peoples. These responsibilities can also trigger CEAA investigations, as outlined below in the section on Aboriginal water rights. Like conflicts with the provinces related to the CEAA, many of these conflicts also end up in the courts.

In the *Water-Powers* reference in 1929, the Supreme Court of Canada determined that the federal government may severely restrict, perhaps even prohibit, provincial water developments in order to preserve federal navigation and fisheries rights (VanderZwaag and Duncan, 1992, 7). In another decision in *Northwest Falling Contractors Ltd v. the Queen* (1980), the court reinforced the federal jurisdiction relating to pollution that was harmful to fisheries. As outlined above, the Supreme Court in *R v. Crown Zellerbach* in 1988 upheld a federal prosecution that broadened the federal government's powers to regulate environmental pollution of water in oceans under the "peace, order, and good government" constitutional provisions when an activity relates to a demonstrable national concern. Although the CEPA refers to toxics as a matter of national concern in the preamble, it was *Crown v. Hydro Quebec* (1997) that upheld the federal government's authority to regulate toxic substances under its criminal law powers. Environmental assessment is another area where the federal government has intervened in regard to projects such as the Rafferty and Alameda Dam in Saskatchewan and the Oldman River Dam in Alberta, both with water resource and environmental implications. However, there have also been Supreme Court decisions that have limited federal powers related to water management, and uncertainty still exists concerning federal powers and the relatively new provincial powers related to natural resources under section 92A of the constitution.

Since the FWP in 1987, the federal government has not introduced a major policy initiative related to water. Although the related legislation outlined above has had implications for federal authorities related to water, the 1990s in large part witnessed a decline in the federal government's role. Two progress reports on the FWP were issued in 1990 and 1994, but water-related policies and programs through Environment Canada witnessed a marked decline as a result of across-the-board budget cuts in the mid-1990s. In January 2000 (just months before the water tragedies in Walkerton, Ontario, and Battleford, Saskatchewan) Environment Canada convened a round table on water management in Canada to engage other jurisdictions and water experts in a dialogue in order to identify key water issues facing the country in the coming decade (Averill and Whelan, 2000).

Despite the identification of significant challenges by policy stake-holders and the water management challenges highlighted by Walkerton and Battleford, the priority of water issues for the federal government remains questionable. It did declare water a sustainable development priority in 2003 and established an interdepartmental committee co-chaired by Health Canada and Environment Canada to develop a Federal Water Framework (FWF) in February 2004. However, a report by the federal Commissioner of Environment and Sustainable Development indicates that the senior-level committees responsible for the FWF have been inactive since the spring of 2004 and the status and future of the framework are uncertain (Canada, Office of the Auditor General, 2005). This same report highlights the need for the federal government to examine its role, including its responsibility for safe drinking water in First Nations communities, on military bases, in national parks, and in relation to transportation, such as trains, aircraft, and cruise ships travelling between provinces and internationally. Stressing the need for a coherent water policy to coordinate the activities of Environment Canada, Health Canada, and the seventeen other federal departments and agencies with water-related responsibilities, the environmental commissioner recommended the need for new steps to be taken on the FWF.

In the midst of the election campaign in 2006, then prime minister Paul Martin announced a $1 billion investment over ten years to clean up major waterways (CBC News, 2006), but the future of federal water policy under the minority Conservative government that came to power after the election is uncertain. In May 2006 the federal government's Policy Research Initiative (PRI) hosted a national conference on water, featuring water experts and representatives from jurisdictions across the country. The emphasis on including representatives from provincial, territorial, and First Nations governments indicates the significance of intergovernmental relations in this policy area. Intergovernmental management of water resources was recognized as important by participants, but a major theme of this conference was defining the federal role in water policy. Although a report from the PRI calls for more federal and intergovernmental policy capacity related to water resource management in Canada (Canada, PRI, 2006b), the issue has yet to make it on to the federal agenda, and given the minority status of the Conservative government and the current focus on climate change, it will likely not be on the federal agenda any time in the near future.

PROVINCIAL AND TERRITORIAL
INSTITUTIONS FOR WATER GOVERNANCE

The evolution of policy development and institutions related to water resource management and policy studies reveals that water quality governance in Canada gives pre-eminence to the powers of provincial governments. The rules in Canada for water quantity and quality management are dominated by provincial regulations within the context of Canadian federalism (Sproule-Jones, 1993). Under section 109 of the Constitution Act, 1982, the provinces in effect own all lands, mines, and minerals within their geographic boundaries that have not been sold or are not subject to Aboriginal rights, and this ownership carries rights to water and other natural resources even though no specific reference is made to natural resources such as water. For the most part, waters that lie solely within a province's boundaries fall under the constitutional authority of that province. As far as Canada's three territories are concerned, the federal Indian and Northern Affairs Canada has as one of its functions in the north the mandate under federal law to manage water resources in the Northwest Territories and Nunavut. In 2003 responsibility for the management of water resources in Yukon was transferred from the federal government to the government of Yukon (Canada, Indian and Northern Affairs Canada, 2007), although under delegated, not constitutional, authority, which still sets it as a territory apart from the constitutional powers of provinces.

Section 92 of the constitution outlines the provinces' constitutional powers. The property and civil rights clause (section 92.13) gives the provinces legislative jurisdiction over the property they own (and private property) and has been used, along with provincial control over natural resources (section 92.5), as a basis for water resource legislation. "Local works and undertakings" (section 92.10) and "generally all matters of a merely local or private nature in the province" (section 92.16) have also been used to authorize legislation in this policy area. The fundamental divisions of power and bases of provincial legal authority did not change with the patriation of the constitution in 1982.[*]

---

[*] Note that the Constitution Act of 1982 did amend section 92 and added section 92(A), making the provinces' jurisdiction over natural resource management more explicit.

These have come to mean property rights over rivers and other wetlands, with the exception of those waters that are found on federal land within provincial boundaries.

The powers of the provinces were reinforced in a constitutional amendment in 1982 (section 92A) that clarified provincial rights over development, conservation, and management of non-renewable resources, forests, and the generation and production of electricity from water (Chandler, 1985, 253–74). In practice, what this constitutional power has meant is that the provinces have been concerned with ensuring that resource-based industries – traditionally, users of large quantities of water – are encouraged to aid in the process of economic development. Provincial governments are therefore constitutionally, politically, and operationally privileged with respect to responsibility for water resource management, and they have historically been more concerned with economic development than with water conservation or quality. In practical terms, this emphasis has resulted in a situation in which Canada's provincial governments have been much less concerned about the quality of their water resources and more concerned about ensuring that the quantity of water necessary for economic expansion is made available to various users.

There are several areas where provincial governments are involved in water resource management. Most early legislative activity was aimed at the use of water for increasing economic development within provincial borders. For example, the province of British Columbia in 1856 passed the Gold Fields Act, which created a commission that would grant exclusive rights for defined quantities of water in return for a rental payment to the provincial government. The Land Ordinance Act of 1865 provided for the diversion of water to cultivated lands. The first statutes to deal exclusively with water rights, the Water Privileges Act, was passed in 1892; it declared that the right to the use and the flow of all water was vested exclusively with the province. By 1909 British Columbia had passed its first Water Act, which delineated the acquisition and control of water rights and established a tribunal primarily to determine the priorities of various claimants and the allocation of water to users. Similar institutions were created in other provinces, each of which began to regulate water for economic development potential early in their history.

Historically, the second area in which provinces passed legislation related to water management was health protection in the nineteenth century. The deplorable state of sanitation throughout Canada during the late nineteenth century resulted in the establishment of a strong provincial presence in the area of public health (Benidickson, 2002). Municipal governments were completely unable to handle the job because of a lack of financial and organizational capacity. Thus with an increase in the number of cases of typhoid, diphtheria, and even malaria, strong action by provincial governments was warranted, and the provinces eventually began to centralize authority and provide administrative and policy leadership. At the time it was not unreasonable to fear that local authorities were likely to be too subject to powerful local influences to act effectively, and thus most provincial governments established some form of centralized authority to deal with the health issues surrounding water quality (Hodgetts, 1995, 19).

Most notable in this regard was the province of Ontario, which in the middle of the nineteenth century faced a number of cholera and typhoid epidemics. The short-term policy response had been to create a board of public health with powers of quarantine, but Ontario, followed by other provinces, passed a Public Health Act in 1884. This act required local (public health) boards to be established and gave the province the power to regulate them. The province then worked with local governments to install sewers, sewage treatment plants, and drinking-water purification plants (Macdonald, 2001, 172). Thus by the end of the nineteenth century, provincial governments had emerged as the primary institutional force in the area of water supply, sewage collection and treatment, health protection, and wildlife management. However, throughout the twentieth century, the actual management of the system was delegated to various municipal or regional agencies or to single-purpose bodies such as hydroelectric utilities and irrigation authorities. Ontario, for example, created the Ontario Water Resources Commission in 1956 under the Ontario Water Resources Act (OWRA) to manage water use and quality in the province. Although the OWRA gave the relevant minister a broad mandate over surface waters and groundwater in the province, the commission's most significant activities were in the area of financing municipal sewage system development and upgrading. In the 1960s and 1970s many provinces began introducing regulations related to water takings, flood control, and management of water systems. Most by this time had natural resource departments responsible for management of public lands, waters, and wildlife, but it was not until the early 1970s that provinces began to establish environmental protection departments.

The Ontario Government Reorganization Act of 1972 created the Ministry of the Environment (MOE) (Winfield, 1994). In that same year the Environmental Protection Act (EPA) was passed and supplemented the OWRA with regard to water pollution management efforts. The EPA prohibited the discharge of contaminants into the natural environment, including water, except where specifically permitted by a certificate of approval (Ontario, MOE, 2000). Implementation remained focused on construction of sewage treatment facilities in partnership with municipalities, point source effluent regulation, prosecution of pollution offences, and the establishment of licensing and monitoring regimes.

Another key area that has involved the provincial governments in water pollution management indirectly has been the environmental assessment process. The Ontario Environmental Assessment Act of 1976 originally applied only to undertakings of the Ontario government and its agencies. This provision was broadened specifically to include undertakings by conservation authorities in 1977 and by municipalities in 1980. Application of the act was extended in 1987 to include private or public waste-management facilities, including landfilling, incineration, processing, and transfer of waste where the facility exceeds a certain size. The act requires these undertakings to undergo an environmental assessment process in addition to municipal assessment requirements.

As well as legislation governing water use and quality, many provinces have water quality objectives and regulatory regimes. In Ontario since 1986, the Municipal Industrial Strategy for Abatement (MISA) program is an initiative under the EPA that establishes regulatory effluent standards based on total loadings that must be approved by the Ministry of the Environment for works that discharge directly into watercourses. The principle goal of MISA is to build on provincial water quality objectives in an attempt to control point source water pollution by establishing total discharge limits (effluent standards) and emphasizing control technologies. The goal is the virtual elimination of persistent toxic substances from effluents that are discharged into Ontario's lakes, rivers, and streams. Originally it was supposed to cover effluent from municipal sewage treatment facilities, but ultimately it placed discharge limits on companies in nine industrial sectors (covering three hundred industries) in the province, rather than on a case-by-case basis. The regulations have been enforceable across the nine sectors since 1998, but the exclusion of municipal sewage treatment facilities is a big gap in Ontario's program.

The Canadian Water Quality Guidelines developed through intergovernmental institutions, discussed below, provide basic scientific information about different water quality parameters, and the provinces use these as reference points in developing their own water quality management guidelines. The provincial objectives are the basis for establishing acceptable limits for water quality and quantity consistent with the protection of the aquatic ecosystem. As a result of the Walkerton Inquiry, Ontario has recently passed the Safe Drinking Water Act and the Nutrient Management Act to proactively try to protect the province's water resources for all users. Other provinces have similar legislation and regulations.

Provincial management of water resources has always been intimately linked to economic development. Provinces are exclusively involved in the creation of hydroelectric power, and most have created state-owned enterprises that have developed this capacity as part of local economic development initiatives or "province-building" (Freeman, 1996). The export of primary resources such as oil and gas, pulp and paper, and agricultural produce is such a large part of most provincial economies that these industries have developed tremendous political and policy influence. These powerful economic actors then oppose constraints that would threaten their access to abundant quantities of water or impose direct costs in terms of environmental improvements.

Some argue that Canada's water has been poorly managed because provincial governments are susceptible to influence and capture by local economic interests. This is an argument that is examined in subsequent chapters. Findings from several of our case studies do little to support it, however. The fisheries are a federal responsibility, and they have been the worst managed in-stream water use in Canada. As well, in recent provincial policy initiatives (water export in all provinces, irrigation regulation in Alberta), the provinces have shown themselves able to withstand economic development interests in the name of resource conservation and stewardship.

Most provinces see themselves as defenders of water, and all have developed new policies and institutions to deal with conflicts over water and ensure that there is "sustainable development" associated with this resource. However, many provinces have been criticized for using rhetoric to overstate their achievements and for not balancing multiple uses despite policy statements to the contrary. For example, the government of British Columbia notes in its Freshwater Strategy:

There has been great progress in recent years with legislation and regulation to clean up many of the major industrial sources of pollution and those efforts are continuing. The focus now is turning towards addressing the less tangible challenges that affect our water resources:

reducing non-point source pollution; efficient and effective water management; harmonization of efforts across the different levels of government; groundwater management and conservation. Above all, we must create an enhanced awareness and understanding of the importance of water and the impact we, as individuals and society, have upon it.

Institutional arrangements vary from province to province, but most have identified similar water policy challenges and approaches. Many have increasingly delegated authority to local governments and agencies to manage water and waste-water systems, groundwater management, and conservation programs. Many have also identified institutional arrangements for intergovernmental capacity-building as central to their new approaches to water resource management and conflict resolution.

INTERGOVERNMENTAL INSTITUTIONS

Despite federal powers with respect to the management of fisheries and navigation and provincial powers related to natural resource management, in reality there exist many intergovernmental arrangements and agreements to manage water resources in Canada. The federal government delegates some power to the provinces, such as over inland fisheries and enforcement of the Fisheries Act (a delegation that has been criticized in the case of Quebec for not being implemented at all), and provinces in turn delegate much of their responsibility to municipal governments in terms of sewage treatment, land-use planning, and water supply systems, even though the provinces themselves are taking an increasingly aggressive role as regulators of these activities. The provinces in turn also oversee the water-related activities of numerous local governments and local bodies. As well, there are other forms of intergovernmental activity, such as federal-provincial conferences, regular meetings of responsible ministers, permanent joint consultative committees, and ad hoc joint working groups and boards for water research and planning.

Since the 1960s, intergovernmental relations have been an important institutional feature of policy-making related to water resource management. "While the federal government is able to deal with some problems that have a national scope, the most-effective problem solving is often accomplished through intergovernmental agreement rather than legislative dictates" (Hessing, Howlett, and Summerville, 2005, 64). Over time, a distinctive set of formal institutions has evolved to manage the intergovernmental character of environmental policy-making and implementation in Canada; many related to fisheries, wildlife, energy, and agriculture have agendas that impact on water policy. The Canadian Council of Resource Ministers, established in 1964, evolved into the Canadian Council of Resource and Environment Ministers in 1971 and became the Canadian Council of Ministers of the Environment (CCME) in 1988. This organization brings ministers of the environment from the federal and provincial levels together annually to discuss environmental policy issues and those related to water resource management. Although part II of the CWA contains provisions for the establishment of joint federal-provincial water-quality management programs and agencies, this provision has never been used. Instead, CCME and multilateral and bilateral agreements have filled this institutional role.

Beyond the political interaction of ministers with water resource management responsibilities, extensive bureaucratic relationships exist to manage shared jurisdictional issues (Sproule-Jones, 1981; Johns 2000). CCME is mirrored by a committee of deputy ministers and supported by its own administrative secretariat, which has had an impact on defining the implementation arrangements of federal-provincial policy. Intergovernmental agreements between the federal government and one or more provincial governments have been the predominant tool for implementing agreed-upon policy goals related to water resource management in recent years. Some are outside the auspices of CCME. The intergovernmental agreement on internal trade, for example, has provisions related to water resources. Another example is the Canada-Ontario agreement regarding the Great Lakes, which is part of the binational Great Lakes Water Quality Agreement under the Boundary Waters Treaty with the United States.

Through CCME the federal government, in collaboration with the provinces, established the Canadian Water Quality Guidelines in 1987. These guidelines are, however, left to the provinces to interpret and implement through their own provincial water quality standards. Intergovernmental agreements related to Great Lakes management and other agreements under the Canada-Wide Accord on Environmental Harmonization, signed by all provinces (except Quebec) in 1998, are other examples. To date, sub-agreements on water quality management have not been negotiated or formalized, although the governments continue to cooperate on water quality guidelines and more recently on developing a multi-barrier approach to drinking-water protection (CCME, 2004a). Environment Canada has also been working with the provinces through CCME to develop a national freshwater quality index tool (Roe, Bond, and Mercier, 2005). The CCME Water Quality Index combines both monitoring data and water quality guidelines into a communication tool that gives an indication of the health of a water body for a range of different water uses. More recently, municipal waste-water effluent guidelines have been on the CCME agenda.

There are also a number of interprovincial boards that facilitate freshwater management across Canada. In the West, for example, the Prairie Provinces Water Board has been responsible for ensuring the equitable sharing of interprovincial waters between Alberta, Saskatchewan, and Manitoba under the Master Agreement on Apportionment. The Mackenzie River Basin Board is responsible for overseeing the Mackenzie River Basin Trans-boundary Waters Master Agreement of 1997, which establishes common principles for the cooperative management of the aquatic ecosystem of the basin (the largest in Canada). The basin lies within the jurisdictions of British Columbia, Alberta, Saskatchewan, Yukon, and the Northwest Territories (Canada, Environment Canada, 2005a).

The impact of intergovernmental institutions on water resource governance is the subject of much debate, which is beyond the scope of this chapter. The degree to which intergovernmental institutions influence provincial actions is a contentious issue. Clearly, intergovernmental institutions and agreements offer the potential for policy exchange and learning across the provinces and federal-provincial domains, but there is some debate about whether bilateral federal-provincial agreements are a means by which provinces keep the federal government at a distance. The case studies illustrate that the significance of intergovernmental institutions varies across different regions and with regard to different types of water uses and conflicts.

ABORIGINAL WATER RIGHTS AND GOVERNANCE

Aboriginal water rights and title related to water are somewhat contested in Canada and are intimately connected to land rights and intergovernmental relations. They also vary with the particular legal circumstances of the community in terms of traditional uses, treaty rights, and reserve rights. Despite the constitutional authority of the federal government under section 91.24 for Indian lands and peoples, Aboriginal rights to access and use water resources predate Confederation. The rights to water for traditional uses are determined by priority

– that is, "time immemorial" – and the priority of rights for other uses is decided by the date of the establishment of water rights on reserved lands through treaty or other means. Rights to water use therefore stem from traditional use, treaty, and riparian or common-law rights.

Riparian rights are a source of water rights founded upon occupation or ownership of riparian land by Aboriginal peoples. These are rights by virtue of proximity to water, which implies rights of occupation and use but not ownership of the water itself. This concept includes "natural uses" that coincide with "traditional uses" protected by Aboriginal title. These riparian rights are not equally applicable across Canada. In the Prairie provinces, provincial governments hold that Aboriginal water rights were abrogated by the Northwest Irrigation Act of 1894. In British Columbia, riparian rights have been effectively abolished for most reserves. It has been noted, however, that the applicability of riparian rights may be limited outside the Territories, "where smaller areas were reserved to the Indians and where more intensive development and contemporary uses were contemplated" (Bartlett, 1986, 226). The application of riparian rights is thus contested.

Indigenous peoples claim inherent rights to their traditional territories, which stem from their possession and use of the land, as warranted in their time-honoured legal and social systems. In the eighteenth and nineteenth centuries many bands ceded lands to the Crown by treaty, but this, it is claimed, did not mean ceding sovereignty or rights to enjoy the use of water. Treaties and agreements do imply water rights (e.g., for fishing), and these rights are now protected under section 35 of the Constitution Act, 1982 (Canada, Royal Commission on Aboriginal Peoples, 1996). Section 25 of the Canadian Charter of Rights and Freedoms recognizes existing Aboriginal and treaty rights. Aboriginal water rights are not as limited as Aboriginal title rights to water (Bartlett, 1988). Hence, while the federal government has always enjoyed exclusive jurisdiction with respect to Aboriginal water rights, since 1982 these rights can "only be regulated or extinguished by constitutional amendment or by agreement with the aboriginal people" (Bartlett, 1986, 128).

Aboriginal rights related to the use of waters have been most contested with regard to major hydroelectric and dam projects and to fishing. In 1990 the Supreme Court, in *R v. Sparrow*, outlined a process for determining if fishing rights have been infringed under section 35 of the constitution. This decision determined that federal and provincial water management measures may be limited in relation to Aboriginal rights.

The more recent Haida Nation and Taku River Tlingit cases detail the requirements for consultation and accommodation of First Nations when their rights are potentially at risk. Important case decisions related to fisheries outlined in chapters 10 and 11 illustrate this process.

Contemporary Aboriginal title settlements in Canada reflect the growing role of Native peoples in the administration of water resources and the affirmation of rights with respect to those resources. The Nunavut Final Agreement of 1993, for example, provides for settlement of Aboriginal title to approximately 350 000 square kilometres of land (Chandran, 2003) and proclaims the rights of the Inuit with respect to water resources on that land. Thus, while First Nations have not been as vocal about water resource issues as many other groups, jurisdictional complexity surrounding the resource can only be exacerbated as Ottawa continues to acknowledge the legitimacy of Native title and rights to use.

The other policy challenge related to water resources in Aboriginal communities is the state and management of these resources where rights are recognized. Indian and Northern Affairs Canada (INAC) provides funding for the construction, operation, and maintenance of water and waste-water systems for First Nations communities. Some Native communities operate these systems themselves, and others have agreements with neighbouring municipalities. The vast majority of communities have only basic water and waste-water management systems, and many have well- and septic-based systems. Most of these systems are managed locally and funded by the federal government. There are no laws and regulations governing the provision of drinking water in First Nations communities (Canada, Office of the Auditor General, 2005). INAC and Health Canada oversee drinking-water management in First Nations communities through their policies, funding arrangements, and administrative guidelines.

Through the finalization of Aboriginal land claim agreements and revisions to legislation, the federal government, in partnership with Aboriginal communities, has also established water boards in some communities. For example, dramatic changes have occurred in recent years in the jurisdictional framework for land and water resource use in the Northwest Territories. The Mackenzie Valley Resource Management Act, proclaimed in 1998, provides for an integrated system of land and water management in the Mackenzie Valley and for the establishment of boards for that purpose.

An assessment carried out by INAC in 2001, based on on-site inspection of all water systems in First Nations communities, found a significant risk to the quality and safety of drinking water in three-quarters of the water systems (Canada, Office of the Auditor General, 2005). In response to this assessment and to the water tragedies in Walkerton, Ontario, and Battleford, Saskatchewan, the federal government introduced the First Nations Water Management Strategy in 2003 with a budget of $600 million over five years (Canada, Office of the Auditor General, 2005). Both INAC and the federal Commissioner of the Environment and Sustainable Development have raised serious concerns about the treatment and management of water in First Nations communities (Canada, INAC, 2003; Canada, Office of the Auditor General, 2005). Despite these documented concerns, the scandalous conditions of water quality made public in Kashechewan, Ontario, in 2005 highlight the significant problems many First Nations communities continue to face in managing their water resources.

LOCAL GOVERNMENTS

Local governments and agencies also play a critical role in water resource management through management systems and protection efforts. Provinces have delegated large areas of responsibility over local matters such as water supply, sewage collection, land-use planning, and water quality regulations to a variety of municipal and regional authorities. Local governments and agencies are the primary actors involved in water and sewage treatment, domestic water supply, and general water infrastructure. Provincial governments have a supervisory and appeal function related to these activities through municipal affairs and natural resource ministries and agencies, but local governments have authorities related to local water-use bylaws, watershed management, and general operations of water and waste-water systems. As outlined in chapter 3, they are also key implementation agents of provincial water policies.

Some provinces also have special-purpose bodies designed to manage water resources with local representation. For example, Ontario has conservation authorities with specific legislative mandates to manage water resources on a watershed basis. Each authority consists of representatives of the provincial government and of each municipality within the watershed. Conservation authorities have a broad range of powers, including the ability to purchase, lease, or expropriate land. They may also make regulations restricting and regulating the use of water in or from surface water bodies within their jurisdiction, particularly related to flood plain management. More recently, conservation authorities have been involved in watershed planning, environmental assessment, and community stewardship of environmental resources.

The fact that most water uses and problems in Canada are local in nature and have involved such things as flood plain management, localized water shortages, and less-than-desirable water quality makes the role of local governments increasingly important. This can be seen vividly with an issue such as groundwater (Karvinen and McAllister 1994). The Walkerton tragedy clearly outlined the significance of provincial-local institutions, the role played by municipalities in monitoring and maintaining water systems, and that of local governments in managing multiple uses of water resources.

NON-STATE ACTORS AND PARTNERSHIP ARRANGEMENTS

In addition to the government institutions engaged in water resource management in Canada, there has been a steady increase in the involvement of non-state actors. Since the 1970s the number of special-interest and community groups in partnership arrangements to manage water resources and address water-use conflicts has grown dramatically. Numerous organizations and associations have water resource management and protection agendas. Some are national, such as the Canadian Water Resources Association, and others are organized for specific water bodies and purposes. There are many examples of these types of stakeholder- and community-based arrangements, which typically involve federal, provincial, municipal, and Aboriginal governments. Their engagement in different water policy communities also varies. Some are active in partnerships with government agencies, others are engaged in voluntary implementation arrangements, as discussed in chapter 3, and still others fill a watchdog and accountability role. Numerous examples can be cited of such arrangements in the management of multiple uses in the Great Lakes, for example (Sproule-Jones, 2002).

In practice, this involvement often means partnerships between stakeholder groups that make suggestions and advise governments. Thus we have recently witnessed the development of "watershed planning and advisory councils," "provincial water advisory councils," and "watershed stewards groups." Such bodies have varying responsibilities that range from monitoring the quality of water to developing best practices, fostering stewardship activities, reporting on the state of the watershed, educating users on water resources, and providing guidance, technical advice, and mentoring.

Bodies such as those mentioned above are part of new partnership structures emerging in all provinces. Such partnerships are an attempt to involve citizens and groups at the national, provincial, and local levels in the planning and implementation of improved water and watershed management. In Alberta, for example, well-organized non-state actors are integrated at the provincial and local levels. A provincial water advisory council provides a high-level overall perspective to the provincial government. This council includes stakeholders from industry, business, agriculture, and environmental groups who report on existing and emerging issues such as conservation and economic activities. They also set priorities for research and consult with provincial residents on an ongoing basis about their priorities in the area of water management. Below this body are a number of watershed planning and advisory councils which report directly to the provincial water advisory council. The councils, six of which are currently in operation, are mostly involved in watershed planning, developing best management practices, fostering stewardship, and reporting on the state of the watershed to educate users. In addition, there are more than forty watershed stewardship groups. They are made up of volunteers, supported by local businesses and industries, who have taken the initiative in protecting local creeks, rivers, streams, and lakes. These groups are a very fast-growing segment of the institutional landscape in most provinces.

CONCLUSIONS

Several themes and conclusions arise from this overview and the water resource management literature more generally. Some of the institutional arrangements designed to deal with the water resource conflicts that stem from the multiple uses of water in Canada predate Confederation. Property rights and common law form the legal foundation on which subsequent constitutional and statutory powers have developed. The review in this chapter highlights the fact that multiple sources of power underpin the institutional arrangements in place to manage water resources in Canada.

As noted above, the federal presence in water resource management has historically been based on its navigation, fisheries, and international treaty powers. Currently, several goals underpin the federal government's involvement in the management of water resources. The first is to protect and enhance the quality of Canada's water resources for a variety of different uses. This goal means in practice anticipating and preventing the contamination of all Canadian waters by harmful substances and working to encourage the restoration of those waters that are contaminated. The other major goal of federal water policy is the promotion of the wise and efficient management and use of water. In practice, this means establishing new ground rules and procedures that respect the value of water to all sectors of society and to the environment. As discussed in chapter 4, the federal government has shifted its instrument choices in recent years and is now much more willing to employ economic incentives (and penalties) to prevent degradation and overuse of water resources. That is, the federal government now emphasizes the promotion of the "polluter pays" principle, with the goal of redirecting the inevitable costs of pollution reduction to those responsible. However, it is equally clear that the quantity and quality management goals of the federal government continue to result in conflict with provincial governments and require intergovernmental negotiation.

In Canada the broad relationship between the provinces and the federal government continues to be guided by the Canada Water Act and the Federal Water Policy but also by the Canadian Council of Ministers of the Environment, which is probably the most important institutional coordinating mechanism between the provinces and the federal government. While there is no Canadian equivalent to the broad water resource management legislation and powers of the US Environmental Protection Agency, the argument has been made that the federal government should be moving in that direction. The timidity of the federal government can be attributed to a variety of factors, including constitutional delegation of much authority over natural resources and commerce to the provinces, enduring federal reluctance to alienate more independent-minded provinces such as Quebec and Alberta, and the substantial physical areas of most provinces, which serve to limit direct cross-boundary conflicts (Skogstad and Kopas, 1992). While under national legislation, various federal agencies are involved in water management issues, the major policy decisions have been left to provincial governments (Kennett, 1991). These delegated powers related to quantity and quality uses are tempered by the federal government's authority and bureaucratic capacity, but in the absence of federal leadership, the provinces have developed their own policies, yet water management institutions are not well integrated with other natural resource policies (Rabe, 1999).

This division of powers for the management of water in Canada has created institutional complexity: as a result, it has been very difficult to develop, let alone implement, an institutional structure to plan and manage integrated water use. It has been noted that problems related to water management are characterized by three main factors: "First, the lack of clarity as well as the overlap of jurisdictional responsibility for environmental matters; second, a shared set of federal and provincial norms which include a preference to avoid coercive regulations and an underlying belief that economic development and environmental quality were antithetical and that resource/economic development (a matter within provincial jurisdiction) must take priority; and third, the presence of well-established mechanisms to facilitate intergovernmental consultation" (Skogstad and Kopas, 1992, 44).

Together, these factors contribute to institutional complexity in many watersheds, which in turn can lead to "buck-passing" and inaction. There is a growing consensus in the literature on Canadian regulatory federalism that "buck-passing" is a defining characteristic of the country's intergovernmental approach to environmental policy-making (VanderZwaag and Duncan, 1992; Harrison, 1996; Skogstad, 1996). This phenomenon suggests a pattern in which both federal and provincial governments attempt to take popular, symbolic steps for which it is easy to claim credit, but blame-avoidance generally prevails, with federal officials reluctant to offend provincial independence and provincial authorities unwilling to do anything that might disturb established patterns or relationships.

In turn, despite the Canadian tradition of "executive federalism," which brings elected provincial and federal officials together to explore issues, there appears to be very limited serious engagement in ideas and innovation across provincial boundaries and between the provinces and Ottawa. There are similar institutional arrangements across provinces yet significant variation in how they manage water resource conflicts. This variation is a major theme in Canadian natural resource and environmental policy and an important one to keep in mind when reading the case studies in this book.

Each province has its own water-related legislation and policies, but generally, provincial policies follow similar patterns. Institutional arrangements also vary at the local level and from watershed to watershed. While the provinces are the dominant actors in water resource management and set the guidelines, the implementation is usually left to regional or local bodies. Increasingly, these authorities find themselves engaged with a variety of groups and community actors in partnership arrangements to manage conflicts and multiple uses. An understanding of the intergovernmental character of water resource management and conflicts in Canada is therefore critical in any study of the issues (Canada, PRI, 2006b; Bakker et al., 2007; Conference Board of Canada, 2007).

In summary, water resource management institutions in Canada can be characterized as decentralized. For some analysts, decentralized arrangements equate to poor management of multiple uses and bad policy outcomes. Such arrangements are criticized for focusing too much on local economic development and limiting the federal government's role. Provinces are viewed as willing and sometimes eager to override their own legislation in face of the need for economic development. For other analysts, the very fact that water resource management issues are so variable across Canada and that there are so many different uses requires a more decentralized approach which allows local stakeholders to use partnership and ecosystem methods to manage multiple-use conflicts. There are also those who argue that a decentralized authority structure has direct implications for how societal interests strategize to change the rules. For example, the "double-crack hypothesis" postulates that if interests are unsuccessful at protecting water resources at one level of government, they can try at another level. This technique has been evident, for instance, in dam projects where environmentalists had little success in blocking the projects at the provincial level and then tried to stop them at the federal level and were, in some cases, successful. Thus there are positives and negatives to both centralized and decentralized institutional arrangements.

It will become evident through the case-study chapters that strengths and weaknesses exist in the current institutional and policy framework for different interests and users of water resources in Canada. As the number of water uses and the demands on water resources increase, there is the potential for greater conflict (both domestically and with the United States). As a result, policy-makers need not only to understand the historical logic and current complexities of existing institutional arrangements but to design institutional arrangements for integrated water use in the future.

The institutional complexities outlined in this chapter set the stage for analyzing conflict not only between different users and stakeholders but also between different orders of government. Generally, shifting the policy approach from conflict resolution to conflict prevention and designing institutions that foster this shift are required. Many guiding concepts, such as a watershed-based approach, an ecosystem-based approach, a multiple-scale approach, a cross-medium (land, water, air) approach, and the precautionary principle all are ingredients that underpin a necessary institutional shift. The case studies in this book illustrate that understanding multiple uses and institutional interplay is the key to designing arrangements which will foster vertical (intergovernmental), horizontal (cross-medium, cross-agency), and stakeholder involvement. Despite the apparent institutional rigidity and tensions inherent in the management of water resources in the Canadian federal system, there is a lot of scope for selecting different policy instruments, designing institutional arrangements to achieve a number of different water resource management goals, and rebalancing the various uses of water in Canada, as the following two chapters outline.

3

Instruments and Implementation Options for Water Resource Management

KAREN THOMAS

As outlined in chapter 2, institutional arrangements for the management of water resources consist of both formal and informal rules. Constitutional provisions authorize the federal and provincial governments to pass legislation (statutory laws) in various water-related areas, and as chapter 4 demonstrates, these statutory laws can modify and override existing water property rights (common laws). Statutes are broad statements of policies, and parliaments and legislatures in Canada usually leave it to public administrators to develop policy instruments and implementation arrangements through consultations with water users, user groups, and the general public, albeit within the guidelines set out in legislation or in policy directives from ministers and cabinets. Statutory laws are then implemented and put into action by government bureaucracies and agencies using a wide variety of policy instruments and implementation tools.

In this chapter, the instruments and implementation arrangements used to govern water resources and conflicts are discussed. The number and diversity of instruments are many and complex. An inventory of different types of water policy and management instruments is provided. Examples of different instruments used in various jurisdictions across the country are included throughout the chapter. In many instances, these result from domestic instrument choice and design decisions, but because some waterways and their uses are shared with other countries, especially the United States, joint international action may be necessary. In addition, a wide range of informal governance and management arrangements related to water policy exist in Canada. As this chapter and the case studies in this book illustrate, a great deal of ingenuity, technical knowledge, and experience is involved in developing the instruments and institutional arrangements for implementation and are central to understanding water policy in Canada.

INTRODUCTION

In any given policy area, government decision-makers have a "toolbox" of policy instruments from which to choose in order to best meet designated policy goals. Policy instruments can generally be defined as "the actual means or devices which governments have at their disposal for implementing policies" (Howlett and Ramesh, 1995, 80). They have been studied to better understand the linkages between policy formulation and implementation, the decision-making process, and how the selection of instruments affect the success or failure of policy goals (Elidias, Hill, and Howlett, 2005).

The range of instruments available for water policies can be categorized along a continuum, as illustrated in table 3.1. The most common continuum moves from binding/formal, or most coercive, mechanisms (regulatory instruments) at one end to non-binding/informal, or least coercive, mechanisms (e.g., information tools) at the other. Among the many typologies of policy instruments that have been proposed, this is an extension of the most frequently used threefold taxonomy: "carrots, sticks, and sermons" (Bemelmans-Videc, Rist, and Vedung, 1998; Conference Board of Canada, 2000; Howlett and Ramesh, 1995).* Sometimes information sharing and education are not considered a policy instrument in their own right but, rather, a necessary or contributing factor in the functioning of the other three categories of instruments.

For government, the choice of policy instrument is part of a complex process involving a combination of political, social, institutional, and economic factors (Howlett and Ramesh, 1993; Rist, 1998; Bressers and O'Toole, 1998). At the most basic level, the choice of policy instrument is influenced by the nature of the problem itself. For example, some issues are simply more technical in nature or pose a higher risk to public health and the environment. In such cases, decision-makers may choose to rely on a regulatory "stick" approach. Some of the factors that may play a role in matching policy instrument choice to policy are illustrated

---

* For examples of other classifications, see Linder and Peters, 1989; Doern and Phidd, 1992.

Table 3.1
Continuum of policy instruments

Coercive Binding/ formal	← ────────────────────────────────────→	Less coercive Non-binding/ informal
Instrument type	*Policy tools*	*Example*
(1) Regulatory	Regulations	Ontario Water Resources Act
	Permits/licences and orders	PEI Groundwater Extraction Exploration Permit
	Guidelines	Canadian Water Quality Guidelines
	Municipal bylaws	City of Toronto Sewer Use Bylaw
(2) Financial/ market-based	Cost-internalizing & revenue- generating tools	
	– buyback and retrofitting incentives	– City of Barrie Water Conservation Program
	– user fees	– City of Nanaimo water metering structure
	Tax-incentive tools	Ecological Gifts Program
	Banking or insurance Programs/requirements	Credit support incentives
	Performance bonds/financial assurance	Ontario financial assurance
	Tradable permits	Ontario Total Phosphorus Management
	Transfer payments	
	– grants/subsidies for farmers and landowners	– National Water Supply Expansion Program
	– grants/subsidies for businesses	– Region of Waterloo's Business Water Quality Program
(3) Voluntary/ Non-Regulatory	Recognition/awards programs	Pollution Prevention Awards Program
	Codes of practice	Responsible Care Program
	Compliance agreements Environmental performance agreements/MOUS	ArcelorMittal-Environment Canada MOU
(4) Information	Public inventories	National Pollutant Release Inventory
	Partnerships for information-gathering	Ontario Lake Partner Program
	Fact sheets/best management practices	British Columbia Well Protection Toolkit

in table 3.2 (Conference Board of Canada, 2000; United States, Office of Technology Assessment, 1995; New Zealand, Ministry of Agriculture and Forestry, 2003; Canada, National Round Table on the Environment and the Economy, 2002).

It is now generally agreed that a mix of policy instruments, incorporating regulatory standards along with economic and voluntary initiatives, should be employed to meet current environmental and economic demands. Furthermore, the "optimal" policy mix of tools will be specific to individual policy processes or issues (OECD, 2001; Conference Board of Canada, 2000). By the 1990s, the traditional command-and-control style of management employing prescriptive standards was viewed as not always most appropriate, or adequate, to deal with existing or emerging problems. Financial/incentive-based mechanisms and voluntary/non-regulatory initiatives are increasingly being used to complement or supplement regulatory standards. The Organisation for Economic Co-operation and Development stated in 2002 that "it is often difficult to design a single policy instrument that will successfully provide the right incentives for a total reduction in resource use or in pollution and waste generation. Instead, it will generally be necessary to employ a mix of policy instruments" (OECD, 2002, 24). Thus it can also be argued that the lines between these categories are becoming increasingly blurred and there is a need to move beyond instrument choice in analyzing environmental policy more broadly (Webb, 2005) and water policy more specifically.

The remainder of this chapter will examine four broad types of policy instruments used to implement water policies – regulatory, financial/market-based, voluntary, and information instruments – as well as the range of mechanisms within each category. Examples of specific programs or policy tools utilized in water policy management in Canada will be provided where possible. The case studies in Part Two highlight various instrument choices of different regulators and management bodies.

REGULATORY INSTRUMENTS

Canada has a history of reliance on regulatory tools that use the threat of penalties to compel behaviour and address water-use conflicts. Regulatory instruments are in many cases the traditional instrument of choice in water resource management, their defining feature being their authoritative or coercive nature. Traditionally, these tools were developed by governments under the authorities and statutes outlined in the

Table 3.2
Criteria for evaluating policy instrument choice

Factors	Description of criterion
Environmental	Level of risk to society or the natural environment.
	Are the pollution issues local or global in nature?
	Likelihood of meeting the targets (effectiveness).
	Is data available for analysis? What is the monitoring capability?
Technical	Is it likely the approach will promote technological innovation and diffusion?
	Does the approach encourage pollution prevention or eco-efficiency?
	Level of adaptability or ease of modifications.
Economic	Potential for cost-effectiveness or savings (to the emitters, the public, and the government).
	Differences in the cost of abatement between emitters/resource users (economic equity).
	Cost-benefit analysis.
Social	Level of public/stakeholder pressure.
	Does the approach promote effective participation?
	Acceptability of the approach to stakeholders.
	Level of vertical equity (distribution of outcomes does not negatively impact the poor more than the rich).
	Level of political will to resolve the issue.
Administrative/ political	Administrative and enforcement capabilities of government authorities.
	Political acceptability (harmonization with policy goals and other instruments) and legal feasibility.
	Feasibility of implementation and enforcement.
	Level of visibility and transparency of issue.
	Are there jurisdictional issues?

previous chapter. They typically derive from enabling legislation at the federal or provincial level whereby the general authority is included in the statute and the discretion of developing detailed regulations is delegated to the bureaucracy. This approach is connected to Canada's regulatory style, which Howlett has called "consultative regulation" – a preference for regulation supplemented by other types of instruments whereby the substance is developed through consultative mechanisms, traditionally with industry but increasingly with other stakeholders (Howlett, 1991). More recently, this style has been influenced by international standards organizations and trading partners, and it takes the form of industry self-regulation (Gunningham, 2005).

Also known as the "command-and-control" approach, regulatory instruments have been criticized as suffering from the systemic limitation of being lengthy, expensive, and not encouraging of technological innovation, as they are often prescriptive* in nature (Whylynko, 1999; Pollution Probe, 2003). The closed-door nature of this approach has also been criticized as the environmental management regime becomes increasingly more open to the public. Moreover, many regulatory instruments tend to be implemented after the fact, after undesirable behaviour is detected. In the 1990s the criticism was that regulatory instruments were expensive, too technical, and required a large bureaucracy to formulate standards, issue permits, and monitor compliance. In an age of fiscal constraints and deregulation, government actors looked increasingly to "alternative" policy tools to supplement established standards, sometimes referred to as the "next generation" of policy instruments or "smart regulation."

The following discussion will provide a brief overview of the key components of the regulatory approach. Specific examples of regulatory mechanisms will be provided to illustrate the application to water quality/quantity management across the country.

Regulations

The highest class of regulatory tools comprises statutes. As outlined in chapter 2, these are established under constitutional authority at both the federal and provincial level (the Canada Water Act and the Ontario Water Resources Act). Statutes are typically general in nature in terms of requirements and have broad policy perspectives. They generally outline which the lead agency will be in developing and implementing regulations. Regulations are made pursuant to authority set out in a statute and provide more specific operational details. Compliance with

---

* Prescriptive regulatory tools typically define the technology or activities that must be used to achieve compliance. Performance standards, on the other hand, leave companies free to adopt whatever means they choose in order to comply with the set requirements or targets.

regulations is mandatory, and most specify penalties and fines for non-compliance. Proposed federal regulations are first published in the *Canada Gazette* for public comment. At the provincial level, there is no universal legal requirement for public consultation. However, some provinces have instituted frameworks that allow the public or interested stakeholders to review and provide comments on new regulations before they are finalized and become mandatory. For example, in Ontario, the *Environmental Bill of Rights* (2005) establishes a formal framework for notifying the public about proposed legislation, policies, and regulations that could have a significant effect on water and the environment. During a specified period, the public is able to submit comments on any proposal, and the government must consider these comments and communicate how those comments affected the final decision. All the case studies in this book highlight key statutes, regulations, and institutional arrangements designed to implement water policies.

In the example of the province of Ontario, the following are some of the regulations established under the Ontario Water Resources Act that set out specific standards related to water quality/quantity.* The Water Takings and Transfers Regulation provides for the conservation, protection, and management of Ontario's waters. The Water Wells Regulation establishes standards for the building and licensing of private water wells in the province. The Licensing of Sewage Works Operators Regulation establishes licensing and operating standards for sewage works. In October 2006 the Ontario government passed the Clean Water Act, representing a new approach to protecting drinking water quality and quantity. A central principle of the new act is the development of source protection plans involving participation by local communities. Since the act came into force, regulations have been passed dealing with implementation activities under the legislation (source protection committees and time limits).

Permits/Licences and Orders

Permits, certificates of approval, or licences are issued to specific parties (industrial facilities, fishers, agriculturalists) by federal and (mainly) provincial agencies, as required under regulations. Permits include information on the type of activities permitted in a water body, such as the level

---

* A full list of Ontario statutes and regulations is available at www.e-laws. gov.on.ca.

of allowable catch, emissions, withdrawals, emergencies, industrial operations, and agricultural, irrigation, and shipping uses. They often include monitoring and reporting requirements. Permits are detailed and industry-, site-, or facility-specific, and compliance with the requirements of the permit is mandatory. Control orders may be issued to permit-holders, usually in response to failure by a regulated party to comply with an act or regulation. Many different regulations related to water quality and quantity uses exist in Canada. In addition to those covered in the case studies in this book, there are many examples of regulations for surface water uses by industry and groundwater uses by residents and agriculture.

In New Brunswick the Water Quality Regulation under the Clean Environment Act directs a process whereby applications for approval of industrial operations are submitted to the government. The approvals cover conditions that control construction and operating activities, including the quality and quantity of contaminants that may be discharged from a facility into water. The Fees for Industrial Approvals Regulation under the Clean Water Act establishes annual fee rates for approval-holders. Fees range from $100 to $42 000 per annum for each approval.*

Groundwater takings are regulated to some extent in most provinces. Although permits for domestic purposes (wells) are generally not needed, requirements vary from province to province, as noted in chapter 2. In Prince Edward Island, exemptions generally apply unless the well is a high-performance one and extracts over 50 imperial gallons per minute. In these cases, the well requires a permit obtained through a two-stage process. First, a Groundwater Extraction Exploration Permit is issued, allowing for the construction of a well, which is hydrologically evaluated. If the results are favourable, a final Water Extraction Permit is issued. The Water Takings and Transfers Regulation under the Ontario Water Resources Act exempts most domestic wells if they use less than 50 000 litres per day, they were installed before 1961, and water is used for ordinary household purposes, direct watering of livestock or poultry, and fire-fighting, but takings beyond those levels require a permit. In general, permits are valid for one to twenty-five years. Much variance exists

---

* Information on the province of New Brunswick's guidelines related to water is available from the Department of the Environment and Local Government at www.gnb.ca/0009/index-e.asp.

among the rates across the country, and the units of measurement are far from standardized; some argue these differences stem from a lack of knowledge about groundwater resources in Canada (Nowlan, 2005).

Guidelines

For many in the regulated community, understanding the specifics of regulations can be difficult. Often, governments will produce guidelines that provide more detail, in laypersons' terms, about the requirements and standards set out in regulations. Guidelines are usually voluntary in nature, although some regulations will reference specific guidelines as direction for those captured under the regulatory requirements. They act like conventions within Parliament, as rules that may be revised after due consideration.

Chapter 2 mentioned the Canadian Water Quality Guidelines drawn up by the Canadian Council of Ministers of the Environment (CCME) as national guidelines that provinces use in developing their own regulations. At the national level, CCME has also developed national ambient water quality guidelines that specify parameters for a list of chemicals in relation to freshwater aquatic life, marine water, sediment, animal tissue residue, and agricultural uses (CCME, 2003). These guidelines are not mandatory, and the degree of uptake may differ from province to province. Currently, CCME is working on municipal effluent guidelines.

Another example at the provincial level, in addition to the permitting regulations outlined above, is the New Brunswick Well Construction and Water Well Testing Guideline, which describes necessary construction and water quality testing standards for private water wells regulated under the Clean Water Act and Water Well Regulation. Guidelines are also used to specify technical requirements of regulatory standards. They have been developed under the province of New Brunswick's Clean Water Act, Watercourse Alteration Regulation, to promote environmentally acceptable design and construction methods for alterations that are permitted under the regulation.

Municipal Bylaws

As outlined in chapter 2, municipalities play an important role in water resource management through their responsibilities for drinking-water systems, land-use planning, and regulation of waste, stormwater, and sanitary sewer discharge limits, wells, and subsurface water supplies, as well as through their provision of water directly to local citizens and businesses. Municipalities can adopt bylaws if statutory authority is provided in a provincial authorizing statute (Pollution Probe, 2003). For example, the Ontario Municipal Act authorizes municipalities in the province to establish bylaws to protect water at the local level. In the city of Toronto, the Sewer Use By-law is intended to protect the sewers, the sewage treatment plant and treatment processes, and the public by prohibiting the discharge of undesirable, toxic, or explosive substances into the sewer systems (Toronto, 2000). Conservation authorities also have designated jurisdiction related to flood control and management.

In summary, regulatory instruments continue to provide the foundation of Canada's water management regime, and as the case studies illustrate, they remain central to managing various water-use conflicts. They have been developed to address water quantity conflicts and water quality issues. However, as outlined above, they have been expensive to develop, implement, and monitor and have often been criticized as not encouraging innovative environmental practices and outcomes. The push for deregulation and alternative instruments began in the 1990s, as governments focused on debts and deficits. Because of budgetary constraints in many water-related bureaucracies and associated reforms under "new public management" and "partnerships," the federal and provincial governments have increasingly utilized other policy tools to augment or replace regulatory instruments and continue their regulatory reform agendas in a new phase of "smart regulation." There is also an emerging consensus that many of the current complex, "third-generation" environmental problems require the deployment of multiple policy instruments, and thus other types of policy tools are increasingly being used as supplementary mechanisms to regulation. The next three sections will describe the role of financial, voluntary, and information instruments in managing Canada's waters.

FINANCIAL/MARKET-BASED INSTRUMENTS

Financial or market-based instruments have been used to address a variety of water conflicts and change behaviour, particularly that of industrial users. Generally, the common purpose of financial instruments is to provide incentives for producers and consumers to alter their decisions and behaviour, in order to internalize environmental costs or by rewarding more sustainable practices. The literature suggests that a number of advantages can be gained through the use of economic instruments

(Lotspeich, 1996; Canada, Environment Canada, 1994b; Canada, National Round Table on the Environment and the Economy, 2002). It is argued that the market is an important initiator of technological change, and if individuals and businesses are given the discretion to develop their own environmental management programs, there will be an incentive for them to produce the most cost-effective method of doing so. Some of the examples below will provide some evidence that technology which improves environmental protection can be more efficient and cost-effective in the long term (i.e., eco-efficient). A market approach also allows for greater flexibility in designing responses to environmental goals such as, for example, process changes and product and materials modification. Additionally, financial instruments can create conditions whereby individuals and businesses can actually be rewarded for environmentally sound practices or activities that exceed regulatory standards. Finally, economic tools tend to be fast-acting. Simply put, actions oriented toward direct impacts on profit margins tend to initiate rapid responses. The major disadvantages identified with this policy tool include administrative complexity, especially if they involve various jurisdictions; difficulty in monitoring; danger of the domination of companies; non-compliance; and reliance on regulatory oversight.

In its 2000 *Economic Survey of Canada*, the OECD stated that "there is a need to increase the use of economic instruments (for instance, charges on toxic emissions and waste, and disposal fees for products containing toxic substances) to reinforce the polluter pays principle" (OECD, 2000, 7). A similar view was promoted by former minister of the environment David Anderson (2000), who stated that "perhaps the most important element [of the new environmental architecture] is an expanded and more sophisticated use of market-based and incentive mechanisms to promote sustainable development." The use of incentives to encourage industry to become more eco-efficient was also identified as a primary theme in Environment Canada's 2001–03 Sustainable Development Strategy. They have been discussed more recently in relation to agricultural uses of water.

The National Round Table on the Environment and the Economy (NRTEE) has been studying the potential use of ecological fiscal reform (EFR) as a policy instrument in Canada. EFR is defined as "a deliberate strategy to use taxation, expenditure, and other economic instruments in a package or suite of measures to provide a comprehensive set of reinforcing incentives for taking environmental action" (Canada, NRTEE, 2002, 6). It differs from the more traditional approach to economic instruments in that it is a strategy (employing several complementary tools) and works over a long time frame. The NRTEE argues that ecological fiscal reform is meant to be employed within a policy package that includes regulatory, informational, economic, and voluntary tools, with the optimal policy mix determined by the characteristics of the issue being addressed.

Although many tools are employed under the typology of financial or market instruments, the following six categories were found to be most prevalent in relation to water conservation and water quality in Canada. Each will be briefly described and examples provided where possible.

Cost-Internalizing and Revenue-Generating Tools

Buyback and Retrofitting Incentives Ultimately, the tools of buyback or retrofitting incentives are designed to change water-use behaviour. They aim to replace inefficient or obsolete appliances, fixtures, and technologies with more water-efficient products and processes or to promote retrofitting of water-consuming fixtures and equipment that might lead to pollution (e.g., leaking toilets can overload on-site systems not designed for large water flows). Some of these tools are designed with water quantity and conservation goals, and others with water quality goals.

Under the province of Ontario's Green Industry Strategy, the city of Barrie initiated a Water Conservation Program. The program implemented a cost-incentive strategy based on rebates for homeowners to replace showerheads and toilets using high volumes of water. Between 1995 and 1998 the program recruited nine thousand households, resulting in a reduction in water demand of 62 litres per person per day (Ontario, Ministry of the Environment, 1998). In British Columbia the town of Qualicum Beach was the first community on Vancouver Island to offer free water-saving devices for toilets and showers to all residents and businesses. Implemented in 1993, the Voluntary In-home Low-Flow Fixture and Retrofit Program realized an average estimated water savings of 40 gallons per household per day. Of this, approximately 10 gallons was hot water, thereby saving homeowners with electric hot-water tanks over $63 per year in hydro costs (British Columbia, Ministry of Water, Land, and Air Protection, 1996b). Such additional cost savings offer an extra incentive for participation in these programs.

User Fees Water pricing by volume can be an effective means of reducing water use, although such policies can be contentious to implement by governments because of a fear they may impose hardships on lower-income people. Nevertheless, metering is increasingly used in munici-palities in Canada as a way to encourage reductions in use and move toward full costing. A report by Environment Canada estimated that in 1999, metered households used about 288 litres per capita per day of water, compared to 433 litres per capita per day for households that paid a flat rate (Canada, Environment Canada, 2001c, xii).

The essential principle behind this policy tool is that those who use more water pay more, and those who use less pay less. Thus user aware-ness increases and provides an incentive to decrease water consumption. Many cities across the country use an "inclining block-rate fee structure" in which water rates increase based on level of consumption. For exam-ple, the city of Nanaimo uses the following metering structure (British Columbia, Ministry of Water, Land, and Air Protection, 2002):

Basic charge:		$0.32 per day
Consumption charge:	0 – 145 gallons per day	$0.00067 per gallon per day
	146 – 220 gallons per day	$0.00311 per gallon per day
	221 – 329 gallons per day	$0.00328 per gallon per day
	330 – 548 gallons per day	$0.00341 per gallon per day
	1 097+ gallons per day	$0.00364 per gallon per day

Although, historically, many users of water such as water bottlers were charged for permits but not the actual water they withdrew, some provinces are beginning to charge for various industrial and commercial water uses. For example, starting in 2009, users such as beverage or ready-mix concrete manufacturers in Ontario will be required to pay a charge of $3.71 per 1 million litres of water (Ontario, Ministry of the Environment, 2007). Other commercial and industrial water-takers will be phased in. The charge does not apply to agricultural operations, in-stitutions such as schools and care facilities, environmental uses such as wetlands projects, private wells, or the water municipalities supply for residential use. This example illustrates that many users of water do not pay for the water they use and that user fees raise difficult questions about fair use, full costing of water, and access issues.

Tax-Incentive Tools

This form of economic instrument encourages water conservation and protection through reduced, deferred, or forgiven property taxes or through the provision of tax credits that can be applied elsewhere. Since 1995, landowners across Canada have been able to receive federal and provincial tax assistance for protecting ecologically sensitive areas. Under Canada's Ecological Gifts Program, eco-gifts are defined as gifts of the full title to a property or the value of a conservation easement, covenant, or servitude attached to that title, as defined under provincial or territorial legislation (Canada, Environment Canada, 1995). Conservation easements, covenants, and servitudes are legal agreements in which a landowner retains ownership of his/her property but conveys certain specifically identified rights to a land conservation organization or a public body. Eco-gifts may include lands that are designated or protected for environmental conservation; are locally important areas; are close to environmentally significant properties; buffer environmentally sensitive areas such as water bodies, streams, or wetlands; or support the conservation of biodiversity in Canada. Individuals receive a tax credit (corporations receive a deduction) for the value of the land donated. Improved income tax rules governing these eco-gifts were implemented in 2001–02 (Canada, Environment Canada, 2003b). Since the program's inception, 650 donations across Canada were completed by 2008, valued at over $379 million, securing and conserving more than 112 000 hectares of sensitive lands (Canada, Environment Canada, 2008a).

Provincial programs and policies are evident as well. The Fish Protection Act in British Columbia includes a provision for property tax deductions for such things as a conservation easement covering an important fish-bearing stream that might be registered against the title of a property, thus preventing future development in and around the stream (British Columbia, Ministry of Water, Land, and Air Protection, 1999a). The province of Manitoba implemented a three-year pilot study covering two rural municipalities. The Municipal Property Tax Credit provided a $1 per acre municipal tax credit to landowners who adopted specified environmentally sensitive land-use practices, such as buffer zones near waterways. The program identified the following water-related benefits: improvements for water quality for drinking and for recreation; reduced flooding, the increase and maintenance of wetlands, preservation of riparian ecosystems, lower expenditures on environmental infrastructure (e.g., lower water treatment costs), and reduced flood control costs (Canada, National Round Table on the Environment and the Economy 2002). Chapter 8 outlines how non-profit land trusts, conservation authorities, and other organizations can be the recipients of land donations that protect waters from runoff and allow for donors to receive income and property tax benefits.

Banking or Insurance Programs/ Requirements

Credit-support incentives provide businesses or individuals with loan assistance (e.g., reduced interest rates, payment deferrals) in exchange for a commitment to perform a specific pollution or conservation management activity. For example, farmers might receive lower financing charges from an agricultural banking institution in return for adopting predefined best management practices, such as fencing off a stream from cattle. Such programs provide a win-win arrangement as farmers are rewarded with mortgage cost savings, banks reduce the financial risk of inheriting an environmental liability, and the quality of receiving waters are improved (British Columbia, Ministry of Water, Land, and Air Protection, 1999a).

Performance Bonds/Financial Assurance

Performance bonds are based on the idea that polluters, not the taxpayers, should bear the responsibility for the costs associated with environmental cleanup or waste disposal. Such tools provide a source of funds in the event that a development or business leads to environmental contamination and the owner or developer is unable (or unwilling) to correct the problem (British Columbia, Ministry of Water, Land, and Air Protection, 1999a). For example, a poorly designed mine might result in acidic runoff or seepage, causing damage to groundwater or a nearby aquatic habitat. Performance bonds are a financial guarantee obtained by the government as a condition of allowing the mine to be opened in the first place; a pool of funds is available to remediate any pollution problems. The possibility of having to forfeit the performance bond is a motivation for "good behaviour," provided that the amount of the bond is set at an appropriate level.

In Ontario, "financial assurance" is imposed by the Ministry of the Environment to ensure that recipients of approvals and orders comply with the stated terms and conditions of their approval and that funds are available for future cleanup, rehabilitation, and decommissioning of sites (Ontario, Ministry of the Enviroment, 1994). Financial assurance may be a mandatory condition of an order or approval or a discretionary requirement, depending on the type of activity being regulated. Forms of acceptable financial assurance include cash, irrevocable letters of credit, surety bonds, and transferable government bonds.

Tradable Permits

Tradable permits have been used in connection with water quantity and quality in many jurisdictions around the world. Water rights transfers have been used in some provinces, such as British Columbia, and as outlined in chapter 6, they are an important part of water conflict and policy in Alberta. Water quality trading (WQT) is a version of pollution trading designed to address issues of water quality, but it has not been used very much in Canada. Like all pollution trading programs, WQT in theory allows firms to meet environmental objectives at lower cost and with more flexibility than other types of regulations. It builds on the fact that polluting sources, generally located in the same watershed or sub-watershed (Canada, PRI, 2006a) and typically representing point sources of water pollution, bear different costs to control their pollution discharges. Trading programs allow businesses facing higher pollution control costs to meet regulatory obligations by purchasing environmentally equivalent (or superior) pollution reductions from another source at lower cost. There are various schemes, but in general the effluent standards remain the same. In theory, efficiency is increased and costs are decreased.

While market-trading programs related to water have been evident in the United States since 1974 (Goodstein, 2001), no such national water quality trading programs existed in Canada at the time of writing. The province of Ontario currently has a program involving water quality trading for phosphorus credits (Conservation Ontario, 2003). Total phosphorus management (TPM) allows municipal and industrial wastewater or stormwater facilities to offset phosphorus from their discharges by investing in non-point or point source control projects. There have also been some policy discussions about the feasibility of using this tool to address agricultural non-point source water pollution (Canada, PRI, 2006a), but examples of using water quality trading tools in Canada are limited. An example from the United States illustrates how this type of instrument works.

In January 2003 the United States Environmental Protection Agency released its Water Quality Trading Policy for a watershed-based trading program across the country (United States, EPA, 2003). In order for a water quality trade to take place, a pollution reduction "credit" must first be created. Sources must reduce pollution loads beyond the level regulated by the most stringent water quality requirements in order to create such a credit. For example, a farmer or landowner could create credits by changing cropping practices and planting shrubs and trees next to waterways. A municipal waste-water treatment plant located within the same watershed could then purchase these credits to meet water quality limits in its permit. The policy includes trading of nutrients (e.g., total phosphorus, total nitrogen) and sediment load reductions. However, it does not currently support trading of toxic pollutants, and it includes provisions to protect against the creation of "hot spots."*

Transfer Payments

This category of economic tools is one of the most widely used in water management in Canada and includes initiatives such as transfer payments (e.g., grants and subsidies) designed for specific environmental actions. There are a wide variety of such programs in Canada, administered by the federal, provincial, and local authorities. Transfer payments designed to improve water quality are available to individuals, farmers, businesses, community organizations, and local governments. Monies are provided as an incentive to change behaviour, leading to increased environmental benefits and more efficient water uses.

Grants/Subsidies for Farmers and Landowners Grants and subsidy programs designed for agri-environmental initiatives are prevalent across Canada. The federal government instituted the National Water Supply Expansion Program, which aims to develop and/or enhance long-term agricultural water supplies (Canada, Environment Canada, 2001c). Projects such as off-stream storage, pasture pipelines, water supply planning, and groundwater studies are eligible for funding under the program. Funding options differ, depending on the type of project, usually with one-third of project costs being covered up to a maximum of $5000 per project (or maximum $15 000 per applicant).

The federal government, through Agriculture and Agri-Food Canada, also provides some funding for provincial governments to deliver environmental farm plan (EFP) programs. EFPs are meant to help identify

---

* For example, under watershed permits in Connecticut and North Carolina, total nitrogen may be traded among waste-water treatment plants to reduce loadings to receiving waters. However, every facility retains a numeric limit on the amount of ammonia (the 'hot spot' pollutant) that may be discharged so that local water quality is protected.

the environmental risks, liabilities, strengths, and assets affecting a farmer's operations. The most comprehensive plans are found in Ontario and Quebec, but they are administered through quite different approaches (Canada, National Round Table on the Environment and the Economy, 2002). As detailed in chapter 8, these can be used to protect water quality. The province of Ontario offers a cash transfer of $1500 to farmers who voluntarily develop and implement farm plans. Many of the measures in these plans protect water quality. In Quebec, farmers are charged an annual fee of $500 to join a "farm club." However, the information and technical assistance offered through these clubs often has a market value far in excess of that charge. Participation in environmental farm plans can lead to enhanced profitability through on-farm environmental improvements or improved market access and eco-labelling through adoption of environmentally safe practices. Development of vs also provide participants with recognition of due diligence.

In Ontario many conservation authorities and municipalities have developed programs to provide technical and financial assistance to help landowners and interested groups improve water quality and quantity management.* Such programs provide benefits to all partners. The public and the region gain improved reliability of water quality. Participating landowners receive assistance to implement measures that, in many instances, provide economic and environmental benefits, such as improved water quality and water levels on lands, improved farm sustainability, and productivity from new equipment. The Nottawasaga Valley Healthy Waters Program is one example of such initiatives. Eligible projects include such activities as grass filter strips, streamside tree planting, livestock access restriction, manure storage, and alternative water sources. Maximum grant rates are 75 per cent of project costs, with a maximum value of between $2000 and $7500, depending on the type of project (Nottawasaga Valley Conservation Authority, 1999).

Grants/Subsidies for Businesses Grants and subsidies for businesses are used in many different ways to address water-use conflicts and both water quantity and quality issues. For example, as highlighted in chapters 5 and 6, the federal government has employed these instruments with regard to fisheries. Similar technical and financial assistance programs

---

* Some examples include the Toronto Conservation Authority Rural Clean Water Program, the Niagara Peninsula Conservation Authority Water Quality Improvement Program, and the Region of Waterloo Rural Water Quality Program.

are available to businesses to help in preventing spills and releases of pollutants into groundwater, surface water, and sewers and to reduce usage of water in manufacturing and processing practices. In the province of Ontario, the Region of Waterloo's Business Water Quality Program* provides grants to businesses to share the cost of best management practices that prevent spills or water pollution. The program lists the following achievements from 2001 to 2003, attained by the twenty-nine participating local companies: water reduction of 110 000 cubic metres of water per year; waste-water reductions in biochemical oxygen demand (BOD), suspended solids, and phenols; reduction of 200 tonnes per year of paint sludge; and elimination of 5000 litres per year of CEPA toxic substances (Waterloo, 2003). The program was renewed in 2003 for an additional five years and $1.5 million in funding.

VOLUNTARY/NON-REGULATORY INSTRUMENTS

The multiple-use water quantity and quality issues we now face are complex in nature, requiring a mix of regulatory and non-regulatory instruments. Both federal and provincial governments have had to face the reality of reduced water resource budgets and personnel in the past decade. The result has been a change in the general policy style surrounding environmental issues and water resource management issues more specifically to one which utilizes the benefits of public-private partnerships and a more cooperative, multi-stakeholder approach.

Voluntary instruments have increased in popularity since the mid-1980s, both within Canada and worldwide. A 1999 review of the use of voluntary mechanisms by the Organisation for Economic Co-operation and Development (1999) found that forty-two voluntary mechanisms were being used in the United States and ninety-five in Canada. Similarly, a 1996 report by the European Environment Agency found that over three hundred voluntary mechanisms were recognized by the countries of the European Union (European Environment Agency, 1997).

Generally, voluntary instruments are seen as the proverbial "carrot," offering such incentives for business interests as:

• recognition through awards and publicity;
• legislative exemptions from regulatory requirements for participating firms;

---

* Another example of subsidies provided to businesses can be found under the Toronto Region Sustainability Program.

- reduced transaction costs as a result of less duplicative regulatory and reporting requirements;
- improved "green image," appealing to environmentally conscious consumers, investors, and suppliers;
- improved relations with government agencies and better linkage to government programs (e.g., technical assistance); and
- reduced costs and increased potential for technological innovation (Gallon, 1997; Gibson, 1999).

However, the voluntary approach has also been highly criticized for having lower visibility and credibility, problems with free riders, uncertain public accountability, and less likelihood of developing rigorous standards and environmental improvements. Thus a considerable literature has developed about the essential design criteria for a successful voluntary program. In 1999 the Commissioner of the Environment and Sustainable Development of Canada evaluated the use of voluntary mechanisms in the federal management strategy on toxic substances (Canada, Office of the Auditor General, 1999). The audit reviewed ten programs that were based on design criteria the commissioner identified as necessary for a successful voluntary initiative. These criteria included clear program goals and targets; standardized performance measures; clearly defined roles and responsibilities; consequences if performance objectives were not met; regular reporting on meeting objectives and credible verification of results (e.g., third-party audits); and continual improvement, with corrective actions to be taken where performance objectives had not clearly been met.

The result of this audit was the development of a formal federal framework for the use and integration of voluntary instruments. The Policy Framework on Environmental Performance Agreements (EPAs) outlines the conditions under which an EPA may be signed, with whom, the necessary design features of eligible programs, the role of Environment Canada in EPAs, and the necessary factors to be considered when determining whether to use an EPA to address a given policy issue (Canada, Environment Canada, 2001a). Participation in EPAs is voluntary; the framework provides only a formalized process for determining the best design and use of such agreements. It is based on the concept of incentives to generate desired environmental and policy outcomes. Incentive measures include technical assistance for participants, public recognition from the government for achievements made under EPAs, economic instruments such as deposit/refund schemes and tradable permits, and statutory discretion to reduce regulatory burdens on companies meeting the requirements of an agreement.

The following section will outline the major categories of voluntary or non-regulatory instruments utilized in Canada to address water quality and quantity concerns. Specific examples of programs will be provided where possible.

Recognition/Award Programs

Many voluntary tools utilize public recognition as an incentive for participation and performance. Evidence suggests that a positive "green image" can affect consumer and investor relations. For example, using a sample of chemical firms, Khanna and Damon (1999) found that firms which were consumer-product oriented were more likely to participate in the 33/50 Program in the United States, since they were more likely to feel pressure from consumers to produce environmentally friendly products.

There are a variety of voluntary pollution prevention programs at the national, provincial, and regional level across Canada. As an approach, pollution prevention programs appeal to businesses since they can lead to economic benefits such as lower production and maintenance costs, improved operating efficiency, reduction in environmental risk, and limits to liability (Ontario, Ministry of the Environment, 2001). Participation can also improve a company's green image, as these programs offer recognition through newsletters, award ceremonies, and certification. Such benefits are often advertised by programs as an incentive for participation.

In 1997 the Canadian Council of Ministers of the Environment launched a Pollution Prevention Awards Program for businesses and organizations in a variety of categories (e.g., small business, group innovation). This program is supported by regional pollution prevention programs across the country. For example, Enviroclub in Quebec provides technical and financial support for in-plant projects leading to improved operating practices and use of resources and reductions in pollutant by-products (Canada, Environment Canada, 2002b). The following example demonstrates how participation in such programs can lead to both environmental benefits for water quality and quantity and financial benefits for member companies. One company under the program processes approximately 18 000 tonnes of potatoes per year, with the washing stage requiring a large volume of fresh water, which the company buys from the municipal drinking-water system. Under the Enviroclub Program, the company implemented a closed-loop water circuit, which resulted in a 50 per cent reduction in water usage, a reduction of 8470 cubic metres a year. The system cost the company $9070, which will be recouped in three years as the reduced water consumption cut the plant's water bill by $3000 a year.

Codes of Practice

Some industry sectors require participation in voluntary initiatives as a condition of membership. The best-known example is the Responsible Care Program, established in 1985 by the Canadian Chemical Producers Association (CCPA), which has now spread to over forty-five countries worldwide. CCPA set out 151 code elements under six main codes of practice for member companies to follow: community awareness and emergency response, research and development, manufacturing, transportation, distribution, and hazardous waste management (CCPA, 2005). In terms of impacts on water quality, Responsible Care member companies achieved a 99.7 per cent reduction in emissions of twelve metals to water between 1992 and 2002 (CCPA, 2002). In addition to such environmental benefits, the program highlights incentives to members such as cost-sharing of resources, knowledge, and expertise and financial savings and company growth through improvements to management systems, reduction in insurance premiums, and lower legal liabilities as participation contributes to a defence of due diligence. The International Standards Association ISO-14000 is another example of a voluntary designation for companies that achieve a level of environmental quality in their productions processes. Part of ISO-14000 certification includes an analysis of water use and efficiency, and as of 2002, some 800 organizations in Canada had received certification, up from 276 in 1999 (Nova Scotia, 2004).

Compliance Agreements

In the case of enforcement, voluntary compliance agreements offer an alternative or precursor to regulatory action. Compliance agreements are agreements made by a regulated business to the regulating agency, describing its plan for resolving a problem of non-compliance (Phyper and Ibbotson, 1996, 19; Commission for Environmental Cooperation, 1998). The goal of these negotiated agreements is to increase compliance and decrease the need to prosecute or seek injunctions. Compliance agreements are used as a tool across the country; however, only

Yukon, Nova Scotia, and Ontario have specific statutory authority for such agreements (Commission for Environmental Cooperation, 1998). These agreements are most effective when offered to those regulated businesses that are "inadvertently" out of compliance. In such cases, voluntary compliance agreements can achieve an acceptable level of compliance at a lower cost to the regulator than if the businesses were prosecuted. However, it is important to maintain a credible and aggressive threat of enforcement for repeat offenders.

Environmental Performance Agreements/Memoranda of Understanding

Many jurisdictions in Canada are using memoranda of understanding (MOUs) or environmental performance agreements (EPAs) to promote environmental improvements. These may take the form of negotiated arrangements between government authorities and specific companies or industrial sectors or between levels of government. Generally, these agreements are more formal arrangements, typically taking the form of regulatory exemption programs in which legal obligations are waived in return for commitments to improve performance beyond existing standards.

An example of a single-company MOU is that made between Dofasco, Environment Canada, and the Ontario government. Signed in 1997, the agreement sets targets for key parameters in the areas of air quality, water quality, waste management, community activities, and environmental management systems. One of the commitments under the agreement is to "use all reasonable efforts to surpass all daily and monthly MISA loading requirements." The Municipal Industrial Strategy for Abatement (MISA) is part of Ontario's provincial regulatory framework for addressing toxic substances of high concern. The program includes specific sectoral regulations for nine industrial sectors. In its 2002 progress report, Dofasco announced that it had surpassed all regulatory requirements for loadings to water of cyanide, lead, zinc, ammonia, and suspended solids (Dofasco, 2003). Proponents of this approach point out the environmental benefits achieved when firms voluntarily go beyond regulatory requirements. Critics argue that MOUs create an uneven playing field by granting concessions to individual companies or sectors.

INFORMATION INSTRUMENTS

Information tools include education, communication campaigns, and knowledge-sharing. Some argue that since information-based approaches rely on sources of behavioural control, the resulting behaviour can be perceived as voluntary in nature (Dietz and Stern, 2002). Here, this type of policy instrument is seen as being on the far end of the policy instrument continuum as the most informal or least coercive tool. Sometimes, however, it is argued that these management tools operate in support of the other forms of policy instruments, rather than as policy instruments in their own right. The following three categories touch on some of the key education and information tools available to help manage water issues in Canada. Specific examples are provided where possible.

Public Inventories

There is growing awareness that public dissemination of environmental information collected by governments is an important component of an environmental management framework. It ensures active public participation, accountability, and awareness of pollution issues in community neighbourhoods. As outlined below, empirical evidence has also suggested that the provision of information indirectly affects markets by generating pressures (e.g., investor response, public concern, or reputation) that influence corporate behaviour toward better environmental performance.

In Canada, reporting of emissions of specified pollutants is mandatory under the National Pollutant Release Inventory (NPRI). The NPRI, established in 1993, is the only legislated, nationwide, publicly accessible inventory of pollutant releases and transfers in Canada. It requires industry to report annually on releases and transfers of a list of substances. As of 2007, 367 substances were being reported to the NPRI, and the list of substances is constantly under revision.

Several studies of the United States' counterpart, the Toxics Release Inventory (TRI), provide some evidence of the important role of these public information inventories. In a study of 612 publicly traded companies, Arora (1999) demonstrated that firms which engage in pollution prevention activities gain market value, as opposed to firms which do not engage in such activities, with public announcements through the Toxics Release Inventory quickly reflected in a firm's stock market value. Hamilton (1995) found a similar result, demonstrating that firms which reported large TRI discharges were more likely to be mentioned in media reports, which in turn resulted in losses in the stock market. As well, O'Toole and colleagues (1997) used data from the TRI to analyze the effectiveness of state right-to-know programs in reducing releases across the United States. Their analysis showed that states with programs which actively promoted access to information on toxic chemical releases were more successful in reducing releases than states without such programs.

Partnerships for Information-Gathering

Cooperative undertakings and cost-sharing arrangements with other government and non-government agencies are an important part of Canada's water monitoring and data collection system. For example, Ontario's Drinking Water Surveillance Program is a voluntary program operated by the Ministry of the Environment (MOE) in cooperation with 169 municipalities to gather scientific data to support drinking-water standards (Ontario, MOE, 2003a). The province of Ontario also operates the Lake Partner Program, in which the Ministry of the Environment monitors water quality in recreational lakes through a voluntary partnership with cottagers and local residents (Ontario, MOE, 2002b). The ministry provides a "Lake Partner Kit" with instructions and equipment for measuring water clarity and nutrient measurements. The public, environmental organizations, and other groups have an important role to play in such partnerships. They often have more knowledge of local issues and also have the ability to provide services (e.g., collect data or monitor water quality and quantity) which the government would be unable to provide on its own.

Fact Sheets/Best Management Practices Information

All levels of government produce a variety of fact sheets and information about best management practices (BMPs) to help educate the public and relevant professionals on how to best protect water quality and quantity. For example, the British Columbian government offers a "Well Protection Toolkit" as part of its management framework to protect the province's groundwater. The tool kit helps communities and the general public to identify threats to groundwater supplies and recommends ways to minimize those threats (British Columbia, Ministry of Environment, Lands and Parks, 2000). Best management practices include principles; guidelines and recommendations to individuals and the private sector on best practices; and technical approaches known to be the most effective and practical means of protecting and conserving water. In some cases, the basis for BMPs is legal in that they are incorporated into conditions of approval. In other cases, BMPs are non-binding guidelines. An example of a water-related BMP in British Columbia is the Provincial Urban Run-off Quality Control Guidelines, which include stormwater management recommendations to assist municipalities and the private sector to minimize impacts of urban runoff on receiving waters.

CONCLUSION

The search for innovative and cost-effective ways to improve water use and management has resulted in the development of a wide array of management tools for ensuring water quality and quantity. In general terms, these tools are the means by which statutes and government policies impact upon water users. They fill the implementation gap between administration of policy and impacts on users. It is clear from this overview that a wide range of tools are available for policy-makers who are dealing with water quantity and quality conflicts and issues. In the past decade, instrument choice has expanded, and the standard regulatory framework has been increasing, supplemented or mixed with incentive-based policy tools designed to change the behaviour of water users. Voluntary, incentive-based, and non-regulatory instruments are increasingly utilized in conjunction with the standard regulatory framework. These instruments supplement and sometimes replace the property arrangements between different rights holders discussed in the next chapter. In summary, many of the examples described in this chapter are, in fact, used as part of a mix of policy instrument approaches and are developed and adapted to existing institutional contexts.

These important tools are often unknown to the general public, and they can frequently be disputed once their impacts are known and existing water uses are challenged. It may take politicians, public servants, the courts, interest groups, the public, and, in some instances, a crisis to change existing instrument choice and design. As the case studies in Part Two of this book highlight, various instruments are used to manage long-standing and emerging water-use conflicts. The cases illustrate that the mix of instruments employed depends on the specific issues being addressed, it changes over time, and it is increasingly contested. The preference for certain water policy instruments is also best understood in the broader institutional context in which they are implemented. In analyzing institutions, it is important to understand that policy-makers, including public servants, make choices and that often the "devil is in the details" of implementation.

4

Property Rights and Water

MARK SPROULE-JONES

Property is an important feature of water resource governance –
indeed, of all resources. Property rights determine who, what, how,
and under what conditions the resources can be enjoyed or used. Historically, the courts were employed to settle disputes among different
owners and users, and then, under our system of law, they became
precedents to referee similar cases of conflict in future years. Property
rights in the modern era are more usually established by government
laws, policies, and regulations, such as those discussed in chapters 2
and 3. In this chapter we spell out some of the implications of the
property rights concept for water use and governance. The attributes
of property rights, or what some scholars call "property rights bundles," are outlined first, followed by an examination of property
rights for surface waters and groundwaters that are the products of
judicial and cabinet/bureaucratic decision-making in varying mixes
from province to province. The chapter will then elaborate on property rights as a tool or instrument of government to induce cooperative behaviour among citizens and users – and perhaps favour one
group of users over others.

INTRODUCTION

The term "property" can cause great confusion since it is frequently used
in different ways and with different meanings. In common parlance, it is
often equated with real estate. In historical terms, the ownership of property could foster widespread social unrest, from the clearances of the
Scottish Highlands (and mass migration to Nova Scotia) through the
communist revolutions of the twentieth century, when all privately

owned property was seized by the state. At various times in history, people were treated as property, even in Canada, where some slaves were bought and sold before the abolition of slavery in 1832. More recently, Canadian women were considered as property rather than as persons, a chattel to be owned and controlled by the head of the household. Hence property is a term that can cause heightened anxiety in many places in the world.

Property is, as we shall see, a reasonably precise concept in Canadian society because of the role of the legal system. No one person has unlimited rights to do as he or she wishes with her/his property. A Canadian's house is definitely not his or her castle. And the Crown, which at one time operated with the dictum "the King can do no wrong," is now severely restrained by statutes and legal decisions on the limits of its power. The legal principles behind these limitations on property owners are found in what lawyers call tort law – essentially that the owners may use property provided the use causes no unreasonable harm to others. So you may pump water from a stream flowing through your property, but you must not cause unreasonable damage downstream – in terms of returning polluted water, for example. These property rights are enforceable rules, historically and typically in the courts (Libecap, 1986). Courts, parliaments, and bureaucracies continue to define and redefine property rights.

Property rights held by one owner can and often do conflict with those of others. The so-called American Wild West was characterized by a clash between farmers who wished and could enclose prairie lands after the invention of cheap barbed wire fencing and the herders, who had been accustomed to move their cattle across wide swathes of land to find better grazing. Many of the case studies in this book are examples of the clash of property rights. Sometimes our legal system and at other times communities of users are called upon to resolve the clashes. Politics is thus intertwined with property.

Chapters 2 and 3 have demonstrated how property rights in the modern era are more usually established by laws, government policies, and regulations. Some trace their origins to customs and legal precedents recognized by the courts. For example, Aboriginal rights to food fisheries were recognized by the courts before they became established in the Constitution Act of 1982. Some rights can even trace their origins to English common laws that were adopted throughout the Commonwealth as a result of colonization. An example is the law of "navigable servitude," which gives commercial shipping priority over other uses of navigable waters unless a province or the federal government has trumped this rule with a new law.

It is often said that property rights are rarely completely integrated. Rather, they consist of "bundles of rights" that, in both legal and practical ways, may be treated as distinct attributes. Frequently, an owner may not use a lake or stretch of river but may lease it to recreational fishers or to municipalities for water supplies. These latter parties will then have a property right, enforceable in court, to use their tenancies in a reasonable fashion. Thus a stretch of river can end up with any of the following rights disaggregated and justiciable before the courts if they are violated: possession or ownership, withdrawals, diversions, transfer of ownership (e.g. sale), exclusion of other uses as well as withdrawals and diversions, and water quality.

Similarly, groundwater could also have its attributes disaggregated and justiciable, although obviously it will not be deployed for as many uses (such as navigation or recreation) and thus is less frequently a subject for conflict and judicial determination of rights. All property rights are legally sanctioned – or, in older communities, sanctioned by customary use – and costs and benefits correspondingly flow from the judicial determination in a particular environment. Communities differ in how they set these rights, and they tend to vary from province to province and from water body to water body.

The large corpus of historical writings on property rights focuses on the possession or ownership feature of property, rather than on other attributes. It is often assumed that ownership title brings with it title to the other attributes in the bundles (as it frequently did). As highlighted in chapter 6 on bulk water exports, some Canadians believe that ownership of a water body signals independence from other countries. Water can thus have connotations beyond the material, as part of our heritage, which we should pass onto future generations in quantities and qualities comparable to those enjoyed today. Many of the actual disputes over water occur over the rights to exclude others, to which we now turn.

EXCLUSION

If one has the legal capability to exclude anyone from using water for any reason, from drinking through irrigation through disposal of wastes such as sewage, then one has a substantial property right over the livelihood of many human settlements. Ownership of this right can be fiercely contested between users and potential users. Four kinds of governance regimes can be based on the rights to exclude people from a water resource (or, indeed, many other resources). These are

- private property regimes in which an individual or a corporation can control access: a British Columbia farmer may fully own access to the underground aquifer on his land, for example;
- state property regimes – called *res publica* in Latin – in which a legitimate government is in charge, such as by selling fishing licences to fishers to fish a salmon stream;
- communal property regimes – called *res communes* – such as a Native band that may have full Aboriginal title to a lake or fish-spawning area;
- *res nullius* – no government or legitimate authority exists to exclude others, and anyone can access and capture a salmon swimming in the high seas.

For many years it was assumed that if *res publica* did not exist for the use of a water resource or its products, then anarchy would prevail. That is, *res nullius* would take over. Then users would compete for the resource beyond any level of long-run sustainability, in case others got there first. A resource could disappear in this regime, just like the Atlantic cod, the North American buffalo, or the migratory blue whales (Hardin, 1968).

Careful empirical investigation undertaken during the last thirty years has discovered that *res communes* are extensive and effective governance regimes for all kinds of water resources (Ostrom, 1990, 2001). A recurring difficulty with large-scale, multiple-use water resources, however, is that they often span political boundaries, and it may be hard to get adjacent jurisdictions to agree on access rules, particularly if the resource use in question is scarce. For example, it is difficult to get the US authorities (state and national) and Canadian authorities (provincial and national) to agree to plans to remediate highly polluted international waters such as the Niagara River when they separately want to set regulations on waste-disposal operators, past and present.

All these concerns about exclusionary rights must be seen in the light of the abundance or scarcity of the water resource in question. A large system such as the Great Lakes is sufficiently abundant to allow navigation and shipping to access the waters, subject only to the physical limits on ship drafts in the connecting channels, locks, and St Lawrence Seaway. But as chapter 9 illustrates, these rights are increasingly being challenged by other water users. As a general rule, when the supply of water is limited or varies widely from season to season, then rules on a variety of uses are developed. Exclusion may be necessary. Ownership of this particular right may make the owner(s) very powerful.

The right to exclude may apply not simply to access to a resource for some purpose such as shipping, recreation, fishing, or waste disposal. It may also apply to withdrawals and diversions. These are the traditional uses of a water body for domestic consumption, stock watering, irrigation, or industrial purposes. At the heart of this issue is one of "packaging" the resource. If the resource can be measured and transferred (perhaps sold on transfer), then it is "packaged" in a technical sense. As outlined in chapter 6, some Canadians recoil at the idea of packaging water resources. Marxist scholars refer to the phenomenon as "commodification" and speculate about how it can facilitate easy water exports from the Great Lakes to the American Southwest.

Whether or not people are "putting" uses into a water body, such as a fishing rod or a waste-disposal pipeline, or taking out water for other uses, such as stock watering, one normally needs permission to do so. The permission may be from a private person, a government or governments (more than one), or a community of persons. Such property rights are allocated, in the Canadian case, either by governments (through statutes, regulations, permits, and other instruments covered in chapter 3) or by custom (through common-law precedents).

SURFACE-WATER RIGHTS

In common-law jurisdictions, flowing or running waters cannot be owned. The use of water, rather than the possession of water per se, may constitute a bundle of legal rights. This bundle of legal rights to use water is, in common law, a derivative of the right of ownership of land. A riparian is one whose land is washed by water and who has the right to the natural flow and quality of that water, subject to the same rights as his riparian neighbour: "No riparian proprietor has any property in the water itself, except in the particular portion which he may choose to abstract from the stream to take into his possession, and that during the time of his possession only" (Lambden and de Rijcke, 1985, S35, 148–54). The riparian is thus enjoined to make reasonable use of (surface) waters, subject to similar reasonable use by his neighbours. However, if the water is diminished by the reasonable use of upstream riparians, then the downstream riparians have no legal recourse. Reasonable use is determined through the judicial process. In common law, it does not include the right to pollute or to obstruct and divert the waters; nor does it include the right to remove unreasonably large quantities (unless so granted by other riparians).

Riparian rights are transferable in that a non-riparian such as an adjacent landowner may negotiate access to the water, subject to the uses of other riparians. However, "in order to obtain secure rights to flow, a non-riparian is likely to have to acquire rights from all downstream and all upstream riparians in order to secure his supply" (Campbell, Scott, and Pearse, 1974, 481). A riparian may also negotiate rights to an extraordinary access to water. Again, the agreement of all riparians is necessary since any one of them can claim compensation for a reduced flow resulting from extraordinary use. The riparian need not exercise her/his right in order to preserve it and, in fact, is entitled to the natural beauty of the water itself.

Thus in common law the use of surface waters for domestic, farming, or other purposes is contingent upon riparian ownership of adjacent lands. These uses may undergo continual change as a result of judicial determinations of reasonable use or through bargaining between riparians, through negotiations between non-riparians and riparians, or through purchase of riparian lands on the open market. The property rights themselves are made adaptable through continual adjustments, as represented by the concept of "reasonable use."

Riparian rights continue to form the basis of water allocation in Ontario (but see below) and Atlantic Canada. That they do so is probably a result of the relative abundance of water in these regions compared with the Prairies and British Columbia. The BC system, for example, was introduced in the late nineteenth century to resolve conflicts between the gold panhandlers, who were diverting streams away from salmon-spawning areas, and the fishers downstream. The civil code in Quebec also provides statutory rights and remedies comparable to those found in riparian rights systems. Both western Canada and the North use systems of water licensing in which the provincial government (in the former case) or the national government (in the latter case, though working through regional water boards responsible to the minister of Indian and Northern Affairs) issues licences based on various use criteria.

The most important of these criteria is that of prior allocation, or first-come, first-served. The province in question (unless in the North) issues a non-transferable licence to take water, with permissible amounts specified in the licence. Ontario enjoys a hybrid system, in which large-scale withdrawals for surface water or groundwater require a permit of approval but not small amounts, which are subject to common-law rules. Currently, the definition of large-scale is over 50 000 litres per day. The director of water resources retains the legal power to limit withdrawals smaller than 50 000 litres per day if they might constitute a nuisance for other landowners. These discretionary powers are authorized under some draconian legislative clauses. Section 11 of the Ontario Water Resources Act, for instance, states: "The Minister, for and on behalf of the Crown, may for the purposes of this Act, acquire by purchase, lease or otherwise or, without the consent of the owner, enter upon, take possession of, expropriate and use land and may use the waters of any lake, river, pond, spring or stream as may be considered necessary for his purposes and, upon such terms as he considers proper, may sell, lease or dispose of any land that in his opinion is not necessary for his purposes" (Ontario Water Resources Act, 1970). Thus the property rights to water in Canada vary by place as well as by use. A large corpus of legal decisions proves necessary to resolve disputes between owners and other users, even if the owners often turn out to be governments.

GROUNDWATER RIGHTS

The common law on groundwater, peculiarly, is not subject to "reasonable use" but to the rule of capture by any landowner with physical access to the aquifer or groundwater basin. While pollution of groundwater is a private nuisance and hence, if unreasonable, justiciable, "this percolating water below the surface in which nobody has, as far as he can, the right of appropriating the whole" (Dubin, 1974). Thus groundwater property rights are attached to the land and are not adaptable, although the bundle of rights as a whole may be purchased in the marketplace.

The only limitation on this rule of capture seems to be that no one can drive a shaft diagonally from adjacent property into a water deposit (La Forest, 1969, 413). In other words, no privatization of percolating water rights exists, even if a new use of the same aquifer on adjacent land affects the water quantities and qualities. Some anecdotal evidence from southern Ontario suggests that new conflicts are emerging between landowners with legal access to the same underground aquifer. The aquifers in question could be ruined if new rules are not established.

In recent years, most provinces have adopted a licensing system for groundwater, thus supplanting the common-law system and its potential problem of coordination among users. There is great variation in groundwater permitting policies and practices across the country, however (Nowlan, 2005). Only British Columbia seems to rely on the common law (for groundwater) and lacks a licensing system for groundwater.

We thus have rules for stream water use and for subsurface water use that vary considerably from province to province. Finally, other uses of water can operate once the generic right of access/exclusion is met. Thus shippers will have attenuated rights to use a body of water for navigation and (delegated) statutory rights of agencies to make "rules of the road" or regulations on the discharge of ballast waters, for example. These other rules and regulations nest within the overall property rights set either by statute or by custom. To the outsider, the system seems unduly complex and perhaps unfair. To the insider, it seems calibrated (by and large) to resolve disputes among interdependent users. The resolution of disputes will, though, create winners and losers; so recourse to political bodies seems inevitable.

PROPERTY RIGHTS AS A META-THEORY

A body of work fashioned largely by lawyers and economists attempts to understand the complex relationships among various property rights. The focus is on the relationships between different types of property rights and the persons who hold, use, or enjoy these rights. It is not simply an exercise in instrumental rationalism but, rather, a broader meta-theory about how persons relate to each other in a network of relationships that we expect to find in any community. It is a meta-theory about socio-legal governance arrangements in which governments play a role as holders of rights.

One of the pioneers of this line of meta-theorizing was the legal scholar Wesley Hohfield, who, writing ninety years ago, distinguished between things, rights to things, and property in law. Property, he argued, is first about rights and not things, and property rights are really not about rights to things as such but about what he called "jural relations" (Hohfield, 1919, 7). Jural relations describe the relationships between a rights holder and others who may have claims on the property holder in some fashion. So I may have a right to access a fishery and withdraw a fish but, as illustrated in chapters 5 and 6, others (e.g., a government agency) may have some claims on my rights, such as requiring

Table 4.1
Schlager and Ostrom's scheme of rights

Positions	Property rights			
	Use	Management	Exclusion	Transfer
Owner	X	X	X	X
Proprietor	X	X	X	
Claimant	X	X		
Authorized user	X			
Squatter[a]				

[a] This author's addition.

me to have a permit, to access the fishery at specified times and places, and to withdraw only particular kinds and sizes of fishes.

The use of a resource for harvesting, withdrawals, or discharges is a privilege. *Management* allows a rights holder to create and annul claims and privileges in a resource. Our BC farmer, for example, may have exclusive privileges over an aquifer under his land, and therefore he may impose a duty on others to respect his resource. *Exclusion* is a property right or claim that determines who will have use of a resource. It is a claim because others owe a correlative duty to the rights holder not to access the resource without consent. There is no reciprocal duty. *Transfer* begins with the transferee relaxing his or her claims on the original rights owner. When the transfer is complete, the transferee may exclude others. A Scottish lord, for example, may, under common law, have the rights to sell the resource (one form of transfer). If the rights to transfer are prevented, the value of the transfer can be attached to an interdependent use. Restrictions on transfers of water withdrawals by permit often get reflected in increases in the value of the lands adjacent to or on the top of the water system in question.

Schlager and Ostrom, in an influential study on the fisheries resource (1992), extend the theory by arguing that these four types of property rights (use, management, exclusion, and transfer) are in fact normally held cumulatively by rights holders. So a rights holder may have rights extending from use through the other three rights (see table 4.1). Schlager and Ostrom use and define the names of different types of rights holders as follows: a proprietor has all the rights to a resource except the right of transfer; an owner adds to these rights the right to transfer; a claimant cannot transfer or exclude but has remaining rights; an authorized user has only the right to withdraw or add to the water; and a squatter has no rights and simply takes.

In this kind of scheme, we can see that the Crown (normally the province) can often own a water body (at least in western Canada). It can lease the use of certain bodies of water to a proprietor, perhaps for a charge, just as the BC government does to the Greater Vancouver Water District. In other regions of the province, a municipal proprietor may not be able to exclude other claimants such as forest companies or recreationists from using a watershed. And a farmer may possess a licence to withdraw only a specified number of litres per day for stock watering and irrigation. In remote regions of the province, a group of squatters may simply homestead in a valley without permission or perhaps without fear of expulsion. Abundance sometimes allows owners to avoid strict implementation of all of his or her rights.

An analysis of water resources in any water body would thus need to explore this web or network of "jural relations." Governance is a mix of elaborate judicial determinations of privileges, claims, duties, and exposures together with governmental rules that create complementary and sometimes conflicting incentives for people.

LIMITS OF THE PROPERTY RIGHTS PARADIGM

Property rights are an integral part of real-world water resource situations, at least in Anglo-American countries. We often think about the need to clarify some rights, adapt other rights to new situations, or develop new rights for new resource situations. For example, a fugitive resource such as ocean-going salmon is a common pool or common property at least while outside the boundaries of a country or a fishing alliance. What happens then if countries decide to extend their maritime boundaries and these overlap with boundaries of other countries? Obviously, some clarification is needed; otherwise, "fish wars" will sporadically break out, as they did in the BC–Alaskan coastal waters in the 1980s and 1990s. Similarly, new situations may arise in which fish-hatchery but migratory salmon mingle with "wild" species, and rights to harvest a traditional fishery (such as the Native food fishery on the Fraser River) may need adaptation. Finally, the invention of new technologies, such as sonar radar for detecting schools of fishes, may require some completely new property rights to prevent capture and potential exhaustion of a fish species on the high seas. The example of fugitive fish species is important, since many countries, including New

Zealand, Australia, and lately Canada, are adopting radically new property rights systems. These are called ITQs, or individual transferable quotas, in which the estimated catch per year is divided up among a group of fishers, and the fishers can choose to catch their share or transfer the right to others. Preliminary evidence, such as from the BC shellfish farmers, suggests that both conservation of stocks and efficiency of fish operations are much improved under this kind of system (Pearse, 1996; Jones, 2003; Tietenberg, 2001).

While the property rights paradigm is useful in the practical world of situations and has fostered a stream of important political theory for a number of centuries, it has limits for analyzing some common-pool problems. The limits are intellectual: the paradigm does not appear to fit or resolve some key problems which, in turn, can have major practical import. Three important limits merit noting.

First, the property rights paradigm is not able to specify or assign liability for some resource uses. One example is non-point source pollution generated from land or from air sources. Soil may be washed off agricultural lands and co-mingle with natural erosion to create a river sediment load, for example, and create damages for other resource uses as varied as shipping (for navigational channels) or fishing (depleted dissolved oxygen levels). Statutory legislation may be needed to assign government agencies with responsibilities to measure and remove some of what in the United States are called total daily maximum loads (TD-MLS). The property rights paradigm presumes that human actors can be located and assigned the property rights to access the water resource with their wastes and thus be held potentially responsible for damages for these rights of access. Of course, the human actors in question may be operating either independently (private dischargers) or collectively (public dischargers). The property rights paradigm is fundamentally about the moral responsibilities of human actors, rather than about natural ecosystems and ecosystem processes that include human actors.

Second, the paradigm offers us little in the way of a theoretical argument to resolve multiple-use competition over water resources. Economic theory takes us some way in that it can specify that the marginal net value of one use should equate with the marginal net values of other uses, where "net" takes into account inter-use damages. The property rights paradigm tells us that courts, bureaucracies, and legislators can specify priorities among multiple uses. So, for example, the concept of "navigable servitude" is a common-law precedent assigning priority for shipping over all other uses of navigable waters (Sproule-Jones, 1993). And many legislators have attempted to draw up a lexicographic list of preferred uses, with human domestic consumption at the top. These regulations build on existing property rights arrangements. In all these cases, the property rights paradigm needs supplementary theory about collective action (governance) to deal with a full allocational process for multiple-use water resources.

Finally, a property rights paradigm generally assumes that rights can be assigned and liabilities enforced within sovereign political jurisdiction. When a resource spreads over two or more sovereign jurisdictions, it necessarily requires supplementary theory about alliances, treaties, and intergovernmental cooperations. The concept of federalism is one major attempt to develop such a theory that includes provinces (states) as potentially harmonized to deal with common property. Even then, breakdowns occur in practice (Sproule-Jones, 2002). And, of course, institutional alliances may lack appropriate effectiveness. There is, in a sense, an issue of institutional scale in which, as the number of sovereign jurisdictions increases, the efficacy of decentralized decision-making by resource uses is threatened (Gibson et al., 2000).

The property rights paradigm thus provides a logical set of arguments about individualism, the use of resources, liabilities for damages to other individuals, and the necessity for interpersonal collaborations over common-pool problems. Once it addresses these last set of issues, however, it needs supplementary arguments about governance to fit the requirements of a paradigm.

CONCLUSION

Property rights are thus rules for the governance of resources. They can be good or bad; they can favour or harm different groups of users and citizens. In arid climates, their distribution can induce social unrest, even revolution. In Canada they may favour different complexes of interests from one province to the next and, indeed, from one water body to the next, as our case studies illustrate.

In any situation, the property rights are bundles of rights – multiple and partitionable rights – to some aspect of the resource. The most important right for classical theorists is that of ownership, but other important ones, such as access and withdrawal and sale of the resource, need not be attached to ownership per se. Ownership can imply possession, and property owners can potentially possess the means of a living for persons who rely on the waters – for fishing or irrigation or drainage, for example. This potential aspect of ownership can be a source of major conflict in fact.

Modern theorists stress the importance of the access and withdrawal rules for the sustainability of the resource. In many situations, unfettered access can lead to resource depletion and degradation. A "tragedy of the commons" can occur. Unfettered access is a rare problem in Canadian waters, as the Crown and private owners work to define and enforce the property rights, albeit with errors of commission and omission. The right to discharge polluted effluent into lakes, rivers, and oceans is probably the most contentious property right leading to degradation in many waters, such as nineteen polluted "areas of concern" on the Great Lakes (Sproule-Jones, 2002). Many of the conflicts highlighted in this book stem from access or withdrawal issues.

Modern theorists also point out the importance of governance arrangements that work to define and amend different property rights. The courts have played a significant role over many centuries in resolving water conflicts and redefining various property rights to water. As outlined in the next chapter, bureaucracies, cabinets, and parliaments are now as important, if not more so, in setting these rules. Only in recent decades have non-governmental communities been officially included in governance processes for water in Canada (Dorcey and McDaniels, 2001).

The transfer and possible sale of water resources is always contentious. Consequently, governments typically enjoin water users and owners from sale. Of particular concern to Canadians is the sale of raw water and a consequent depletion of the stock of water that sustains many traditional uses and users. Some economic theory would suggest that transfers by sale would reallocate the resources to its highest valued use, thus placing this kind of theory in direct conflict with deeply held beliefs of many Canadians. Currently, the issue is resolved in favour of conservation rather than transfer.

Canadian governments, federal and provincial, have set rules for determining what property rights may be held by whom, for what specified period of time, and when and how they may be changed. Complex bundles of rights have been developed in different provinces and on different bodies of surface and underground waters over time. In many instances they have been (and are) developed to referee conflicts among rival users of the resource. Property rights are also a product of instruments and government policies. Often they are only changed by governments with great trepidation. They can be respected by courts, for example, almost as if they are constitutionally reserved clauses of the Constitution Act (Mullan, 1996). In the United States they are constitutionally entrenched.

Scholars often refer to property rights and regulations as operational rules since they create the frameworks within which users may go about their activities in mutually productive ways. They are rules for day-to-day governance. Naturally, such rules can become outdated, disputed, or conflictual with each other, and then some governmental process is needed to resolve the conflicts and sort out the operational difficulties. Courts may do this, or groups of users or governmental officials.

Property rights are thus subject to legislative and legal scrutiny. In turn, these forums can act only if authorized by the constitution. Thus there are three levels of decision-making in our governance system: the operational level, the level of parliaments and courts (sometimes called the collective choice level), and the constitutional level in the form of the Constitution Act and other major conventions of government (Buchanan and Tullock, 1962; McGinnis, 1999; Sproule-Jones, 2002). These constitute a hierarchy of rules.

Property rights and other regulations/instruments are thus the lowest level of rules in a three-tier stack. They can be changed by collective choices at the statutory level or by constitutional choices. Property rights can therefore be seen as important elements in a framework of rules for governance, management, and change. Some economists believe that well-designed property rights are the central fixtures of an efficient economy and society. Hence recommendations for property rights changes are often made by economists seeking greater efficiencies and the reduction of social costs in the economy (for review, see Schmid, 2004). An example would be allowing water permit holders to resell their permits. Other examples are outlined in chapter 3.

Property rights are in constant need of adaptation. In some regions, communities of users are engaged in co-management and co-production of the resource with other users and regulatory agencies. A variety of forums are involved in dispute resolution and water resource decision-making. The case studies in this book show how governance involves a variety of forums that must come to terms with different users who have different property rights and differential powers in their waters. Historically, we have relied on disputes between users to bring issues and conflicts to the attention of courts to resolve. The resulting decisions are political ones and have enduring impacts on institutional arrangements. More recently, conflict resolution has involved decisions and collective choices by politicians and bureaucrats under various statutory authorities. The case studies in Parts Three, Four, and Five of this book outline how historical property rights and these collective choices define the politics of water withdrawals, pollution, and in-stream uses in Canada.

PART THREE
The Politics of Water Withdrawals

5

Enough for Everyone: Policy Fragmentation and Water Institutions in Alberta

KEITH BROWNSEY

Southern Alberta is one of the most water-scarce parts of Canada, and competition for water can be intense, particularly during periodic droughts. Managing water withdrawals in this region has become an increasing challenge as urban populations have grown, oil exploration and extraction has increased, and the uncertainties of global climate change loom large. However, by far the largest user of water in southern Alberta is irrigated agriculture, and this chapter shows that irrigators continue to maintain their long-standing water rights in the region, despite increasing pressure from new users. Irrigators' water rights are institutionally entrenched in the prior allocation system, a system of water rights dating from the nineteenth century, and they have been able to protect these rights largely because of the continued rural bias of the Alberta legislature. In the 1990s the Alberta government introduced a number of policy changes to address the increasing rivalries in water withdrawals and the growing problem of environmental decline, but the integrity of the prior allocation system remained intact. Although the system may seem anachronistic and ineffective today, this case study illustrates that institutions such as these can long persist when their supporters are advantaged in political processes.

INTRODUCTION

In June 2003 the two-year drought that had devastated a large part of Alberta was declared over. Environment Canada issued a statement declaring that "a wet spring has spelled an end to the driest conditions in decades." Summer rains were predicted to set the conditions for a normal crop year in the province; indeed, the summer forecast called for above-normal precipitation. This was described as good news for farmers and ranchers who had suffered through up to four years of drought. The dry conditions had seen grain production cut by half, while hay and pasture crops had also declined. The resulting feed shortage had forced some ranchers to sell off large parts of their herds. But the spring rain and snow had boosted precipitation levels well above stated normal levels, and meteorologists, politicians, farmers, and ranchers declared nature's gentle balance restored (*Edmonton Journal*, 2003).

There is, however, a problem with this conclusion. No reliable measures of either normal rainfall or how much water exists in Alberta have been compiled. While some progress has been made toward an overall assessment and strategy for water allocation and conservation, there are no reliable surveys of groundwater, and records are too sparse to estimate average or normal rainfall with any accuracy. Instead, policymakers have assumed that high levels of rainfall are normal and that there are abundant, if not limitless, supplies of groundwater.

Water allocations to households, farmers, ranchers, and industry, moreover, are predominantly based on institutions and policies established in the late 1800s, when the population of the region was a fraction of its current size. The main policy principle governing the extraction of water is the concept of "first in time, first in right." As a result, the industries established in the early settlement period, such as agriculture and oil and gas production, benefit disproportionately from water resource allocation. More recently, however, some effort has been made to find a balance among different resource users such as recreation, wildlife conservation, waste disposal, industrial use, and household consumption. Even among established interests such as farmers and oil and gas producers, there is increasing conflict over the use of water resources. The problem of negative interdependencies has pitted upstream oil and gas producers against local communities and the agricultural sector. Simply put, the failure of the province to find a balance between multiple users of water resources has led to conflict and the depletion of a common pool that is essential for continued economic and social harmony in a semi-arid environment.

Water has always been important to Alberta. The first European settlers in the western edge of the Canadian prairies – what is now the province of Alberta – were unsure that there was sufficient moisture to

grow crops. Only after much experimentation and a massive public relations campaign did settlement begin on a large scale. Many of the
early fears were realized in the 1930s. The late 1920s and 1930s saw
much of the Canadian prairie devastated by a drought that lasted close
to a decade. Only the determined effort of the federal and provincial
governments, along with the cooperation of various farm organizations,
allowed the reclamation and continued farming of prairie lands. Irrigation projects, soil restoration schemes, and genetic modification of
crops permitted agriculture to prosper on the semi-arid prairie of southern and central Alberta in the following decades (Gray, 1996).

In the late 1990s and early 2000s, however, crisis struck once again.
Grasshopper infestations destroyed crops and made walking the streets
and roads of the eastern-central region of the province difficult; an incident of bovine spongiform encephalopathy (BSE, or mad cow disease)
sent cattle prices tumbling and the ranching industry into near collapse;
and abnormally low rainfall resulted in years of lost crops and severe
damage to the soil. Plagues, locusts, and especially droughts have become all too familiar to the residents of Alberta (van Herk, 2001; *Edmonton Journal*, 2003).

The response of the federal, provincial, and local governments to recent water shortages has revealed a system of water management that is
uncoordinated, fragmented, and ineffective. While there have been
some successes in dealing with the economic impact of the recent
drought, various policies and programs have not addressed the problem
of continuing water shortage. They have focused, instead, on price-
support schemes, public relations campaigns, and massive water diversion and dam proposals that would, many believe, only exacerbate the
current freshwater shortfalls. Little effort has been made to improve irrigation technology and practices, to curb increasing freshwater use by
the oil and gas industry, to regulate urban growth patterns, or to coordinate policy among a variety of federal, provincial, and local departments and agencies. The result of these uncoordinated and short-term
policies has been to exacerbate an already difficult situation and to ensure that water shortages will increase in the future.

WATER IN ALBERTA

Alberta is a landlocked province. Approximately 22 million square kilometres in area, it is bordered on the west by British Columbia and the
Rocky Mountains and on the east by Saskatchewan and the prairies. In

the north, Alberta faces the Northwest Territories, while in the south it lies adjacent to the American state of Montana. About two-thirds of its population of 3.3 million residents are found in the two largest cities of Calgary and Edmonton, although smaller regional centres such as Fort McMurray, Red Deer, and Lethbridge also contribute to the 80 per cent of the province that resides in urban areas.

Alberta is at the epicentre of the western Canadian sedimentary basin, which contains – in one form or another – vast amounts of oil and natural gas. The hydrocarbon resources have made Alberta the wealthiest province in Canada. This wealth has attracted thousands of new residents and contributed to a booming economy. With an increasing population, rapid economic growth, and wealth derived from natural resources, what happens in Alberta is of great importance to the rest of Canada. If, for example, the Bow River, which supplies the Calgary region with water, were to dry up in the next twenty-five years, as some environmentalists and geographers believe, the economic, environmental, and demographic consequences for the city, province, and country would be significant.

Most of Alberta's major waterways originate in the Rocky Mountains. The Columbia and Fraser rivers flow into the Pacific, while the Athabasca and Peace rivers form the headwaters of the Mackenzie River system. It is the Saskatchewan River system, however, that is vital to Alberta's supply of fresh water. This system of rivers begins in the Rockies and flows through Alberta, Saskatchewan, and Manitoba, ending up in Hudson Bay. There are seven major river systems or basins in the province – the Milk River, the North and South Saskatchewan river basins, the Beaver River, and the Peace, Athabasca, and Hay river basins (figure 5.1). While the stream-flow data from the river basins is known, the groundwater situation in Alberta, as in other provinces, is not. There are no accurate figures on either how much groundwater is available or how much is used. As a result, aquifers in the province are an uncertain source of supply.

The total amount of water in the seven river basins is approximately 7 755 137 000 cubic decametres. The river systems all originate in the Rocky Mountains and represent an enormous geographic area. The flow of each of these river basins is dependent on rain and snow in the Rockies, which can vary enormously from year to year. As a result, it is inaccurate to speak of a "normal" level of precipitation or surface water in Alberta. Yet the water from the seven river basins is used for hydroelectricity generation, irrigation, industry, oil and gas extraction, recreation,

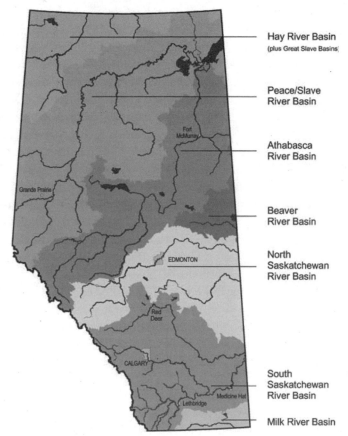

Figure 5.1 The seven major river systems or basins in Alberta.

and household consumption. As with Alberta's rivers and lakes, the province's groundwater originates in the Rockies. From the high elevation of the mountains, gravity forces water through numerous subterranean aquifers. Seepage from the aquifers is the source of much of the wetlands and lakes on the prairies.

WATER USES (AND ABUSES)

The province's lakes and rivers have always been characterized by multiple human uses. They are a source of food and water for a variety of animal species and are essential to human habitation. Native peoples camped, hunted, and fished along these waterways, while early European explorers and settlers used them for transportation and as a source of food and trapped and traded for the rich fur-bearing animals living in the region. In the latter part of the nineteenth and the early twentieth century, settlers established communities along the shores of rivers and lakes. Today surface water is used for a variety of purposes, including irrigation, industry, oil and gas extraction, commercial and sports fishing, transportation, recreation, domestic consumption, and waste disposal. While surface water is still used for transportation in some regions of Alberta, an increasing amount is consumed for purposes of commerce. The two major users of surface water are irrigation at 70.95 per cent and commercial-industrial operations at 14.8 per cent. Municipal water supplies account for 5.39 per cent of surface water consumption.

The three main groundwater users are commercial-industrial operations at 58 per cent, agricultural users at 25 per cent, and municipalities at 18 per cent of total groundwater consumption. In southern Alberta there are approximately 5000 licensed commercial users of groundwater. This water is employed for various industrial and resource extraction purposes, such as in oil and gas exploration and production. Private residential users, on the other hand, require no licence for personal consumption. The only requirement for residential users is that they contract a qualified well driller and limit their use to 6250 cubic metres per year. There are no restrictions on the use of water by residential property owners (Eckert, 2004; Alberta, 2000b; Alberta, Alberta Environment, 2002). There is no comprehensive inventory of Alberta's groundwater resources. A survey was undertaken in the 1970s, but no tally of the overall resource base was ever made. During the provincial restructuring of the mid-1990s, the Department of the Environment lost its capacity to map groundwater reserves, and a groundwater inventory has yet to be completed.

The southern portion of Alberta is divided into thirteen irrigation districts. All the districts are located within the South Saskatchewan River basin, withdrawing water from rivers such as the Oldman, the Bow, and the South Saskatchewan. In 2002, 2 784 000 irrigation licences were issued on 1 224 581 acres (Taylor, 2003, 7, 8, 10). The total volume of surface water diversion in the thirteen districts that year was 2 208 479 cubic decametres. The irrigation districts pay no fees for the withdrawal of water, but they are required to charge their members for the construction and maintenance of irrigation infrastructure such as dams and canals.

The agricultural sector comprises approximately 30 per cent of Alberta's total land area. Crop and livestock production is one of the province's largest economic sectors. Agricultural water consumption involves stock watering, crop production, and domestic use. A farm may depend on surface water, groundwater, or a combination of the two. Because it requires minimal treatment and is generally available, groundwater is most often used for domestic purposes. Surface water comes from a variety of sources, including lakes, ponds, rivers, and dugouts. Some of this water is used for intensive livestock operations such as feedlots. It is also used for the spreading of fertilizers and pesticides as well as for irrigation. Irrigation is an essential part of the agricultural industry in Alberta. Without it some parts of the province could not sustain a viable farming or ranching industry. Irrigation also allows for the improvement of agricultural productivity and crop diversification.

Outside the thirteen southern Alberta irrigation districts, there were 2828 private irrigation licences in Alberta, for a total of 283 254 acres of farmland. These irrigation projects vary in size from 3 acres to several thousand of varied use. Each of these projects is licensed to an individual or group of producers. The feasibility of the various applications is assessed by Alberta Agriculture, while the licensing is regulated by Alberta Environment. There is no charge for approved (licensed) withdrawals (Taylor, 2003, 15).

The oil and gas industry was licensed to use 4.6 per cent of all water allocated in Alberta at the end of 2001. Less than half a per cent of this amount is used in water and steam injection operations (enhanced recovery of hydrocarbons). Water diverted for these purposes declined from 88.7 million cubic metres in 1972 to 47.5 million cubic metres in 2001, of which 37 million cubic metres was saline or brackish (Alberta, Alberta Environment, 2003a). Water is used in the recovery of oil and gas in several ways. Drilling rigs use it to make a fluid called mud in their operations. The mud helps to bring rock chips to the surface and to keep the drill bit cool. Water for this process usually comes from a surface source, but groundwater is also used. Water is also used in the recovery of in-situ oil sands where the hydrocarbons are too deep to mine. Steam is injected into the oil formation to heat and push the liquid to the surface. In oil sands mining, water is used to separate the oil from the sand. Oil sand upgraders, oil refineries, and petrochemical plants use water for heating and cooling in the refining process (Alberta, Alberta Environment, 2002, 32).

About two-thirds of the water used in drilling and enhanced recovery of oil sands is fresh water from groundwater sources. In 2003 the oil patch was licensed to use more than 51 billion litres of groundwater – 26 per cent of all groundwater extracted in the province. It is estimated that nearly half of Alberta's oil production of 1.5 million barrels per day comes from oil recovery using fresh water. Much of this water is permanently polluted by hydrocarbon, sulphur, and salt contamination. Although required to bear the cost of the infrastructure for extracting water, the oil and gas industry – upstream and midstream – does not pay for its use (Schmidt, 2003).

About 10 per cent of Alberta's surface and groundwater is used in manufacturing and forestry. The seven pulp and paper mills in the northern boreal region of the province use high volumes of water from several rivers. Water is used to break down wood fibers for the bleaching and cooling of pulp. The seven pulp mills in northern Alberta obtain their water from rivers (Alberta, Alberta Environment, 2002, 33). Lumber mills use large amounts of water for debarking of logs and cooling of saws. While much of the water employed by the forestry industry is returned to the several water systems from which it is drawn, a good deal of it is polluted because of the inability or unwillingness of small producers to remove various contaminants.

Another important use for fresh water in Alberta is in the generation of electricity. A number of hydroelectric dams and related storage reservoirs are located in the province. In 2002 there were twenty water power developments: eleven hydroelectric plants on the Kananaskis/ Bow River system, two on the North Saskatchewan/ Brazeau River system, and seven smaller facilities on various canals and rivers in central and southern Alberta. The province's hydroelectric facilities generate 5 per cent of the province's electricity. All the hydroelectric power generation plants are owned by individuals and private corporations.

Alberta uses a mix of surface and groundwater for domestic use, which consists of drinking, cooking, washing, sanitation, and yard watering. Only a small proportion of the province's water is employed for these purposes – 5.9 per cent of surface water and 18 per cent of groundwater extracted (Alberta, Alberta Environment, 2002, 27–8). Surface water for domestic use comes from lakes, reservoirs, and rivers. Most of the province's population gets water from these sources. Groundwater comes from wells or springs that are fed from an underground source. About 2 million of Alberta's 3.3 million residents obtain their drinking water from large municipal systems in Edmonton, Calgary, Lethbridge, Red Deer, and other major urban centres. About 400 000 people in the province get their supplies from smaller municipal systems. Over 600 000 Albertans use water from wells, from co-operatives, or distributed by truck.

THE INSTITUTIONS OF WATER
GOVERNANCE IN ALBERTA

As outlined in chapter 2, under the BNA Act (1867; now the Constitution Act), the provinces were given jurisdiction over the natural resources within their borders, including most water resources. The Prairie provinces were an exception, however, and did not obtain control over their natural resources until the Natural Resources Transfer Agreements of 1930. As a result, it was the federal government that set the pattern of water allocation in the province of Alberta early in its history. Through the subjugation of Native peoples and the extermination of the buffalo herds, the prairie west was cleared for European settlement. A policy of accelerated economic development and cultural ethnocentrism seems to have guided federal decision-makers in determining who would benefit from the resources of the area, especially in the case of water.

The dominant group in early Alberta society – the recently arrived ranchers and farmers –were the primary beneficiaries of federal water allocations. Because early Alberta was a rural society, the political support of farmers was critical for any democratically elected government. Both the federal and provincial governments therefore catered to the interests of the agricultural community, ensuring residents a safe and secure supply of water for crops and livestock through a government-mandated water allocation system (Levi, 1988, 10–40).

The water allocation principle used to support agricultural expansion in the prairies was the concept of "first in time, first in right," an approach borrowed from existing water allocation practices in the American West. To adapt this approach to the Canadian context, however, all water was retained as Crown property, and allocations were granted as licences rather than as private property. Some riparian rights for stock watering and domestic use were preserved, but all large water uses were licensed on the basis of temporal priority. This has meant that the first agricultural settlers had priority in access to water resources, laying claim to them through the government licensing process.

Although Alberta has become an urbanized, industrial society, the early pattern of water allocation has continued with only some modifications. When the Alberta government took ownership over the province's water resources in 1930, it maintained a policy of benefiting the agricultural community over other groups. The rural bias in the distribution of seats in the provincial legislature has meant that the influence

of the agricultural community has continued, even as the demographic
and economic importance of rural Alberta has gradually declined.

In sum, the federal government established a system of water allocation that maximized its own political benefit and accelerated agricultural expansion in the prairie region. When the Alberta government
later obtained jurisdiction over its natural resources, it maintained this
pattern of water distribution for similar reasons. As a result, the allocation of water has changed little since the early days of European settlement. In more recent times, this situation has resulted in increasing
conflict between a declining rural, agricultural community and an increasingly powerful urban community. Some legislative changes to the
water allocation rules have been undertaken as a result, but the licences
granted under the "first in time, first in right" system have been preserved, and they remain the dominant feature of Alberta water policy.

While the province owns the water resources in the right of the provincial Crown, local authorities, through a variety of institutional arrangements, are licensed by the province to distribute fresh water for
drinking, sewage, recreation, and irrigation. The most important of
these institutions are the thirteen irrigation districts established under
the provincial Irrigation Act (detailed below). Irrigation districts are
self-governing cooperatives that construct and manage the distribution
of surface water for agricultural and other purposes in the southern
portion of the province. The federal government intervenes only when
water consumption and diversion issues involve Native reserves, military bases, and interprovincial and international waterways. Also, a
number of private corporations have licences from the province to withdraw water from aquifers, rivers, and lakes for a variety of purposes
ranging from oil and gas production to intensive agriculture. The myr-
iad of institutions involved in contemporary Alberta water governance
are outlined in further detail below.

The Government of Canada

When the federal government handed over control of natural resources
to Alberta in 1930, water management became the responsibility of the
province. But the national government's role in water did not end entirely. As outlined in chapter 2, the division of powers in the BNA Act
assigned most authority over water to the provincial governments, but
this authority is limited by the existence of several federal constitutional
powers. These powers allow the government of Canada to legislate in

respect of water for several purposes, limiting provincial authority in the areas of fisheries management, navigation, and transboundary waters. Accordingly, a number of pieces of federal legislation are relevant to water management in Alberta, many of which have already been described in chapter 2. The most important pieces of federal legislation are summarized in table 5.1.

The Province of Alberta

The province is the central player in water resource policy in Alberta, and various provincial departments and agencies play key roles in water management. Alberta Environment issues licences for water use in the province and records all the water that is allocated. In 2001 the province allocated 9.4 billion cubic metres of water for a variety of purposes. Allocations from surface flows constitute 97.5 per cent of the total, while the other 2.5 per cent is from aquifers (Alberta, Alberta Environment, 2002, 27).

Eight pieces of provincial legislation impact on water policy in Alberta, the most significant of which are described in more detail below: the Water Act, the Environmental Protection and Enhancement Act, the Wildlife Act, the Forests Act, the Public Lands Act 1949, the Provincial Parks Act, the Wilderness Areas Act, and the Irrigation Act. The Crown in right of the province owns most of the water in Alberta and regulates most developments and activities that affect rivers, lakes, and groundwater. This ownership gives the province a great deal of power to regulate water use.

The central piece of legislation in the regulatory and legal framework of water management is the Water Act. Its main principles have been in place since the 1890s. The federal government passed the Northwest Irrigation Act in 1894, vesting ownership of all water in the Northwest Territories (which at that time included what are now Alberta and Saskatchewan) in the federal Crown and introducing the "first in time, first in right" approach to water allocation. State ownership was subsequently transferred to the provinces in 1930 and then extended to include groundwater in 1962. The current Water Act covers virtually all water use and management in Alberta. It prohibits the diversion or uses of water except those approved under the act and its regulations.

In 1996 the Water Act underwent significant legislative reforms after seven years of public consultations. The new act created four categories of water rights holders: existing licensees, household users, agricultural

Table 5.1
Federal legislation relevant to Alberta water management

Legislation	Description	Significance
Canada Water Act	Provides for federal–provincial agreements on water inventories, data collection, management, and implementation of water resource plans.	Has resulted in increased monitoring of river flows and data gathering on water uses, but produced no substantive changes to water allocations or water usage.
Fisheries Act	Includes protection of fish habitat, prohibition of obstruction of fish passage, and rules against water pollution.	Has been instrumental in triggering environmental assessments of controversial projects such as the Oldman River Dam, the Pine Coulee project, the Little Bow project, and the Alberta Pacific pulp mill.
Canadian Environmental Assessment Act	Requires that an environmental assessment be undertaken before a federal authority carries out a project, before it provides financial assistance for a project, and before it transfers administration or control, sells, or leases federal land to allow a project.	The environmental assessment process has provided environmentalists, Natives, and other groups key input into many water projects (such as those listed above), even though the federal government has not always followed the assessments' recommendations.
Canadian Environmental Protection Act	The principles of the act include a federal-provincial framework for cooperation in matters affecting the environment (including water), environmental quality guidelines, control of toxic substances, control of material that promote growth of aquatic vegetation such as phosphates, and guidelines for federal works and lands.	In accordance with the act, the governments of Canada and Alberta have signed An Agreement on the Equivalency of Federal and Alberta Regulations for the Control of Toxic Substances in Alberta. The agreement requires Alberta to set standards for environmental protection that are equivalent to those prescribed under the various regulations of the Environmental Protection Act in areas such as testing, standards, penalties, enforcement, and the public's ability to request investigations.
Navigable Waters Protection Act	Designed to protect the public right of navigation on all waterways deemed navigable by the minister of Fisheries and Oceans; it can apply to any permanent work on any provincial waterway.	While the act has not always been vigorously enforced, recent litigation by several groups looking to alter or stop several major projects on various provincial waterways speaks to its continuing relevance.

users, and new licensees. The existing licensees are those who were granted licences under the "first in time, first in right" system, and these licences continue to hold force. Househould users and agricultural users are those riparians and groundwater users who use water for domestic and stock-watering purposes respectively, and these rights are similarly maintained. New licences, however, are issued at the discretion of the act's director, usually the minister of the environment, for specific terms, and the director must take into account environmental, human health, and public safety factors in the distribution of new licences. He or she also has the power to reserve water for his/her discretionary use and to issue moratoriums on the issuance of new licences. This system for the allocation of new licences differs considerably from the long-standing "first in time, first in right" system that continues to define and protect existing licences (Percy, 1996).

One of the more novel features of the Water Act is a provision for "water management plans" for each of the province's sub-basins, negotiated by various user groups and government administrators and adopted in an effort to strike a finer balance between economic and environmental uses of the province's water. These plans also offer an opportunity to establish ground rules for voluntary transfers of licensed water allocations through market exchanges. Such transfers were permitted for the first time under the Water Act, but all transfers had to be either approved by cabinet or compliant with a cabinet-approved water management plan (Percy, 2005). These tenuous moves toward co-management and water entitlement trading have put Alberta on course to reforms already adopted in other semi-arid regions such as the western United States and southeastern Australia. Thus far, however, only the South Saskatchewan Basin has produced an approved water management plan, and the volume of water traded under this plan remains relatively small. The status quo water allocations remain well entrenched.

Water management under the act also includes powers to prevent the disruption of rivers, lakes, streams, and aquifers (groundwater). The construction of dikes, erosion control, pipelines, telecommunication lines, and water crossings may require the approval of Alberta Environment. The Water Act also authorizes the province to construct, maintain, repair, or appropriate various works related to water if they are declared by the province to be in the public interest.

The province owns $4 billion worth of water resources infrastructure. These assets are managed by Alberta Environment under the Water Act. There are approximately 1400 dams, which supply water to irrigation districts, control flooding, and provide water for domestic, municipal, and industrial use. The act prohibits the bulk export of water as well as any inter-basin diversions of water. It also forbids people from diverting or using water to carry on an activity that affects water unless a licence is obtained. Licences are granted for diversions or other purposes, which may include municipal water supply, power generation, and industrial, irrigation, or conservation projects.

The Irrigation Districts Act is another important part of the water policy regime in Alberta. Irrigation has a long history in the province, but its growth really began with the passage of the federal Northwest Irrigation Act in 1894. Most of the irrigation projects in southern Alberta started as private or corporate enterprises, and many of them quickly ran into financial difficulties. The provincial Irrigation Districts Act in 1915 allowed the farmers involved in the various irrigation projects to purchase them from their corporate owners and operate them as farmer-owned cooperatives, known as irrigation districts. This gradually became the dominant business model among Alberta irrigators, and it remains so today.

The current Irrigation Districts Act dates from 2000. The purpose of the act "is to provide for the formation, dissolution and governance of irrigation districts in order that the management and delivery of water in the districts occurs in an efficient manner that provides for the needs of the users" (Alberta, 2000a, 12). The act also establishes a province-wide Irrigation Council. The minister of agriculture is responsible for appointing this council, not to exceed seven members. It consists of five public members, one from the Department of Agriculture, and one from Alberta Environment. The council is directed to make recommendations to the minister, monitor the operations and financial performance of the districts, and hear appeals on the rulings of the thirteen irrigation districts. The minister of Agriculture, Food and Rural Development is responsible to the legislature for the administration, supervision, and enforcement of the various sections of the act (Alberta, 2000a, 13–14).

The Irrigation Districts Act also establishes the thirteen irrigation districts. Each is required to have a board. The members of the board are chosen by election, and the number of board members is determined by resolution at the annual board meeting. The board may also appoint members, but these appointees are not to exceed 50 per cent of the total membership. The terms of the elected and appointed members are three years. The full board may be elected every three years, or a partial slate of directors may be chosen annually. The district irrigation board is elected by those farmers and ranchers recorded as irrigators on the most recent assessment role of the district or appointed under written authorization as agents for corporations that are irrigators in the district (Alberta, 2000a, 44). As a result of these provisions, the membership of the various irrigation district boards varies. The boards are responsible to the minister of agriculture, the provincial Irrigation Council, and the local irrigators (Alberta, 2000a, 38–42).

Water allocations are made from the province to the irrigation districts and from the irrigation districts to irrigators. While the irrigation districts have provincial licences to divert specific volumes of water, their boards have considerable discretion in allocating water to the irrigators within their respective districts. An irrigation district board may, for instance, stop delivery of water to a parcel of land if any future delivery may exceed the amount prescribed by a district bylaw or if the owner or lessee has used or is using irrigation water in such a manner that it has or may cause damage to property or loss or injury to any person. The irrigation district may also terminate delivery if the board believes it cannot deliver a sufficient quantity of water to some or all of the designated irrigated land (Alberta, 2000a, 19). Private irrigators, outside the irrigation districts, have licences directly with the province and are largely responsible for the delivery of their own water.

Other legislation that affects Alberta water policy includes the Environmental Protection and Enhancement Act. Administered by Alberta Environment, this legislation monitors the quality of drinking water, regulates waste water, storm drainage, groundwater, and drilling, and provides for environmental assessments. The Environmental Protection Act establishes two administrative bodies. The first is the Sustainable Development Coordinating Council. The council coordinates, reviews, and makes recommendations to the minister on interdepartmental matters concerning sustainable development and environmental protection. The second administrative body is the Environmental Appeal Board (EAB). The EAB hears appeals of decisions made under the Environmental Protection Act and makes recommendations to the minister. Members of the appeals board are appointed by order-in-council for terms ranging from one to three years.

The Municipal Government Act (MGA; *Statutes of Alberta,* 1996) gives municipalities direction, control, and management of rivers, streams, watercourses, lakes, and other bodies of water. The local government is subject to any other legislative enactment, including the Water Act and the Environmental Protection Act. Municipalities with a population over

3500 must create a development plan consistent with provincial land-use policies. These plans must contain provisions for the protection of water bodies and natural riparian habitat. Fisheries are also a significant part of water policy in Alberta. Administered by the Department of Sustainable Resource Development, the provincial Fisheries Act sets out rules for the protection of fish habitat to be followed by municipal governments and the various provincial departments.

INTERNATIONAL AND DOMESTIC TRANSBOUNDARY INSTITUTIONS

Alberta water is affected not only by national and provincial laws and regulations but by a number of international treaties, conventions, and protocols. Once again, the Canada–US International Boundary Waters Treaty and the International Joint Commission are of particular importance. Under an apportionment agreement dating to 1921, the Milk and St Mary rivers are treated as a single hydrological unit, despite their existence in separate basins, with the United States guaranteed 75 per cent of the Milk's flow and Canada guaranteed 75 per cent of the St Mary's flow. The latter is of particular importance to the thirteen irrigation districts in Alberta, as the St Mary flows from Montana into the Canadian portion of the South Saskatchewan Basin, where most of the intensive irrigation in Alberta takes place.

The central interprovincial water management institution is the Master Agreement on Apportionment (MAA), overseen by an intergovernmental organization known as the Prairie Provinces Water Board (PPWB). An agreement between the federal government and Alberta, Saskatchewan, and Manitoba in the 1930s established the PPWB; initially, however, it acted only as a forum for intergovernmental coordination and debate with no defined apportionment of the shared prairie rivers. This situation changed in 1969 when the MAA was signed. While water quality is mentioned in the MAA, the focus of the accord is on a formula for sharing interprovincial water.

In normal climatic conditions, Alberta may divert, store, and consume a quantity of water equal to one-half of the natural flow of the South Saskatchewan River, measured at the Alberta-Saskatchewan border. In drought conditions, however, Alberta is entitled to a minimum of 2.1 million acre feet per year, even if this exceeds 50 per cent of the available flow. While this provision is not usually a problem, in the late 1990s and early 2000s the amount of water flowing in the South

Saskatchewan has declined because of drought. As a result, the amount of water Alberta extracted in this period exceeded 50 per cent of the river's volume. Water consumption in Alberta therefore impinges on Saskatchewan users, particularly in times of drought.

The PPWB is mandated to review water quality and encourage sound environmental management practices. A list of water quality objectives has been created which include such chemical and biological contaminates as arsenic and fecal coliform, but these are only objectives. Like most other intergovernmental institutions in Canada, the PPWB has no enforcement mechanism.

POLICY-MAKING AND WATER INSTITUTIONS

Within the institutional context of water policy in Alberta, one concept is central – "first in time, first in right." The rules governing most water extraction and allocation in the province are premised on this principle. As the primary economic activity of the first European settlers, agriculture was given precedence over almost any other activity. With what appeared to be abundant surface and groundwater, irrigation became an early priority of the federal and provincial governments, especially in the semi-arid regions of the southern half of the province. This situation has continued until the present for several reasons. The first is the fragmentation of water policy in the province. A variety of interests compete for the attention of policy-makers. The water policy community is diverse, with no coherent focus. Facing no organized alternative, the traditional agricultural sector and the oil and gas industry dominate the decision-making process in Alberta. The second reason is the centralization of decision-making in the executive. The political composition of Alberta's legislature heavily favours rural areas. This rural bias has helped to maintain the pre-eminence of agricultural interests in provincial policy-making. In a premier/cabinet-centred government whose support lies in rural areas, the interests of the traditional agricultural community dominate.

Within the water policy community there are dozens of voices. The Pembina Institute maintains a directory of over four hundred environmental groups in the province. While most of these organizations have local objectives, many are provincial and even national in scope. These groups comprise such diverse interests as the privately held TransAlta Utilities Corporation, which operates six storage and eleven hydroelectric plants in the Bow River basin. The federal, provincial, and municipal governments all play important roles in water policy and management. The federal government, for example, through the Department of Canadian Heritage, Parks Canada, operates Jasper, Waterton, and Banff National Parks. Within park boundaries, Heritage Canada licences and regulates all water extraction and allocation. Municipalities also play a key role in the water policy community. As with almost all municipalities within the province, Calgary and Edmonton, with close to 2 million residents between them, operate their own water systems. Their collective voices play an important role in determining provincial water policy.

The thirteen irrigations district are very influential voices within the water policy community. The rural bias of the legislature creates a situation where rural – that is, agricultural – interests have a disproportionate influence compared to their population within the province. While over 2 million of Alberta's 3.3 million residents live within the metropolitan areas of Calgary and Edmonton, these cities have only 42 of the legislature's 83 seats. The rural areas and small towns dominate Alberta political life. As a result, the irrigation districts have a greater influence on provincial political life than their populations would otherwise suggest.

There are numerous non-governmental organizations within the water policy community. In the Calgary region is the Alberta Conservation Association (ACA), which is composed of seven different groups – Trout Unlimited Canada, Western Walleye Council, Alberta Fish and Game Association, Professional Outfitters Association of Alberta, Alberta Trappers Association, the Federation of Alberta Naturalists, and the Treaty Eight First Nations of Alberta. The ACA runs several water-related programs, including the Fisheries Management Enhancement Program and Fisheries Habitat Development Program. Other non-governmental organizations involved in the water policy community include Ducks Unlimited, and Partners for the Saskatchewan River Basin. These interest groups vary in their orientation and have not presented a consistent message on water. The interests of the Treaty Eight First Nation of Alberta, the Sierra Club, and the Bow River Basin Council are also often in conflict.

As outlined above, four provincial departments have a direct role in water policy: Alberta Agriculture, Food and Rural Development; Alberta Environment; Alberta Sustainable Resource Development; and Alberta Community Development. Despite the numerous pieces of provincial legislation and the various departments that deal with water issues, no cabinet coordinating committee exists with an environmental or water policy focus. Within the executive decision-making apparatus, moreover, the rural backbench members of the Legislative Assembly (MLAs) have a great deal of influence. Many of the rural MLAs are committed to the maintenance of the status quo. As a result, the principle of "first in, time, first in right" continues to dominate policy.

WATER-USE CONFLICTS
AND INSTITUTIONAL CHANGE

The construction of the Oldman River Dam in the front ranges of the Rocky Mountains in southern Alberta during the late 1980s and early 1990s brought a great deal of attention to provincial water issues. The Oldman project witnessed the Alberta and federal governments and a well-organized and well-funded irrigation sector confronting local landowners, environmental groups, and the Peigan First Nation. For years, the dispute over the damming of the Oldman River in order to supply farmers with water for irrigation brought southern Alberta and the province's environmental and water policies a great deal of attention in the local, national, and international media. Federal environmental reviews, a Supreme Court decision, and the determined efforts of the Peigan and their supporters in the environmental movement failed to dissuade the province from completing the project. The river's annual flow of 3.5 million cubic decametres is now controlled by a dam that the court-mandated environmental assessment review, the Oldman River Dam Environmental Assessment Panel, recommended be decommissioned (Glenn, 1999).

Although a variety of lessons can be learned from the construction of the Oldman Dam, the most important for provincial water issues is the strength of the irrigation lobby. This group of thirteen districts in southern Alberta and their supporters successfully lobbied the province for a dam that invaded traditional Native lands, displaced anglers, upset local landowners, and made the province the target of every legitimate environmental group in North America. All of this was done in an effort to grow crops that many environmentalists say would be better grown in less arid climates (Nikiforuk, 2003).

With the attention of a number of environmental groups now trained on Alberta's water policies, the province was forced to undertake a variety of studies. Unfortunately, the politics of deficit reduction intervened, and Alberta Environment faced reductions in funding of 20 per cent. As part of restructuring, it was decided that the department would cancel a number of programs, including those related to the study of groundwater.

The consequence was that all the hydrologists who studied groundwater were dismissed, and there is no accurate survey of the amount of groundwater present in the province. Other water-related programs were affected in a similar fashion.

In the mid 1990s the federal Department of Agriculture and Alberta Agriculture, Food and Rural Development, under the Canada-Alberta Environmentally Sustainable Agriculture Agreement, undertook to study the impact of agriculture on the province's water quality. The key finding of the study was that agricultural practices were "contributing to the degradation of water quality" in Alberta. The study found a link between fertilizers and herbicides and poor or hazardous water quality. It also described three causes of water pollution from current agricultural practices. Among these were nutrients such as nitrogen and phosphorus, which often exceeded water quality guidelines for the protection of aquatic life in surface water, while nitrate concentrations sometimes exceeded guidelines for drinking water in groundwater sources such as wells and shallow aquifers. Fecal coliform bacteria were also found to be a problem, often polluting surface water and irrigation systems in agricultural areas. While other sources of fecal coliform, such as human activities and wildlife, contributed to the problem, agricultural stocks were found to be the primary source. Pesticides were a third, but not significant, cause of water pollution from agriculture. Although some of these contaminants originated in domestic gardens and lawns, agriculture was the major source. The study showed that concentrations of several herbicides were higher in irrigation canals that in other water sources (Canada-Alberta Environmentally Sustainable Agriculture Water Quality Committee, 1998).

Though the first major study of agricultural pollutants and water quality undertaken in Alberta, the report received very little publicity or action. Facing opposition from rural MLASs through both the caucus and the standing policy committees in the Alberta cabinet, Alberta Environment failed to act upon the recommendations, with the exception of those concerned with encouraging the agricultural community to adopt practices to better protect ground and surface water.

A number of individuals and groups have also raised concerns about the use of fresh water for oil and gas production. Alberta Environment licenses and records all water that is allocated in the province, except that allotted to the irrigation districts, which is recorded by Alberta Agriculture, Food and Rural Affairs. In 2001 the province allocated 9.4 billion cubic metres of water for all purposes. The oil and gas industry was licensed to use 4.6 per cent of all water allocated in the province in 2001 (Alberta, Alberta Environment, 2003a). By 2004, over 7 per cent of total water allocations (surface water and groundwater) was for the production of oil and gas, and the proportion of groundwater allocations, at 37 per cent, was far higher (Griffiths et al., 2006). However, the Alberta government reports that water diverted for this purpose has declined from a high of 88.7 million cubic metres in 1972 to 47.5 million cubic metres in 2001, of which 37 million cubic metres was fresh water and 10.5 million cubic metres was saline. Oil and gas operators are encouraged by Alberta Environment to use alternative methods of enhanced recovery, such carbon dioxide injection. If no other technology is economically feasible, the department will grant a licence. The problem, as many environmental groups claim, is that this water is not recoverable. That is to say, it is contaminated with pollutants such as benzene, or it becomes too brackish for agricultural or domestic consumption. This water use has led to several serious conflicts between oil and gas companies and local towns. Capstone Energy, for example, has been licensed to extract water from the Red Deer River, an important source of fresh water for a number of local communities in central Alberta. Already running low on potable reserves, these communities are making plans to bring in fresh water by pipeline and tanker truck.

In response to growing concerns over a possible lack of fresh water as a result of a four-year drought, the Walkerton tragedy in Ontario, and, closer to home, the E. coli contamination in the water supply of North Battleford, Saskatchewan, the province of Alberta responded in 2003 with a set of proposals to ensure sufficient quantity and quality of fresh water called *Water for Life* (*Edmonton Journal*, 2003; Alberta, Alberta Environment, 2003a). As the introduction states, Alberta "is facing significant pressures on its water resources" and a "fluctuating and unpredictable water supply in recent years." The demands of population growth, intensive agriculture, industry, and drought have placed an increasing and unsustainable burden on the province's water supplies. In the past, Alberta has managed its water through a series of ad hoc and uncoordinated policies and programs that have been in place for most of the province's history. The principle of "first in time, first in right" has guaranteed agriculture primacy in the use of Alberta's surface and groundwater. But increasing demand and unpredictable supplies have necessitated an effort to regulate the now apparently limited supplies of fresh water available for consumption. As well, *Water for Life* addresses the issue of water quality and healthy aquatic systems. It promises performance measures to ensure that Albertans will have safe drinking water and that aquatic life will be protected.

While the proposals contained in *Water for Life* constitute the provincial government's response to the problem of maintaining sufficient reserves of fresh water for a growing economy and population, they are not policy. *Water for Life* is seen as the first step in the construction of a comprehensive scheme of water conservation and planning for the province. It is a policy document that recognizes the finite amount of water available for domestic, industrial, and agricultural consumption. Nevertheless, the political economy of water policy has not changed in Alberta. The largest users of water – the agricultural sector and the oil and gas industry – are still protected by the policy of "first in time, first in right." This principle has laid the foundation of Alberta water policy since the 1890s, and the water rights allocated under this system continue to be protected, even as the *Water for Life* initiative takes some tentative steps in the direction of a more comprehensive, coordinated approach to water management.

CONCLUSION

Since the early days of European settlement, the extraction and allocation of water in Alberta has been dominated by the principle of "first in time, first in right." This principle has framed the legal and policy debates surrounding water resources in favour of agriculture and, to a lesser extent, the oil and gas industry. When conflict has arisen, the long-established industries and their various institutional and social networks have worked to defend these rights.

The constitutional, legal, and political framework within which water policy is made has also helped to create a situation of administrative and policy fragmentation. The result of divided jurisdictional responsibility between Ottawa and Alberta and within the provincial government has been the lack of a coherent plan for water extraction, allocation, and conservation. Municipalities have been given the responsibility of costing water, while irrigation districts have the ability to extract water based on previous allocations with no obligation to charge their members other than for the construction and maintenance of physical infrastructure. There are no requirements that irrigation districts conserve their allotments even in periods of drought. This situation is unlikely to change because of the political influence of the agricultural sector, resulting from rural overrepresentation in both the legislature and the governing Progressive Conservative Party.

Similar political influence is exercised by the oil and gas industry. The oil patch is Alberta's most important economic sector, generating between 20 and 40 per cent of provincial revenues on an annual basis, and the province has been very reluctant to impose any restrictions on the use of fresh water in the recovery of petroleum resources. Oil industry practices are also restricted only by the principle of "first in time, first in right." Increased water scarcity as a result of population growth, agricultural expansion, and drought has brought pressure on the oil sector to change its practices, yet Alberta Environment has been reluctant to challenge a politically and economically powerful industry, an industry that has the regulatory support of the most important provincial regulatory agency, the Alberta Energy and Utilities Commission, the governing Progressive Conservative Party, and a large segment of the public.

The provincial response to water scarcity has been to make minor amendments to the Water Act for the allocation of new water licences and to introduce the *Water for Life* strategy. While *Water for Life* is the first attempt to bring some coherence to water policy in Alberta, it is unlikely to succeed in its stated goals of a safe and secure supply of drinking water, healthy aquatic systems, and reliable reserves of water for industrial and agricultural use. The unwillingness to regulate water use has caused a lack of policy direction which has resulted in waste and pollution. While diversion schemes from the northern watersheds to the arid south are viewed by the province as a possible solution to increasing shortages, the management of water continues within a framework of conventions, rules, laws, jurisdictional authority, and institutions appropriate for a small agricultural society of the early 1900s. Little is likely to change in this system until the conventions and institutions of water management are reformed to better reflect the realities of a growing urban and economically diverse society.

6

Against the Flow: Institutions and Canada's Water-Export Debate

JOHN K. GRANT

One of the most contentious water-withdrawal issues in Canada concerns a type of water withdrawal that has not yet even occurred: bulk withdrawals for the purposes of export. The potential bulk export of Canadian water has been a recurring political issue since the 1960s, but it has acquired increased attention and urgency since Canada entered the North American Free Trade Agreement (NAFTA) in 1993. Although water exports have yet to commence and water-export advocates remain few and politically unorganized, Canadian nationalists and environmentalists view water exports as a serious threat and have lobbied extensively for a national export ban. Yet Canadian governments have not developed a comprehensive national policy banning or regulating bulk water exports. This chapter argues that a primary reason is the widespread institutional fragmentation shaping this policy issue. As the chapter shows, rules relating to potential water exports exist at both the federal and provincial levels of government as well as in NAFTA, creating substantial jurisdictional rivalries and a lack of clarity that have made it extremely difficult to form a comprehensive water-export policy.

INTRODUCTION

Even to talk about selling it is ridiculous. You do not sell your heritage.

(Bennett, n.d.)

Canada is said to be the single largest holder of freshwater resources in the world, possessing at least 7 per cent of the total renewable supply (Canada, Environment Canada, 2004a). Exploration, transportation, and energy production have all been dependent on this nation-building resource. Yet Canadians have predominantly viewed water as part of their national heritage, not just an economic commodity, and there is continuing debate and analysis around whether water is a tradable commodity (Canada, Policy Research Initiative, 2007). It is for this reason that the ongoing debate over bulk water exports has stirred public sentiment in Canada. Bulk water exports refer to the selling of large volumes of Canadian water to foreign buyers by means of either tanker ships or large-scale diversion projects. Thus far, the debate has largely ignored the already thriving international trade in bottled water, mostly because the volumes involved are relatively small and this trade seems to be a reciprocal exchange rather than a one-way drain. While some Canadian business people see trade in bulk water as a source of untapped wealth and a potential growth industry for the twenty-first century, many others view it as a looming environmental catastrophe and a major threat to Canadian sovereignty. Current federal and provincial policies in Canada have stymied the bulk water-export business thus far, but it remains a prospective new economic user of Canadian water, clearly challenging the institutionalized status quo.

As outlined in chapter 2, under Canada's constitutional framework, jurisdiction over water removals and international trade is divided between the federal and provincial governments. Since there is no real consensus among the provinces or between the provinces and the federal government on water issues, policy-making proceeds in an ad hoc manner. As such, rivalry, conflict, and jurisdictional overlap have necessitated different kinds of decision-making in the policy area. Moreover, First Nations' land and resource claims are further clouding jurisdictional divisions.

One of the key problems facing Canadian regulators is the fact that bulk water exports are no longer just a domestic Canadian issue. This concern now extends beyond Canada's traditional geographical boundaries and, possibly, the jurisdiction of the national and provincial governments. The Free Trade Agreement (FTA) and, later, the North American Free Trade Agreement (NAFTA) have given rise to concerns that, like culture, water could be characterized as a commodity. It is often argued that Canadian sovereignty over water resources is compromised under the provisions of these agreements. The implication that bulk water has legal status as a "good" or "commodity" suggests to many that Canada could be vulnerable to future access claims by various agricultural and commercial interests in the United States. Public-sector interest groups (e.g., the Council of Canadians and the Canadian Environmental Law Association) have warned that, under free trade, if water export to the United States begins, Canada will be unable to turn off the tap (Council of Canadians, n.d.(a); Muldoon, 2000). The sale and export of bottled drinking water is minimally regulated, and these groups argue that bulk water exports need further regulation for social, environmental, and ecological reasons. One issue for the federal government is that an outright ban on water exports could be even a tacit recognition that water in its natural state is a tradable commodity or good under the NAFTA. Thus, while it has consistently opposed the export of Canadian water, a comprehensive federal policy on exports has never been formally codified. In part, policy formulation has been excessively cautious, as the federal government is unwilling to challenge the legal parameters of the constitution and the NAFTA.

Currently, in order to avoid trade challenges, the federal government has chosen to treat bulk water export as an environmental issue. To this end, it has taken the following steps: referred the issue to the International Joint Commission (IJC), which has jurisdictional authority over Canada–US boundary waters; attempted to persuade provincial governments, via the Canadian Council of Ministers of the Environment (CCME), to legislate against bulk water removal and/or make such removal subject to environmental assessment; and amended the Canada–US International Boundary Waters Treaty Act in order to prohibit the bulk removal of boundary waters from Canadian basins.

The purpose of this chapter is to highlight the apparent conflicts that exist around the issue of bulk water export in its various forms. Indeed, there would appear to be limits to the ability of governments to reconcile the many and varied interests in this area. The chapter will briefly examine the history of the policy problem and review the policy initiatives undertaken in response to public attention to the issue. It will then evaluate the current and previous institutional arrangements that have impeded the development of a single, comprehensive bulk water export policy in Canada. The discussion will conclude with an analysis of current progress on bulk water export policy, which centres on the transborder region of the Great Lakes.

THE HISTORY OF THE BULK WATER ISSUE

During the 1960s, nine proposals were advanced for bulk export of Canadian water, the most ambitious of which was one by the North

American Water and Power Alliance (Day and Quinn, 1992, 37). The concept involved diverting water from major rivers in Alaska, British Columbia, and Yukon to a reservoir in the Rocky Mountain Trench. From there it would be redirected for consumption in the western United States and Canada. Hostile public reaction and the question of feasibility quashed the idea in its infancy.

The Great Recycling and Northern Development (GRAND) Canal scheme in the early 1980s was a revival of a project first proposed in 1959 by Thomas Kierans. In this scheme, James Bay was to be diked, creating a freshwater lake, the waters of which could be diverted to the Great Lakes and on to the southwestern United States and even Mexico. First Nations were the most vocal opponents, fearing the project would destroy the local ecosystem. Again, the $100 billion scheme lacked feasibility.

While most of the early water-export proposals generated controversy and debate, they were never economically or technically viable. Most were, in fact, initiated by Canadians, which made foreign demand on Canadian water a made-in-Canada controversy (Canada, Inquiry on Federal Water Policy, 1985, 25). Simon Reisman, for example, was a project director of the GRAND Canal proposal prior to becoming Canada's chief free trade negotiator (Day and Quinn, 1992, 37).

More recently, as bulk water export schemes have been developed that are less sophisticated and more realistic (e.g., by tanker or pipeline), public attention and concern has focused on the issue once more. In 1991 Sun Belt Water Inc. of Santa Monica, California, won a contract to supply a small state town with Canadian water. Sun Belt was to acquire the water from a Canadian company, Snowcap Waters of Fanny Bay, British Columbia. The deal was eventually killed by a provincial moratorium on water exports by container ship, and both companies attempted to sue the federal government. Sun Belt claimed that its firm had not received "fair and equitable treatment" under article 1105 of the NAFTA. In this case, however, the federal government dismissed the claim as invalid since Sun Belt had been treated no differently from any other (Canadian) company (Canada, International Trade Canada, 2004). To date, the company has not pursued any further action.

In 1998 a consortium known as the Nova Group was granted a five-year water-taking permit by the Ontario Ministry of the Environment, which allowed the company to draw up to 10 million litres of water per day from Lake Superior for export to Asia. After a huge public outcry from both sides of the border, Nova agreed to drop the proposal, provided it was first in line should bulk water become tradable (Council of Canadians, 2006). Essentially, it was argued that the scheme would violate a long-standing (tacit) policy against water exports from the Great Lakes Basin. Moreover, the granting of such a permit by the province of Ontario ran counter to principles of conservation and cooperative management set out in joint province-state declarations such as the Great Lakes Charter, a non-binding agreement drawn up in 1985 between the provinces and states of the Great Lakes Basin aimed at protecting their shared water resources.

Later in 1998 the McCurdy Group of Newfoundland applied to export 52 billion litres of water per year from Gisborne Lake in Newfoundland. The proposal did not receive provincial approval, and late in 1999 the government of Newfoundland and Labrador passed legislation prohibiting bulk water removal. In 2001, however, a ministerial committee was formed to re-examine the export issue. As a result of the committee's report, the province decided not to rescind or amend the 1999 legislation. Notwithstanding the decision, it was still determined that

- There is no public policy reason not to proceed with bulk water export.
- There is no legal impediment to a bulk water removal project.
- There is no compelling environmental reason not to allow such a project to proceed (Newfoundland and Labrador, 2001).

There are a few existing cases that may already qualify as examples of bulk water export. Three small transborder pipelines divert water from the communities of Coutts, Alberta, Gretna, Manitoba, and St Stephen, New Brunswick, for consumption by small nearby US border towns. However, since these projects do not involve any large interbasin transfers, they have not raised public concern (Fritz and McKinney, 1994, 72).

In the Great Lakes Basin, the Chicago Diversion, which became operational in 1900, provides the city's drinking water and facilitates the shipment of goods from Lake Michigan to the Mississippi River. The average outflow from this diversion is 91 cubic metres per second (Michigan, Department of Environmental Quality, n.d.), and many claim that this constitutes a form of water export, since international waters are indirectly affected. The problem for Canadians concerned with potential water exports through the Chicago Diversion lies in the fact that Lake Michigan is, legally, a domestic US body of water.

Another, much smaller diversion has been constructed to take water out of the Great Lakes Basin through the Erie Canal; however, at the present time, more water is diverted into the basin than is removed. The major inflow comes from the Albany River system in northern Ontario at Longlac and Ogoki. Other existing diversions do not remove water from the basin itself. In most cases, these intrabasin diversions serve to facilitate such things as hydroelectric generation (e.g., Niagara Falls) and shipping (e.g., Welland Canal).

Aside from these diversions, there are two important factors that bear directly on the availability and supply of potable water in the Great Lakes Basin. According to the Great Lakes Commission's[*] water-use database, approximately 3.2 trillion litres per day of water is withdrawn from the Great Lakes Basin for industrial, domestic, and agricultural uses, as well as for power generation and sanitation (Great Lakes Commission, 2000a). For consumptive uses, water is withdrawn and not returned to the area from which it was taken. This includes water for crops, that consumed by humans or livestock, water used in industrial processes, water incorporated into manufactured products, and that which is lost as a result of evaporation in hydroelectric plants. When water is used for irrigation, over 70 per cent is consumed, while at the other end of the scale, when water is used for thermoelectric power, less than 1 per cent is consumed (International Joint Commission, 2000). While impacts on water levels by *individual* consumptive uses are relatively small, "considered cumulatively, they are equivalent to a large scale diversion out of the Basin" (Frerichs and Easter, 1990, 564). Moreover, for non-consumptive uses such as industrial processes, water that is withdrawn is often returned in a degraded state: that is, it may be contaminated with, for example, "toxic substances from industrial and mining uses and with human and animal wastes" (Farid et al., 1997, 21–2).

Also, "there is no unified, consistent mapping of boundary and transboundary hydrogeological units" (International Joint Commission, 2000), and this lack has serious implications for the management of

---

[*] The Great Lakes Commission is a public agency that was established in 1955 by way of legislative action of the eight Great Lakes states (Great Lakes Basin Compact). The agency addresses basin-wide public policy issues such as environmental protection, resource management, and sustainable development. Ontario and Quebec were granted associate member status in 1999.

water supplies, particularly, those of groundwater. For example, there are approximately five hundred municipal water suppliers in the province of Ontario, and of these, three hundred use groundwater sources (Ontario, Ministry of Environment and Energy, 1992, 76). However, during periods of decreased precipitation and/or increased demand, underground aquifers are often temporarily mined; that is, the water table drops and wells go dry. In southwestern Ontario during the early 1990s, water quantity problems accounted for 34 per cent (the largest single category) of all water complaints investigated (Ontario, Ministry of Environment and Energy, 1992, 75). In addition to supplying drinking water, however, groundwater supports wetland habitats, and "local shortages may still pose significant threats to the ecosystems that depend on groundwater for survival" (McCulloch and Muldoon, 1999).

The foregoing considerations are more significant in light of the fact that only 1 per cent of Great Lakes water is naturally renewed (by rain, snow, or runoff), and the comparatively small drainage area of the basin means that outside sources bring in relatively little water to the lakes themselves (Farid et al., 1997, 18). Thus, although there is a relative abundance of water in the Great Lakes Basin, these supplies are not limitless.

INSTITUTIONS PERTAINING TO BULK WATER EXPORT

The International Boundary Waters Treaty of 1909 was the first institution designed to deal with the issue of large-scale diversion or export. The treaty delineated the rights and obligations of the United States and Canada with respect to the protection of natural levels and flows of their shared boundary waters. It gave vetoes to each federal government and to the panel of IJC commissioners collectively over any proposed diversion in boundary waters that would substantially affect water levels on the other side of the international border. Though the relevance of the treaty to water-export issues is readily apparent, a diversion for the purpose of bulk export has never been considered for approval.

Apart from the International Boundary Waters Treaty, the other existing international water-management institutions were designed to address water quantity issues related to hydroelectricity and commercial navigation and did not pertain directly to bulk water exports. The Lake of the Woods Regulation Act, 1921, for example, established federal control of that lake's levels and outflows as a means of resolving a dispute between Ontario and Manitoba over hydroelectric interests. Another initiative, the *Water-Powers* reference of 1929, was an attempt to clarify "the respective limits of the federal navigation and declaratory powers ... as opposed to provincial powers based on ownership." However, while the Supreme Court of Canada offered some general guidelines, they were far too broad to be of real use (Percy, 1988, 26, 27).

One outstanding example of inter-jurisdictional cooperation in water resource development concerns the Columbia River Treaty, which was formally approved in 1964. "Through its terms, the United States acquires large quantities of Canadian storage to meet certain power and flood objectives, and Canada receives a share of the increase in power produced at U.S. generating plants plus payment for its storage contribution toward flood damage reduction within U.S. borders." The complex technical, economic, and political issues that were overcome in order to reach such an agreement is remarkable in light of the fact that they involved not only the interests of Canada and the United States but also those of British Columbia, which has constitutional jurisdiction over its natural resources (Krutilla, 1967, v). However, it should be noted that the treaty negotiations spanned more than twenty years and illustrated fundamental differences between the electric-power interests in British Columbia and Washington State and the broader environmental and social interests expressed through the national governments, especially in Canada (see also Swainson, 1979).

The 1970 Canada Water Act established joint federal-provincial management of Canada's water resources but did little to clarify jurisdictional divisions. Mostly, it provided for consultative arrangements over water resource matters but failed to supply policy direction on any issues other than those of water quality (Canada, Environment Canada, 1997a). It was, in essence, only a framework for action; it did not "in and of itself direct such action" (Saunders, 1988, 30).

By the 1980s, the re-emergence of proposed continental water diversion schemes and the prospect of Canada–US free trade sparked public concern about bulk water export and prompted the Canadian government into action. In 1984 the Canadian government began its Inquiry on Federal Water Policy. The aim of the inquiry was to determine the adequacy of federal water policy, and to seek the views of citizens. The Pearse Report (1985), as the final document came to be known, acknowledged that water policy development is "inextricably involved with environmental concerns, the economy, political relations, and social and heritage values" (Canada, Inquiry on Federal Water Policy, 1985, 7). In all, the report outlined fifty-five recommendations for a coherent water policy and the development of an administrative framework to deal with future water issues. Further, it recommended a cautious approach to water transfer/diversion and suggested procedures to assess the environmental, societal, and economic implications of such transfers. It also highlighted the need for a strong lead agency to develop and administer water policy as part of an ongoing process designed to meet emerging priorities.

In 1987, with free trade on the horizon, the federal minister of the environment, the Honourable Tom McMillan, announced a federal water policy "in which he stated unequivocally that the federal government was opposed to large-scale exports of our water and would take all possible measures within the limits of its constitutional authority to prohibit such exports by interbasin transfers" (Johansen, 1990, 1). The government cited potential harm to society and the environment, especially in the North, where the delicate ecology and Native cultures could be devastated. Two important bills were tabled in this regard: Bill C-156, the Canada Water Preservation Act, which set parameters for small-scale export of water; and Bill C-130, an amendment to the Act to Implement the Free Trade Agreement between Canada and the United States. This amendment stated that the Free Trade Agreement would not apply to water, except as part of a manufactured beverage, and was intended to remove any doubt as to the matter of bulk water export. Both bills, however, died with the dissolution of Parliament. The need for a water-export policy was acknowledged again in 1990 in *Federal Water Policy: A Progress Report* (Canada, Department of the Environment, Interdepartmental Committee on Water, 1990), but as before, the report offered no solutions.

In 1993, to alleviate public concerns over the NAFTA, Canada, the United States, and Mexico issued a joint statement asserting that the agreement created no rights in the water resources of any NAFTA country; nor did it force the exploitation of water for commercial use (excluding bottled water). Although this statement could be used as an interpretive guide in a future dispute over water trading, it is important to note that it was merely an expression of intention, with hortatory but not mandatory effect.

The *Federal Water Policy: Report No. 2* of 1994 identified the quality and availability of fresh water as a major global issue (Canada, Department of the Environment, Interdepartmental Committee on Water, 1994). At this point, it is evident that Ottawa was beginning to frame future water-export policy as an issue of environmental sustainability, rather than of international trade. The report urged the wise use of water consistent with socio-economic and environmental needs, although these needs were never clearly delineated. A key recommendation was the prohibition of interbasin water export; however, any relevant trade issues were deftly avoided by stating that the NAFTA applied only to water packaged as a beverage or in tanks.

Important non-governmental organizations also began to emphasize the need to develop a water-export policy. In 1988 the Science Council of Canada reported on the sustainability aspect of water removal/diversion and identified two key aspects of all water issues: they require an interdisciplinary approach to research policy development and implementation, and they are international in scope (Science Council of Canada, 1988, 17). The report concluded that the consequences of policy inaction were too great to ignore.

The World Commission Report on Environment and Development (the Brundtland Report, 1987), which was endorsed by Canada, recommended that governments consider the ecological/environmental dimensions of policy-making at the same time as they study the economic dimensions of policy-making, such as trade. Moreover, the report argued that protecting the regenerative capacity of renewable resources is a prime component of sustainability, and it urged industrialized countries to strengthen their environmental protection and management agencies (World Commission on Environment and Development, 1987, 313–19). Notably, at the same time as the report was published, Environment Canada was accused of displaying "a lack of economic capability, absence of legal support and timidity in fulfilling its role as advocate for the environment" (Canadian Environmental Advisory Council, 1987, 44).

Paradoxically, as reports, recommendations, and policy statements on the status of bulk water export proliferated, the federal government was beginning to downgrade water as a policy priority. As Pearse and Quinn noted, "The downgrading of water as a policy interest by the Government of Canada is even more perplexing in light of the fact that it runs counter to a growing consensus that water is emerging as a critical need around the world" (Pearse and Quinn, 1996, 336).

Following the round of tanker export proposals in the 1990s, the federal government announced a strategy to prohibit the bulk removal of water from Canadian watersheds. By framing bulk water removal as an environmental management issue, the Department of Foreign Affairs and International Trade hoped to avoid trade challenges since an outright federal ban on water exports was contrary to the trade rules of the General Agreement on Tariffs and Trade (GATT) and, subsequently, the NAFTA. The logic underlying this approach is that water in its natural state – in rivers or lakes, for example – is not considered a good or product and is not subject to international trade rules.

The 1999 federal strategy was comprised of three key elements: proposed amendments to the International Boundary Waters Treaty Act; a proposed Canada-wide accord on bulk water removals; and a joint Canada–United States reference to the International Joint Commission to study the effects of water consumption, diversion and removal, including for export, from the Great Lakes (Johansen, 2001, 15). Although under the Canadian constitution the provinces possess proprietary rights over water resources, the federal government has legislative jurisdiction over boundary waters by way of its treaty-making powers. Thus, in order to prohibit the bulk removal of boundary waters from Canadian basins, Bill C-6, An Act to amend the International Boundary Waters Treaty Act, was introduced in the House of Commons on 5 February 2001. The bill was debated and enacted into law later that year, with the related amendments and regulations coming into force on 10 December 2002. In essence, the amending act deems that the cumulative effect of bulk removals of boundary waters outside their (Canadian) basins alters the natural level or flow of waters on the US side of the border (Canada, Department of Justice, 2001). This position is consistent with the original intent of the International Boundary Waters Treaty Act, which established a mutual obligation between Canada and the United States to protect the natural levels and flows of shared waters.

Because of shared jurisdiction over water, the federal government's strategy also included a proposed Canada-wide accord to prohibit bulk water removal. In November 1999 and again in May 2000, the Canadian Council of Ministers of the Environment (CCME) met to discuss bulk removal of surface water and groundwater from the five major Canadian basins. However, while there was unanimous agreement that this type of export should be banned, a formal consensus could not be reached as to what policy tools or instruments should be utilized to achieve this goal. In all, nine of fourteen jurisdictions endorsed the Accord for the Prohibition of Bulk Water Removal from Drainage Basins. Quebec and the four western provinces declined to endorse the accord as presented (Quebec opted to set out its own position later) (CCME, 1999a). Some provinces, such as British Columbia, wanted the federal government to implement trade legislation to ban exports as part of the agreement. Other provinces viewed the issue as one of provincial resource ownership and resented any federal involvement. They were unwilling to relinquish what they felt was their jurisdictional prerogative to implement their own water removal policies (Heinmiller, 2003).

Notwithstanding the limited support for the accord, several problems with such an approach aimed at protecting Canadian water have been identified. First, the accord is not legally binding. Provincial governments, "perhaps upon a change of political administration, would be free to abandon obligations they may have agreed to." Second, the accord would "do nothing to actually prohibit export initiatives that might be undertaken by provincial governments, municipalities, Crown agencies, corporations, or even private parties. This would require legislation, and when it comes to international trade, it is the federal government, and not the provinces that has the constitutional authority to regulate" (Shrybman, 1999, 5). Finally, by allowing the provinces to develop their own approaches to attaining the accord's objectives, the federal government is re-emphasizing the traditional diversity of policies and regulations across the country. Federal legislative powers cannot change provincial proprietary powers and interests in water resources.

In November 1999 the governments of Canada and the United States referred the issue of boundary water use, especially that in the Great Lakes Basin, to the IJC. The commission was requested "to examine, report upon, and provide recommendations on ... matters that may affect levels and flows within the boundary or transboundary basins and shared aquifers" (International Joint Commission, 2000). In its final report, the commission determined the following:

> International trade law obligations – including the provisions of the Canada–United States Free Trade Agreement (FTA), the North American Free Trade Agreement (NAFTA), and World Trade Organization (WTO) agreements, including the General Agreement on Tariffs and Trade (GATT) – do not prevent Canada and the United States from taking measures to protect their water resources and preserve the integrity of the Great Lakes Basin ecosystem. Such measures are not prohibited so long as there is no discrimination by decision makers against persons from other countries in their application, and so long as water management policies are clearly articulated and consistently implemented so that undue expectations are not created. Canada and the United States cannot be compelled by trade laws to endanger the

waters of the Great Lakes ecosystem. The public, however, remains deeply concerned that international trade law could affect the protection of these waters. (International Joint Commission, 2000)

These conclusions suggest that bulk water exports may be proscribed on the basis that they could adversely affect the integrity of ecosystems; however, as the commission itself is aware, many still remain concerned that international trade laws could indeed impinge on the protection of natural waters, particularly after trade in water has commenced.

THE INSTITUTIONAL COMPLEXITIES
OF PROTECTING CANADA'S WATERS

As outlined in chapter 2, the Canadian provinces exercise legal rights over waters located within their boundaries, since, under section 109 of the Constitution Act, 1867, they have effectively been granted proprietary rights to natural resources. These stem from jurisdiction over property and civil rights (section 92.13) and the management and sale of public lands (section 92.5). More recently, section 92A of the *Constitution Act, 1982*, conferred upon the provinces the right to exclusive legislative jurisdiction in relation to the development, conservation, and management of non-renewable resources. It should also be noted that provincial powers have been supplemented by various federal-provincial accords, such as the western Natural Resources Transfer Agreements (1930) and those relating to control of hydroelectric generation (Barton, 1986, 235).

Some provinces, such as Ontario, have a number of their own agencies which have various levels of authority over water management (e.g., Ministry of the Environment, Ministry of Natural Resources, and the Ministry of Agriculture, Food and Rural Affairs), reflecting the diversity of water uses and interests within government. In most provinces, permits or licences are required to withdraw large quantities of water (except that which is used for domestic or emergency purposes), but the permits are subject to very different provisions and regulations. After the Sun Belt application in 1991, British Columbia placed a moratorium on bulk water removal for export, pending a policy review. Certainly, the implications of Sun Belt's proposal were not lost on Ottawa either; in 1994 a federal committee was created to report on the issue of water export from British Columbia.

The Bloc Québécois, in response to the Nova stir in 1998, asserted that Quebec's water belonged to Quebecers; hence the people of Quebec reserved the right to use the resource as they saw fit (*Canada Official Report*, 1999). Quebec actively supports the bottled water export industry but has implemented an out-of-province ban on bulk water export under its Water Resources Preservation Act (1999). By 2002, all provinces with the exception of New Brunswick had formulated some kind of policy restricting bulk water removals for the purpose of export, following the lead of British Columbia and its 1995 Water Protection Act (Heinmiller, 2003, 507–8).

Federal interests in water exports are derived from the government's treaty-making powers (enshrined in section 132 of the Constitution Act, 1867) and jurisdiction over waters that cross provincial and national boundaries. There are over twenty different federal departments and agencies that deal with water (Canada, Environment Canada, 1985, 151), demonstrating in part the diversity of different water uses and interests as reflected in the federal government. Among these organizations are the Department of Fisheries and Oceans (which, under the Fisheries Act, protects fish habitats in most regions), Transport Canada (which administers the Canada Shipping Act and the Navigable Waters Protection Act), Environment Canada (by way of the Canadian Environmental Protection Act), Indian and Northern Affairs, Natural Resources, Foreign Affairs, and Agriculture Canada. Additional federal jurisdiction involves trade and commerce, the spending powers, criminal law, and the protection of federal lands.

Jurisdictional complexity is exacerbated by two other important factors. First, the physical nature of the resource makes it even more difficult to separate jurisdictional responsibilities. As many scholars have pointed out, the fugitive or transitory nature of water and its many interrelated uses do not permit it to fit neatly within well-defined categories of property rights that are recognized under common law (see Lucas, 1986; Barton, 1986; Sproule-Jones, 2002). While there are certain clearly defined property rights within the provinces, these become less clear when the resource straddles or flows across provincial or territorial boundaries. Hence "the legal character of water [has] made it more difficult than other resources to fit into the constitutional division of powers" (Lucas, 1986, 42). The relative lack of success in providing a structure for water management suggests that common-law notions of ownership may be inadequate to deal with complex international water resource transfers.

Further difficulties involve the legal rights of Aboriginals in Canada. Aboriginal water rights and title contemplate rights of occupation and use, which extend protection for traditional and domestic uses of the resource. The rights to water for traditional uses are determined by priority – that is, "time immemorial" – and the priority of rights for other uses is determined by the date of the establishment of water rights on reserved lands through treaty or other means. An earlier priority limits the water rights of other users, riparian or otherwise. Rights to water held by bands on reserves are generally considered to be more substantial than rights that protect the traditional uses of water since they also include those derived from riparian ownership. It has been pointed out, however, that the applicability of riparian rights may be limited outside the territories, "where smaller areas were reserved to the Indians and where more intensive development and contemporary uses were contemplated" (Bartlett, 1986, 226).

Contemporary Aboriginal title settlements in Canada reflect the growing role of Native peoples in the administration of water resources and the affirmation of rights with respect to those resources. The Nunavut Final Agreement of 1993, for example, provides settlement of Aboriginal title to approximately 350 000 square kilometres of land (Chandran, 2003) and proclaims the rights of the Inuit with respect to water resources on that land. Thus, while First Nations have not been as vocal on the bulk water export issue as many other groups, jurisdictional complexity surrounding the resource can only be exacerbated as Ottawa continues to acknowledge the legitimacy of Native title and rights to the use of water resources.

The bulk water export issue therefore involves interdependencies between federal, provincial, and Aboriginal decision-making processes. As J. Owen Saunders once lamented, "In sum, there is lacking, both within the federal government and between the federal and provincial levels, any [one] mechanism that could qualify as a comprehensive and effective means of coordinating – let alone harmonizing – interjurisdictional arrangements affecting water management in Canada" (Saunders, 1988, 46). Currently, the CCME is probably the closest to such a mechanism, but, as seen in its failure to find consensus on the proposed bulk water removal accord, it is plagued by jurisdictional jealousies, divergent regional interests, and a lack of enforcement capacity. A reformed and empowered CCME could go a long way to overcome some of the institutional fragmentation in protecting Canada's waters, but this is unlikely given the current decentralized nature of Canadian federalism.

Further complicating the domestic jurisdictional issues are concerns that water could be a "good" and therefore subject to export under the NAFTA. The implication that bulk water has legal status as a good or commodity suggests to many that Canada could be vulnerable to future access claims by other states. Although the NAFTA cannot force Canadians to begin bulk water export, most observers agree that "its provisions do ensure that once bulk water exports are started, stopping them becomes significantly more difficult" (Biro, 2002).

According to David Johansen, there are three separate but related issues that arise from international trade agreements such as the GATT and the NAFTA. The first concerns whether or not water in its natural state can be treated as a good. The second issue is whether allowing water to be extracted from lakes, rivers, and other bodies and sold as a good would create a precedent whereby other such requests must be automatically granted. The third issue deals with chapter 11 of the NAFTA and questions regarding the national treatment obligation as it applies to bulk removal for domestic purposes or export (Johansen, 2001).

Under both the NAFTA and the FTA, a "good" is that which is concomitantly considered a "product" under the General Agreement on Tariffs and Trade. Tariff heading 22.01 of the GATT (which is appended to the FTA and the NAFTA) itemizes "water" as including "natural or artificial waters and aerated waters, not containing added sugar or other sweetening matter nor flavouring; ice and snow" (Canada, 1992a). In effect, this definition covers natural waters of all kinds (excluding sea water). However, "goods" are domestic products as understood in the GATT and are therefore stored, bottled, or "produced" in some way. The Canadian government argues that since a good must be produced, something must be done to water for it to be a product. Thus water in its natural state is not a product (or good), any more than oil or gas in the ground is a product. Once removed, however, water could be considered an article of commerce subject to free trade rules.

Opponents of bulk water export (the Council of Canadians, the Canadian Environmental Law Association, and others) argue that, indeed, water carried by tankers or pipelines would be classed as a product under the GATT and a number of consequences would follow if this was truly the case. Under the "national treatment" provision of the NAFTA, governments cannot accord economic advantage to their own residents over those of other NAFTA countries. If Canada allowed a Canadian firm to divert, remove, or export water from the country, it would be required to allow a US or Mexican firm to do the same. Moreover, once water is exported, the total output available would have to be maintained at a constant rate, even if the export customers were to waste the water. In effect, it would be difficult to "turn off the tap."

The national treatment principle is extended further under the NAFTA to include investment and services. Thus "the provision of construction, engineering services and investment, all of which are key to any large-scale water export development scheme, could not be impeded by a domestic government" (Farid et al., 1997, 71). Further, any attempt by an exporting country to tax or limit export of water must be met by a similar tax or restriction on domestic consumption under article XI of the GATT. Quantitative restrictions are permitted only in critical situations, such as to protect human health during a water shortage (Farid et al., 1997, 71), which is unlikely to occur in Canada. While restrictive measures are also permitted for the purpose of conservation (provided there are matching restrictions on domestic production or consumption), WTO dispute-settlement panels that have considered previous cases concerning the protection of environmental or natural resource interests have ruled against those interests without exception (Elwell and Sierra Club of Canada, 2001, 175).

Some have also expressed concern that the commencement of bulk water exports by any single province would set a policy precedent that other jurisdictions would have to follow. In this regard, the Department of Foreign Affairs and International Trade has argued that "the fact that a government in Canada has allowed the extraction and transformation of some water into a good, including for export, does not mean it (or another government within Canada) must allow the extraction and transformation of other water into a good in the future" (Johansen, 2001, 10). This view was reinforced by the IJC study on the protection of the waters of the Great Lakes: "even if there were sales or diversions of water from the Great Lakes Basin in the past, governments could still decide not to allow new and additional sales or diversions in the future" (International Joint Commission, 2000, 36). It should be noted, however, that the conclusions of the IJC have been limited in scope to a review of trade obligations regarding water as a good and not to water as a service and investment (Elwell and Sierra Club of Canada, 2001, 176–7).

Many of the concerns expressed mimic those of 1960s over oil and gas exports; however, the major difference is that natural waters – that is, those which are unprocessed or unrefined – may indeed be considered "goods" under the terms of the FTA and the NAFTA. Specific exceptions do exist for export controls over raw goods, such as logs or unprocessed fish, in order to encourage domestic production, but not for water. As Steven Shrybman, of West Coast Environmental Law, has argued, "under both U.S. and international law, water in its natural state is considered a commercial good. Moreover, a very large portion of Canadian water resources would already have to be considered as having entered into commerce, because it is being used to generate power, irrigate crops, support industry and service individual consumers" (Shrybman, 1999, 1).

Under these international trade rules, the Canadian government finds itself in a policy dilemma because if it proposes an outright ban on bulk water export, it risks a trade challenge from the other NAFTA signatories. Ottawa has therefore focused on the environmental sustainability aspect of the issue. One of the main problems, however, is that the NAFTA does not integrate environmental and trade issues. The existence of the North American Agreement on Environmental Co-operation (the environmental side agreement to the NAFTA) suggests that environmental concerns were an afterthought to the NAFTA. Furthermore, the large-scale movement of water was neither raised nor discussed during the negotiations.

REGULATING BULK WATER EXPORTS IN THE GREAT LAKES BASIN: A CASE OF INSTITUTIONAL FRAGMENTATION?

Some of the changes that threaten the waters of the Great Lakes are driven by global forces. This makes it difficult for residents of the region to influence them ... We now see troubling contradictions between the Great Lakes Charter, water protection laws and ... trade agreements.

(Farid et al., 1997, 6)

Internationally, the Canada–US Boundary Waters Treaty is the main legal instrument dealing with the boundary and transboundary waters of the Great Lakes Basin. The treaty provides that no action can be taken which affects levels or flows of waters, except under prescribed procedures for coordination and agreement between the United States and Canada. The problem is that the treaty does not deal with all basin waters in a similar manner. For example, tributaries of boundary waters and transboundary rivers remain under national jurisdiction and control, specifically with respect to use and diversion. Furthermore, the treaty makes no explicit reference to groundwater, an important source of recharge for basin surface waters.

The International Joint Commission was formed in 1909 as an independent, objective body to deal with transborder water issues. As well, it administers portions of the Boundary Waters Treaty. The commission is binational, consisting of three representatives from each country, and serves two basic functions. First, it controls water movement in the Great Lakes (e.g., any diversion that would alter natural levels or flow of boundary waters would require the approval of both the US and Canadian governments and the IJC). Secondly, the commission investigates and reports on important questions submitted to it by the US and Canadian governments. In administering the Boundary Waters Treaty, then, the IJC attempts to resolve questions of rights and obligations that arise between the two countries and/or the eight states and two provinces affected by the treaty. The IJC has limitations, however, since it possesses neither the legal powers of enforcement nor the means to make any of its recommendations binding. Yet the commission remains a strong investigative and quasi-judicial authority, well regarded and respected by the governments it serves. Indeed, as a result of its study on water-taking in the Great Lakes Basin, the IJC has emerged as an influential source of support for Ottawa's decision to take an environmental approach to the bulk water export issue.

In order to strengthen the ability of the eight Great Lakes states and two provinces to protect their shared water resources, a non-binding agreement between them was drawn up in 1985. Among other things, the Great Lakes Charter aims to protect levels and flows of the Great Lakes, their tributaries and connecting waters, and the integrity of the basin ecosystem. The charter also provides for data collection on consumption and diversion uses greater than 380 000 litres per day (averaged over a thirty-day period). Further, any states or provinces considering the issuance of a permit or approval to take in excess of 19 million litres per day (averaged over a thirty-day period) must notify the other states and provinces and, if necessary, the International Joint Commission through a Prior Notice and Consultation procedure. If any objections are voiced, the permitting jurisdiction is required to seek input and devise agreeable solutions (Council of Great Lakes Governors, n.d.).

The 2001 Annex to the Charter and Implementing Agreements reaffirmed the commitment of the Great Lakes governors and premiers to the broad principles originally set out. More importantly, the annex put forward several directives aimed at creating a set of basin-wide binding agreements. The purpose of such agreements is to "retain authority over the management of the Waters of the Great Lakes Basin and enhance and build upon the existing structure and collective management efforts of the various governmental organizations within the Great Lakes Basin" (Council of Great Lakes Governors, 2001). In December of 2005, in order to meet these objectives, the eight states and two provinces signed the Great Lakes–St Lawrence River Basin Sustainable Water Resources Agreement. The agreement establishes a virtual ban on diversions, a basin-wide environmental standard for water uses, better conservation measures, and an increased role for science in decision-making (Ontario, Ministry of Natural Resources, 2006). Importantly, the agreement also sets out procedures for public participation, as well as for consultation with First Nations or federally recognized tribes, with respect to regionally significant proposals involving new or increased withdrawals, diversions, or consumptive uses of water (Council of Great Lakes Governors, 2006).

While most environmental groups lauded the agreement as a positive step for the protection of basin waters, they did so with some reservations. One problem is that the agreement allows for access to basin water by US communities that lie within "straddling counties" (those counties that cross the hydrological boundaries of the basin). This provision, some claim, raises the likelihood of a NAFTA trade challenge by corporate water investors within these counties. Another problem is that the agreement does not apply to the diversion at Chicago, which many fear could be increased in the future. Finally, the export of bottled water from the basin still remains an ambiguous issue at best (see Canadian Environmental Law Association, 2006; Council of Canadians, 2006). Whether the agreement will take legal effect or remain just a political commitment is still an open question, as only a handful of Great Lakes jurisdictions, including Ontario, had ratified it at time of writing.

In sum, the Great Lakes water management institutions are such that the regulation of bulk water exports is considerably fragmented, and efforts at regulation in any one policy arena, while necessary, still result in incomplete management. Overcoming this institutionalized fragmentation remains the primary challenge in this issue, both in the Great Lakes region and throughout Canada.

CONCLUSION

Recently, the issue of water export has reached a significant position on the Canadian political agenda. The economic viability of export schemes is one reason that may have contributed to this development. Attention now centres upon the social and environmental consequences of the resource's appropriation. However, Canada has had a history of passive/reactive responses to water-based issues. Irrigation, power, and diversion schemes all originated as private or municipal projects (Scott, Olynyk, and Renzetti, 1986, 196), and often, policy has only been articulated as a result of negative public opinion.

As suggested in this chapter, there are three key problems that complicate policy development: the unique nature of the resource and the multitude of uses and users; the complexity and institutional fragmentation related to jurisdictional divisions within Canada (including the large number of stakeholder agencies); and the domestic policy implications inherent in the free trade agreements, which are exacerbated by the prevailing tensions between business and the environment.

The physical attributes of water make its management unique. As was alluded to earlier, water has been characterized as a fugitive resource, in that it is always moving and changing. It is therefore difficult to ascribe given units to a specific location at any particular time. Water flow, for example, is not a constant, and such factors as cyclical flows, measurement inadequacies, and monitoring deficiencies (particularly with respect to groundwater) cause management uncertainties. Thus separate institutional arrangements have developed in response to water's various physical characteristics as well as its uses. Institutional responses to the quantity and quality aspects of water have also evolved separately (Doerkson, 1978, 515).

The third problem is notable in that it is one of the consequences of economic globalization – domestic policy must now be formulated within the constraints of international obligations and duties. The number of relevant actors and institutions has expanded in a rather obtuse way through the NAFTA, and they now officially include other national and sub-national governments. This issue is further complicated by the absence of international legal instruments that address the issue of shared freshwater resources, such as those of the Great Lakes Basin, to which Canada's governments and agencies might possibly refer.

All these factors combine to create an institutional context of fragmentation and uncertainty, characteristics that are clearly reflected in the prevailing bulk water export rules found at the provincial, federal, and international levels. Whether this ungainly web of rules can be fashioned into some kind of coherent management policy remains the open question in the bulk water export issue. Meanwhile, this issue continues to be either a political hot potato or a candidate for serious institutional reform.

PART FOUR
The Politics of Water Pollution

7

Politics and Pollution on the Great Lakes: The Cleanup of Hamilton Harbour

MARK SPROULE-JONES

The Great Lakes Basin lies at the heart of the North American continent, is home to more than 33 million people, and supports some of the most important industries in the United States and Canada and many multiple uses of water. Long-standing institutions such as the International Joint Commission have needed to take multiple uses of the lakes into account as they advise governments about water quantity and quality issues in the Great Lakes. In addition to the well-established uses for shipping and commercial fishing, water quality concerns in the Great Lakes have emerged on the political agenda in the last half-century, and policies such as the Great Lakes Water Quality Agreement have been developed to address some of these issues. As this chapter shows, one of the most challenging aspects of implementing the Great Lakes Water Quality Agreement has been the effective engagement of relevant stakeholders in local remediation processes, despite the new institutional arrangements designed for this purpose. In the case of Hamilton Harbour, consensus-based processes and institutions have been designed to involve environmentalists and industrialists, but their legitimacy has been seriously undermined by the willingness of industrialists to bypass these processes when it has suited their interests. This case study suggests that institutions not only shape conflicts but can be seriously undermined by conflicts when their legitimacy is uncertain.

INTRODUCTION

Pollution control in Canada and other countries is sometimes viewed as a "command and control" system of regulation. In this perspective, one or more government agencies develop standards for water or air emissions from stacks and pipes based on the best scientific evidence about the pollution, about best available technologies of control, and about best knowledge of the ambient environment. The agency can then issue regulations and enforce compliance from industries, municipalities, and other waste dischargers such as hospitals and universities (Dryzek, 1997, 63–83). A different perspective views pollution control as a product of negotiations and bargaining between regulators and dischargers. Parties negotiate standards, technologies, and impacts in the context of debatable scientific information (Dorcey and Riek, 1987). The process is seen as largely collaborative, although government regulators may have a variety of possible instruments besides standards and implementation, as Karen Thomas shows in chapter 3.

Both these perspectives are simplistic and have been superseded by the newer environmental processes in the post-1980 period. (Hessing and Howlett, 1997; Parson, 2001b). Parties generally recognize that decisions are made in the light of scientific and engineering uncertainties. They also acknowledge, as Carolyn Johns shows in chapter 8, that effective point source regulations may be nullified by non-point sources such as runoff from urban and agricultural sources. Finally, it is now recognized that different river basins, lakes, and marine coasts may have varying ecologies and that appropriate solutions to the disposal of anthropogenic waste streams may not be easily transferable by site.

Before we look at the case of remediating pollution in one harbour on the Great Lakes, we need to describe the environment of the basin and provide an overview of Hamilton Harbour in order to place the pollution-control institutions in the context in which they operate. The effectiveness of changes in controlling current pollution inputs and dealing with past pollution discharges can only be assessed against the baselines of the environment in the areas under study. Following this review of the state of the environment, we will develop our case of environmental management of polluted sediments in Hamilton Harbour. Finally, in the concluding section we assess the case in terms of our framework on conflicts and institutions.

WASTE DISPOSAL IN THE GREAT LAKES

The Great Lakes of North America are one of Canada's (and the United States') treasured resources. They exceed half a billion square kilometres, have a combined shoreline of 17 000 kilometres, and hold over 22 000 cubic kilometres of water. Bigger than many oceans, they contain about 20 per cent of the world's freshwater supply. The Great Lakes Basin experienced massive population increases during the nineteenth century. Over 10 million people had settled on its shores by 1900, the large majority of these in the Lake Michigan and Lake Erie subsystems (Canada, Environment Canada and the US Environmental Protection Agency, 1995). Urbanization and industrialization occurred with major population nodes created around southern Lake Michigan, western and southern Lake Erie, and the northwest shores of Lake Ontario. Heavy manufacturing, such as steel, paper, and chemicals, provided the primary sources of urban employment, and water and electrical power supplied cheap sources of energy (Sproule-Jones, 2002). In this context, the Great Lakes have been used for transportation of people and goods, fisheries, hydroelectric generation, recreation, and, of course, the disposal of waste products by individuals, industries, and governments. It is the last of these uses that is the primary focus of this chapter, but the impact of waste disposal and pollution on other uses will become evident.

The watershed is home for some 33 million people, 80 per cent of whom live in seventeen metropolitan areas, the industrial heartlands of Canada and the United States (Colborn et al., 1990, 67). Historically, expanding human settlements were largely cavalier in their disposal of wastes. Many cities such as Chicago and Toronto experienced cholera epidemics through contaminated well and near-shore water intakes. Solid wastes were frequently dumped into marshlands, which were considered non-valuable sites that could not support buildings and roads. Industrial wastes were either buried or diluted and dumped into near-shore waters and wetlands. Some communities were proud of their air pollution, believing it a sign of progress. The impacts of human settlements are now well documented.

One estimate suggests that each of the 33 million residents of the Great Lakes Basin generates about 2 kilograms of solid wastes. Most of these kinds of wastes are landfilled rather than dumped into rivers or lakes. However, rainfalls and snowmelts exceed evaporation throughout the basin, and consequently the leachates are likely to enter some parts of the water courses. In addition to these dumps, some 116 sites on the US side of the basin are considered hazardous (and were part of the US Superfund program), and roughly 5 per cent of 342 Ontario dumps are comparable. Liquid wastes are directly disposed into the lakes and streams. It has been estimated that some 57 million tonnes of liquid wastes are poured into the Great Lakes annually by the 33 million basin residents, industries, and municipalities (Colborn et al., 1990, 64).

Wastes are also disposed into the ecosystem through soil erosion, pesticide use, and manure management from agricultural lands. Estimates of the scale of these activities are available, but no estimates exist of the extent to which they end up in non-point source pollution. Similarly, wastes washed into storm drains, creeks, rivers, and bays from non-agricultural lands may be highly polluted, but no quantity estimates are available (Canada, Environment Canada, SOLEC, 2005).

The impacts on the environment of these waste-disposal activities intermingle with the impacts caused by direct human alterations of the ecosystems. Human settlements alter habitats through land development or resource extraction. They alter hydrology through diversions and dredging. Increased sedimentation and sediment transport change the physical processes on the near-shores at least. And biological structures are altered through human disruptions of food webs in ecosystems. The exact contributions of each of these various sources are impossible to estimate. The overall consequences show up in degraded water and impaired natural ecosystems. Some of these consequences are well-known.

The bottom waters of Lake Erie showed the first signs of anoxia in 1953. By the 1960s, the lake was often characterized as dead, which meant that massive algal blooms were occurring and several near-shore areas were largely devoid of aquatic life. Erie was subject to cultural eutrophication, whereby phosphorus as a nutrient was imposing an algal bloom in a relatively shallow lake with relatively low dissolved oxygen levels in the summer months. Public concern about Erie was in large part instrumental in establishing the Great Lakes Water Quality Agreement between the United States and Canada, to be discussed below. The practical consequence of the agreement was to reduce phosphorus loadings by improved sewage treatment, such that targets and objectives were attained by 1991, and chlorophyll a (an indicator of nuisance algal growth) was at acceptable levels by the early 1990s. Conversely, the introduction of the zebra mussel has increased water clarity (77 per cent between 1988 and 1991) because of its filtration activities, and aquatic plants are thus spreading into deeper waters (Canada, Environment Canada, SOLEC, 1995).

The Love Canal, near the Niagara River in New York State, was declared a federal disaster area by President Jimmy Carter in 1976. The Hooker Chemical Company had buried 20 000 tonnes of chemical wastes that were now, thirty years later, seeping into water and air. The effects were showing up as human skin rashes and irritated eyes and in detectible levels of persistent toxic chemicals in downstream fish tissue (Canada, Environment Canada, SOLEC,1996). The leachate from the Love Canal is now contained and treated, but the Niagara River is still the most significant source of toxic chemicals entering Lake Ontario. Upstream and downstream monitoring indicates that point and non-point sources on the river itself are significant modes of entry for these toxins.

These two well-known cases of environmental degradation cannot tell the full story of the Great Lakes environmental situation. In 1985 the two national governments began a new wave of joint efforts to clean up the Great Lakes. This endeavour identified so-called impaired beneficial uses in forty-three polluted bays, harbours, and river mouths on the lakes. These are called "areas of concern" (AOCs) and were identified by the International Joint Commission and its scientific bodies pursuant to the Great Lakes Water Quality Agreements (1972, 1978, and revised) between Canada and the United States. The AOCs are identified in figure 7.1 and the fourteen use impairments in table 7.1. They are sites where toxic pollution is more easily measured and remediated than in open waters. They reflect the negative effects of many decades of waste disposal and environmental degradation. Other valued uses, such as sustaining a fishery, have been impaired and not "balanced" in some way with tolerable levels of water quality.

There are four major indicators of the impacts of waste disposal on the human and living systems in the lakes (the SOLEC volumes published by Environment Canada list over a thousand indicators):

Aquatic Habitat and Wetlands There are major losses throughout the basin: Ontario has lost 80 per cent and the other lakes some 60 per cent since the 1780s. Enhancement and restoration programs cannot keep up with current habitat losses, with perhaps the exception of brook trout habitat in the Upper Lakes. The aquatic food web is severely impaired in all the lakes except Superior, and it is subject to newer threats from invasive species.

Persistent Toxic Substances Loadings of persistent toxic contaminants have been reduced to 50 per cent of their 1970 levels, although the weights of chemicals remain constant. Contaminant concentrations in waters, sediments, fish, and wildlife are declining. In urban areas (AOCs) and for certain species, however, levels are high enough to cause concern. For instance, human consumption of top predator and forage fish is discouraged, and the effects of alteration in biochemical function,

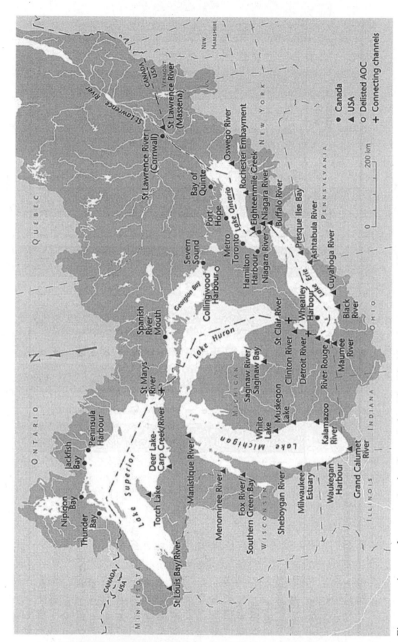

Figure 7.1 Areas of concern in the Great Lakes identified by the International Joint Commission.

Table 7.1
Great Lakes areas of concern: impaired uses

| | | Use impairment categories[a] | | | | | | | | | | | | | |
| | | Ecological health and reproduction[b] | | | | | | Habitat[c] | Human health[d] | | Human use/welfare[e] | | | | |
Water body	Area of concern	(3)	(6)	(13)	(8)	(4)	(5)	(14)	(1)	(10)	(2)	(7)	(9)	(11)	(12)
Superior	Peninsula Harbour	✓	✓					✓	?			✓	✓		
	Jackfish Bay	✓	✓			✓	?	✓	?			✓		✓	
	Nipigon Bay	✓	✓	✓	✓	?		✓	✓		✓	✓		✓	
	Thunder Bay	✓	✓	✓		✓	?	✓	✓	✓		✓		✓	✓
	St Louis Bay/River	✓	✓			✓	?	✓	✓	✓	?	✓		✓	
	Torch Lake	✓	✓												
	Deer Lake–Carp Creek/River								✓						
Michigan	Manistique River		✓					✓	✓	✓		✓		✓	
	Menominee River	✓	✓					✓	✓	✓		✓		✓	
	Fox River/Southern Green Bay	✓	✓	✓	✓	?	✓	✓	✓	✓	?	✓	✓		
	Sheboygan River	✓	✓	✓	✓	✓	✓	✓	✓			✓			
	Milwaukee Estuary	✓	✓	✓	✓	✓	✓	✓	✓	✓		✓		✓	
	Waukegan Harbor	?	✓	✓			?	✓	✓	✓	?	✓	?		
	Grand Calumet River/Indiana Harbor Canal	✓	✓	✓	✓	✓	✓	✓	✓	✓	✓	✓	✓	✓	✓
	Kalamazoo River	✓	✓	?			?	✓	✓			✓		✓	
	Muskegon Lake	✓	✓	?	✓		?	✓	✓			✓	✓	✓	
	White Lake	✓	✓	?	✓		✓	✓		✓		✓	✓	✓	
Huron	Saginaw River/Bay	✓	✓		✓				✓		✓				
	Collingwood Harbour													✓	
	Severn Sound	✓	?					✓				✓			
	Spanish Harbour	✓	?				?	?	✓	✓		✓			✓

Table 7.1
Great Lakes areas of concern: impaired uses (Continued)

| Water body | Area of concern | Use impairment categories[a] | | | | | | | | | | | | | |
| | | Ecological health and reproduction[b] | | | | | | Habitat[c] | Human health[d] | | Human use/welfare[e] | | | | |
		(3)	(6)	(13)	(8)	(4)	(5)	(14)	(1)	(10)	(2)	(7)	(9)	(11)	(12)
Erie	Clinton River	✓	✓	✓	✓	✓		✓	✓	✓		✓	✓	✓	✓
	Rouge River	✓	✓	✓	✓	✓		✓	✓	✓		✓	✓	✓	✓
	River Raisin	✓	✓						✓			✓			
	Maumee River	✓	✓		✓	✓	✓	✓	✓	✓		✓	✓	✓	✓
	Black River	✓	✓	?	✓	✓	✓	✓	✓	✓	?	✓		✓	✓
	Cuyahoga River	✓	✓	?	✓	✓	?	✓	✓	✓	?	✓	?	?	
	Ashtabula River	✓	✓		✓	✓		✓	✓	✓		✓	✓	✓	
	Presque Isle Bay	?	?			✓			✓			✓			
	Wheatley Harbour	?	?		?	?		✓	✓	✓		✓			
Ontario	Buffalo River	?	✓				?	✓	?		?	✓	✓		
	Eighteen Mile Creek	?	?	✓				?	?			?			
	Rochester Embayment	✓	✓	✓	✓	?	✓	?	✓	✓	?		✓	✓	✓
	Oswego River	✓	?	?	✓	?	?		✓	✓				?	?
	Bay of Quinte	✓	✓	✓	✓	?		✓	✓			✓		✓	✓
	Port Hope								✓			✓		✓	
	Metro Toronto	✓	✓	?	✓	?	?	✓	✓	✓		✓	✓	✓	✓
	Hamilton Harbour	✓	✓		✓	✓	✓	✓	✓	✓		✓	✓	✓	✓
Connecting channels	St Marys River	✓	✓			✓		✓	✓	✓		✓	✓	✓	✓
	St Clair River	✓	✓	?		?		✓	✓		?	✓	✓	✓	✓
	Detroit River	✓	✓		✓	✓		✓	✓	✓		✓	✓	✓	✓
	Niagara River (Ontario)	✓	✓				?	✓	✓	✓		✓	✓	✓	✓

Table 7.1
Great Lakes areas of concern: impaired uses (Continued)

Water body	Area of concern	Use impairment categories[a]														
		Ecological health and reproduction[b]						Habitat[c]	Human health[d]		Human use/welfare[e]				
		(3)	(6)	(13)	(8)	(4)	(5)	(14)	(1)	(10)	(2)	(7)	(9)	(11)	(12)
	Niagara River (New York)	?	✓	✓		✓	?	✓	✓			✓			
	St Lawrence River (Cornwall)	✓	✓	?	✓	✓	✓	✓	✓	✓	?	✓	✓	✓	
	St Lawrence River (Massena)	?	?			?	?	✓	✓						✓

SOURCE: Adapted from Progress in Great Lakes Remedial Action Plans, 1994, DF: 6/8/94.

a The Great Lakes Water Quality Agreement lists 14 beneficial uses that may be impaired and in need of restoration. The four general categories contain 14 impairments that are identified by number in the subsequent footnotes, based on the sequence in which they appear in the agreement.

b Degradation of fish and wildlife populations (3); degradation of benthic populations (6); degradation of phytoplankton and zooplankton (13); undesirable algae/eutrophication (which may cause low dissolved oxygen levels and may, in turn, cause other impairments) (8); fish tumours and other deformities (4); bird or animal deformities or reproduction problems (5).

c Fish and wildlife habitat (14).

d Restrictions on fish and wildlife consumption (1); beach closings (bacteria) (10).

e Restrictions on fish and wildlife flavour (2); restrictions on dredging (7); taste and odour in drinking water (9); degradation of aesthetics (11); added costs for agriculture or industry (12).

? = impairments being investigated.

pathological abnormalities, tumours, and reproductive abnormalities in well-studied species such as the herring gull have been observed. Pharmaceuticals represent a major threat. Birth control pills and increased estrogen levels in animals are leading to feminization of a number of species. Some newer chemicals such as flame retardants, chlorinated paraffins, and pesticides currently pose additional problems. Many persistent toxics reside in sediments and represent pollution loadings from previous years and generations.

Thirty-eight of the forty-three AOCs have restrictions on dredging because of the potential impacts of toxic pollutants in sediments. In-place contaminated sediments can have direct impacts on aquatic life, such as fishes, and these may get redistributed through the food chains. Indirect impacts can occur when sediments are resuspended (through ship movements) or dredged and dumped in confined disposal facilities or shallow waters and on beaches. Unless in-place treatments of contaminated sediments are possible, sediments must be dredged and then normally coupled with biological, chemical, or thermal treatment technologies. Typical contaminants in the sediments of AOCs are heavy metals, polyaromatic hydrocarbons (PAHs) and polychlorine biphenyls (PCBs) caused by industrial discharges, as well as persistent pesticides and herbicides from non-point sources. Many point source controls are ineffective against toxic discharges, and municipal sewage treatment plants rely on metals and organic chemicals attaching themselves to suspended sediments in the effluent, which can then be drained and landfilled.

Eutrophication Loadings of total phosphorus are at good or restored levels under the Water Quality Agreement targets. These objectives were also achieved by 1990 for total phosphorus concentration in open water. Outside some twenty-one AOCs, levels of chlorophyll a are also considered as good or restored. Levels of dissolved oxygen, outside Lake Erie's central basin in the summer months, are similarly restored. Nitrate-plus-nitrate levels for the open lakes show some increases, however, especially for Ontario.

Human Health Effects Thirty-five of the AOCs have fish consumption advisories, as noted above. The impacts of toxic substances in general on humans are both complex and uncertain. Several recent studies associate increased tissue levels of toxic substances with reproductive, developmental, neurological, endocrinological, and immunological effects. And studies have linked PCB (and some other organochlorides) levels in blood plasma with the consumption of fish. Ontario and the Great Lakes states have had fish-consumption advisories (recommended portions per annum) since the 1970s. Twenty-four AOCs have beach closures or recreational body contact restrictions as a result of pathogenic pollution. Forty-four per cent of Canadian Great Lakes beaches are closed for at least some of the three summer months (June–August), and 23 per cent of US beaches are also closed on the same basis. (Monitoring of beaches varies by jurisdiction, as do criteria for closures.) There is some more recent evidence and concern that the use of chlorine as a major cheap disinfectant in water supply systems from the lakes (as well as sewage inputs) is associated with bladder and colon cancers. The dose-response linkages remain unclear, however.

This suite of indicators provides a cursory overview of the pollutant impacts of waste disposal from the humans and their activities throughout the Great Lakes Basin. Particular sites, including Hamilton Harbour, can differ. We will now examine the Hamilton case to see how pollution can differ from site to site.

HAMILTON HARBOUR POLLUTION AND WASTES

Hamilton Harbour[*] itself lies at the western edge of Lake Ontario, the deepest and most populated lake on the Canadian side of the whole Great Lakes Basin. The harbour measures 40 square kilometres and is accessible to the lakes by a human-made ship canal (completed in 1830) through a natural sandbar. The watershed of 500 square kilometres is divided by three main tributaries. The harbour itself was, over time, reduced in size by 25 per cent, and this phenomenon was replicated throughout the urbanized portion of the Great Lakes.

The watershed has a population of more than 500 000 residents, 95 per cent of whom live in urban locations and 60 per cent in the older central city of Hamilton. Manufacturing accounts for 56 per cent of employment, including that provided by the largest concentration of iron and steel industries in Canada. These industries, in turn, support the largest commercial port on the Great Lakes, with over a thousand vessel arrivals per annum.

---

[*]   The discussion and evidentiary basis for this section can be found in Sproule-Jones, 1993, chapter 9, but updated with recent Remedial Action Plan Reports.

Some 25 per cent of the harbour is reclaimed land, and only 25 per cent of the wetlands that existed in 1800 still remain. Seven industrial and four municipal waste point source discharges account for 27 billion gallons of liquid waste, or 40 per cent of the volume of harbour waters. Water quality concerns include elevated levels of phosphorus, ammonia, heavy metals, and polyaromatic hydrocarbons (coal tar). There is some evidence that many water quality parameters (measures), such as dissolved oxygen levels, have improved in the last forty years as a result of pollution controls.

The state of Hamilton Harbour differs from the Great Lakes in five key ways:

1 The dissolved oxygen levels in the harbour vary by season, and levels in the water column, unlike Lake Ontario levels generally, where dissolved oxygen levels are at saturation as a result of natural re-aeration from the atmosphere. In the harbour the water levels stratify in the summer months, preventing the natural circulation and re-aeration of waters (see figure 7.2).
2 Water clarity in the harbour can now exceed 2 metres in places. Before 1995, suspended solids discharged from the sewage-treatment plants (STPs) and the steel mills on the waterfront could obscure sunlight and hence plant growth.
3 Pathogens come largely from the STPs and from storm drains (many of which take sewage overflow on rainy days). As a result, water contact sports are banned, and beaches frequently closed.
4 Hamilton Harbour is nutrient-rich as a result of phosphorus loadings and basin retention times. The peak years occurred in the late 1960s, and loadings from the STPs and the steel mills were slashed in the 1970s and 1980s. But eutrophication has been radically slowed because dissolved oxygen levels, water clarity levels, and elevated concentrations of iron in the water column (which are converted into ferrous phosphate, a non-nutrient) have masked nutrient impacts.
5 Heavy metals and toxic compounds are harder to measure in the water column than in sediments. Some ten heavy metals are found in provincial Ministry of Environment levels (objectives), but concentrations of persistent organics such as PCBs and PAHs are at alarming levels in particular hot spots, as we shall see below.

The consequences of these pollutants will be familiar to many; among these are that six of twelve sport-fish species have elevated levels of mercury, PCBs, and mirex, such that limited consumption is officially

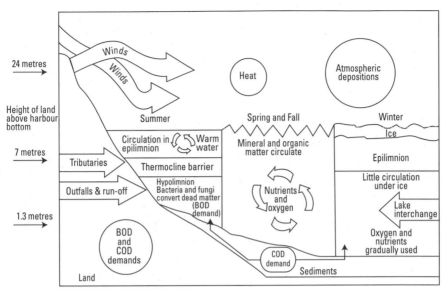

Figure 7.2 Water circulations in Hamilton Harbour.

advised; some trace contaminants are detectable in herring gull eggs and in the tissue of flightless domestic ducks; and human health effects seem to mirror those found throughout the Great Lakes Basin.

INSTITUTIONS IN THE HAMILTON HARBOUR ENVIRONMENTAL MANAGEMENT SYSTEM

This description of the state of the environment in the Great Lakes and in Hamilton Harbour gives no real picture of the key organizations and actors associated with the politics of waste disposal. With millions of people living and working in the basin and with thousands of businesses, local governments, and non-profit organizations all using products and services that create residuals and other leftovers, the number of potential political actors seems overwhelming. We can distinguish between actors that own and can potentially sell property (such as water, land, food, widgets, and services) and actors that can regulate others when they dispose of unneeded wastes. The former have property rights and can include governments (especially provincial governments under Canada's constitution) as well as private organizations. The regulators are normally government agencies at federal, provincial, or local levels, but occasionally businesses will "organize" themselves through business

associations such as Responsible Care, the arm of the Canadian Chemical Producers Association. With the exception of some twenty-five toxic
compounds regulated by the federal government under the Canadian
Environmental Protection Act as products that cannot be used unless
proven safe to do so, the activities of other actors are permissible unless
governed in some way by a regulatory agency. Most regulation in
Ontario is handled through the provincial Ministry of the Environment
(MOE) unless delegated to a municipality or expressly shared with a federal agency such Environment Canada, the Canadian Environmental
Assessment Agency, or Fisheries and Oceans Canada. A premium is
placed on negotiated implementation, fair administrative processes, ver-
ifiable impacts of regulation, and intergovernmental coordination when
two or more agencies and/or levels of government are drawn into the
regulatory processes. In the case of international waters, of course, the
activities of US agencies such as the Environmental Protection Agency
and international agencies such as the (largely advisory) International
Joint Commission can affect property owners and residents and their
uses of resources.

   In Hamilton Harbour the usual actors are evident. The Ontario Ministry of the Environment regulates emissions from point sources directly
into harbour waters or into the air by using certificates of approval (effluent permits). The adjacent municipalities (Hamilton and the Region of
Halton) operate STPs and regulate the households and firms that discharge into the sewer systems. Eleven pipes owned by landowners on the
harbour discharge wastes into the bay; the most significant (in volumes
and composition) are owned by Steel Company of Canada (since a 2007
buyout, it is officially called US Steel Canada, but we will use the older
shortened and more recognizable name Stelco) and Dominion Foundry
and Steel Company (Dofasco, now ArcelorMittal). Environment Canada
(EC) is involved as the major regulator of toxic wastes (especially air
emissions in Hamilton) and as the principal stakeholder and coordinator
of the remediation of the harbour under the IJC cleanup processes mentioned above. The other key actor is the Hamilton Port Authority
(HPA), a successor organization to the Hamilton Harbour Commissioners,
which has managed commercial shipping and associated industrial lands
since 1911. The HPA owns the bed of the harbour and many of the water
lots adjacent to the foreshore (much of which it also owns). It has large
potential powers because the courts have declared that shipping and navigation is a use that trumps all other uses of the harbour and lakes. Thus
the Hamilton Harbour Commissioners were able to successfully reclaim

most of the productive marshlands of the harbour (especially between World Wars I and II) in order to construct lands for industrial development. This took place notwithstanding the ostensible environmental protections provided by the federal Fisheries Act. The only other major actors are the two municipalities that collect and partially treat or remove water pollution in their sewage treatment plants. The larger one is the city of Hamilton, and the other is the Region of Halton, which services the sewage and water needs of the city of Burlington on the northern shores of the bay. Under a remedial action plan, these major actors and some other public bodies are grouped into a Bay Area Implementation Team (BAIT) with designated functional (voluntary) responsibilities. A Bay Area Restoration Council provides an organizational means for citizen and interest-group stakeholders/users to articulate their interests in public and comment on the remediation progress.

Remedial action plans (RAPs) were and are established for the aforementioned forty-three areas of concern on the Great Lakes. In 1985 the IJC asked the governments of Canada and the United States to organize stakeholders in each area to develop a plan to restore the impaired beneficial uses particular to each AOC. Local stakeholders were to be included and resource interdependencies recognized within an ecosystem planning approach. RAPs were to identify problems and solutions in the sites (stage 1), develop implementation strategies (stage 2), and report on the successful remediation of beneficial uses (stage 3). Hamilton is currently at stage 2, and the original target date for stage 3 appears to be highly optimistic.

The Hamilton pattern of organization is not atypical of the environmental management system found in urbanized bays and harbours in Ontario, and the key actors and legal powers of governments are comparable. The access of citizen and group stakeholders to the environmental management system is more structured and systematic in the Hamilton case, with its Bay Area Restoration Council as a confederation of forty or more stakeholder groups. There is some concern in other AOCs that Hamilton enjoys a preferred status as the result of the direct funding of a BAIT coordinator from Environment Canada, rather than from provincial funds. However, two other AOCs in Ontario also enjoy this status.

We will now look how the multiple agencies and members of the public operate. There have been successful cases of remediation in Hamilton, such as restoring fish and bird habitat and deploying tighter standards from point sources of effluent (the pipes coming from

municipal sewage-treatment plants and from industrial operations located on the bay). Our case was selected to show how conflicts occur
between different interests and how a particular group of interests (the
waste disposers, the port authorities, and the federal public servants)
seem to win over environmental and recreational interests whenever
such conflicts occur.

THE CASE OF RANDLE'S REEF

Randle's Reef is a natural rocky reef some 5 to 8 metres underwater near
a shipping pier used for the offloading of coal and owned by Stelco. The
reef and surrounding harbour bed form a water lot owned by the Hamilton Port Authority. An outfall from the steel company discharges into the
region, and a spill from the company was certified as appropriately
dredged and removed by the Ontario Ministry of the Environment in
1984. The HPA also reports that it conducted shipping-lane maintenance
dredging in adjacent waters in the late 1980s but that its paperwork is
now missing. However, interviews reveal that the dredged material was
shipped to an industrial landfill in Sarnia, Ontario, and classified as
hazardous waste.

In 1988 the Randle's Reef area was characterized as a sediment "hot
spot" by scientists at the National Water Research Institute (an agency
of Environment Canada), and the Remedial Action Plan of 1991 recommended it be remediated through removal and treatment or through in
situ treatment. Like many other AOCs, Hamilton Harbour revealed extensive sediment contamination, with hot spots adjacent to the steel
companies and to sewage-treatment outfalls (see figure 7.3).

The sediments at Randle's Reef were contaminated largely by coal tar
compounds and metals. The PAH levels exceeded 800 parts per million
in some sediment cores, levels only exceeded in Canada at the infamous
Sidney Tar Ponds in Nova Scotia (figure 7.4). Many metals (especially
iron) exceeded MOE "severe effect levels," and detectable levels of
PCBs, dioxins, furans, and organochlorines are present. The problem is
compounded by wave action from ships berthing nearby and redistrib-
uting the sediments across the harbour bed.

By 1994 Environment Canada, in consultation with the MOE, had devised a plan to remove some 30 000 cubic metres, or approximately the
volume of sediments at Randle's that exceeded 800 parts per million. At a
public meeting of the Bay Area Restoration Council (BARC), over a

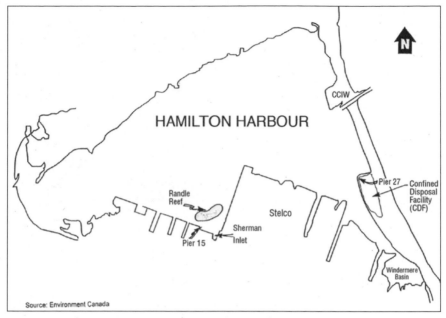

Figure 7.3 Sediment contamination in Hamilton Harbour.

hundred stakeholders and citizens unanimously endorsed this cleanup strategy. Now the politics really began. As in all organizational processes, a key person is mandated to deal with negotiating and implementing corporate strategy. This person develops a virtual veto power over organizational responses as a result of his/her mandate, information, and staff loyalty.

Naturally, successful individuals scan their own environment to ensure that their power base is continually reconfirmed "in house." The key actors for Randle's Reef became the director of Environmental Conservation (or EC, as it was called throughout most of this history) for the Ontario region and two other locally based public servants (the RAP coordinator and the Sustainability Fund manager); the regional director for the South Central Region of the MOE; the manager (later vice-president) of Environmental Services at Stelco; and the former and current port manager (now named president) of HPA. These persons engaged in a series of bilateral and multilateral discussions over many months and years. They also helped to form the core membership of a Randle's Reef Remediation Steering Committee with other invited stakeholders.

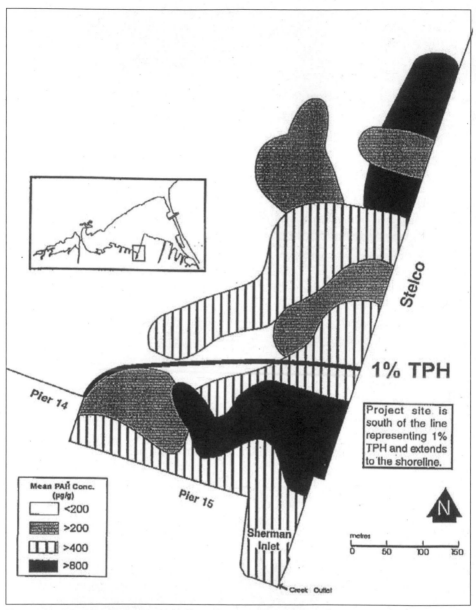

Figure 7.4 Mean concentration of polynuclear aromatic hydrocarbons in Randle's Reef, 1994.

In terms of strategies, EC early in the process determined it did not want to risk losing a court case against Stelco for violating the *Fisheries Act*; it had no unambiguous proof that the contaminated sediments may not have originated from another point or from non-point sources. Stelco naturally argued for its innocence. EC also wanted to demonstrate that it could engage in productive partnerships with industries such as Stelco and provincial agencies such as the MOE. It thus proposed a three-way split of the cleanup costs. Interestingly, this was neither government policy nor was it endorsed by senior management. Stelco refused to endorse any plan (at this stage). The MOE let EC take the lead and later moved its request for support to a political level. The 1990s were an era of cutbacks at all levels of government, and the MOE found its resources reduced by 40 per cent in the mid-decade. Thus special political intervention was needed to keep it as a key actor. The HPA was content at this stage to allow the parties to consider an empty pier a site for remedial work. It made no financial contribution.

The logjam was broken by a public announcement in June 1995 by the federal minister of the environment (who was also a Hamilton MP). She discovered, in her briefing notes in a car on the way to a public meeting, that some $5 million of a federal Great Lakes Cleanup Fund was going to be spent on the Randle's Reef cleanup. She then made the announcement and publicly demonstrated her skill at delivering needed pork barrel. The allocation of funds had in fact bypassed normal channels in EC headquarters (and in the Privy Council Office) and gone straight to the minister's political office from the Great Lakes Cleanup Fund office. EC was now publicly committed by pre-emptive local bureaucratic action. The MOE was virtually committed by mid-summer too. The Ontario minister of corrections (a local MP) gave a verbal commitment to the BARC president that the $5 million would be matched at the provincial level. One week later, however, an election was called, and four weeks later a new provincial government was elected. Stelco just sat tight and waited for public-sector largesse. Within a year, the new provincial government had contributed $1 million.

EC now began a "comprehensive study," which is an analysis of technical options required under the Canadian Environmental Assessment Act. A review of sixteen technical options by the steering committee resulted in a recommended option for dredging, dewatering, treatment, and reuse, with estimated costs ($15 million) attached to these processes. Significantly, the port authority vetoed any infill option on the site as contrary to its navigational interests.

Stelco moved to the offensive. Letters to the president of Stelco from the regional director of EC had requested fulfillment of the three-way split of the cleanup costs advanced by EC bureaucrats. Stelco was backed into a corner. It changed strategy. In meetings with EC, it pressed for a removal of the RAP coordinator and author of the comprehensive study from the Randle's Reef process, a freeze on the release of the comprehensive study and its preferred recommendation, and an examination of two new technical options involving incineration of the sediments in Stelco's scrap metal furnace. EC complied, of course, except that the first request took a while to finesse. Needless to say, the remediation process stalled.

But Stelco did not stall. In February 1997 it convened a meeting of the twelve largest employers in Hamilton in a venerable downtown private club, incidentally only accessible to women in recent years. It announced that the RAP should be abolished as it had "lost the confidence of the community." The RAP would be replaced by an endowment of $1 million provided by the employers' group. This proposal was rejected.

Another strategy was needed. By the fall of 1997 and into 1998, Stelco was pushing for EC, the MOE, the HPA, and Stelco to form a consortium to use untendered outsourcing (to Stelco client organizations) for the necessary cleanup work. This was only twenty years after a commissioner on the Harbour Commission had been jailed for dredging kickbacks. This time EC did not comply. The Department of Justice legal advisers to EC questioned the legality of such contracts.

By 1999 another new option was being promoted, studied, and pushed by Stelco and EC, this time acting bilaterally. This was for the incineration option mentioned above. However, a Stelco union local (1006 of the Steelworkers Union) objected, even before the required public consultation, on the grounds that incineration would increase dioxin and furan emissions (albeit in non-measurable amounts). EC was in another dilemma. It was coincidentally trying to establish objectives for sintering plants as part of a national process for managing air emissions (Stelco had the only sintering – scrap-metal – furnace in Canada). EC could have been accused of helping to pay for increased air pollution by Stelco, while at the same time making it more difficult to limit the polluted air. So it nixed the proposal.

By 2001 EC had begun again. The two local EC officials reorganized the defunct steering committee, and with judicious attention to detail, it now constituted a new "Project Advisory Group." This group consists of seventeen public servants, two Stelco managers, one Stelco unionist, five neighbourhood community representatives, two representatives from BARC, and one environmentalist. The composition of the group was rationalized as being full of technical experts no matter what their organizational allegiances. The deck was thus loaded for a "consensual decision" by supporters of the EC strategy. EC officials promote the preferred remediation favourite of the director: namely, "confine, fill, and cap," which meant dumping more contaminated sediments on top of Randle's Reef and then covering it all with a clay soil and an asphalt hard surface. The EC officials privately persuaded the HPA that the port official policy against aqua fill on navigational grounds should be removed in view of potential port-pier expansion on the new infill. They then persuaded the MOE and other public officials that an aqua fill could collect contaminated sediments from other sites. The city of Hamilton was easy to persuade. It had budgeted $10 million for removal of sediments emitted into a smaller sub-basin near its STP. (Suspended solids are a major component of municipal treatment plant emissions and are themselves frequently bound to persistent organic chemicals discharged into the sewer system itself). The Project Advisory Group could then approve the new plans for the reef, with only one vote (that of the environmentalist) dissenting. At a later strategic time, the EC officials and the group inflated the initial size of the proposed dump from 9 to 50 acres of infill in order to make the site commercially viable for the port. In the next three years, almost $2 million of public funds were spent on studies estimating the scope of dredge material from different sites in the harbour and the technical issues involved in transportation and dumping. By 2006 the original project to remove 30 000 cubic metres (revised early to 20 000) had transformed itself into a shipping pier made up of 630 000 cubic metres of contaminated sediments, a clay overlay, and a hard surface surrounded by steel walls built by Stelco (perhaps an in-kind contribution).

The saga continues. Currently, EC is satisfied that a project has been agreed upon. The MOE is content that EC is taking the lead and the potential criticism. Stelco is ecstatic; it has spent twenty years successfully avoiding liability for the Randle's Reef contamination. The HPA now gets another fifty-acre pier for shipping and leasing. And the public purse gets to contribute $90 million to bury contaminated wastes in a water environment, untreated and reserved for future generations to deal with. In an environmental management system where the key actors are largely confined to industry, bureaucracies, and commercial shipping ports, we should perhaps expect no better. The closed nature of environmental/pollution control in Hamilton and on the Ontario side of the Great Lakes basin is not atypical of environmental management across the country.

Efforts by Environment Hamilton, an environmental interest group, and the Sierra Legal Defence Fund (now Ecojustice) to get the bureaucracies to reconsider their strategies and financing have been unsuccessful. Federal Fisheries and Oceans claims that since no fish spawn or swim around the contaminated sediments, the Fisheries Act does not apply. The only fish that try suffer burns to fins and skins. EC claims that since the aqua fill site can be used for commercial shipping, it is consistent with sustainable development, notwithstanding the case of future generations.

There are no really effective appeals on decisions made under this system, except to a political level, and ministers are constantly persuaded by public officials that they need to avoid discussion on "technical" issues. Most technical issues have major political considerations, however. Not the least of these is financial in nature. In August of 2007, two months before a provincial election, the Ontario Liberal government announced that it would donate $30 million to the "burial" of Randle's Reef, thus illustrating the primary incentive and concerns of ministers and governments. This contribution was matched by the federal government in November 2007. In this milieu, even appeals to the courts are generally limited to "due process" appeals, which are difficult to invoke in an organizational system where documents can get shredded and agreements made without written acknowledgments.

CONCLUSION

We use the natural environment to dispose of wastes, some treated, some partially treated, and some just benign junk. The Great Lakes, which were once known for their fisheries and recreational attributes, were a convenient location for industry and municipalities to dispose of wastes. Gradually, through legislation and tenacious interest-group activity, regulations on discharges were revised, implemented, improved, and reimplemented, and institutional arrangements evolved accordingly. The process was slow and focused on point sources. We have, however, been able to document the impacts on the water quality and on the living systems, whether in a large environmental site such as the Great Lakes or in smaller sites such as Hamilton Harbour. The results all appear negative.

In the light of these impacts, governments claim to have refocused on both remediation and pollution prevention strategies. In practice, however, there remain major disputes. These are signalled by continual fights between and among the stakeholders: the industrial polluters, the municipal polluters, the Environment Canada bureaucrats, the provincial bureaucrats, the port and shipping interests, the recreation interests, the environmental NGOs, and others. The alliance between government bureaucrats and industry bureaucrats seems to trump others. The Randle's Reef case is one of remediation, but similar struggles occur between actors over discharge permits and amendments to these permits.

In the case of Randle's Reef, we saw how the actors included both federal and provincial organizations, with Environment Canada taking the lead role in negotiating with Stelco and devising a solution acceptable to government and waste disposer. Other government agencies were included to the degree that their agreement to the technical solutions to Randle's might involve a government permit, such as a navigable waters permit from the Canadian Coast Guard or a letter of consent from Fisheries and Oceans Canada. The port authority, as a property owner of the reef, of adjacent fast lands, and of potentially a new large pier, was obviously a natural participant. Environmental groups were initially active but got reduced to minor players through the strategic realignment of advisory groups. Interestingly, the other major steelmaker on the waterfront, ArcelorMittal, is agreeing to planning, financing, and implementing its own solution to the removal and treatment of contaminated sediments in its shipping lanes.

The decision forums in this case were plural, sometimes bilateral, sometimes in a small group, sometimes in chosen larger groups of user interests, and sometimes in large public meetings of eight hundred or more citizens. The process was initially organized by BARC after EC reviewed scientific evidence about sediments in formulating the first RAP. EC soon took charge after concerns were raised by Stelco about the direction of negotiations. EC and Stelco bargained as equals and secured a solution that would gain the support of the port authority and the city of Hamilton. Other users of the harbour, including the environmentalists, were discounted or excluded from the forums.

In sum, pollution control is a political process in which dischargers are accustomed to the freedom to negotiate limits on their pollution activities. On the Great Lakes the limits have been minimal, at least until recently. Public agencies and dischargers have developed long-standing alliances, and the rights of dischargers are reflected in institutional arrangements. Agreements between public agencies and dischargers are negotiated with limited public scrutiny and despite the interests of other users in a multiple-use site. Conflicts are resolved by a strategy of search for and agreement on a so-called technical solution amenable to waste disposer and regulator. Courts and ministers are perceived as unpredictable and best avoided. The big picture, such as sustainable development, is not on the agenda.

8

Non-point Source Water Pollution Institutions in Ontario before and after Walkerton

CAROLYN JOHNS

In some instances, the multiple and conflicting uses of water and the shortcomings of existing institutional arrangements are not fully or publicly recognized until a serious problem or crisis emerges. This was the case with the Walkerton water tragedy in May 2000, when agricultural runoff contaminated the local drinking-water supply with E. coli O157:H7 bacteria, resulting in widespread illness and seven deaths in the community. The complex causes of this tragedy highlight the variety of institutions and policy instruments involved in water governance and the significant implications of agricultural uses for drinking-water supply and water quality. This chapter recounts how the Walkerton tragedy focused unprecedented political attention on the issue of drinking-water pollution, highlighted conflicting water uses, and resulted in some reform of the institutions, policies, and policy instruments used to regulate water resources in the name of human health and clean drinking water. The Walkerton case is a good example of how relatively mundane water management issues can be vaulted into the political spotlight and reveal conflicting water rights, uses, and choices for policy-makers. It is also a case that highlights the challenges of changing water management institutions, even in the context of public pressure and political commitment.

INTRODUCTION

As in all jurisdictions across Canada, surface water and groundwater are key natural resources for a number of different users and uses in

Ontario. Much of the province's historic settlement patterns, industrial development, and economic growth derive from water resources. All of the multiple uses outlined in chapter 1 are significant in Ontario and have been central to its economic progress. Surface water and groundwater are important sources for agriculture, commercial development, industrial production, a variety of domestic uses, and drinking water. Of the province's population of 11 million, 8 million residents have their drinking water supplied from a water-treatment facility. The rest of the population get their water from municipal or private wells. An urban population of approximately 1.5 million is dependent on groundwater, and an additional 1.3 million rural people obtain their water supplies from private wells and groundwater sources. It is estimated that more than 500 000 water wells have been constructed in Ontario since 1945, with an annual addition of 12 000 to 20 000 (Singer et al., 2003).

Walkerton is like many other small communities in Ontario with a mix of water users reliant on surface water and groundwater. It is a community in which agricultural water uses and domestic water uses have for the most part coexisted, but not without impacts on the water quality for human and ecological uses. The tragedy that unfolded in Walkerton in May 2000 illustrates the significant human impacts when water quality is taken for granted and the institutional failure when multiple water uses are not well managed.

The Walkerton tragedy highlighted the fact that policy-makers have to balance these multiple uses and that an imbalance can have serious social, environmental, cultural, and economic costs. As a result of Walkerton, the significance of water for human health and the importance of safe drinking water were brought to the top of the policy agenda. This chapter outlines the institutional arrangements and policy-instrument strategies used in Ontario before and after the Walkerton tragedy to address non-point source water pollution problems and related drinking-water issues. The chapter focuses on the institutions, legislation, policies, and programs in existence prior to the tragedy and how the shift in policy stemming from the Walkerton Inquiry resulted in institutional change and in Ontario adopting a more coercive and less fragmented mix of instruments to address water pollution in the province, particularly related to drinking water.

NON-POINT SOURCE WATER POLLUTION

Some eight years after the events referred to as the Walkerton tragedy and nearly fifty years after the introduction of water pollution legislation in

Canada, water pollution remains an important public policy problem. In most jurisdictions, water pollution management regimes have been developed and designed according to the source of the pollution. As outlined in chapter 1, water pollution can be divided into two broad types: point source and non-point source. "Point source" water pollution refers to inputs into natural ecosystems (such as creeks, rivers, and lakes) that come from easily identifiable "end-of-pipe" sources – for example, industrial effluent and outfall from municipal water- and sewage-treatment facilities. "Non-point source" (NPS) water pollution refers to inputs that come from multiple sources – for example, agricultural waste and pesticide runoff, urban sewage overflow, nutrient and herbicide runoff from golf courses, and runoff of heavy metals and toxic substances that may contribute to surface water and groundwater contamination. The major groundwater sources of pollution are septic tanks, underground storage tanks, abandoned waste and well sites, and NPS surface water contributions (United States, Environmental Protection Agency, 2000). Although in many industrialized countries, non-point sources are recognized as the primary barrier to meeting water quality objectives, policy-makers in Canada, particularly before Walkerton, tended to limit the scope and focus of water pollution management to the more easily identifiable point sources.

Three important aspects of NPS water pollution influence policy approaches, institutional design, and the choice of policy instruments: scale, complexity of sources, and property rights. All three aspects are complicated by the lack of information about NPS water pollution and water resources generally. The first important aspect – namely, scale – is common to all pollution problems. As outlined in chapter 1, ecosystems and watersheds are interconnected at different scales. Hydrology, typography, and seasonality all make water pollution problems highly variable. The total land surface from which a system of streams receives its waters is termed the "drainage basin" or "watershed"; from it the water flows into lakes or oceans as the receiving bodies downstream. Generally, NPS water pollution occurs in the upstream portion of drainage basins and significantly affects the water quality in the receiving body or groundwater downstream. The natural upstream and downstream boundaries of watersheds do not necessarily correspond with political boundaries.

Another important dimension of NPS water pollution is the complexity of sources. By the early 1980s, research in the United States indicated that non-point sources were contributing as much as two-thirds of surface water pollution (United States, Environmental Protection Agency, 1995, 46).

No data are available for Canada or Ontario, but comparable data from the United States indicate that the largest contributor of NPS water pollution by volume is sediment runoff from agricultural land use. The second largest group of sources consists of nutrient loadings (primarily nitrogen, potassium, and phosphorus). The third largest group of sources is made up of pathogens such as coliform bacteria from livestock waste and human waste, either in inadequately treated sewage or in sewage overflows (United States, Environmental Protection Agency, 1995). Other toxic substances such as pesticides, herbicides, and heavy metals also find their way into surface water and groundwater along with runoff. The distinction between point source and non-point source water pollution can be viewed along a continuum (Russell and Shogren, 1993, viii). For example, some agricultural sources such as large manure-management facilities can be regarded as point sources. However, given that a typical watercourse may contain numerous such sources, it can be difficult to identify and attribute specific sources to individual polluters. The sources of NPS water pollution, in comparison with point sources, are diffuse and extremely variable.

Understanding the cross-medium connection between air, land use, and water quality is critical to understanding the source dimension of NPS water pollution problems. Streams, creeks, and rivers are best viewed as fragile ecosystems that are easily affected by human use of land and water. "Streams are the collectors, concentrators and integrators of all the impacts of man on watersheds and they truly reflect whether we know how to manage our environmental affairs" (Larkin, 1974, 14). Virtually any pattern of land use is reflected in the drainage basin. Watersheds are therefore important units of analysis in assessing NPS water quality problems and in implementing solutions, particularly related to the land-water interface. In addition, air deposition can also be a non-point source of water pollution, adding another non-point source dimension to this class of water pollution problems.

Property rights, which are related to the land-use–water quality interface discussed above, are a third important dimension of NPS water pollution. Property rights within a given ecosystem influence, in many ways, the type of institutional arrangements needed and available to manage NPS water pollution problems. As outlined in Part One of this book, in any given watershed, a number of individuals may own property close to a watercourse. Most watercourses can be classified as common-pool resources (CPR). With CPR, one person's use directly reduces the common pool's value to others. For example, if a farmer were using a creek that ran through his property as a water supply for his cattle and as a waste disposal site for his agricultural wastes, his use would directly reduce the quantity and quality of water for users downstream. If all the users of the creek decided to use the watercourse in the same way, the stream would become polluted, and collective action would be required to restore it or prevent a "tragedy" from occurring (Hardin, 1968). This example illustrates a problem that arises when individuals do not cooperate to achieve a goal that is in both their collective and their individual interest to pursue –namely, water quality.

The challenge for policy-makers is to change the rules and design institutions to better manage the creek ecosystem collectively. The rules of water pollution management in Canada have evolved from property rights and common law and ultimately been replaced by regulations and statutes, but NPS pollution challenges the traditional regulatory framework because there is no clear-cut relation or causal link between clearly identifiable polluters and those affected by the pollution (Söllner, 1994, 75). Further complicating the setting of rules and standards for surface waters and groundwater is the difficulty of determining which land user or polluter is responsible – the problem of assigning responsibility (Shortle and Abler, 1997, 114). The actions of the individual, or the discharges caused by these actions, cannot always be observed directly, and thus regulation based on effluent standards is very difficult. In addition, monitoring NPS pollutants is in some cases technically infeasible and in many cases prohibitively expensive (Ribaudo et al., 1999, 26). Different policy instruments have been used in various jurisdictions to address these distinctive dimensions of NPS water pollution.

POLICY INSTRUMENTS USED
TO MANAGE NPS WATER POLLUTION

As outlined in chapter 3, a combination of policy instruments and organizational strategies are typically employed to remedy complex water policy problems. Governments in many industrial countries have used similar policy instruments to deal with water pollution. Although these governments recognize that solving NPS pollution problems is increasingly important in meeting water quality objectives, authorities worldwide and in Canada have tended to limit the scope and focus of pollution management to more easily identifiable point sources (Organisation for Economic Co-operation and Development, 1996; Johns, 2000). Thirty years after legislative action and the development of regulatory regimes, the traditional point source framework is increasingly being criticized for failing to curtail further degradation of water resources. The policy instruments used across Canada to remedy point source pollution are very similar. The preferred instruments have been, first, public spending on the infrastructure for water and sewage treatment and, second, monitoring and regulation of large, stationary industrial and municipal point sources. This is not to say that end-of-pipe regulation and enforcement are not important components of a comprehensive water quality management approach and cannot be improved; however, upstream water pollution inputs – a significant source – demand different public policy approaches and solutions. The challenges are, first, to match appropriate instruments and implementation institutions with the nature of the problems and, second, to shift the approach from treatment and remediation to prevention.

As in the case of point source water pollution, many jurisdictions are using similar instruments to resolve NPS pollution. As Karen Thomas outlines in chapter 3, policy-makers can use a wide range and mix of instruments, including "sticks" in the form of regulation (land use and regulation of agricultural practices, through permits, licences, and prohibitions), "carrots" in the form of economic instruments (subsidies, taxes, and tax incentives), and "sermons," in the form of information or communicative instruments (moral suasion, education, and outreach) (Bemelmans-Videc et al., 1998). The instruments vary in terms of coerciveness, intervention, and design features.

Subsidy-Based Best Management Practices

The most common instruments used to prevent NPS water pollution are different forms of cost-shared subsidies. These instruments are typically designed to subsidize the individual or firm in implementing best management practices (BMPs). BMPs attempt to reduce the likelihood of pollutants entering surface water or groundwater by managing adjacent lands with ecologically sensitive practices (such as protection of stream banks and proper manure and chemical storage) and encouraging alternative agricultural production methods. Public funding of BMP cost-sharing programs covers a variety of temporary and permanent water protection measures. These typically include improving waterway buffers, controlling nutrients and pesticides, stabilizing stream banks and grades to prevent erosion, upgrading wells, constructing and relocating manure storage facilities, erecting livestock fencing, upgrading stormwater runoff facilities, and constructing filtration units and retention basins. The cost-sharing aspect of these instruments requires the individual or firm to partially fund the BMPs at various rates.

Regulation

Since many NPS water pollution problems are directly related to land-use activities, land-use regulation is another instrument that has been used to address these water pollution problems. For example, there are regulatory limitations on the size and location of agricultural operations and land-use restrictions through protective zoning in areas close to sensitive watercourses and groundwater recharge areas. The coercive element of this approach often requires mandatory review, approval, permitting, and licensing processes for different types of current and proposed land uses in a geographic area. Typically, this instrument is implemented at the local level because of the variable nature of land-use patterns across jurisdictions. However, many jurisdictions have not directly linked this instrument to water quality protection and objectives. Nonetheless, land-use regulation is one set of policy tools being used in some jurisdictions to abate NPS water pollution.

Tax Instruments

Taxes are another set of instruments that have been used in the management of NPS water pollution. Negative taxes on certain types of undesirable behaviour are used in some jurisdictions (for example, Sweden, Norway, and Finland have a tax on chemical fertilizers; see Eckerberg, 1997), but tax incentive schemes are more common. These instruments are less direct and attempt to achieve water quality objectives through income and property tax credits and deductions that encourage private protection and stewardship of land and water resources. They are often connected to land-use or land-protection strategies such as conservation easements and covenants. Two-part schemes are applied in some jurisdictions: if pollutant levels exceed a certain limit, the polluter pays a tax on the excess; if the discharges are lower than the set limit, the polluter receives a subsidy or tax credit (Segerson, 1988, 90). In practice, carrots combined with sermons are the preferred instruments to address NPS water pollution problems. The tendency is to use a combination of instruments and implementation arrangements through policy instrument strategies.

NPS WATER POLLUTION MANAGEMENT
IN CANADA AND ONTARIO BEFORE WALKERTON

As outlined in chapter 2, there are several constitutional areas where the federal government has authority related to water pollution management. The emphasis of federal water policy has primarily focused on toxic substances, point source pollution, and other ecosystem-based efforts, such as remediation of water pollution in the forty-three "areas of concern" on the Great Lakes under the Canada–US Great Lakes Water Quality Agreement. As chapter 7 illustrates, the results related to historical point source regulation have been slow and mixed, despite efforts to develop institutions to address water pollution in the Great Lakes. NPS efforts under remedial action plans (RAPs) have also been limited because governments on both sides of the border have focused on the remediation of high-cost point source problems. The federal government has not been actively involved in defining the problem of NPS pollution beyond Environment Canada's role in some basic research on selected watercourses (Canada, National Water Research Institute, 1998). Federal legislation and implementation efforts before Walkerton reflected the federal government's role in research and its emphasis on providing infrastructure funding to manage point source pollution. The federal government has also been involved in the intergovernmental process of developing water quality standards and sponsoring water policy workshops through the Canadian Council of Ministers of the Environment (CCME). As well, as described below, the federal government has been involved in funding some agro-environmental initiatives, but there was no indication in the pre-Walkerton period that this policy position and capacity was changing (Canada, Environment Canada, 2000b; Johns, 2000).

Chapter 2 in this book also highlights the fact that water resource management in Canada is primarily the responsibility of provincial governments. Surface water quality and groundwater quality are primarily dealt with under provincial legislation. Although all provinces have legislation to regulate point sources of water pollution, only British Columbia had a five-year program to deal specifically with NPS water pollution before Walkerton (BC, Ministry of Environment, Lands and Parks, 1999). The economic costs of several NPS-related pollution events resulted in the BC Ministry of Environment, Lands and Parks taking responsibility for implementing the action plan under existing legislation (BC, Ministry of Environment, Lands and Parks, 1999).

Most other provinces, including Ontario, had only indirect instruments to deal with NPS water pollution.

Between 1884 and 1956 the primary legislative instrument in Ontario used to address water quality issues was the Public Health Act (primarily focusing on bacterial pollution). The Ontario Water Resources Commission was established in 1956 under the Ontario Water Resources Act (OWRA) to manage water use and water quality in the province. Although the OWRA granted the minister a broad mandate over surface waters and groundwaters in Ontario, the commission's most significant activities were in financing municipal sewage system development and upgrading. In 1972 the Ontario Environmental Protection Act (EPA) supplemented the OWRA as the basis of water pollution management efforts. Since then the Ontario Environmental Protection Act and the Ontario Water Resources Act have been used interchangeably by Ontario's Ministry of the Environment (MOE) to abate water pollution through regulation of point sources, investments in sewage-treatment facilities, and monitoring systems (Estrin and Swaigen, 1993). This regime indirectly addressed some non-point sources since in urban areas runoff is normally drained into storm sewers and hence transformed into a point source as part of the municipal treatment and effluent system. Overall, the main thrust of Ontario government policy before Walkerton was to regulate point sources of water pollution, not non-point sources (Johns, 2000, 2002).

The MOE has been the lead agency in point source water pollution management, but its efforts to address NPS water pollution were much more limited. Progress in addressing non-point source water pollution management was also impacted by the funding and staff cuts the MOE endured in the 1990s. The ministry's operating budget declined from a high of $454 million in 1989–90 to $164.8 million in 1999–2000. The most significant cuts have been since 1994, bringing the operating budget of the ministry in 1998 dollars down to 1973–74 levels. Staffing levels at the MOE dropped from a high of 2450 in 1990 to 1460 in 1999 (Ontario, MOE, 1999, Krajnc, 2000; Merritt and Gore, 2002; O'Connor, 2002, 1: 414–15).

The province relied largely on its agricultural ministry to manage the largest non-point sources, the agricultural industry. In Ontario the environmental effects of farming practices have been defined as part of agricultural policy rather than environmental policy (Montpetit and Coleman, 1999, 701). Agricultural waste and the negative ecological implications of farming practices were thus not covered directly by

Ontario's Environmental Protection Act but, rather, left to the discretion of the Ministry of Agriculture, Food and Rural Affairs (OMAFRA) under the Farm Practices Protection Act (Montpetit and Coleman, 1999, 701) and other agro-environmental policies and programs based on best management practices. The province used BMPs as a basis of a small subsidy-based instrument strategy.

By the late 1980s the MOE and the OMAFRA did recognize that rural sources of water pollution were an important contributor to water pollution in the province. The Land Stewardship program was initiated by the OMAFRA in 1989 to encourage farmers to make conservation farm plans by using grant incentives. In 1991 the then newly elected New Democratic Party government approved a ten-year $60 million program called Clean Up Rural Beaches (CURB). The program was designed to subsidize farmers to change farming practices to address the problem of beach closures as a result of bacterial contamination. The program began to build organizational capacity to address agro-environmental pollution problems in the government's main environmental agency in partnership with conservation authorities, but it was cancelled with the election of a Conservative government in 1995 (Montpetit and Coleman, 1999, 708).

A movement by farmers in 1992 to take comprehensive action on the environmental impacts that farming has on land and water quality gained momentum when the voluntary Ontario Environmental Farm Plan (EFP) was initiated. The EFP was an initiative by the Ontario Environmental Farm Coalition, a group of farmers' organizations that included the Ontario Federation of Agriculture, the Ontario Farm Animal Council, the Ontario Christian Farmers Federation, and AGCare (Agricultural Groups Concerned about Resources and the Environment). The voluntary program was designed to encourage farmers, through moral suasion and economic incentives in the form of small cost-share subsidies, to implement BMPs (Weersink et al., 1998; Johns, 2000). The goal was to have all forty thousand farmers in Ontario develop and implement EFPs by the year 2000 (Ontario Environmental Farm Coalition, 1997). A subsidy was designed as an incentive for farmers to implement environmental improvements on their farms in the form of livestock fencing around water courses, relocation of manure storage facilities in proximity to water, and similar measures.

Funding for the program originally came from Agriculture Canada under the federal Green Plan and the Canada-Ontario Environmental Sustainability Agreement. A total of $3.9 million from federal Green

Plan funding was earmarked to provide up to $1500 per farm over four years in order to implement EFP action plans (Canada, Agriculture and Agri-Food Canada, 1996). The Ontario Environmental Farm Coalition and the Ontario Soil and Crop Improvement Association were responsible for implementing and administering the program. On termination of the Green Plan in 1995, funding for EFPs in Ontario then came from the CanAdapt Program of the federal government's Canada Agricultural Adaption Council. Provincial support for the program was limited to the MAFRA's role in providing technical assistance and staff time to develop BMP guidelines and technical materials.

The EFP program was designed to deal with a variety of environmental problems at a micro-level. A 1997 report indicated that federal funding had provided $3.4 million in grants and that farmers' contributions were estimated at more than $10 million (Ontario Soil and Crop Improvement Association, 1997). By March 2000 a reported 16 000 farmers had participated in the workshops, 9700 had undertaken the peer review process, and 3000 projects had been completed and funded through the incentive part of the program (Fitzgibon et al., 2000). Although initially farmers were interested in the plan-preparation workshops and the program was technically sound, uptake by farmers tailed off over time, and the objectives of the program were not tied to provincial water quality policies (Johns, 2000).

The Ministry of Natural Resources (MNR) also plays an important policy role in protecting wetlands, forests, fish habitat streams, and other aspects of water resource management in Ontario. It is the primary managing agency for non-agricultural rural land. Like the Ministry of Environment, the MNR has faced significant budget reductions. Its operating budget was reduced from $519 million in 1995 to $364 million in 1999–2000. Budget reductions were reflected in a staff layoff announcement in 1996 that 2170 MNR employees would be eliminated over a two-year period (Kranjc, 2000, 114–15). These reductions in resources have narrowed the focus of the ministry and affected its capacity to contribute to non-point source water pollution management efforts in the province. Increasingly, the ministry has had to devolve its responsibilities to statutory agencies in the province called conservation authorities.

Under the Conservation Authorities Act (1970), which is administered by the MNR, conservation authorities manage flooding and other issues in watersheds in the province. There are thirty-six conservation authorities in Ontario, which existed prior to Walkerton (see figure 8.1). Their functions include the control of potential flood damage and, in many

Figure 8.1 Conservation authorities of Ontario.
SOURCE: Conservation Ontario, 2005.

cases, watershed management, such as planning, education, prevention, treatment, and monitoring. Conservation authorities have a broad range of powers, including the ability to purchase, lease, or expropriate land. They may also make regulations related to flood-plain management within their jurisdiction. Each authority consists of representatives of the provincial government and of each municipality within the watershed. The relevant municipality (or municipalities, if the watershed extends into others) appoints the members. They are financed through user fees, municipal levies, and provincial grants (Canadian Institute for Environmental Law and Policy, 2002). A substantial portion of the province (containing about 10 per cent of the population) is not covered by a conservation authority (CIELP, 2002).

As NPS water pollution is intimately related to land use, land-use planning and regulations are another set of instruments employed to address NPS water pollution problems. Pursuant to enabling legislation under the provincial Planning Act, municipalities in Ontario manage land use on behalf of the province through approved "official plans" (OPs). Local governments are involved in land-use regulation through local bylaws and regulation of land-use designations by means of OPs. Where two tiers of government exist, the lower-level OPs must conform with regional official plans (ROPs) developed by "upper-tier municipalities" or regional governments. In addition, special regional planning authorities – for example, the Niagara Escarpment Commission – deal with planning issues on a larger scale. In some cases, the policies of these authorities take precedence over regional and local planning decisions.

Ecologically sensitive areas, including water resources, are protected through the land-use planning and approvals system. Certain lands have provincial protection through designations such as "provincially significant wetlands," "areas of natural or scientific interest" (ANSIs), and "natural heritage areas." Many ROPs also include designations that regulate development in or close to "environmentally sensitive areas" (ESAS). ESAS are designated ecological areas that are protected on the basis of certain ecological criteria, many of which relate to water quality. Operational rules require that development in or close to ESAS undergo environmental assessment prior to development approval. In some cases, approval of development or a land-use change may be accompanied by conditions or measures designed to protect water quality: for example, setback, buffers, and water quality protection measures during construction. In addition, the Planning Act provides for the establishment of environmental advisory committees composed of volunteers to monitor,

review, and report to municipal or regional planning staff and council-
lors. Under the act, municipalities also have the ability to pass and enforce bylaws related to agricultural operations, such as nutrient
management, but many have not done so.

Early in 2000, prior to the Walkerton tragedy, the Ontario Municipal
Board upheld a municipal zoning bylaw passed under section 34(1) of
the Planning Act permitting municipalities to regulate large or intensive
livestock operations (Mitchell, 2000). The bylaw allows for limits on
the number of livestock units permitted on one site or regulation of manure storage facilities until a nutrient management plan is completed.
Some municipalities were also involved in surface water quality monitoring and watershed and sub-watershed studies and programs in partnership with conservation authorities. Despite the fact that the MOE,
the MNR, and the Ministry of Municipal Affairs had published a document entitled *Integrating Water Management Objectives into Municipal
Planning Documents* prior to Walkerton, land-use planning and management tools were only indirectly connected with provincial water
quality objectives (Johns, 2000).

Tax instruments, land trusts, and conservation easements are another
set of instruments used to address NPS water pollution by encouraging
environmentally responsible management of land adjacent to water
bodies. The incentive for landowners to participate lies in the tax system, primarily income and property tax legislation. The federal Income
Tax Act has permitted "ecological gifts" of land to non-governmental
registered charities, municipalities, and Crown agencies since 1997. The
basis for obtaining these benefits is the appraised market value of the
donated land (Attridge, 1997, ix). Organizations such as conservation
authorities and their spinoff foundations are the primary recipients in
Ontario (Canada, Environment Canada, 1997b, 6). Direct promotion
of these tax measures is still very much linked to land and habitat protection, rather than to water quality management (Johns, 2000).

In Ontario, under the Ontario Heritage Act and the Conservation
Land Act, property tax rebates (pre-1998) and exemptions (post-1998)
have also been used. The MNR determines which lands are eligible under the Conservation Land Tax Incentive Program, and on approval,
landowners receive a full property tax exemption (Ontario, MNR,
1999). Landowners and organizations such as conservation authorities
can also receive property tax exemptions for the lands they own but not
those under easements. Easements held by non-profit land trusts for
land and water quality management have not been a popular tool for

municipal governments and conservation authorities in Ontario. Although used in other jurisdictions, these tools have not been employed in the province to encourage effective land conservation and water quality management (Attridge, 1997, xv; Johns, 2000).

Prior to Walkerton, no specific policy instrument strategies had been initiated to address NPS water pollution problems, though a combination of provincial and municipal policy instruments did deal indirectly with this type of water pollution. Despite the existence of these instruments, the province of Ontario had little institutional capacity to address NPS water pollution compared to other jurisdictions (Johns, 2000). It had few instruments, declining bureaucratic capacity, and very little water quality monitoring capacity (Johns, 2000). Cuts to the MOE (Kranjc, 2000) and the Conservative government's dismantling of environmental policy capacity (CIELP, 2002; Prudham, 2004; McKenzie, 2004) left the province with reduced capacity to address this increasingly important kind of water pollution. In addition, the government used very little of its regulatory power over agriculture to address agro-environmental policy issues (Montpetit, 2002). While conservation authorities in some watersheds tried to fill this gap (Johns, 2000; CIELP, 2002), the institutions and legislative, policy, and existing instruments were weakly designed to address NPS water pollution problems. Even given this context, it would have been difficult to forecast the severity of the public policy crisis that unfolded in May 2000.

THE WALKERTON TRAGEDY AND INQUIRY

As mentioned in the introduction to this chapter, there is little to distinguish Walkerton from many other small towns in Ontario or other provinces. It is an agricultural town located in close proximity to a river and reliant on groundwater as a source of drinking water. In 2000 rain fell heavily in Walkerton from 8 to 12 May, and much of the runoff from this rainfall made its way across the land, into surface water and groundwater, and ultimately into three wells that supplied the town's drinking water. Well no. 5 was a shallow one, supplied by a groundwater source that was under the direct influence of surface water. In the following days, Walkerton's drinking-water system became contaminated with deadly bacteria, primarily *Escherichia coli* O157:H7, seven people died, and more than 2300 in a town of 4800 residents became ill. The economic impacts of the Walkerton tragedy itself were estimated to be more than $64.5 million (Livernois, 2002). This figure does not include the event's great impact in terms of human suffering and loss of life and the environmental costs to ecosystem health. The tragedy sounded alarm bells in Ontario and across Canada about the safety of drinking water and the uses and management of water resources.

The Walkerton Inquiry

In Canada two types of public inquiries have been used by the executive branch of government in relation to policy development and review (D'Ombrain, 1997). Investigative inquiries are quasi-judicial commissions established in response to crisis events and political pressure. Policy inquiries, in contrast, are usually set up as a result of the government's desire to go beyond the confines of the normal policy process. The Walkerton Inquiry was established as an independent commission by the government of Ontario under the Public Inquiries Act in June 2000. Justice Dennis O'Connor was charged in the terms of reference with inquiring into (a) the circumstances of the tragedy; (b) the cause of the events, including the effect if any, of government policies, procedures and practices; and (c) any other relevant matter that the commission considers necessary to ensure the safety of Ontario's drinking water.

As Justice O'Connor stated, "the purpose of the Inquiry is to inquire into and report on what happened and the causes of the tragedy, including how it might have been prevented. It is not unusual for public inquiries to have both an adjudicative-type role, to determine why a particular tragedy occurred, and a forward-looking policy function, to make recommendations so that a similar tragedy will not occur again." O'Connor structured his inquiry in two parts, combining the two general types of inquiries into one. Part 1 was set up as a quasi-judicial investigative inquiry, and Part 2 as a more traditional policy inquiry. The total budget for the two-year inquiry was an estimated $9.5 million, divided roughly equally between the two parts (O'Connor, 2002, 2: chap.16, sec. 16.11).

Although the written terms of reference for the inquiry stated that the inquiry was to focus on drinking water, Part 2 allowed Justice O'Connor to comprehensively examine water resource management in Ontario. In that phase of his inquiry, he undertook a comprehensive review of all aspects of the drinking-water system in the province, including the protection of sources; the treatment, distribution, and monitoring of drinking water; the operation and management of water systems; and the full range of functions involved in the provincial regulatory role. The Part 2 process involved the appointment of a Research Advisory Panel consisting of leading practitioners and academics in the field to assist in determining the topics to be addressed and papers to be commissioned and to offer research advice on the issues being examined by the inquiry (O'Connor, 2002, 2: chap.16). O'Connor granted standing to parties who might be directly affected by the recommendations or represented a distinct viewpoint that needed to be separately represented in that phase (O'Connor, 2002, 2: chap.16). The principal difference between parties with standing and the public was access to some of the documents collected by the commission and the ability to apply for funding. These parties were also were actively involved in writing submissions and in the expert meetings on eleven different issue topics in Part 2. As outlined in table 8.1, thirty-six parties were granted standing in the Part 2 process.

Operation Clean Water

As the inquiry got underway, the Harris government moved quickly to adjust the policy instrument strategies that had failed to protect Ontario's drinking water. One of the first policy responses after Walkerton was Operation Clean Water. The Ontario Drinking Water Objectives were changed to the Ontario Drinking Water Standards (and ultimately the Ontario Drinking Water Protection Regulation under the Safe Drinking Water Act, 2002) for large waterworks,* as regulations under the OWRA in August 2000. Under this initiative, the Harris government also established a provincial groundwater monitoring network, made data from the Drinking Water Surveillance program more available to the public, and initiated consultations on regulation of small waterworks, nutrient management, and groundwater management. The government also commissioned a management review of operations of the MOE from Executive Resource Group (ERG), a consulting firm under the leadership of a former Ontario deputy minister, Valerie Gibbons.

Premier Harris praised *Managing the Environment: A Review of Best Practices* (also known as the Gibbons Report on the Future of the Ontario Ministry of the Environment) when it was released in February 2001, saying that it supported the major changes his government had

---

* Large waterworks are those that use more than 50 000 litres of water per day and serve more than six residences.

Table 8.1
Individuals, groups, and organizations with standing in the second phase
of the Walkerton Inquiry

ALERT/Sierra Club Coalition	Ducks Unlimited Canada	Ontario Métis Aboriginal Association
Association of Local Public Health Agencies	Energy Probe Research Foundation	Ontario Municipal Water Association
Association of Municipalities of Ontario	Government of Ontario	Ontario Pork Producers' Board
	Grand River Conservation Authority	
Azurix North America (Canada) Corp.	Indian Associations Coordinating Committee of Ontario Inc. (Chiefs of Ontario)	Ontario Public Service Employees Union
Bruce-Grey-Owen Sound Health Unit		Ontario Society of Professional Engineers
Canadian Environmental Defence Fund and Pollution Probe Coalitionow	Dr Murray McQuigge	Ontario Water Works Association
	Office of the Chief Coroner of the Province of Ontario	Professional Engineers and Architects of the Ontario
Canadian Union of Public Employees	Ontario Cattle Feeders Association	Public Service
Christian Farmers Federation of Ontario	Ontario Cattlemen's Association	Professional Engineers of Ontario
Concerned Walkerton Citizens/Canadian Environmental Law Association	Ontario Farm Animal Council	Sierra Legal Defence Fund Coalition
	Ontario Farm Environmental Coalition	Uxbridge Conservation Association
Conservation Ontario and the Saugeen Valley Conservation Authority	Ontario Federation of Agriculture	Walkerton and District Chamber of Commerce
Dairy Farmers of Ontario	Ontario Medical Association	Walkerton Community Foundation

SOURCE: O'Connor, 2002, 2: section 16.5.3.

tried to implement. In response, the government established a new cabinet committee on the environment, appointed Elizabeth Witmer minister of the Environment, and hired Bob Breeze, a member of the ERG study team, as associate deputy minister of the environment. In 2001–02 the commitment to moving forward with recommendations in the Gibbons Report were integrated into the MOE's business plan. As the Walkerton Inquiry was underway, senior bureaucrats in the MOE were moving forward with a transition plan for the MOE and referencing the

Gibbons Report. This voluntary approach was in direct contrast to the more regulatory-based approach presented by the government a year later when Justice O'Connor tabled his findings and recommendations. These two distinct and contradictory approaches were simultaneously adopted. The more regulatory approach recommended by O'Connor began to reframe the drinking-water policy regime, and the more voluntary approach continued to be applied in most other environmental policy areas in the province.

O'Connor's Findings and Recommendations

In Part 1 of his report, released in January 2002, Justice O'Connor concluded that "the primary, if not the only, source of the contamination was manure that had been spread on a farm near Well 5" (O'Connor, 2002, 1: 105). The owner of this farm "followed proper practices and should not be faulted in any way. He used what were widely accepted as best management practices in spreading the manure" (O'Connor, 2002, 1: 129). In addition to pinpointing well no. 5 as the source of the contamination, O'Connor also observed that the existing Ontario Drinking Water Objectives (ODWO) had failed in 2000. He stated, "I am satisfied that matters as important to water safety and public health as those set out in these guidelines should instead have been covered by regulations – which, unlike guidelines, are legally binding" (O'Connor, 2002, 1: 30). In addition, O'Connor found that for years, the Public Utilities Commission (PUC) operators, Stan and Frank Koebel, had engaged in a number of improper operating practices, including failing to monitor, false reporting, and ignoring MOE guidelines and directives. And he found that the PUC staff lacked the training and expertise to identify the vulnerability of well no. 5 and that the MOE had taken no steps to inform them of the requirements for continuous monitoring or to require training that would have addressed that issue.

In Part 2 of his report O'Connor stated, "I am satisfied that if the MOE had adequately fulfilled its regulatory and oversight role, the tragedy in Walkerton would have been prevented or at least significantly reduced in scope" (O'Connor, 2002, 2: 00). He concluded that "the most significant deficiencies associated with the MOE relate to the approvals program, the inspections program, the preference for voluntary rather than mandatory abatement, and the water operator certification and training program" (O'Connor, 2002, 2: 00). Recognizing that the MOE had been the target of much attention from the Harris government's

Red Tape Commission (O'Connor, 2002, 1: 393, 464) and that the ministry had been subject to significant resource cuts, he outlined how the MOE's weak regulatory and oversight role contributed to the tragedy. Others have argued that the shortcomings of the MOE stemmed directly from the Harris government's rounds of budget cuts (Kranjc, 2000), anti-regulatory climate (Whorley and Winfield, 2002), preference for voluntary rather than mandatory pollution abatement (Cooper, 2003), and ideological dismantling of environmental policy and administrative capacity (Prudham, 2004; McKenzie, 2004).

Despite the capacity issues of the MOE before the Walkerton tragedy, Justice O'Connor, in Part 2 of his report, recommended that the MOE, not the OMAFRA, be the lead provincial agency with regard to all aspects of providing safe drinking water, including watershed-based source protection. He also recommended that existing institutional arrangements be used to develop and ultimately implement several new pieces of legislation.

THE POLICY AND INSTITUTIONAL RESPONSE

The Safe Drinking Water Act, 2002

In terms of a policy shift, Justice O'Connor's report adopted a multi-barrier approach that involves a series of measures to protect water beginning at its source – whether in underground aquifers or surface waters – all the way through the water-treatment and distribution system, monitoring system, and response system for adverse conditions. This approach was also adopted by the intergovernmental committee of CCME, which develops these standards at the national level (CCME, 2004b). Source protection was identified by O'Connor as the first critical step in a multi-barrier approach. On the basis of this approach, he recommended that the province develop a comprehensive source-to-tap, government-wide drinking-water policy and enact a Safe Drinking Water Act embodying the important elements of that policy. He suggested that the MOE take the lead in developing and implementing the policy to gather all legislation and regulation relating to treatment and distribution of water in one piece of legislation.

The Safe Drinking Water Act (SDWA) was passed in 2002 after broad public consultation under the Environmental Bill of Rights, with input from municipalities, laboratories, health units, waterworks owners, environmental organizations, and other stakeholders. The act's purpose is to

Table 8.2
Walkerton Inquiry recommendations related to safe drinking water

Recommendation 65	The provincial government should develop a comprehensive "source to tap" drinking water policy covering all elements of the provision of drinking water, from source protection to standards development, treatment, distribution, and emergency response.
Recommendation 66	The Ministry of the Environment should be the lead ministry responsible for developing and implementing the "source to tap" Drinking Water Policy.
Recommendation 67	The provincial government should enact a Safe Drinking Water Act to deal with matters related to the treatment and distribution of drinking water.
Recommendation 69	The provincial government should create a Drinking Water Branch within the Ministry of the Environment to be responsible for overseeing the drinking water treatment and distribution system.
Recommendation 80	The Drinking Water Branch should prepare an annual "State of Ontario's Drinking Water Report," which should be tabled in the Legislature.

SOURCE: O'Connor, 2002, 2.

protect human health through the control and regulation of drinking-water systems (including treatment and distribution systems) and testing. It provides legislative authority to implement 50 of the 93 recommendations made in Part 2 of O'Connor's report. The act covers the accreditation of operating authorities and municipal drinking-water systems and drinking-water testing, inspections, compliance, and enforcement. It establishes the authority to set mandatory drinking-water standards, require the certification of all system operators, require mandatory licensing and accreditation of laboratories that perform drinking-water testing, and strengthen compliance and enforcement provisions; creates the new position of chief inspector; and requires the government to submit an annual "State of Ontario's Drinking Water Report" to the legislature (Ontario, MOE, Media Backgrounder, 11 December 2002).

Together with the SDWA, the Eves government introduced the Sustainable Water and Sewage Systems Act, also subject to public consultation under the Environmental Bill of Rights. This piece of legislation was designed to address O'Connor's references to the need for municipalities to ensure that their water systems are fully costed and adequately financed. The act made it mandatory for municipalities to assess and report on the full costs of providing water and sewage services and prepare plans for recovering those costs. It was amended in 2006 and at time of writing was still not in force (Ontario, 2002). When these two pieces of legislation were enacted, they were criticized for not including enough emphasis on source protection, and later, parts were revised under the Clean Water Act, detailed below. The Conservative government also promised that it would move forward in the coming months and address critical agricultural and municipal sources through a new nutrient management policy.

The Nutrient Management Act, 2002

In Part 2 of his report, Justice O'Connor stated, "I envision requiring large farms in all locations and smaller farms in sensitive areas to develop water protection plans for MOE approval. In addition, I recommend that there be minimum regulatory requirements for agricultural activities that create impacts on drinking-water sources. The objective of these recommendations is to ensure that the cumulative effect of discharges from farms in a given watershed remains within acceptable limits. For smaller farms in areas that are not considered sensitive, I recommend continuing and improving the current voluntary programs for environmental protection" (O'Connor, 2002, 2: 10).

In June 2001, a year after the Walkerton tragedy, the Harris government and the MOE put forward the proposed Nutrient Management Act (NMA) for comment. After consultations with interested stakeholders, including agricultural associations, environmental groups, municipalities, and water and waste-water industry groups, the act passed on 27 June 2002. It builds on the largely voluntary system that existed prior to Walkerton by giving current best management practices the force of law and creating comprehensive, enforceable, province-wide standards to regulate the management of all land-applied materials containing nutrients. The act also contains amendments to the Environmental Protection Act, the Highway Traffic Act, the Ontario Water Resources Act, the Pesticides Act, and the Farming and Food Production Protection Act.

The NMA provides a comprehensive nutrient management framework for Ontario's agricultural industry, municipalities, and other generators of materials containing nutrients, including provisions for the development of strong new standards for all land-applied materials containing nutrients, a proposal to ban the land application of untreated septage over a five-year period, and proposed strong new requirements such as the review and approval of nutrient management plans, certification of land applicators, and a new registry system for all land applications (Ontario, MOE, 2005b). Regulatory changes under the act included a ban on the land application of untreated septage over a five-year period, extension of winter spreading restrictions, and a requirement that municipalities prepare a strategy on how they will manage untreated septage. Traditionally, the private sector has collected and managed disposal of untreated sewage, with much of it spread on agricultural land. The other standard disposal method is to take it to a municipal sewage-treatment plant.

The act established the authority of the MOE to develop regulations in three stages. Stages 1 and 2 related to municipal nutrient management plan bylaws and were to be in force by 2003. Stage 3 regulations were to deal with livestock access to waterways, setbacks, and manure haulage, transfer, and disposal. Large livestock operators whose existing operations generate 300 nutrient units or more were required to comply with the Nutrient Management Act by submitting a nutrient management strategy (NMS) by 1 July 2005 for approval. A nutrient management plan (NMP) must then be completed by 31 December 2005, at which time large livestock producers must be compliant with the act. Small farms were not to be covered under the new regulations until 2008 at the earliest.

An NMS sets out an environmentally acceptable method for managing all materials generated at an agricultural or non-agricultural operation. An NMP details how nutrients are to be applied to a given land base. Such a plan is based on both the characteristics of the nutrients and the land to which they are applied. The plans are designed to optimize the utilization of the nutrients by crops in the field and minimize environmental impacts (Ontario, Ministry of Agriculture, Food and Rural Affairs, 2003). They include information on storage, nutrient application, tillage practices, and so on and must be renewed every five years. The role of the OMAFRA was to work with farmers to ensure compliance by allowing them to access financial assistance, communicating the new policy, and providing training courses for farmers who have to prepare NMS/NMPs. Farmers had two options for the preparation of their plans: hire the services of a consultant holding an Agricultural Operation Strategy and Plan Development certificate awarded by the OMAFRA or become certified (or have an employee certified) to prepare their NMS/NMP (Ontario, MAFRA, 2004).

Agricultural organizations have been very suspicious of enforceable regulations to control the storage and spreading of manure. In addition, they do not welcome having to deal with MOE staff but preferred to deal with staff at the OMAFRA. Operators also fret that they will be subject to municipal regulations as many municipal councils have drafted bylaws to control livestock operations. They argue that regulations must be science-based and recognize the variation in farming operations and practices across the province, thereby allowing for more flexibility in the design of their nutrient management strategies and plans. The position of agricultural organizations with regard to the regulatory regime is not surprising or new (Johns, 2000; Montpetit, 2002).

Other stakeholders were critical of the NMA for not incorporating sound, comprehensive source-protection principles. Some argue that the focus on nutrient management in Ontario is not based on science at all and that in other jurisdictions pathogen, not nutrient, abatement is viewed as the way to protect water resources (Stiefelmeyer, 2003). It is interesting to note that, as table 8.3 demonstrates, Justice O'Connor referred to such plans as "farm water protection plans" and argued that large farms and small farms in sensitive areas should be required to develop water-protection plans that were consistent with watershed-based source protection plans.

The Clean Water Act, 2006

Arguably, the most significant and wide-ranging policy shifts were related to Justice O'Connor's recommendations for source protection. On the basis of his terms of reference, O'Connor noted, "I restrict my recommendations to those aspects of watershed management that I think are necessary to protect drinking-water sources, but I want to emphasize that a comprehensive approach for managing all aspects of watersheds is needed and should be adopted by the province" (O'Connor, 2002, 2: 9). He recommend that the province adopt a watershed-based planning process, led by the Ministry of the Environment and by the conservation authorities (where appropriate), and that it involve local actors to develop a source-protection plan for each watershed in the province.

O'Connor also recommended that to "ensure that local considerations are fully taken into account, and to develop goodwill within and acceptance by local communities, source protection planning should be done as much as possible at a local (watershed) level, by those who will be most directly affected (municipalities and other affected local

Table 8.3
Walkerton Inquiry recommendations related to nutrient management

Recommendation 11	The Ministry of the Environment should take the lead role in regulating the potential impacts of farm activities on drinking water sources. The Ministry of Agriculture, Food and Rural Affairs should provide technical support to the Ministry of the Environment and should continue to advise farmers about the protection of drinking water sources.
Recommendation 12	Where necessary, the Ministry of the Environment should establish minimum regulatory requirements for agricultural activities that generate impacts on drinking water sources.
Recommendation 13	All large or intensive farms, and all farms in areas designated as sensitive or high-risk by the applicable source protection plan, should be required to develop binding individual water protection plans consistent with the source protection plan.
Recommendation 14	Once a farm has in place an individual water protection plan that is consistent with the applicable source protection plan, municipalities should not have the authority to require that farm to meet a higher standard of protection of drinking water sources than that which is laid out in the farm's water protection plan.
Recommendation 15	The Ministry of the Environment should work with the Ministry of Agriculture, Food and Rural Affairs, agricultural groups, conservation authorities, municipalities, and other interested groups to create a provincial framework for developing individual farm water protection plans.
Recommendation 16	The provincial government, through the Ministry of Agriculture, Food and Rural Affairs in collaboration with the Ministry of the Environment, should establish a system of cost-share incentives for water protection projects on farms.

SOURCE: O'Connor, 2002, 2.

groups)" (O'Connor, 2002, 2: 9). He argued, "Where possible, conservation authorities should coordinate the plans' local development." Otherwise, the MOE itself should undertake the coordination role. On institutions charged with implementing source protection policies, Justice O'Connor stated:

I have approached the recommendations with a view toward using existing structures and institutions wherever those structures are able to carry out my recommendations. For example, I recommend that the provincial government's responsibility for protecting water

Table 8.4
Summary of Walkerton Inquiry recommendations related to source protection

Source protection (chapter 4)	**Recommendation 1** Drinking water sources should be protected by developing watershed-based source protection plans. Source protection plans should be required for all watersheds in Ontario. **Recommendation 2** The Ministry of the Environment should ensure that draft source protection plans are prepared through an inclusive process of local consultation. Where appropriate, this process should be managed by conservation authorities. **Recommendation 3** Draft source protection plans should be reviewed by the Ministry of the Environment and subject to ministry approval. **Recommendation 4** Provincial government decisions that affect the quality of drinking water sources must be consistent with approved source protection plans. **Recommendation 5** Where the potential exists for a significant direct threat to drinking water sources, municipal official plans and decisions must be consistent with the applicable source protection plan. Otherwise, municipal official plans and decisions should have regard to the source protection plan. The plans should designate areas where consistency is required.
Provincial government (chapter 13)	**Recommendation 7** The provincial government should ensure that sufficient funds are available to complete the planning and adoption of source protection plans. **Recommendation 8** Conservation authorities (or, in their absence, the Ministry of the Environment) should be responsible for implementing local initiatives to educate landowners, industry, and the public about the requirements and importance of drinking water source protection. **Recommendation 17** The regulation of other industries (recommendation 11–16 related to agriculture) by the provincial government and by municipalities must be consistent with provincially approved source protection plans. **Recommendation 70** The provincial government should create a Watershed Management Branch within the Ministry of the Environment to be responsible for oversight of watershed-based source protection plans and, if implemented, watershed management plans.

sources be implemented on a watershed basis through the already existing conservation authorities, rather than by establishing new local bodies to fulfill this role. If a conservation authority is unable to carry out the new responsibility, the MOE itself should do so. I expect that the use of existing institutions will facilitate the adoption of these recommendations and reduce the costs of implementing them. (O'Connor, 2002, 2: 7)

The plans would be approved by the MOE and would be binding on provincial and municipal government decisions that directly affect drinking water safety. O'Connor recommended giving the MOE powers to trump other agencies' mandates, including overseeing municipal land-use plans, which would have to be consistent with source-protection plans (Cooper, 2003, 24). In this regard, he recommended that source-protection plans should be a subset of broader watershed management plans.

In November 2002 the Eves government established a seventeen-member, multi-stakeholder Advisory Committee on Watershed-Based Source Protection Planning, which released its report in April 2003 and made fifty-five recommendations, including broader consultation, establishment of a technical committee, and development of specific source-water protection legislation, rather than amendments to the Environmental Protection Act. A year later, in November 2003, the newly elected Liberal government established two committees with expertise from the conservation, resource, agricultural, environment, and health sectors to advise on the draft legislation and policy. The sixteen-member Technical Experts Committee was tasked with providing advice on an Ontario-based threat assessment process and appropriate risk management tools for various levels of threat, and the twenty-one-member Implementation Committee was given the job of providing advice on tools, innovative funding mechanisms, and incentives to implement watershed-based source protection planning. In February 2004 the Integrated Environmental Planning Division of the MOE released a *White Paper on Watershed-Based Source Protection Planning*, another part of its public consultation process to develop legislation.

As first proposed, the Drinking Water Source Protection Act was posted on the Environmental Registry on 23 June 2004. It was later renamed and introduced as the Clean Water Act for first reading on 5 December 2005. This bill became law in December 2006. The legislation requires the development of source water protection plans for watersheds in Ontario. Under the leadership of the MOE, the act requires the establishment of source-protection authorities (SPAS) as the primary agencies responsible for implementation; SPAS will also be grouped into source-protection regions. They are to establish multi-stakeholder source-protection committees (SPCS). Conservation authorities in most instances are the institutions mandated to implement the legislation at the watershed scale to oversee the development of source-protection plans (SPPS) for watersheds.

SPPS are to include information identifying those drinking-water re-sources under significant and direct threat, actions and measures needed to address immediate threats to drinking-water sources, an implementa-tion plan for the management of the identified source-protection issues, a detailed monitoring and assessment program, a description of the process that will be undertaken to ensure a transparent local consultation process based on requirements sent by the ministry, and a description of any out-standing or unresolved issues and how they will be dealt with. Local com-munities would be responsible for developing and implementing risk management strategies through existing local programs. For example, ag-ricultural threats may be minimized through environmental farm plans (Ontario, MOE, 2005b).

The legislation is consistent with Justice O'Connor's recommenda-tions that the MOE be the lead provincial agency in establishing the framework for developing the watershed-based source water protection plans. The MOE would help to fund and participate in the development of SPPS and would approve the completed plans. The legislation also follows O'Connor's recommendation that other policies and regula-tions such as provincial permits to take water, certificates of approval, and even municipal official plans and zoning decisions be consistent with the source-protection plans. However, it remains to be seen to what impact this legislation will have on altering the rules of the game for those, such as agriculture, with institutionalized interests related to the economic uses of water in Ontario.

One concern about source-protection plans is that they focus on drinking-water sources and not on NPS water pollution more broadly. How such plans will be integrated with existing watershed-level instru-ments and institutions is still to be demonstrated. SPPS are just now being established on the basis of provincial directives and local representation at the watershed level. The structure and operation of these watershed-based institutions are nonetheless notable institutional changes that may have broader impacts on water quality policy in the province.

Institutional Change and Implementation Costs

In their book, Eugene Lee and Anthony Perl hypothesize that a short-coming of an existing environmental policy may trigger a "conscious effort to change administrative structures and jurisdictional boundaries in order to enhance environmental policy capacity" (Lee and Perl, 2003, 256). The Walkerton tragedy can be viewed as a publicly recognized policy failure that has triggered an institutional response. Justice O'Connor explicitly approached his recommendations "with a view toward using existing structures and institutions wherever those structures are able to carry out my recommendations." No new institutional arrangements were deemed necessary to implement the recommendations. Rather, adjustments to the authority and structures of existing institutions resulted from his recommendations.

One of the central issues of the Part 2 process was whether the downsizing and privatization policies of the Harris government contributed to the Walkerton tragedy. In analyzing this question, O'Connor stated: "The reductions were initiated by the central agencies of the government, including the Management Board Secretariat, the Ministry of Finance, the Cabinet Office, and the Premier's Office rather than from within the MOE, and they were not based on an assessment of what was required to carry out the MOE's statutory responsibilities. Before the decision was made to significantly reduce the MOE's budget in 1996, senior government officials, ministers, and the cabinet received numerous warnings that the impacts could result in increased risks to the environment and human health" (O'Connor, 2002, 1: 404–16). As a result, he recommended that the government strengthen the capacity of the MOE and establish two specialized branches within the ministry, one responsible for overseeing drinking-water treatment and distribution systems with a chief water inspector responsible for the inspections system and another for watershed planning.

In April 2003 the Eves government announced the creation of the new division, led by an assistant deputy minister and chief water inspector, and claimed that it had added more than three hundred positions to the ministry since 2000 (Ontario, MOE, 2003b). Figures 8.2 and 8.3 outline the organizational structure of the MOE before and after Walkerton. To date, the recommendation to establish a second division for source protection and watershed planning has not been implemented. Some functions were also taken over from other ministries. The new

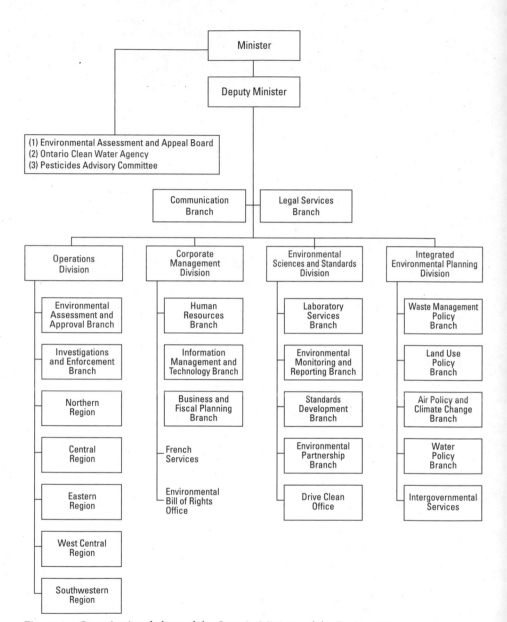

Figure 8.2 Organizational chart of the Ontario Ministry of the Environment, 1999.
SOURCE: http://www.ene.gov.on.ca/envision/org/orgchart.htm; accessed December 1999.

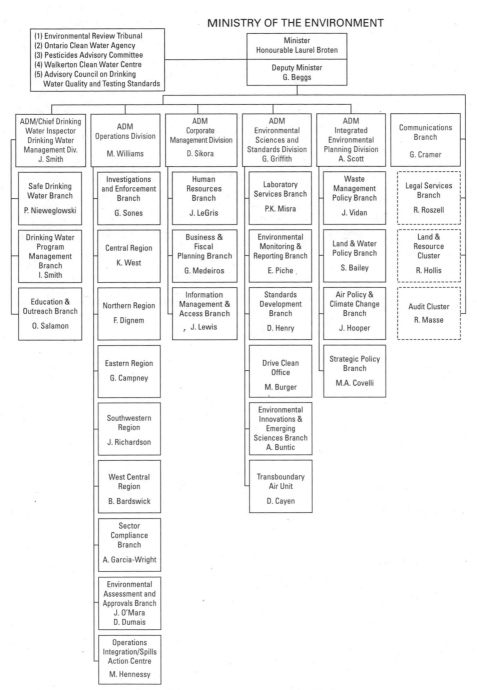

Figure 8.3 Organization chart of the Ontario Ministry of the Environment, 2007.
SOURCE: http://www.ene.gov.on.ca/en/about/org/orgchart.htm; accessed May 2007.

chief inspector for drinking water took over the regulation of agricultural discharges from the Ministry of Agriculture, Food and Rural Affairs, and the new drinking-water branch took over the regulatory responsibility of nutrient management plans where the OMAFRA had previously overseen the voluntary Environmental Farm Plan program.

Organizational restructuring was not enough. Justice O'Connor also argued that "it is essential for the Province to strictly enforce drinking water regulations and to commit sufficient resources, financial and otherwise, to enable the MOE to play this role effectively" (O'Connor, 2002, 2: 18–30). He also recommended developing new administrative and analytical capacity within the MOE, a recommendation that would require a significant reinvestment in staff and programs.

O'Connor commissioned a consulting firm, Strategic Alternatives, to estimate the costs of steps that the provincial government had taken by 2002 and the costs of implementing all the recommendations in Parts 1 and 2 of his inquiry. One-time costs of steps taken by the provincial government from 2000 to 2002 were estimated at $100–520 million, with ongoing annual costs between $41 and $200 million (Strategic Alternatives et al., 2002). The same report estimated the one-time cost of implementing the inquiry's recommendations to be in the range of $99–280 million and ongoing annual cost in the range of $17–49 million (Strategic Alternatives et al., 2002). Citing the consulting report, O'Connor stated that "the total costs of my recommendations, including the one-time costs amortized over 10 years at 7% interest, would amount to an average of between $7 and $19 per household per year. Comparing the average water rates with those for less essential services such as cable television, telephones, or Internet access makes this point powerfully" (O'Connor, 2002, 2:7).*

CONCLUSION

Ultimately, the way policy-makers define public policy problems influences which strategies, instruments, and institutions are used to solve them. In addition to grappling with the scope and complexities of the problems, policy-makers face the challenge of designing new instruments, adapting existing instruments, and reforming institutional arrangements within a context of limited resources and well-established

---

* These estimated costs relate only to implementing Ontario Regulation 459/00 and Ontario Regulation 505/01.

historical uses. In relation to water resources, they must do so in a context of existing institutions, powers of different policy actors, and other uses of water.

Policy-makers in other jurisdictions have realized for some time that NPS water pollution problems vary in a number of different dimensions: scale, scientific character, property rights, and risk (human health and ecosystem health). Prior to Walkerton, as in most other provinces, non-point source water pollution was not the focus of provincial water policy in Ontario. Water pollution was framed as a point-source problem, and institutional arrangements were designed and funded to focus on these more easily identifiable sources. Other jurisdictions such as the United States have passed federal and state legislation* to address non-point sources and realized that water quality objectives would not be met without this important part of a water policy framework, but Canadian jurisdictions have lagged behind in recognizing the significance of non-point source pollution and source protection (Johns, 2000). Canada and Ontario have had very limited capacity to address this type of water pollution, and institutional arrangements reinforced a medium-based approach (Johns, 2000; Rabe, 1999).

Federal involvement in addressing NPS water pollution before and after Walkerton has been both low and indirect. The federal government has only indirectly dealt with NPS water pollution through research, focus on some "areas of concern" under the Great Lakes Water Quality Agreement, low levels of funding for agro-environmental programs, and the rhetoric of pollution prevention and the ecosystem approach. Representatives from Health Canada were observers of the Part 2 process of the Walkerton Inquiry from a drinking-water standards and risk assessment perspective, but Environment Canada was not present from a water quality and ecosystem health perspective. In the eight years since Walkerton, the federal government has invested in NPS water pollution research through the Canadian Water Network and funded the development of water quality indicators through the National Roundtable on the Environment and the Economy and the CCME Water Quality Task Group. It has also participated actively in the standards-setting process through CCME and in CCME water policy workshops. This limited

---

* In the United States, section 319, under which the federal EPA required and funded state non-point source programs, was added to the federal Clean Water Act in 1987. Some states such as Wisconsin had their own policies and programs in place in the late 1970s.

role is not surprising given the pre-eminence of provincial powers and institutions, as outlined in chapter 2, but there have been continual calls for increased federal involvement in water policy (Pearse and Quinn, 1996; Pearse, 1998; Johns, 2000; Canada, Policy Research Initiative, 2006b), and some groups have even called for a national water protection policy (Council of Canadians, 2000). Nevertheless, the role of the federal government did not change even after another water pollution incident shortly after the Walkerton tragedy, this one in Saskatchewan.

In April 2001 more than 5800 residents became infected when sewage-treatment plant effluent flowed into the North Saskatchewan River upstream from the raw water intake for the water treatment plant. The cryptosporidium parvum parasite resulted in many residents in North Battleford, Saskatchewan, becoming very ill. In the North Battleford Water Inquiry, Justice Robert D. Laing made twenty-eight specific recommendations for the city of North Battleford and the province of Saskatchewan to improve the quality and safety of drinking water within its jurisdiction. Laing recommended several policy and institutional changes, including an independent unit to protect watershed and groundwater sources of drinking water. A year later the Saskatchewan government created the Drinking Water Quality Section in Saskatchewan Environment, and source water protection responsibilities were to be managed by a new Saskatchewan Watershed Authority. As in Ontario, non-point source water pollution policies were framed as source-protection policies designed to protect human health. Other provinces have followed and adopted watershed-based approaches and source-protection frameworks.

Ontario had no explicit policy regarding NPS water pollution prior to the Walkerton tragedy. Although sector-specific programs such as the Ontario Environmental Farm Plans were trying to address non-point sources such as agricultural runoff through voluntary participation and small incentives that promoted BMPs, the connection of this program to water quality objectives was only indirect, and the impact on protecting water resources was negligible. This outcome is not surprising, given the typical Canadian approach to agricultural pollution, entrenched agricultural interests, and weak bureaucratic capacity in the environmental sector and strong state-sector relations in agriculture (Montpetit, 2002, 275).

Overall, Ontario has begun to build the policy and institutional capacity to manage this complex type of water pollution. In contrast to the pre-Walkerton period, the instrument choice has shifted from a voluntary approach based on moral suasion to a more regulatory approach focusing on watersheds. As outlined in chapter 3, in practice a mixture of instruments are being employed to address NPS water pollution problems in Ontario. As a result of similar pollution problems and the lesson learned across jurisdictions, similar policy approaches seem to be emerging across Canada.* In terms of water quality, these approaches and standards have been promoted through intergovernmental forums such as CCME, which has produced a document on the multi-barrier approach to safe drinking water that provides guidance to water-system owners and operators on how to apply the concept and give decision-makers at all levels of government a structure for integrating health and environmental issues and setting implementation priorities (CCME, 2004b). More recently, there has been an emphasis on developing municipal effluent guidelines.

Research indicates that the choice, design, and comparative effectiveness of different policy instruments depends largely on the way that problems are defined and the capacity of the institutions implementing these instruments (Bemelmans-Videc, Rist, and Vedung, 1998; O'Toole et al., 1997; Johns, 2000; also see chapter 3 in this book). In the area of water pollution, Ontario had a lot of catching up to do compared to the United States, which has outperformed Canada in water pollution management in the past two decades (Hoberg, 1992; Rabe and Zimmerman, 1995; Rabe, 1999; Johns, 2000). US states were far ahead of their Canadian counterparts in preventing pollution, integrating cross-medium policies, and measuring environmental outcomes more comprehensively (Rabe, 1999; Johns, 2000) at the time of the Walkerton tragedy. Research on water pollution instruments and arrangements used in the Great Lakes Basin also shows that governments which adopt "integrated regulations" perform better than those which rely on "fragmented regulations" (Rabe and Zimmerman, 1995). An outstanding challenge will be for policy implementers to integrate the various policies, regulations, and institutional arrangements at different levels and across land-use–water-use lines.

Walkerton clearly brought drinking-water policy to the top of the provincial policy agenda in 2000. The focus on source protection as part of the drinking-water policy framework also helped to bring the significance of NPS water pollution problems to the attention of policymakers. However, the connections between human health and ecosystem

---

* For examples of recent strategies and policy instruments, see Canada, Environment Canada, 2003c, 6.

health are not clearly integrated in the post-Walkerton policy frame-work, and a broad integration of drinking-water policies and non-point source water policies remains to be implemented under the province's source water protection legislation. Another challenge will be to sustain the political commitment and implementation momentum at the provin-cial and local levels. As the definition of the water pollution problems has shifted to incorporate both point sources and non-point sources and as a prevention approach has been adopted in the form of source protec-tion, local governance structures will arguably become increasingly im-portant in the implementation of new provincial legislation, regulations, and programs.

The post-Walkerton policy response to the Walkerton Inquiry and Jus-tice O'Connor's recommendations has resulted in significant capacity-building in the past five years, but there is still a long way to go in terms of implementing source protection and addressing NPS water pollution from a human health and, more broadly, ecosystem health perspective. Other instruments with the potential to address NPS water pollution by integrating land use and water use, such as tax incentives, easements, and non-profit land trusts, remain the most weakly developed in On-tario. Policy-makers may need to incorporate these instruments into the policy mix if water quality objectives are to be met. The capacity to monitor and measure the environmental impacts after Walkerton will also be a challenge unless the weak monitoring capacity of surface water and groundwater (Johns, 2000; CIELP, 2001) is also addressed.

The developments in this case clearly indicate that historical water rights, interests, and institutional arrangements related to point source water pollution management are firmly entrenched in Ontario. Despite the nerve that the Walkerton tragedy hit with policy-makers and the public and the resulting policy efforts and resources in the aftermath of the inquiry, agricultural interests retain a firm economic stake in ensur-ing these institutions are not altered significantly and that point source instruments are not applied to non-point source problems. By framing Walkerton as a public health issue, rather than as a pollution and envi-ronmental issue, some substantive policy and institutional change did occur. The province's current approach to source protection, which fo-cuses on drinking-water uses, highlights the enduring impact of institu-tions and rights of users even in the aftermath of a significant water pollution event and public inquiry. Since Walkerton, the watershed ap-proach seems to be a significant institutional approach being adopted across Canada. However, although the Walkerton Inquiry presented an important opportunity for broader institutional reform and redesign, its impact in terms of addressing water quality and water pollution in the province is in need of further analysis and assessment.

PART FIVE
The Politics of In-Stream Water Uses

9

The St Lawrence: From River
to Maritime Superhighway

B. TIMOTHY HEINMILLER

As outlined in chapter 1, commercial shipping has long been one of the most economically important in-stream water uses in Canada, and the St Lawrence River continues to be the country's most important commercial shipping route. For centuries, the St Lawrence has been the maritime gateway to the heart of the North American interior, providing a crucial transportation link to export markets for Canadian timber, grains, minerals, and manufactured goods. This chapter provides a historical institutional analysis of the political-economic development of the St Lawrence River, describing its transformation from pristine river to regulated maritime superhighway. This analysis reveals how the early economic uses of the St Lawrence have been entrenched in the domestic and international governance institutions for the river, ensuring their priority over environmental and recreational uses that have more recently emerged. This situation has not only created rivalries between established and emerging uses but ensured that these rivalries are played out on unequal terms, with established uses enjoying the privileges of the entrenched status quo. The contested evolution of the St Lawrence clearly reveals that in-stream water uses are not immune from the conflicts and user rivalries more commonly associated with water withdrawals and water pollution.

INTRODUCTION

Because of its size and geographic location, the St Lawrence has long been regarded as a key maritime artery to the heart of the North American interior. Nevertheless, since its discovery by French explorers in the sixteenth century, it has undergone a conceptual and physical evolution from the St Lawrence as "river" to the St Lawrence as "seaway." This transformation has been quite significant for both the users of the St Lawrence and for the waterway itself. While a river is regarded as something wild and natural with inherent value, a seaway is seen as something that can be captured and developed to produce economic value, primarily through navigation and shipping. The St Lawrence's transformation from river to seaway has occurred incrementally over nearly five centuries, but it has been neither complete nor uncontested.

Today, the institutions governing the St Lawrence clearly reflect its ascendancy as seaway, having entrenched the rights of shipping, industrial, and hydroelectric interests and given them priority over other users. However, these entrenched rights are being challenged by environmentalists and other user groups, who put forward a strong case for the restoration of at least some elements of the St Lawrence's riverine characteristics. This chapter traces the evolution of the St Lawrence from river to seaway, emphasizing the political-economic factors that have driven this change and the institutions that have symbolized and formalized it.

THE ST LAWRENCE AS A RIVER, 1535–1840S: EARLY INSTITUTIONS

When Jacques Cartier sailed up the St Lawrence in 1535, he was not really interested in the river at all. The river and its overgrown banks were a novelty and a revelation, but he was most interested in finding the fabled Northwest Passage to India. In other words, Cartier viewed the river as a potentially profitable maritime trade route and was probably the first person to see it as a seaway, though in a much different sense from the way it is perceived today. Unfortunately for Cartier, his dream of a maritime trade route ended just west of Hochelaga (present-day Montreal) at a set of impassable rapids now known as the Lachine Rapids, and the river would remain "just" a river for the next three centuries.

To the Aboriginals whom Cartier encountered on its banks, however, the river was home and had been for as long as they could remember. All along the fertile Great Lakes–St Lawrence lowlands, dozens of Native tribes had thrived for millennia, living from the land as hunters, anglers, and farmers. To them, the St Lawrence was not a means to an end but an end in itself: it was a source of water, a source of food, and a vital transportation link between tribes. The river was not something that could be owned or conquered but something that existed as it was meant to exist: an ecological and cosmological constant in the world.

The St Lawrence area was the crucible of European settlement in North America, and as Europeans confronted Aboriginals, the first conflict between river and seaway was played out. As the French established settlements along the banks of the St Lawrence and began to exploit the wealth of natural resources in the area, the river quickly became the focal point of a thriving trade route. As Donald Creighton has argued in his seminal book *The Empire of the St. Lawrence*, "The lower St. Lawrence was for the French, as it is for the Canadians of today, the destined focus of any conceivable northern economy [in North America]" (Creighton, 1958, 11). This economy was driven by a "staples" trade that started with furs and gradually evolved into other goods such as timber, wheat, and potash, and the St Lawrence served as a ready shipping link to move these goods between the northern colonies and Europe (Creighton, 1958, 89).

At the heart of the St Lawrence, the city of Montreal emerged as one of the continent's most important ports and the centre of maritime trade for the Canadian colonies. In large part, it enjoyed this status simply because of its location. The rapids west of the city were impassable to large ships; so the various staples harvested from the North American interior were trekked to Montreal, where they were traded and loaded onto Europe-bound ships. However, as other colonies spread rapidly along the Atlantic seaboard, Montreal's ascendancy as the main transportation link between Europe and the North American interior would come to be challenged by rivals from the south.

The challenge came in the form of the Hudson River, which also offered shipping access to the North American interior, flowing past New York City into upper New York State. It was in this early rivalry between the St Lawrence and the Hudson that the transformation from river to seaway really began. In their natural flow, both rivers offered access to the interior, but with some excavation and construction, this access could be greatly extended. In the case of the St Lawrence, it meant the excavation and construction of a canal to bypass the Lachine Rapids, while in the case of the Hudson, it meant the excavation and construction of a canal to link the Hudson with the Great Lakes Basin. Both projects offered the prospect of shipping access all the way to Lake Ontario and perhaps beyond. It was merely a question of who would build first (St Lawrence Seaway Management Corporation, 2003, 2). As the rivalry intensified, those relying on the St Lawrence felt the need to make it competitive and, as a result, took the first conceptual steps toward a seaway: rivers do not compete, but seaways do.

Though the users and regulators of the St Lawrence in the Canadian colonies were well aware of their competition to the south, they trailed the Americans from the start. The Erie Canal linking the Hudson River to the Great Lakes Basin was undertaken in 1817 by the New York state government, and the governments of Upper and Lower Canada responded in 1818 by forming an ad hoc commission to study the potential improvement of St Lawrence navigation. Though some very small canals had been constructed around Montreal as early as 1779, they were not designed for large commercial vessels, and the building of larger canals had been continually thwarted by the fragmentation of governance authority between the two Canadian colonies and the British government (Creighton, 1958, 198). Even after the commission recommended the construction of new canals no smaller than those underway in New York, the only action taken was the completion of the Casson Canal bypassing the Lachine Rapids in 1824, and it was just over half the size of the Erie.

Until the 1840s, the push toward seaway development was prevalent in the St Lawrence but continually frustrated. The main source of frustration was the inability of the Canadian colonial governments to work together on the construction of a comprehensive canal system, but there were other obstacles as well. One was the considerable time and expense of undertaking such a project, as the government of Upper Canada found out when it proceeded unilaterally with the construction of a number of navigation works in the upper St Lawrence in the 1830s. Another was the small and unstable nature of the Canadian economy, which put into question the soundness of such large infrastructure investments. So, even though the motivation to move from river to seaway was present, colonial Canadians could not muster the collective will and resources necessary to reshape the river to their commercial needs, and the push from river to seaway was stymied for a number of decades.

SEAWAY I (1840S–1950S): THE EMERGING DOMINANCE OF SHIPPING AND HYDROELECTRICITY

In the 1840s, however, dramatic changes in the political economy of the Canadian colonies enabled them to overcome their differences and take a gamble on the construction of a large-vessel waterway through the St Lawrence and Great Lakes system. The first major change was the creation of a unitary Canadian colonial government along the length of the St Lawrence, replacing the former colonies of Upper and Lower Canada with a single government. Then the combination of a world-wide economic depression and the planned withdrawal of trade advantages by Britain prodded the new Canadian government into action. In the words of Donald Creighton, the Canadians acted "feverishly to complete the canals in the hope that while the diminished protective system still lasted in England, Canada could establish the superiority of the St. Lawrence route" (Creighton, 1958, 365). The result of this concerted governmental action was the construction of new canals at Cornwall in 1843 and Beauharnois in 1845 and the expansion of the Casson Canal, renamed the Lachine Canal, in 1848. By 1850 an "embryonic seaway" was constructed along the length of the St Lawrence, capable of moving vessels up to 2.4 metres in draft, a capacity quite competitive with the Hudson-Erie system (St Lawrence Seaway Management Corporation, 2003, 2).

For the rest of the nineteenth century, the St Lawrence and Hudson-Erie waterways were locked in competition for the pre-eminent maritime trade route into the North American interior. As commercial vessels increased in size and draft, so did the canals and locks of these competing waterways. In the St Lawrence, the Lachine Canal was expanded for a second time, and the Soulanges Canal was constructed to replace the Beauharnois Canal. By 1904 all the canals and locks between Montreal and Lake Erie were capable of hosting vessels with a 4.3 metre draft, almost double what they had been fifty years earlier (St Lawrence Seaway Management Corporation, 2003, 3). Similar expansions were made in the Hudson-Erie canal system, but as the end of the century approached, it became increasingly clear that the Americans were losing the maritime trade competition. The St Lawrence was, by nature, a much wider and deeper river than the Hudson, and commercial ships were simply starting to outgrow the latter. By the early twentieth century, the traffic on the Hudson-Erie system had been reduced largely to barges, and today most traffic is comprised of recreational boats. In short, the St Lawrence succeeded in becoming the favoured route for most of the heavy maritime traffic into the North American interior, while the Hudson-Erie system was relegated to smaller regional and recreational shipping.

During this period, Montreal established itself as one of North America's premier shipping ports, and communities along the St Lawrence grew precipitously. By the 1880s, greater Montreal had a population of almost 300 000, and urban and industrial uses of the St Lawrence began to have a noticeable impact on the river. Industries such as agriculture, shipbuilding, pulp and paper, textiles, and metal processing relied on the St Lawrence as both a water source for manufacturing processes and a waste discharge outlet. Similarly, Montreal and other urban areas along the river used it as both a drinking water source and a garbage dump. In 1827, for example, a regulation was introduced requiring Montrealers to discard their garbage into the river, where it would be carried away downstream, and this sort of approach was also used for the discharge of untreated municipal sewage until well into the twentieth century (Francoeur, 2000, 145; Sancton, 1985, 126). Not surprisingly, environmental and public health problems resulted from these practices. In the nineteenth century these were manifested in periodic outbreaks of water-borne diseases such as cholera, which were eventually controlled through better treatment of municipal drinking water. Later, in the twentieth century, these problems would be apparent in much larger-scale environmental degradation.

Just as the St Lawrence started to claim permanent ascendancy over the Hudson-Erie system in the late nineteenth century, a new transportation network emerged to compete with it, bringing different kinds of competitive pressures. This competitor was the burgeoning railway system, and it offered advantages over any seaway in the St Lawrence, even an expanded one. The railways provided the potential to carry loads comparable to those moved through the seaway, but on a year-round basis, not just the seven-month shipping season of the St Lawrence (St Lawrence Seaway Management Corporation, 2003, 2). As a competitor, the railways would prove more daunting than the Hudson-Erie system had been, particularly because of the political influence and acumen of the railway interests.

In addition to these changing competitive pressures, the political institutions of the St Lawrence area also evolved considerably in the latter half of the nineteenth century. Obviously, the most important of these changes was the creation of Canada as an independent, federal country in 1867. The new federal division of powers in the British North America Act (now known as the Constitution Act, 1867) had significant implications for St Lawrence governance, as sovereign authority over water was divided between the new federal and provincial governments. While Ottawa was given authority over such water-related areas as fisheries (section 91.12) and navigation and shipping (section 91.10), the provinces retained proprietary rights to most of the waters within their borders (section 109), allowing them to regulate most riparian uses (Kennett, 1991). An added wrinkle for the St Lawrence, an international waterway shared in part with the United States, was the provision regarding international treaties. According to section 132 of the British North America Act, the British government would continue to negotiate international treaties on Canada's behalf, so that until 1926[*] the negotiation of international treaties relevant to the St Lawrence was a somewhat awkward three-way exercise between the governments of Canada, the United Kingdom, and the United States (Monahan, 2002).

Almost as important as Confederation was the drastic improvement in Canada–US relations, which ultimately led to a more cooperative, binational approach to the regulation and use of the St Lawrence. As the British and the Americans turned from foes to friends and the rivalry between Canadian St Lawrence advocates and American Hudson-Erie advocates cooled, many Americans realized that a thriving seaway in the St Lawrence had much to offer them. Cities such as Chicago, Cleveland, and Detroit were emerging industrial powerhouses, and an expanded seaway offered the potential for even further growth in the American Midwest. Consequently, closer cooperation between Canada and the United States became the norm, starting with the Treaty of Washington in 1871. This treaty established the exact international border in the St Lawrence and granted American navigators increased access to the Canadian portion of St Lawrence waters. In 1895 even closer cooperation was undertaken with the formation of a joint Deep Waterways Commission to investigate the prospects for an expanded St Lawrence seaway. Despite the commission's endorsement of expansion, however, the project was blocked by American railway interests, fearful that an expanded seaway would hurt their business (St Lawrence Seaway Management Corporation, 2003, 4).

Close Canadian-American cooperation in their shared boundary waters, including the St Lawrence, was eventually institutionalized in the International Boundary Waters Treaty of 1909. A remarkable achievement for its time, the treaty created the International Joint Commission (IJC), a body comprised of three Canadians and three Americans, to manage competing uses and intergovernmental conflicts in Canada–US boundary waters. If a proposed project in a boundary water "substantially affects"

---

[*] In 1926 it was agreed at an imperial conference that Canada would henceforth negotiate international treaties on its own behalf.

water levels on the other side of the border, it must gain the approval of the US president, the Canadian prime minister, and the IJC before it can be undertaken. The IJC was also given the power to investigate questions referred to it by its two member governments, and in recent years, it has taken on the role of watchdog for the 1972, 1978, and 1987 Great Lakes Water Quality Agreements. For the St Lawrence, the creation of the IJC ensured that any further expansion of the seaway infrastructure would occur under its auspices and under a new set of international rules.

The undertaking of a seaway expansion, however, was still a matter of political will within the respective governments, and US railway interests successfully undermined the American political will for a number of decades. After the recommendations of the 1895–97 Deep Waterways Commission were shelved, technological changes created another potential use for the St Lawrence that rekindled interest in development on both sides of the border. This was the prospect of hydroelectric power generation, and the US and Canadian governments began talks in the 1920s about simultaneously expanding the locks and canals of the St Lawrence while harnessing its flow to generate electricity.

The result of these talks was the Great Lakes–St Lawrence Deep Waterway Treaty of 1932, which was signed by both countries and outlined ambitious plans for the construction of both navigation and hydroelectric improvements. However, when the treaty was submitted to the US Senate for ratification, the railway interests rallied and successfully lobbied enough senators to have it rejected. Frustrated but undeterred, the United States and Canadian governments tried again in the Great Lakes–St Lawrence Basin Agreement of 1941, but its ratification was also eventually blocked in the US Senate (St Lawrence Seaway Management Corporation, 2003, 4).

Much like the initial push for seaway construction in the St Lawrence, there was general agreement in the early twentieth century that seaway expansion was desirable, but collective action among the necessary actors proved exceedingly difficult. In this case, it was not the unwillingness of the relevant governments to cooperate and invest in expansion but the influence and tactics of a dissenting special interest at a crucial veto point that thwarted collective action. Like most efforts at international cooperation, it was not just the positions of the relevant governments but also the support, or lack thereof, of key domestic interests that influenced the outcome. In order for seaway expansion to proceed, either the political influence of the US railway interests would have to decline or the US Senate would somehow have to be bypassed.

In the end, a combination of the two would eventually lead to the construction of the world-renowned St Lawrence Seaway in the 1950s.

SEAWAY II (1950S TO THE PRESENT): INSTITUTIONAL EVOLUTION

By 1951 the Canadian government had become quite frustrated with the inability of its American counterpart to ratify a treaty on St Lawrence seaway expansion, a project that it regarded as crucial to Canadian trade; so it decided to proceed with expansion on a unilateral basis. The Canadian Parliament passed the St Lawrence Seaway Authority Act and the International Rapids Power Development Act, developing plans for both navigation and hydroelectric improvements along the length of the St Lawrence and into the Great Lakes. But because the construction of a hydroelectric dam across the St Lawrence would substantially affect water levels on the American side of the river, the 1909 International Boundary Waters Treaty came into effect, and the US government became involved in the process.

After obtaining President Eisenhower's approval for the proposed dam, the Canadian and American governments submitted a joint application for approval to the IJC in 1952. The application was only for the hydroelectric dam, but it was made with the tacit understanding that Canada would also construct and operate navigation works in the St Lawrence that could accommodate vessels of 8.2 metre draft. The IJC gave its approval in October of 1952, but construction was delayed another two years because of challenges in the US courts and difficulties in passing the necessary enabling legislation through the US Congress (St Lawrence Seaway Management Corporation, 2003, 5). The American railway interests resisted until the end, but their influence in Washington had declined, and the threshold required to pass the dam appropriations bill in the Senate was much lower than it had been to ratify the earlier international treaties.* With the last key remnant of domestic opposition effectively overcome, the legislation was passed, and construction was slated to begin in 1954.

Between September 1954 and April 1959, millions of dollars and man-hours were poured into construction along the St Lawrence, transforming

---

* To pass a regular bill in the US Senate, only a simple majority of senators (50 out of 100) must vote in favour. However, to ratify an international treaty in the Senate, two-thirds of the senators (67 out of 100) must vote in favour.

it from a functional "seaway" into a formal and proper "Seaway." By the time construction was completed, the level and flow of the St Lawrence had been brought under almost complete human control. The primary means of this control was the new Moses-Saunders power dam, constructed near Cornwall at the outlet of Lake Ontario into the St Lawrence. The operation of this dam, in conjunction with two smaller dams, gave administrators the ability to substantially regulate the outflow of water from Lake Ontario into the St Lawrence, thereby allowing them to manipulate water levels in both of these bodies within centimetres of targeted levels. In this way, the construction of the seaway not only increased the St Lawrence's shipping capacity; it also transformed it from a naturally flowing river to an engineered hydraulic system.

Nevertheless, the St Lawrence remained a complex, multi-jurisdictional water resource, and rules had to be developed to govern water levels both upstream and downstream of the Moses-Saunders dam. Primary responsibility for developing these new rules fell to the IJC, and it eventually did so through a 1956 order of approval and a regulation plan known as 1958–D. Administrative responsibility for maintaining desired water levels in Lake Ontario and the St Lawrence was assigned to the International St Lawrence River Board of Control, an affiliate of the IJC comprised of five Americans and five Canadians appointed by their respective governments. The Board of Control sets Lake Ontario outflows on a weekly basis but must operate within the rules established in Plan 1958–D. Since the construction of the seaway, it is these rules that have established the prevailing rights to the use of the St Lawrence, notwithstanding those riparian rights that have long existed as a matter of common law in Ontario and civil law in Quebec (Yee et al., 1990; Percy, 1988).

With the expansion of the seaway and the construction of the Moses-Saunders power dam, the conflicts between the competing uses of the St Lawrence were brought into sharp focus, and development of regulations for water levels was a precarious balancing act between the various interests of these uses. Industrial and municipal riparians, for instance, generally favoured moderate water levels and stable flows because these provide a reliable source of water for withdrawals and discharges, with minimal property damage from flooding. Periodic flooding had long been a problem in Montreal, and municipal authorities saw the new water control structures as a means of preventing future flooding disasters. At the same time, navigators and power generators generally favoured high water levels and faster flows because these allow them to carry larger cargo loads and generate more electricity.* They believed that the seaway had been built primarily for these purposes, and so it was not unreasonable to give them priority over riparian flooding concerns.

In Plan 1958–D the IJC established rules for the operation of the Moses-Saunders power dam that attempted to balance what were regarded as the most important uses of St Lawrence water at that time. Essentially, the plan set up a hierarchy of water rights that prioritized riparian and navigation rights over hydroelectric generation rights. Thus, in regulating outflows from Lake Ontario to the St Lawrence, the Board of Control is obliged, first and foremost, to protect riparian and navigation interests in the river. If these uses are satisfied, then hydroelectric power generation is to be the second consideration (International Joint Commission, 1956, 4). In normal circumstances, all three water uses can be satisfied simultaneously, and the Board of Control is required to maintain Lake Ontario water levels in the target range of 74.2 to 75.4 metres to attain this balance (International Joint Commission, 1956, 6). However, when water levels are lower or higher than "historical levels," the board has some discretion in how it satisfies the identified water uses: "in the event that supplies exceed supplies of the past, the works should be operated to provide 'all possible relief' to the riparian owners upstream and downstream. In the event that supplies less than the supplies of the past occur, the works should be operated to provide 'all possible relief' to navigation and power interests" (Yee et al., 1990, 9). So even though a complex of rules was created to manage user conflicts over St Lawrence water, the dams and diversion works are normally operated to satisfy all identified users and to avoid this kind of conflict in most circumstances.

If we look at the design of Plan 1958–D, it seems like a shining example of political compromise and positive sum cooperation: potentially competing uses were accommodated to ensure mutual security and prosperity – in an international body of water, no less. Though there is some validity in this analysis, another, more critical interpretation is revealing. To some extent, it can be argued that the riparian, navigation, and hydroelectric generation rights institutionalized in the plan created a cartel over St Lawrence water that has seriously deprived other uses

---

* "[O]ne additional centimetre of water in the St. Lawrence allows a container ship to carry six more containers, at an average value of $2,000 each" (Vaillancourt et al., 2003, 27).

not included at that time. In other words, the riparian, navigation, and hydro interests have succeeded in capturing water rights in the St Lawrence to the exclusion of such uses as recreational boating, swimming, commercial fishing, and environmental preservation. To be fair, most of these potential uses were excluded simply because they were not prevalent at the time – the environmentalist movement did not get into full swing until the late 1960s – but the effects of their exclusion have been very significant.

Since Plan 1958–D has been in effect, riparian, navigation, and hydroelectric interests have benefited considerably. While some riparians have noticed little change resulting from St Lawrence regulation, many others have experienced a significant decrease in seasonal flooding. Particularly around Montreal, seasonal and annual fluctuations in water levels have greatly decreased, and property damage from flooding has also decreased (Canada, Department of the Environment, 1998, 5). Navigational interests have also profited handsomely from the St Lawrence Seaway as more than 2.2 billion tonnes of cargo – mostly grain, iron ore, coal, and steel – worth an estimated $265 billion have been transported through it since it was opened in 1959 (Canada and the United States, n.d.). These benefits have been facilitated by increased dredging efforts* to allow for the passage of increasingly larger ships through the seaway's navigational channels and by technological innovations to inhibit ice formation in canals and locks that have extended the shipping season to about nine months each year (St Lawrence Seaway Management Corporation, 2003, 9). Since it has become fully operational, the Moses-Saunders power dam has regularly produced enough electricity to meet the needs of a city of over one million people, and this does not include the power generated at two smaller dams in the international section of the river or the dams operated by the government of Quebec on various St Lawrence tributaries. The availability of this hydro power has attracted a variety of energy-intensive industries, such as aluminium smelting in Quebec, contributing further to economic growth.

Unfortunately, many of these benefits have come with severe environmental costs, a set of St Lawrence water uses not institutionalized in Plan 1958–D. One of the most serious environmental problems was a

---

* Dredging is the process of scraping sediments from the bottom of the river to create deep-water shipping channels in some parts of the seaway. Because these channels will refill with sediment if left untended, dredging is a continuous maintenance task.

steep decline in water quality during most of the twentieth century. While 42 per cent of the pollution in the St Lawrence has it origins upstream in the industrialized areas of the Great Lakes, local industries, municipal sewage systems, and farmers along the river are responsible for the release of thousands of tonnes of pollutants into the St Lawrence each year themselves (Francoeur, 2000, 142). Despite cleanup efforts over the past twenty years, about half the beach areas east of Montreal are unsafe for swimming for extended periods of time, and anglers are warned not to include St Lawrence fish as a staple in their diet because of its toxicity (Vaillancourt et al., 2003, 8–9).

Biodiversity has also suffered in the course of the St Lawrence's transformation to seaway as the number of threatened or endangered species in the area continues to rise. Habitat destruction through dredging, damming, riverbank erosion, and wetland drainage has been the primary threat to biodiversity, while the introduction of around 160 invasive species, often through ships' ballast water, have devastated natural ecosystems (Francoeur, 2000; Munk Centre for International Studies, 2004). The seaway works have altered water temperatures, currents, and river depths to such an extent that fish migration paths have been disrupted and native species such as eel, tomcod, shad, smelt, and yellow perch are being replaced by invasive species such as walleye, shorthead redhorse, bass, lake whitefish, sea lamprey, and zebra mussel, a veritable transformation of the ecosystem (Francoeur, 2000, 144–5).

One of the clearest indicators of the declining health of the St Lawrence has been the plight of the beluga whale. The belugas are often cited as an indicator of river health because they are near the top of the river's food chain and, through biomagnification,[*] have been most affected by the deterioration of water quality and biodiversity. Since 1900 the population of St Lawrence belugas, which primarily reside in the lower reaches of the river, has declined steadily from about 5000 to a low of around 700, and they are now considered a species at risk (Great Canadian Rivers, 2003). While overfishing explains a significant part of this decline, the recovery of the belugas continues to be inhibited by habitat destruction, water pollution, and noise disturbance from human activity (Canada, Environment Canada, 2004e). Cancers and other deformities have become increasingly evident among the St Lawrence

---

[*] Biomagnification is the process in which pollutants tend to accumulate in those species at the top of a local food chain because they consume vast quantities of other species that also contain pollutants.

belugas, and the pregnancy rate of females is only around 3 per cent, as compared to 35 per cent for Arctic whales (Great Canadian Rivers, 2003). Recent efforts to protect the St Lawrence belugas have resulted in a slight increase in their numbers, but they remain a long way from full recovery (Canada, Environment Canada, 2004e).

Until the 1970s, most of the environmental problems in the St Lawrence went unnoticed or unremedied by the governments sharing the river. However, over 60 per cent of Quebec's population lives along the banks of the St Lawrence, and 45 per cent of the province's drinking water is drawn from St Lawrence waters; so the decline of the river could not be ignored forever (Quebec, 2002). Between 1973 and 1978, an intergovernmental River Water Quality Committee worked to scientifically assess problems with the St Lawrence that were increasingly evident through anecdotal evidence. The committee's report, *A Plan for the St Lawrence*, was the first real eye-opener about the river's decline and prompted some governments into action. In 1978 the government of Quebec undertook an ongoing program to upgrade the province's sewer and waste-water treatment facilities (Quebec, 2002). By 2000 the number of municipalities treating their waste discharges into the river had risen from 2 per cent to 98 per cent, a remarkable increase (Francoeur, 2000, 144).

A major initiative was then launched in 1988 when the Quebec and federal governments signed a cooperation agreement on the restoration of the St Lawrence, known as the St Lawrence Action Plan. The plan was focused on industrial cleanup and identified fifty specific industrial plants as priorities, establishing measurable pollution reduction targets for each. The Action Plan enjoyed such success that it was subsequently renewed by the participating governments in both 1993 and 1998, renamed St Lawrence Vision 2000, and given an expanded mandate to include greater community involvement in non-industrial cleanup issues. Since its inception, this cooperative intergovernmental approach has resulted in just over $600 million in government spending on St Lawrence restoration and an over 90 per cent reduction in the toxicity of the effluents released by 106 identified plants (Vaillancourt et al., 2003).

While the successes of St Lawrence Vision 2000 and its predecessors are encouraging, these programs are not a permanent solution to degradation of the river system. The underlying cause of environmental problems in the St Lawrence is its transformation into a seaway and the institutionalized hierarchy of water-use rights that supports this. Programs such as St Lawrence Vision 2000 have achieved admirable outcomes in mitigating the negative byproducts of prevailing water-use rights, but they have not fundamentally altered the rights themselves. Until this sort of institutional reform takes place and environmental uses are incorporated into the hierarchy of recognized water rights, it is unlikely that water quality or biodiversity will be permanently restored.* The problem, however, is that many of the existing water rights could be significantly impaired by the introduction of new water rights, and so there is considerable conflict about any such reform. This conflict challenges the very nature of the St Lawrence's definition as seaway and is one of the pressures facing the waterway as it struggles to find an identity for the twenty-first century.

SEAWAY III? THE STRUGGLE FOR THE FUTURE OF THE ST LAWRENCE

The fundamental definition of the St Lawrence is probably more contested today than at any time in the past. Until the last thirty years or so, its definition as seaway was generally accepted by most of its water users. Those who dissented did so on the grounds that other transportation networks, such as the Hudson-Erie waterway or the railways, were economically preferable for the movement of goods. In recent years, this seaway consensus has broken down, and an increasing number of interests now favour defining the St Lawrence as river. The result is a situation where two radically different visions have emerged for the future of the St Lawrence: one sees an expanded seaway, while the other sees a restored river.

As with past campaigns to expand the shipping capacity of the St Lawrence, the current push to enlarge the seaway infrastructure is the result of competitive pressures from other transportation networks. This time, however, the competition is on a global scale, as seaway advocates increasingly feel the need to accommodate large-draft ships that can be hosted by many of the world's deepwater ports. In 2003 the St Lawrence Seaway had 3886 vessels move through the system, carrying 40.982 million metric tonnes of goods valued at approximately $7 billion, but some business people feel that the seaway, together with the St Lawrence

---

* To some, the idea of environmental property rights may seem unusual, but they have been adopted in other places. In the Murray River of Australia, for instance, the recent Environmental Flows Initiative has allocated a defined share of Murray water to environmental uses, creating, in effect, an environmental water right.

region, is losing out to other areas around the world (Canada and the
United States, n.d., 4). "In the past 30 years international maritime traffic
has grown 600 percent; meanwhile, closer to home, the St. Lawrence Seaway has seen its traffic *decrease* 20 percent in the last 20 years" (Jacquez,
2002b, 3). The seaway seems to have lost its competitive edge, and advocates of expansion, such as the US Army Corps of Engineers and the
St Lawrence Seaway Development Corporation,* argue that the very viability of the seaway is now at stake: "Basically two choices are on the table: an inland waterway capable of providing a modern, vibrant
maritime link to world markets or one that does not. The first offers
hope for a brighter tomorrow founded on the proven expertise of the entire marine transportation industry; the latter vision is defeatist, suggesting that the Seaway's time has come and gone, that it should drift
gracefully into irrelevance and the history books" (Jacquez, 2002b, 3).
The construction costs of seaway expansion are likely to be formidable,
but the economic costs of not expanding are said to be even higher. In
this regard, the Army Corps of Engineers has completed a preliminary
study of seaway expansion but is still awaiting permission to proceed
with a more detailed follow-up study (Jacquez, 2002a). The expansion
issue is on the public agenda, but action does not appear imminent.

The opposing view of the future of St Lawrence not only rejects an
expanded seaway but demands at least a partial restoration of the natural water flows and levels that characterize it as a river and ecosystem
rather than an engineered waterway. This would be achieved through
the introduction of substantial water property rights for recreational
and environmental uses. There are a number of interest groups throughout the Great Lakes–St Lawrence basin who advocate this vision, but
the stated goal of a group known as the International Water Levels Coalition (IWLC) is typical: "To have the International Joint Commission's
Order of Approval amended to include recreational boating and the environment" (IWLC, 2004). Most advocates of this vision accept that
some sort of seaway is bound to persist in the St Lawrence because of
its economic importance, but they insist that institutional changes, such
as amendments to Plan 1958–D, are necessary to restore water quality
and biodiversity in the St Lawrence area on a large scale.

---

*   The US Army Corps of Engineers is a federal agency that has a long history of investigating and constructing large-scale water diversion projects in the United States. The
St Lawrence Seaway Development Corporation is the American federal agency responsible for operating the navigation works in the US portion of the St Lawrence Seaway.

The antagonism between those advocating an expanded seaway and those arguing for a restored river is quite obvious and has escalated to the point where governments have become involved in considering the future of the St Lawrence. In December of 2000 the IJC established the International Lake Ontario–St Lawrence River Study Board to undertake a five-year study "to assess and evaluate the current criteria used for regulating water levels on Lake Ontario and in the St Lawrence River" (International Lake Ontario–St Lawrence River Study Board, 2004). In particular, the board was asked to investigate whether any changes to Plan 1958–D are necessary to protect water uses that are currently excluded. The board is binational in nature and has engaged user groups, academics, and the general public in an effort to determine if a consensus vision for the future of the St Lawrence is possible (International Lake Ontario–St Lawrence River Study Board, 2004). In March 2006 it issued its report, recommending three new regulation plans as candidates to succeed Plan 1958–D, each of which, in its view, would increase aggregate economic and environmental benefits from the river. All the recommended plans continue to serve the interests of the shipping, hydroelectric, and riparian users, while a plan that would return the St Lawrence to more natural flow patterns was considered by the study board but ultimately rejected (International Lake Ontario–St Lawrence River Study Board, 2006). The IJC has yet to designate a new regulation plan at time of writing, but the St Lawrence's status as seaway seems in little jeopardy.

The current debate over the future of the St Lawrence is even further distinguished from past discussions by the development of a large-scale ecological phenomenon without precedent: human-induced global climate change. Through computer modelling and various other forms of educated guessing, the Canadian Climate Change Centre predicts that water levels in the St Lawrence could decline 30–80 centimetres over the next one hundred years (Francoeur, 2000, 146). Even if these figures are inaccurate, a decline in water levels of some magnitude can reasonably be expected: if humans stopped producing greenhouse gases today, there is still enough in the atmosphere that some climate change is virtually assured over the next few decades.

Declining water levels in the St Lawrence would adversely affect navigation and hydro generation, perhaps leading to calls for seaway expansions just to maintain shipping and power generation at current levels. Riparians may also suffer from declining water levels, particularly if a warmer climate prompts an increase in irrigated farming in the

Great Lakes–St Lawrence region, a voracious consumer of water. Furthermore, under current institutions, all of these uses would have priority over environmental and recreational uses, which would likely suffer
most from reduced water supplies in the St Lawrence. Though this scenario is still hypothetical, there is a growing amount of data to support
it, and the current debate about the future of the St Lawrence could be
further complicated by the various interests contending to position
themselves in a water-scarce future.

CONCLUSION

For the foreseeable future, the St Lawrence is likely to remain an un-
wieldy combination of river and seaway. Shippers, riparians, and hydroelectric generators continue to enjoy priority rights to the use of the
St Lawrence, entrenched in the IJC order of approval, and it is unlikely
that environmentalists and recreational users of the river will succeed in
substantially diminishing these rights as long as the seaway remains economically viable. At the same time, however, there has also been a
growing awareness of the St Lawrence's riverine ecosystem, and the federal and provincial governments have invested considerable resources in
preserving and restoring some of the river's natural features. While this
environmentalism has not succeeded in returning the St Lawrence to a
pristine state, it is likely to act as a serious political barrier to future
efforts to expand the existing seaway further.

And so the St Lawrence effectively exists in a state of political equilibrium. Neither river nor seaway advocates have been able to make a case
compelling enough to convince the IJC and the two federal governments that significant institutional change is necessary, and so the prevailing hierarchy of property rights has remained in place and seems
likely to continue so. Past experience, when there was a relative political consensus about the necessity of an expanded seaway, suggests that
the difficulties of binational cooperation can impede significant policy
change, and these are an even greater impediment today, when a political consensus for change – in either direction – is entirely lacking. The
contest between river and seaway is far from settled, but neither side
has yet to muster the political influence necessary to run the institutional gauntlet and tip the balance one way or the other.

10

Chasing Whose Fish? Atlantic Fisheries Conflicts and Institutions

PETER CLANCY

In terms of in-stream uses, water is valued not only as a transportation network (see chapter 9) but also as a habitat for a wide variety of marine species. In Canada, commercial fishing is one of the most economically and culturally important in-stream water uses, and the management of the Atlantic fisheries has become one of the country's most contentious resource management issues. In this chapter the coexistence, conflict, and tension of different marine fisheries are examined, with particular attention to the institutions in which these conflicts are played out and the types of knowledge that various actors draw upon in defining their interests. Particular attention is focused on the management of the northern cod, Gulf of St Lawrence herring, and harp seals, as well as the ongoing contention over harvesting rights for Aboriginal fishers. The cases highlight how, in the past, coastal water resources were centrally managed by the federal government, a practice that led to the development of intensive user rivalries and the collapse of a number of important fisheries, most notably the Atlantic cod. With failures such as these and greater demands for stakeholder participation, centralized federal management is gradually giving way to various co-management arrangements in which the divergent perspectives pervading the Atlantic fisheries have a greater chance of being expressed and, it is hoped, reconciled. Like the previous chapter, this chapter shows the great diversity of interests involved in in-stream water uses and how failure to manage rival interests can result in significant resource degradation.

INTRODUCTION

Beyond Canada's coastal provinces and territories, fisheries may be viewed as a distant and somewhat marginal concern. On the nation's three oceans, however, where marine resources, harvesters, and regulators constitute a significant socio-political sector, the reverse is true. The oceans economy is currently valued at more than $22 billion (Canada, Department of Fisheries and Oceans, 2005), and the Supreme Court of Canada has confirmed that the country's fisheries resources are a common property, belonging to all the people of Canada. Recent fisheries management disasters, such as the collapse of the Atlantic cod, have shown that the centralized institutions traditionally used to manage this common property resource are no longer effective. Accordingly, governments and stakeholders have embarked on an ongoing pursuit of institutional reform, the outcomes of which are still uncertain. Moreover, recent court decisions recognizing Aboriginals as holders of significant fisheries harvesting rights have introduced a new group of stakeholders and increased demands on already scarce resources, complicating the situation even further. Altogether, this confluence of factors has put the Atlantic fisheries in a state of institutional flux, and this chapter explores how the old centralized institutions have been largely discredited and what institutional reforms are being developed in their place.

FISHERIES INSTITUTIONS IN ATLANTIC CANADA

As outlined in chapter 2, the current Fisheries Act is recognized as one of the strongest pieces of legislation to protect aquatic ecosystems in the country. It also grants significant management powers to the federal Department of Fisheries and Oceans (DFO), which is involved in all fisheries-related issues in the Atlantic region. In federal government circles, the department is often seen as a middle-level portfolio with a producer or consumer clientele (alongside agriculture, natural resources, labour, industry, and veterans' affairs). This perception may well prevail around the cabinet table and even in Parliament. However, it overlooks some key features of the fisheries and oceans portfolio. The central statute, the Fisheries Act, confers extensive powers over the resource, its use, and its habitats. As a result, the department wields broad regulatory authority that may be the envy of other clientele agencies. Ministers of Fisheries and Oceans enjoy considerable discretionary authority under the act, which has allowed departmental staff to design and implement sweeping regulatory and management regimes. There have been some notable realignments over time. More than a century ago, for example, inland fisheries management was delegated to provincial governments. However, marine fisheries and oceans remain very much with Ottawa.

The department is a significant part of the federal civil service establishment, ranking among the top five departments by size (Clancy, 2000). Furthermore, it is a highly decentralized bureaucracy. Some 90 per cent of the positions are situated outside Ottawa, in six regional and dozens of area offices across the country. While legal enforcement may be the most visible part of DFO activities on the ground, the department maintains significant scientific expertise, particularly in the disciplines of biology and engineering. The first federal fisheries research stations were established a century ago, and the Fisheries Research Board was a leading producer of science studies in its day (Johnston, 1977). This activity continues within the department today, in support of the dual fisheries management and habitat protection mandates. The advent of Ottawa's "oceans" program in recent years calls for a further broadening of the science mandate and a paradigm shift from species biology to ecosystems (Canada, DFO, 2002a, 2002b). Indeed, its dual mandates create formidable challenges in fashioning integrated management measures across its own specialized branches, which range from fisheries enforcement to science, habitat protection, oceans, harbours, and other issues. This is a large organization to be sure, but it is being asked to assume ever larger and more complicated responsibilities at a time when hiring and expenditure budgets have been frozen or slashed.

Within the government of Canada, the DFO faces a struggle for attention at both the cabinet and the budget tables. Ministerial turnover is rapid; there were seven ministers between 1994 and 2007 – Brian Tobin, Fred Mifflin, David Anderson, Herb Dhaliwal, Robert Thibault, Geoff Regan, and Loyola Hearn – for an average tenure of less than two years. Fisheries is not an easy portfolio to manage, with its constant bursts of clientele dispute and jurisdictional challenge. For federal politicians, the DFO has a reputation as politically difficult and loaded with minefields that are dangerous to an aspiring career. Equally, the department is hemmed in by a tangle of rival federal agencies, including Indian and Northern Affairs, Natural Resources, Justice, Environment, and Transport, to name only the most prominent (Clancy, 2000). Like other departments, the DFO was forced to implement deep program and personnel cuts during the Chrétien-Martin Program Review of 1994–95.

There are three principal policy thrusts to contemporary fisheries and oceans programs. The first, and the traditional core, program is fisheries management, rooted in section 91.12 of the Constitution Act, 1867, which deals with the living resources of "seacoast and inland fisheries." This responsibility has expanded dramatically since the assertion of the

200-mile offshore zone in 1977 (Pross and McCorquodale, 1987). A second policy thrust is for marine infrastructure. What began with harbours, wharves, and navigational aids such as charts and buoys has expanded, through time, to embrace the Canadian Coast Guard, safety and rescue, and marine traffic control. Many of these business "service" activities have found their way into the DFO from other departments such as Transport and Public Works. Unlike fisheries management, where budget cuts have been a secondary source of political difficulty, marine infrastructure was in the front lines of commercialization and privatization during program review. The oceans mandate is the third and latest policy thrust in the DFO. The enactment in 1997 of Canada's Oceans Act paved the way for a management shift from species to ecosystems and from single-purpose to integrated programming. Appearing in the midst of the Liberal fiscal clampdown, the challenge for the oceans program is to win sufficient resources to adequately address this new and complex mandate (Clancy, 2000).

Despite the DFO's size and scope, it far from exhausts the marine fisheries policy sector. Mention must be made also of the federal-provincial relationships, which are omnipresent. This factor derives in part from closely aligned provincial powers over shore-based activities such as fish processing and coastal zone activities such as aquaculture siting and the pollution of internal waters. Newfoundland's vigorous interest in supporting the Atlantic seal hunt, discussed later in this chapter, is a case in point. Many of these issues have found their way into formal federal-provincial forums such as the Canadian Council of Ministers of Fisheries and Aquaculture.

The parliamentary process also needs to be factored into this model of the "fisheries state." This is because the House of Commons Standing Committee on Fisheries and Oceans has proven to be a vigorous and creative force in recent decades. It has demonstrated a significant degree of cross-partisan purpose in auditing departmental activities, delving into controversial issues, and providing channels for fisheries interests and coastal communities to be heard. Through a series of broad-ranging inquiries, the committee has proven to be an effective critic, calling ministers and senior bureaucrats to account and making positive policy contributions along the way (Canada, House of Commons, Standing Committee on Fisheries and Oceans, 1998a, 1998b, 1998c, 1998d, 1998e, 1999, 2002, 2004).

Another key institution of fisheries governance is the judicial system. The recent importance of the courts in the East Coast fisheries distinguishes them from most other aquatic resources, as the courts have played a comparatively lesser role in most other water-related issues. Since 1990, the Supreme Court of Canada (and to a lesser degree the Federal Court of Canada) has adjudicated a number of cases with policy implications of the highest order. Some of these involve questions of federalism, as with the *Ward* case, which challenged Ottawa's powers to regulate the trade in seal products (Canada, Supreme Court of Canada, 2002). Others involve administrative law, as with the Ecology Action Centre's initiative to require a federal environmental review of the habitat impacts of deep-sea dragging (Canada, Federal Court of Canada, 2004). Finally, there have been a series of cases concerned with Aboriginal fishing rights that served to redefine the basis of licensing and harvest allocation. The *Marshall* case, discussed below, is a prime example in point.

Regardless of policy subject, the courts have a distinctive style of resolving resource conflicts compared to other institutions. The interest-holders or clients must retain professional experts (lawyers) to speak on their behalf in an adversarial setting. Arguments are advanced in a technical legal discourse centred on jurisdiction, precedent, and procedure. A judicial elite, operating at the apex of this system, determines outcomes. The logic of decision-making is zero-sum or winner-take-all, compared to the compromisory and negotiable logic of conventional legislative and executive institutions. Consequently, litigation offers a high-risk path for settling political disputes.

The institutions have clearly evolved to manage both an increasingly complex fishery and the interface of commercial fisheries uses with other water uses such as shipping, recreation, and coastal waters as outlets for municipal and industrial wastes. Even within the Atlantic fishery there are multiple uses. Although the users are in many instances the same fishers, the cases which follow indicate that there is inter-use conflict on a variety of fronts which has significant institutional impacts, particularly on the institutional dominance of the federal Department of Fisheries and Oceans.

GROUNDFISH AND THE COD COLLAPSE

The Euro-Canadian fishery began more than five hundred years ago, when the baskets lowered from John Cabot's ships lifted cod from schools so dense that the ocean was described as seething. Since then, the Atlantic ground fishery (bottom-dwelling species including Atlantic cod, haddock, halibut, and redfish, among others) has been exploited for a variety of purposes and by a variety of techniques (Innis, 1954). In the early centuries the European states that fished the western Atlantic skirmished over imperial strategies, territorial claims to new lands, and rights of shore use. Following the American Revolution, the United States joined these contests. Tensions between rival fleets and nationalities, involving both the three-mile limit of territorial sovereignty and the delineation of international maritime boundary limits, surfaced regularly. Disputes over export market access were also a continuing theme. All these issues became the grist for diplomatic manoeuvring, treaties, and legal challenges. As recently as the 1980s, Canada and the United States appeared before international courts to settle their conflicting claims over fishery rights to the East Coast Georges Bank (VanderZwaag, 1983).

Tensions arising out of the commercial ground fisheries were also prominent in domestic politics in both Canada and Newfoundland. Resident fishers and settlers tended to use small boats in inshore waters. Permanent residents depended upon government support in ways that foreign fleets (and seasonal residents) did not. The fishers who produced the commodity were also locked in rivalry with buyers and processors over the terms of sale, along with the broader colonial mercantile role. All these questions were prone to political challenge, as rival interests sought advantages in both market and state circles. By exercising regulatory powers, governments could favour one class of fishers, buyers, or processors over others. Bounties or subsidies could tip the scales in favour of one enterprise, in boat building, wharf provisioning, customs staffing, or fish transport. Statutory regulations could authorize or proscribe key harvest activities by designating open and closed seasons, catch size, permissible gear types, boat numbers, or processing plant locations. In the ground fishery of the 1920s, for example, small boat fishers opposed the introduction of company-owned trawlers, which dragged cone-shaped nets along the bottom to scoop up large numbers of fish. Following a royal commission in 1927, Ottawa restricted the trawler fleet to a handful of vessels. This restriction was lifted after World War II, but it benefited the small-boat, inshore sector while it lasted.

The rise of the factory trawler fishery, beginning with foreign fleets in the 1950s, marked a transformation that would have catastrophic consequences for northwest Atlantic groundfish stocks. The combination of trawling gear, improved fish-finding instruments, vastly expanded storage capacity, side-by-side trawls, and unregulated access took a dramatic toll. It is estimated that some 8 million tonnes of northern cod were caught in the twenty-five to forty generations produced between 1500 and 1750. An equivalent 8 million tonnes was taken in the one to two generations in the factory-freezer era from 1960 to 1975 (Hutchings and Myers, as quoted in Harris, 1998, 63–4).

The story of the northern cod collapse is too complex to be reprised here. However, the political process of groundfish quota determination, which lies at the heart of the conservation question, is revealing. After World War II, the chief mechanism of groundfish conservation was the International Commission for Northwest Atlantic Fisheries, or ICNAF (Chepel, 2000). While the commission was committed to the goal of maximum sustained yield and created a science establishment together with a policy and administrative arm, it was handicapped in the 1950s and 1960s by the requirement for unanimity among member states before measures could be approved. In 1978 ICNAF was replaced by the North Atlantic Fisheries Organization, an equally impotent management institution that established internationally negotiated total allowable catches (TACs) for some Atlantic fisheries but had no means of enforcing them. In consequence, at the international level the Atlantic fisheries were treated, in essence, as an open-access resource, and fishers from all over the northern hemisphere rushed to capture a piece of it (Harris, 1998, 72–7).

In 1976 Canada expanded its coastal jurisdiction to a 200-mile Exclusive Economic Zone, and the DFO stepped up its efforts to improve fisheries management in Canadian waters. Grounded in the scientific management perspective, formal procedures were established to channel science advice to managers setting quotas. Central to this process was the Canadian Atlantic Fisheries Scientific Advisory Committee, or CAFSAC. Here staff scientists deliberated on stock assessments made in species subcommittees (e.g., for groundfish), while departmental directors and some invited outside scientists sat on the steering committee that prepared advisory documents for senior management. By the 1980s the department found itself faced with apparently conflicting information regarding groundfish (Harris, 1998). Newfoundland inshore fishers, drawing on local, experiential knowledge, reported serious declines in catches, which they linked to declining overall stocks. Yet offshore harvests remained consistently strong, suggesting healthy stocks. The inshore fishers were sufficiently concerned to commission an autonomous scientific panel in 1986 that audited DFO methods and concluded that the groundfish stock assessments, based principally on offshore catches, were seriously overestimated. Yet that same year the

CAFSAC advisory document on groundfish that covered areas 2J, 3K, and 3L (combined as 2J3KL on figure 10.1) estimated that cod biomass was growing. Here, in microcosm, is the dilemma of science serving management in a politicized policy network.

There are several pressing issues worthy of note. The first involves shortcomings in the quality of research, including bureaucratic insularity in defining and reviewing population studies, inflexible adherence to modelling assumptions and parameters (even in the face of formal challenges), and the failure to address alternative data or findings that run contrary to officially accepted results (Finlayson, 1994). A second issue concerns the absence of effective links between research findings and administrative decision-making. Partly this has involved the presentation of data without reference to the range of scientific uncertainties and analytic debates that are inherently part of the research process. The result tends to narrow the interpretation and exclude the complexity of the issues as the data move to a lay administrative audience, contaminating the deliberative process along the way (Hutchings et al., 1997). Third, there was significant reluctance at senior administrative and ministerial levels to apply a precautionary conservation ethic in situations which risked damaging social and economic consequences. After 1988, when advisory bodies urged more than a 50 per cent cut in the total allowable catch, ministers opted instead for a cut of less than 10 per cent (Harris, 1998).

It should be evident that there are no simple solutions to perfecting the science-management nexus. However, the extreme consequences that flowed from the groundfish collapse and the 1992 moratorium constitute a devastating political legacy (Schott, 2004). It continues to shape relations between DFO scientists and managers, harvester groups, conservationists, and the public at large on a variety of separate issues.

MARINE MAMMALS AND THE SEAL HUNT

One of the most complicated and intractable issues in Canada's Atlantic fisheries deals not with a fish species but with a marine mammal – the seal. In fact, seals have had important economic and political roles on all of Canada's coasts. In the Arctic, Inuit have hunted ringed seals since time immemorial. In the Pacific the commercial assault on fur seals and their ensuing collapse led to an international treaty as early as 1911. Finally, in the case of the Atlantic, profiled below, harp and hooded seals have been hunted commercially since the late 1700s (Ryan, 1994).

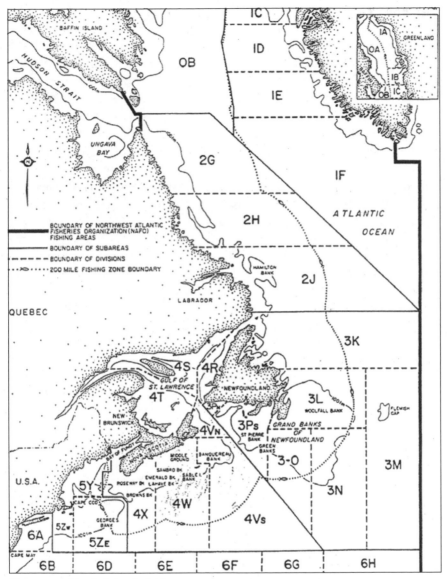

Figure 10.1 North Atlantic fishing zones.
Courtesy Fisheries and Oceans Canada.

Today sealing represents a significant, though not overwhelming, source of seasonal cash income, particularly in outport Newfoundland. The spring seal hunt became intensely politicized in the late 1960s, fuelled by the animal rights movement that gained ground rapidly in both Europe and North America. Almost immediately, the scientific and management context became more contentious, as opponents demanded the abolition of the seal hunt. Direct action protests, broadcast electronically around the world, disrupted the hunt and sparked bitter confrontations in sealing communities (Watson, 2002). A royal commission was struck to review the issues, boycotts were declared in Europe, and the fur seal market collapsed. The Department of Fisheries and Oceans found itself embroiled in a very "modern" management problem situated between animals, harvesters, and third-party interests.

Two species of seal, harp and hooded, are found in numbers in the Atlantic waters, though the political dispute centres on the more numerous harp seals, whose newborn display the archetypal white coats. In the early spring, female harp seals emerge onto the ice to give birth and nurse their young. The two principal whelping areas are in the central Gulf of St Lawrence and off the Labrador coast north of Newfoundland. For a period of several weeks, the animals are exposed above water, and it is at this time that the seal hunt occurs. For centuries, thousands of Newfoundlanders have hired out on vessels to kill and skin seals in the hundreds of thousands each year. It is hard and dangerous work, and the history of the seal hunt is littered with the names of ships and men lost at sea. Though the pay is relatively marginal, it has provided a seasonal cash income to generations of outport men, and the experience of going "o'er the side" onto the ice became a rite of passage for young Newfoundlanders. The commercial fishery centred traditionally on seal oil and fur skins, most of which were exported by Newfoundland and Norwegian companies.

The political challenge to the spring seal hunt dates from 1964, when the anti-sealing movement was born. Radio-Canada broadcast a film, *Les Phoques de la Banquise*, with footage from the Gulf hunt off the Magdalen Islands that showed a seal being skinned alive on the ice. In the face of public condemnation, Ottawa adopted a set of seal protection regulations the following year covering seasonal limits, quotas, kill methods, and the licensing of both vessels and sealers. The anti-seal campaign picked up steam after 1969, when Brian Davies (previously an activist with the New Brunswick Humane Society) established the International Fund for Animal Welfare, or IFAW. Within a few years, its annual revenues exceeded half a million dollars, which funded direct-action resistance as opponents blocked vessel movements, sprayed seals with paint, and filmed seal kills. The movement broadened with the entry of Greenpeace in 1976 and the beginnings of celebrity protest a year later, when Brigitte Bardot ventured onto the ice off Newfoundland. Henke (1985) discusses the panoply of anti-sealing actors of the 1980s. In response, the province of Newfoundland launched a campaign to defend the hunt and the sealers, a position that it continues to hold today. In 1982 the federal government supported the establishment of a harvester voice, the Canadian Sealers Association.

The stakes intensified in 1983 when the European Community, responding to the anti-sealing lobby and to public pressure, imposed a ban on all products derived from whitecoats (Herscovici, 1985, chaps. 5–6). Overnight, the market for seal products collapsed (including that for ringed seal pelts produced by Inuit in the Arctic). The 1984 harvest was only one-third that of the year before, and none went for export. Momentum accelerated when IFAW orchestrated a successful lateral boycott on Canadian fish products among British grocery chains.

In an effort to gain purchase on the debate, the federal government appointed a Royal Commission on Seals and Sealing in 1984. Led by Quebec Justice André Malouf, the inquiry was charged with investigating all aspects of sealing and seal management. Timing was significant here, as it was hoped (in vain, as it turned out) that the inquiry could report before the European Community revisited its ban in 1985. In a three-volume report, Malouf addressed the heart of the anti-sealing debate with his finding that most seal kills were humane (Canada, Royal Commission on Seals and Sealing, 1985). He did, however, advise a blanket prohibition on the commercial hunt for baby seals prior to moulting (about two weeks for whitecoats and fifteen months for bluebacks, or young hooded seals). By adopting this measure in 1987, Ottawa signalled that the highly emotive slaughter of helpless whelps was over. The federal government also followed Malouf's advice by permanently closing the offshore (large ship) segment of the hunt, while endorsing the inshore, community-centred hunt from small boats of less than 65 feet. Today more than 11,000 persons hold commercial licences, while shoreline residents qualify for personal-use seal licences for up to six animals per year.

More generally, it became clear that for the seal hunt to gain political legitimacy, it would have to be managed on a scientific basis. New marine mammal regulations were promulgated by the DFO in 1993, prohibiting the sale, trade, or barter of whitecoats or bluebacks. Following a legal challenge to its constitutionality (on grounds that only a province could regulate the marketing of seals), the Supreme Court of Canada ruled in Ottawa's favour in 2002 (Canada, Supreme Court of Canada, 2002). In the uncertain decade that followed, the EC ban, annual harp seal harvests averaged 51,000 animals, which was less than one-third of the total allowable catch. With much lighter commercial takes, the estimated total harp population, which had dropped below two million in the early 1970s, rose to over five million animals by the 1990s. The regulations also governed hunting seasons (basically from mid-November to mid-May) and TACs. As well, they provide for the training and professional licensing of commercial sealers.

By the 1990s, the seal resource was increasingly being framed in an ecological manner. The northern cod moratorium played an important part in this debate. In the fishing sector, questions were being raised about the impact of burgeoning seal numbers and seal predation upon the prospects for groundfish recovery. These issues became more intense as years passed with little or no evidence of rebuilding stocks. In their long north-south migrations, harp seals consume millions of tons of fish. The favoured species are capelin, sand lance, and Arctic cod – forage fish rather than commercial species. However the inter-species relationship goes further, if seal predation diminishes the food base for Atlantic groundfish recovery. After extensive review of the prevailing data, the DFO's Eminent Panel on Seal Management demonstrated the complexity of inter-species dynamics and concluded that, in general, "the belief expressed by some stakeholders that reduction of seal numbers will rapidly restore cod numbers is overly optimistic" (MacLaren et al., 2001, 71). Nevertheless, the panel found that in certain zones, a reduction in seal predation might have a substantial positive effect on groundfish by protecting spawning and juvenile stocks.

The Atlantic Seal Hunt Management Plan of 2003–05 offered a striking example of flexible management supported by research (Canada, DFO, 2003a). It identified a series of population reference levels keyed to the estimated maximum of 5.5 million harp seals. A three-year TAC of 975,000 was estimated to reduce total stocks by not more than 30 per cent (or 3.85 million animals) over the period. In the event that the total fell below 70 per cent of maximum, more stringent management measures would come into effect, and if it fell below 50 per cent of maximum, very stringent measures, including closure, would be triggered. This plan aimed to meet standards of sustainable management together with incorporating channels of adaptive feedback. Notably, the basic principles (derived largely from the expert panel report) were received positively by several hundred stakeholders at the DFO's 2002 Seal Forum in St John's.

The current Atlantic Seal Management Plan (2006–10) continues in this vein, with control rules and reference points guiding year-to-year adjustments. The harp seal TAC was set at 325,000 in 2006 and at 270,000 in 2007. The plan also had to deal with a 2006 quota overrun in the Gulf of St Lawrence that prompted new measures governing season length and daily vessel reporting in the following year (Canada, DFO, 2006, 2007). These speak further to the changing processes of Atlantic marine resource regulation.

Of the aquatic policy cases considered in this chapter, the seal controversy is distinctive for being fuelled by non-fisheries interests. Opposition from animal rights or anti-harvest forces is not common in the Atlantic wild fishery and has not challenged existing institutional arrangements. The effective exercise of political leverage through mass-media mobilization, direct-action protests, and trade sanctions is equally rare in this sector. Only in the face of the most grave crisis were Canadian authorities able to partially displace the established economic users of the seal population and mount a fundamental revision to the management regime, eliminating the most devastating flashpoint (the whitecoat kill) and presenting the residual seal hunt in a context of scientific and professional practice. The case against sealing is unlikely to disappear; however, this analysis illustrates that it can be contained by successfully transforming the debate and altering institutions and the public perception of the hunt.

HERRING DISPUTES
IN THE GULF OF ST LAWRENCE

In the last week of October 2003, a group of local fishermen and friends rushed to the wharf in Souris, Prince Edward Island. They circled their cars and pickup trucks to form a barrier across the wharf road and announced that no fish would move from the four New Brunswick seiner boats that had tied up the night before to unload their catches. The several hundred local protesters made it clear that they meant business, and any trucker or fisherman who defied them could count on rough treatment. The blockade continued for several days, until the herring in the holds and in the trailers on the dock had spoiled (Willis, 2003).

The intensity and the scale of this protest were not typical of Souris, a small town of several thousand residents situated on the province's eastern shore. Islanders are generally calm and relaxed in their ways, overt conflict is frowned upon, and the political tradition is decidedly conservative. Yet the Souris mayor was quick to offer support to the local protest. On the front line, the Island fishers demanded that Robert Thibault, then federal fisheries minister, intervene to protect their herring stocks. One Souris fisherman declared that they had tried to secure change through normal channels, but to no effect. So the time had come for direct action. Besides, he said, "This is how they seem to get things done in Quebec and New Brunswick."

Herring is a small pelagic species that gathers into schools in the Gulf of St Lawrence during the spring and fall spawning periods. The adults overwinter in the ocean off the east Cape Breton coast. A visual feeder, herring consumes plankton at all stages of life. It, in turn, is prey for marine birds and mammals as well as groundfish (cod and hake) and tuna (Canada, DFO, 2003c). The strategic place of herring in the gulf aquatic food chain explains, in part, the PEI fishers' concern with stock size and health. By contrast to the groundfish, herring stocks remain regionally strong and constitute the major landed fish by volume.

Herring has been fished in East Coast waters since the 1800s. Until thirty years ago, it was considered a low-value fish, used for bait in other fisheries, ground into fish meal, or processed into farm fertilizer. Then in the late 1970s a new commercial food market transformed herring into a higher-value fish and value-added products. This development was due partly to the decline of overseas fisheries, which opened demand for Canadian herring fillets in Europe and herring roe (fish eggs) in Japan. The gulf catch rose dramatically and then crashed abruptly in the early 1980s (Kinnie, 2001).

This is a fishery in two segments. Inshore harvesters use gillnets, set from small boats, in shallower inshore waters near spawning grounds. Positioned with buoys and weights, the nets are suspended in the water column for a period of time. Fish swimming through the nets are trapped in the mesh and then prevented from backing out by the flaring of their gills. The nets are later lifted to recover the adult fish. By far the majority of herring fishers use gillnet or "fixed" gear. Today some 3,300 licences are held in the four Atlantic provinces (over 800 of them in Prince Edward Island). The licence-holders are based in small ports and form part of the small-enterprise backbone of the inshore fishery. The inshore sector operates on a competitive basis, with licensees free to operate within designated herring fishing areas, or HFAS (within area 4T of figure 10.1). Once an area's total allowable catch has been attained, that area is closed for the season.

The other segment of the herring fishery is the seiner fleet, conducted from larger (over 65 foot) boats. Here the technique involves a net that hangs vertically in the water, with floats and weights, but is "mobile" in the sense that it is hauled through the water in a circular pattern to enclose the catch. After the ends are connected, the bottom of the net is "pursed" by tightening a cable running along the base, trapping the fish inside. With the seine boat pulled up alongside the net, the catch can be lifted out of the net and stored aboard. At the time there were thirty licensed seiners in the Gulf of St Lawrence (eight from New Brunswick and none from Prince Edward Island). Seiners operate according to individual transferable quotas (ITQS) that can be filled in designated HFAS. Obviously, far more fish can be captured much more quickly in this way, and it was not long before tensions emerged between the two sectors.

Traditionally, the herring fishery was, from a government point of view, an open-access resource. Then in 1973, following biological studies, the first catch limits were imposed. By 1981 the seiner fleet accounted for 80 per cent of total landings, which peaked at around 350 000 tons. Then the gulf stock crashed. The combination of much reduced TACs and soft markets left the herring fishery in disarray in the early 1980s. The DFO was forced to alter its management approach, which became more nuanced over the next decade. The gulf seiner fleet was reduced in size when many vessels were assigned to separate Scotia-Fundy waters. Also, the seiners were allocated transferable quotas, thereby limiting their total share. In 1984 separate inshore fisheries were designated for the spring and fall, with specified seasons and quotas for each. The goal here was to prevent the overfishing of spring spawners and also to better distribute the catch across the region. In 1987 the gulf waters were divided into seven herring management areas corresponding to the major spawning grounds. This more detailed basis for TACs and other regulations made it possible to spread fishing effort, reallocate fisher access, and devolve management responsibilities to area DFO staff. By the 1990s the proportions were effectively reversed, with about 75 per cent of the catch allocated to the gillnet fishers and 25 per cent to the seiners. These proportions continue today.

In 1999 the DFO introduced a new approach, an Integrated Fisheries Management Plan, for herring in Area 16. This was advanced in response to falling catches and unused quotas. The main change lay in the policy-making arrangements for setting quotas, seasons, and other regulations. An advisory mechanism was established to involve fisher groups in a consultative capacity. This operated at two levels, with area or regional advisory bodies for each HFA and an umbrella Gulf Small Pelagics Advisory Committee (covering herring, mackerel, and caplin) for Area 16 as a whole. The latter includes a dozen fisher organizations, fish processor associations from the four provinces, provincial Aboriginal groups, the five provincial governments, and the DFO (Canada, DFO, 1999b).

The PEI inshore fishermen were the driving force behind the October protests. With the inshore season effectively over, these fishers were aware that five New Brunswick seiners were still working the waters north of the Island, chasing their fall quotas for 2003. The PEI people had just finished a disappointing season in which catches fell far short of the inshore quota. Many blamed this outcome on the cumulative effect of several years of seiner activity in local waters. They argued that the seiners were only working off Prince Edward Island because they had depleted the New Brunswick areas. It was only a matter of time, the gillnetters said, before the same effect hit the Island, and that time was now. Part of their complaint involved seine fishing in shallower coastal waters, which overlapped with traditional gillnet grounds and, they said, damaged lobster habitat. DFO enforcement personnel from Charlottetown said that they could only enforce the regulations as written and could not push the seiners farther out.

Ministers in the government of PEI tended to side with the gillnetters, and the Island's federal MPs also expressed support for the home gillnet fleet. However, federal fisheries minister Robert Thibault defended the existing herring regulations. The TACs were set on the basis of the best available science, he said, with input from fisher groups represented on the Gulf Small Pelagics Advisory Committee. DFO enforcement personnel monitored on the water, by air, and on the wharf to ensure that seiner quotas were complied with. Furthermore, he pointed out that the local protests were illegal and threatened legitimate fishers with the loss of their legal catch. The Mounted Police were dispatched to police the situation at wharf-side in Souris.

After the season was over, the DFO hired a consultant to meet with all stakeholders and set out future policy options (Surette, 2004). The department, however, reserved the prerogative of determining the 2004 regulations, which were revealed as a carefully crafted compromise. In addition to marginal increases in the herring TACs (totalling 85 000 tons), the new minister, Geoff Regan, extended the seiner exclusion zone to the 20-fathom, or 150-foot, depth (the inshore fishers wanted 25 fathoms). Finally, to deal with the habitat concerns, Regan announced a three-year scientific study of seiner activity in 17–20 fathom depths, with independent observers and careful controls (Canada, DFO, 2004e, 2004g). Extensive efforts, continuing throughout the 2004 fall season, were made to persuade the PEI fishermen to endorse these measures.

ABORIGINAL FISHING RIGHTS
AND THE *MARSHALL* CASE

Today the DFO describes its aquatic resource mandate in terms of precautionary management, with non-governmental interests being involved not only as clients but also as partners. As former minister David Anderson put it in 1999, "co-management and shared stewardship are key to managing Canada's fisheries effectively. By introducing new roles for stakeholders in program-delivery, we aim to create environmentally sustainable, economically viable, self-reliant and self-adjusting fisheries" (Canada, DFO, 2000b).

One of the most demanding tests of this pledge involves the Aboriginal fishery. Throughout the 1990s, The DFO faced a continuing challenge to accommodate mounting numbers of Aboriginal fishers as a new class of harvesters not traditionally acknowledged within existing institutional arrangements and commercial management regimes. That this challenge occurred at a time when virtually all fixed coordinates of fishery policy were coming into question and when core groundfish and salmon stocks were in precipitous decline made the politics of Aboriginal fishing even more complicated.

The decade began with a historic judicial ruling from the Supreme Court of Canada in the *Sparrow* case. Here the court found that members of the Musqueam band in British Columbia possessed an Aboriginal right to fish for food and ceremonial purposes and that management schemes should give priority to these rights once valid conservation measures were met (Canada, Supreme Court of Canada, 1990; Sharma, 1998). In response, the DFO launched its Aboriginal Fishing Strategy in 1992 as a way to create space for Aboriginal peoples in fisheries across the country (Canada, DFO, 2003d). Initially this strategy focused on issuing communal licences and providing economic support for food and ceremonial fishing. (Two years later an Aboriginal Allocation Transfer Program was announced, to buy back commercial licences and transfer

them as communal holdings to Aboriginal authorities.) It was in 1993
also that Ottawa ratified the Nunavut Final Agreement. Its terms, which
settled the comprehensive land claims by the Inuit of the eastern Arctic,
included path-breaking co-management arrangements by which Aboriginal and government delegates jointly set a variety of conservation rules
and allocations under the authority of the Fisheries Act. This process
represented a powerful model of joint decision-making, which the department had only accepted after much deliberation and compromise
(Canada, 1992b; Clancy, 1999). For Aboriginal peoples, however, the
struggle to win recognition of fishing rights and generalized opportunity
for their exercise was long and difficult. By 1999 the Aboriginal Fishing
Strategy was being pursued in every region, though the number of new
entrants remained modest.

The East Coast counterpart to *Sparrow* was the *Marshall* judgment,
released by the Supreme Court in September 1999. Where *Sparrow* involved assertion of an Aboriginal right to food and ceremonial fishing,
Marshall sought recognition of a Mi'kmaq treaty right to fish for commercial sale. Prins (1996) and Henderson and Tanner (1992) outline the
background to Mi'kmaq harvesting and treaty rights litigation in general. Donald Marshall was charged with fishing and selling eels from
Pomquet Harbour, Nova Scotia, in violation of federal fisheries regulations (Wicken, 2002). After his conviction was registered at trial and
upheld by the Nova Scotia Court of Appeal, its reversal by the Supreme
Court of Canada came as a thunderbolt to both the DFO and the Atlantic commercial fishing industry. In short order, it triggered a firestorm of
political conflict.

Writing for the Supreme Court majority, Justice Ian Binnie found that
the 1760–61 treaties conferred a right to Mi'kmaq to sell fish. This
finding was based on a trade clause that granted the "right to bring"
products of hunting, fishing, and gathering to government-established
truckhouses to secure "necessaries" through exchange. Where the prior
courts had found that this right to trade had disappeared, since the
truckhouse system had fallen into disuse by the 1780s, Binnie ruled that
continuing access to a harvest of wildlife for trade was a necessary part
of the treaty transaction (Canada, Supreme Court of Canada, 1999a).
Thus the court majority found a continuing right to sell equivalent in
the contemporary context to a "moderate livelihood" for individual
Mi'kmaq families (Underhill and Legge, 1999). Binnie made clear in his
ruling that this constitutionally protected treaty right was subject to
valid conservation measures imposed by appropriate jurisdictions.

However, the ruling was widely (if incorrectly) construed, by both Native and non-Native fishers, as conferring an unlimited and categorical right to fish any stock or species.

Six weeks later the *Marshall* judgment was thrown into some confusion by the release of a unanimous Supreme Court "clarification" of the original decision (Fife and Hamilton, 1999). An intervenor in the *Marshall* appeal, the West Nova Fishermen's Coalition, had applied for a stay of the September judgment and a rehearing of the case. Though the Supreme Court denied the motion, the November clarification served to modify the original judgment by re-examining the issues raised in the original decision at considerable length (Canada, Supreme Court of Canada, 1999b). At least two new major points emerged. The court stressed that the *Marshall* decision applied to one specific resource, and it cautioned that findings related to eels did not apply necessarily to other Crown resources. In addition, the court suggested that the Crown's regulatory jurisdiction could extend beyond conservation objectives, to ensure fairness to and recognize historic participation by non-Native fishers.

The first sector to feel the impact of these rulings was the inshore lobster fishery, which was only two months away from the opening of the 1999 season. Flush with enthusiasm from the newly confirmed right, some Aboriginal fishers put to sea almost immediately. This action triggered a bitter, multi-track protest from non-Native lobstermen and from fishers more generally, who feared that their licensed positions under DFO management had been placed in peril. Well-organized into regional and species-based groups, these interests forced the political agenda with threats of direct action if the department was unable to assert control. Intense and sometime violent disputes continued for several lobster seasons after 1999, with the epicentre at Burnt Church, New Brunswick (Coates, 2000). Initially, the department offered each of the thirty-four Mi'kmaq bands a transitional program for immediate commercial fisheries access, through the retirement and reallocation of non-Aboriginal licences and the transfer of vessels and equipment to First Nations groups. Most, though not all, band authorities signed agreements. At Burnt Church, for example, the band sought the right to implement its own fisheries conservation plan, as opposed to falling under the federal Fisheries Act (Ward and Augustine, 2000). In 2001 Ottawa announced a longer-term Marshall Response Initiative for additional commercial fisheries access through multi-year agreements extending to March 2006. This program provides for additional licences and vessels (including new vessel construction) and capacity-building measures such as fisher mentoring and business training. By 2004, twenty-nine bands had agreed to terms that were estimated to have created 310 new fishing enterprises and over 1250 full- and part-time jobs (Canada, DFO, 2004a).

While the future of Aboriginal fishing in Atlantic waters is far from resolved, a number of significant institutional features and implications are worthy of note. First, the DFO was caught without contingency plans as the courts imposed a dramatic shift in the balance of harvester rights. The long-established, though somewhat vulnerable, fishing rights of non-Native fishers were suddenly threatened by the even longer established, but only recently recognized, fishing rights of local Aboriginals. Perhaps more important was the glaring lack of structured channels through which the department could bring together the full range of interests to pursue, much less achieve, reconciliation. Indeed, the Native and non-Native fishers seemed to share a mutual alienation from and distrust of the federal authority. It is telling that, at a moment of intense social confrontation, a non-governmental track of group-to-group talks produced the most positive outcomes. These negotiations, which bear features of the "community fisheries" model (Kearney, et al., 1999), led to local agreement between inshore fisher groups and Mi'kmaq bands in several southwest Nova Scotia harbours to accept a modest number of "licensed" Aboriginal boats into the fall lobster fishery. The agreement between licensed fisher groups and the Acadia First Nation proved to be tenuous, however, and vulnerable to negative pressure from both sides (Hamilton, 1999).

The DFO response to the *Marshall* decision was to accelerate the rate of commercial licence buybacks in Atlantic Canada over the next five years and transfer these to Aboriginal communities. Working documents from the cabinet and the Finance Department set the cost of this initiative at $500 million over the period (Fife, 1999). At the time of writing, the level of political tension has subsided, though this lull seems likely to be as transitory as the passage of the fishing seasons.

A NEW POLICY PARADIGM AND INSTITUTIONS?

As the millennium approached, the DFO launched a sweeping review of its East Coast fisheries management regime. The timing was propitious, as the tight fiscal years of the 1990s were over and the groundfish adjustment strategy that followed the cod moratorium had run its course.

There remained, however, pressing problems of stock status, harvester access, gear and quota issues, and habitat quality for many of the thirty federally managed fisheries on the Atlantic. So when Minister Anderson announced the Atlantic Fisheries Policy Review (AFPR) in May of 1999, it was justified by the need to acknowledge declines in certain key resources, pressures and tensions for harvester access, and possibilities for new approaches to management. The extent of flux was underlined just four months later when the Supreme Court of Canada released its *Marshall* ruling.

Over the next six years, the DFO engaged in what was, for the department, an almost unprecedented political review of its East Coast operating coordinates. Most generally, the goal was "to create a framework for managing East Coast fisheries and build consensus around a renewed vision for the fishery" (Canada, DFO, 2004f). The result was a multi-stage process combining internal policy review and external political consultation, with the minister and his AFPR working group directing the overall process. Ongoing liaison with the provinces took place through the Atlantic Council of Fisheries and Aquaculture Ministers, a body established to coincide with the fisheries policy review.

The first phase was to define new goals and visions for East Coast fisheries management, culminating in a new policy framework document. Phase two involved the design and implementation of measures to realize the new approach. Phase one began with a series of stakeholder meetings in the summer of 1999, at which the department was warned against a "quick and dirty" fix. The following year a thirty-person External Review Board was appointed to advise the department over the life of the review. In February 2001 the DFO released a discussion document (already vetted by the review board) to serve as a springboard for a public consultation. Nineteen community meetings were convened for this purpose in the spring. Departmental staff then went back to the drawing board, spending the next two and a half years preparing the framework document.

Along the way, two particularly sensitive issues were carved out for separate treatment. One involved the question of "access" to expanding or emerging fisheries, a matter of ongoing concern to almost all categories of fishers and their associations. In June 2001, five experts were appointed to an Independent Panel on Access Criteria, or IPAC (Canada, DFO, 2001a, 2001b). In less than a year, the panel met with more than fifty stakeholders, and it presented a report in April 2002. In his fall response, the minister accepted the thrust of the panel's report. The second issue involved the status of the small-boat segment in any future fishery scenario. Particularly in light of past federal fisheries strategies, the inshore associations regard any "restructuring" initiatives with a jaundiced eye. In this case, the DFO chose a different approach. In late 2003 the department released its own discussion document on the independence of the inshore fleet (Canada, DFO, 2003b). A series of public hearings (separate from the main AFPR) were held the following year, and the process continues at time of writing. In effect, these two issues were fast-tracked to achieve policy results before phase one was over.

When the framework document was ultimately released in April 2004, there was much to interest the fisheries policy network and important potential implications for institutional arrangements (Canada, DFO, 2004d). For example, it suggested that a common sense of stewardship could be enhanced between the DFO and harvesters through the use of incentives and administrative sanctions, as opposed to legal prosecution (as outlined in chapter 3, a trend related to policy instruments evident in other water policy areas). Similarly, the framework document pointed to a shifting sense of the DFO role "from one focussed on day-to-day management of fishing activity to one more focussed on conservation, setting policy direction, establishing incentives for conservation and evaluating performance" (Canada, DFO, 2004b). Related to this change was a new vision of cooperative management in the medium to long term, since "as resource users increase their ability to assume management responsibilities and as they demonstrate their commitment to sustainability, the DFO plans to delegate authority over specific decision-making areas to them" (Canada, DFO, 2004b). Overall, the framework document outlined a rationale for the introduction of co-management in the Atlantic fisheries and plotted the incremental steps to its introduction. The institutions envisioned would therefore more prominently reflect the ecological perspective outlined in the first section of this chapter and engage more stakeholders beyond the DFO.

Although, politically, some of the momentum generated by the review process was blunted by the Martin government's slip to minority status in 2004, the DFO, in its *2005–2010 Strategic Plan: Our Waters, Our Future*, stated that one of its priorities over the next five years was "to develop a new governance model for fisheries management" and modernize the Fisheries Act. The stated vision for the department was "excellence in service to Canadians to ensure the sustainable development and safe use of Canadian waters" (Canada, DFO, 2005). Strategies to achieve the vision have been developed through consultative exercises on both coasts, including the Atlantic Fisheries Policy Framework, Pacific New Directions, the Joint Task Group on Post-Treaty Fisheries, and the First Nations Panel on Fisheries (Canada, DFO, 2005).

Two years later, however, the Harper Conservatives tabled Bill C-45, "An Act respecting the sustainable development of Canada's seacoast and inland fisheries," in December 2006; it represented a comprehensive revision to the Fisheries Act, which had not undergone any significant overhaul since it came into force in 1868. Bill C-45 offered a variety of significant changes that had the potential to alter institutions governing the fishery uses in coastal and inland waters (Canada, Library of Parliament, 2007). Significant features of Bill C-45 (currently cited as the Fisheries Act, 2007) included provisions to curb the minister's absolute discretion over licensing by stipulating seven "application principles" to guide fishery decision-making, a section outlining federal-provincial relations, a new "Canadian Fisheries Tribunal" reflecting the significance of conflicts and to shift many infractions out of the criminal courts for more rapid adjudication, and new formal provisions for shared management roles. At time of writing, the future of this bill within the minority Parliament is unclear. Nonetheless, its very tabling altered the standards and expectations for fisheries policy and institutional change in future years. How adequately it will be able to address the conflicts sketched earlier in this chapter remains to be seen. The bill itself, however, reflects how fisheries are increasingly viewed as part of a broader set of water uses in Canada.

CONCLUSION

The cases of resource use, conflict, and adjudication discussed above provide a cross-section of Atlantic ocean fisheries politics today. It should be remembered, however, that there are dozens of additional species and stocks in the Atlantic region that are also subject to scientific monitoring and harvest management. In addition, there are a plethora of interactions among ocean fauna and other water uses that have not been adequately integrated into institutional arrangements to date. A common institutional element in these cases is the central role of the Department of Fisheries and Oceans, which anchors the fisheries policy sector on all of Canada's coastal regions. The department's legal and administrative powers are substantial. Yet this strength does not ensure that they will be effectively applied or that the desired outcome of sustainable fisheries will be realized.

The Atlantic fisheries sector also reveals a striking range of organized voices – of harvesters, processors, wildlife advocates, fisheries and ocean scientists, bureaucratic managers, lawyers and judges, and governmental leaders. Many of them are anxious about the health of the resource, the security of livelihoods, and the condition of coastal and ocean environments. In trying to sort out the competing claims, it is far from clear where guidance should be taken. Given the experiences of the past twenty years, there is little lingering deference to scientists, managers, or political leaders. Neither is there a single canon of legitimate knowledge available to frame fisheries policy. Almost all the coordinates of fisheries management are contestable today. To some extent, the boundaries between traditional or local knowledge and natural science knowledge are relaxing, and the beginnings of dialogue can be seen and reflected in institutional arrangements, particularly the tentative shift to co-management outlined in the AFPR and Bill C-45. This cooperation has been particularly necessary in cases where organized science has failed to acknowledge legitimate harvester perceptions or where management initiatives have ignored the informal institutional arrangements and the social and political dimensions of harvester communities.

The cases in this chapter also suggest how institutions have shaped the management of East Coast fisheries, contributing to many of the problems currently faced and influencing how actors have sought redress to these problems. With Newfoundland groundfish, a world-class resource was decimated in less than two generations, as a fractured regulatory system focused on the parts rather than the whole, while an embedded decision-making process was insulated from reflective review. With the harp seal question, by contrast, the creative role of political pressure served to dislodge traditional practice and open the way for new deliberative arrangements. While no harvest management system is unlikely ever to fully meet the concerns of animal rights advocates, the terms of discourse were significantly altered by broadening the participating constituency. The Gulf of St Lawrence herring dispute reminds us of a classic form of resource dilemma in which harvester interests based on gear type, catch level, or residence compete for fair shares. As with seals, ecological issues are raised when the regulation of one species may impact on the status of others. There is little evidence that present stock planning for herring can acknowledge, much less accommodate, possible broader trophic impacts, suggesting another challenge of institutional design that fishers and regulators will need to confront in the future.

Aspiring Aboriginal fishers faced a different challenge – to recover a significant stake in a livelihood that was once integral to their society. They were forced to resort to the judicial system to challenge the entrenched fishing rights already held by non-Aboriginal commercial fishers. The uncertainties, resentments, and hostilities that followed both the *Sparrow* and *Marshall* rulings point to the need to build bridges between user groups as well as with state authorities, as the institutions of East Coast fisheries management are reconfigured to incorporate new classes of fishing rights.

As a policy area, that of fisheries and oceans is complicated across space, species, knowledge domains, and technical instruments. The level of institutional interplay in this sector is high. In the terminology of this volume, it extends in both horizontal and vertical dimensions. As the core department, the federal DFO remains at the centre of the network. But its days of monopoly are long gone. Instead, the courts, the provinces, Parliament, and emerging co-management institutions enjoy substantial roles. So, too, the East Coast fisheries sector can no longer be viewed as a classic case of "producer capture" politics. The discussion above reveals trenchant challenges from prospective new users of water resources, both fishers and other groups.

Finally, it is worth noting the fluidity of fisheries arrangements in this era of institutional change. New bureaucratic decision-making rules and procedures are being explored at the same time as traditional legal mandates are being reformed. A powerful established bureaucracy bears a mixed legacy of management success and failure, while a growing constellation of stakeholder groups claim an expanded role in all stages of the policy process. The recent DFO strategy proposals – with their vision of delegated decision-making, more emphasis on conservation and habitat, alternative enforcement measures, and collaborative planning – are a potentially bold offer. No doubt they will be greeted with initial skepticism from some harvester communities hardened by traditional battles. However, there is also an intriguing possibility in this vision of new mechanisms for resolving local conflicts, for reconciling the informal rules of harvester culture and the formal legal rules of licensing and contracts, and for synthesizing a rounded understanding of aquatic systems that draws upon many types of knowledge. Certainly, this is the path suggested by the cases studies presented above. As the next chapter reveals, the institutional features and challenges are similar, yet different, on Canada's Pacific Coast.

11

Conflict and Institutional Reform in the British Columbia Salmon Fishery

RICHARD SCHWINDT

AND AIDAN R. VINING

In this case study the BC salmon fishery is used to highlight how a single in-stream water use can result in different sources of conflict and require different institutions to manage it. The conflicts on our Pacific Coast and in the open Pacific waters between commercial, recreational, and Aboriginal fishers, as well as conservationists, are examined. They are not just over fishing limits, licences, and places to fish; they have extended in the last two decades to conflicts over wild salmon versus hatchery or farmed salmon. One key actor remains constant, the federal Department of Fisheries and Oceans, which has substantial powers related to this water use and over fisheries policy and instruments generally. Just as in the Atlantic case, the DFO as an institution and its regulations are challenged. In contrast to the Atlantic case, however, contests have also arisen from other institutional actors, such as the BC government and its Ministry of Agriculture, which licenses fish farms, and from foreign salmon fishers and governments. Similarly, the DFO must now, as a result of legal decisions made by the Supreme Court of Canada, include Aboriginal fishing first as a ceremonial food fishery (starting on the West Coast) and secondly as a commercial fishery (starting with East Coast lobsters). Readers are encouraged to refer back to chapter 10 for details about the DFO and Aboriginal rights, as they will not be repeated again in this chapter. The last section of this case study outlines how institutions underpin various options for policy reform.

INTRODUCTION

A review of commercial fisheries around the world concludes: "The world's fisheries face the crises of dwindling stocks, overcapitalization, and disputes over jurisdiction" (Grafton, Squires, and Kirkley, 1996, 90). Several major Canadian fisheries face all three of these problems, as well as several other major issues. Partly as a result, several commercial fisheries in Canada are among the most contentious, conflict-ridden policy arenas that politicians, civil servants, and interest groups face. The observation that many fisheries around the world suffer from similar problems suggests that the underlying nature of these problems are at least partially fundamental, rather than idiosyncratic Canadian policy failures.

Why is fisheries conflict endemic? First and most obviously, fisheries involve the ownership and allocation of valuable resources. Second, they generally impinge on large and important ecosystems that support or affect multiple fishery and non-fishery uses and interests (Sproule-Jones, 1999). Third, jurisdiction over fisheries often involves multiple levels of government, ranging from the supra-national to the regional and local (Sproule-Jones, 1999; Potter, 2003). The distribution of property rights by governments exacerbates many of these conflict points. Because of inadequate property rights, there is conflict within individual fisheries as fishers inefficiently compete with one another for the harvest. This inefficient competition occurs either because additional fishers can access the resource (the "open access" problem) or because existing fishers invest in additional harvesting capacity (the "open effort" problem). Many of the aquatic ecosystems upon which a specific fishery depends also support other fisheries and uses. This is especially true for inshore fisheries, where marine transportation, aquaculture, recreational users, and coastal communities all claim rights to the use of the water resource. Fourth, many fish stocks move across different government jurisdictions, leading to frictions between these various governments over ownership and control of the resource. Finally, the rise of aquaculture in many parts of the world has placed open-water fisheries in direct competition with farmed salmon. This is partly a function of intensified market competition: the increased supply of farmed product has generally put downward pressure on prices. But, as we discuss below, aquaculture can also generate externalities that affect wild stocks, although there is disagreement as to their extent.

However, it is worth noting that while serious fishery problems are endemic globally, they are not universal. There is evidence that some countries – Iceland and New Zealand are two notable examples – have successfully reformed their fisheries and eliminated open access and open effort. This outcome demonstrates that, at least in some circumstances, effective institutional design is achievable.[*]

The purpose of this chapter is to review the problems and conflicts that beset the BC salmon fishery and to consider institutional impacts and reforms that might transform it once again into a sustainable, wealth-creating industry, reduce environmental concerns, and diminish the conflict with aquaculture. In this effort, we briefly review the history of the small-boat Pacific salmon fishery[†] in order to clarify the fundamental nature of the economic and environmental problems. We demonstrate that the economic and ecological issues are inseparable, and we conclude that current policy reforms have institutional implications, are costly, and will not be sufficient either to reverse the economic situation or to mitigate the threat to specific salmon stocks. To address the implications of an expanding aquaculture industry and its implications for the wild salmon fishery, we review the growth of aquaculture in British Columbia and, to some extent, around the world. We then consider several alternative policy options, instruments, and institutional options for the salmon fishery in terms of the broad policy goals of efficiency, ability to preserve the species diversity of the salmon stocks, and impacts on various groups that have a claim to special consideration (equity or distributional issues).

The focus of this chapter is primarily on the wild salmon, commercial, small-boat fishery. The federal government manages the fishery through the Department of Fisheries and Oceans (DFO), much as it has over the past thirty-five years. In simple terms, the number of vessels is fixed through a licensing program. Each year, government fisheries biologists attempt to determine the number of fish migrating toward their natal spawning grounds. From this estimate they deduct the number that must escape harvest in order to reproduce and then allocate the surplus to different users, primarily the commercial small-boat fleet,

---

[*] It should be noted, however, that both countries do have the advantage of relative geographic isolation, which somewhat insulates them from international property rights disputes.

[†] The fishery is classified as a small-boat fishery because most of the harvest is taken by seine, gillnet, and troll vessels that are small relative to "high-seas" fishing vessels.

First Nations fishers, and recreational users. Thus the federal government distributes valuable property rights to both the harvesting and the sale of salmon.

Because the harvesting capacity of the commercial fleet far exceeds a sustainable catch and because individual fishers have the incentive to catch as much as possible, policy-makers have imposed increasingly restrictive regulations on "time, place, and gear." As a result, commercial fishers are severely limited as to when they can fish, where they can fish, and the type of gear (e.g., net size) they can use. In order to comprehend the current state of the fishery, it is necessary to understand the historical development of public policy with regards to the problems of open access and open effort in the Pacific salmon fishery.

Open-access and open-effort problems are nearly always more severe when there are large profits from catching and selling a common-pool resource such as BC salmon. The value of seafood often exceeds (in some cases, far exceeds) the cost of harvesting and transporting it to market. This difference between value and cost, which economists label "rent," can potentially be quite significant in many fisheries. However, fishers may engage in behaviour that increases costs, thereby reducing or completely eliminating (dissipating) the rent. Perverse incentives can result from the way the fishery is organized. Fishers may find it in their self-interest to fish until the cost of catching an additional fish (their marginal cost) just equals the price of the fish (their marginal benefit). But their individual efforts (as well as the efforts of new entrants) can reduce the stock of fish available for catching and the value of the fishery for all. Under either open access or open effort, an efficient equilibrium (i.e., a level of effort that just maximizes the rent) is almost impossible to achieve or sustain. It is not surprising, therefore, that a good deal of fisheries policy in British Columbia has been aimed at attenuating the deleterious effects of open access and then open effort: most importantly, the propensity of fishers to overharvest the resource.

A BRIEF HISTORY OF THE BC SALMON FISHERY AND INSTITUTIONS

In the distant past a fishery existed in which salmon were essentially "free goods," so that the catches of individual Aboriginal fishers did not increase the marginal costs borne by other fishers (Higgs, 1982; Weinstein, 2000). But there is evidence that, even before European contact, increasing demand for fish prompted Aboriginals to develop their own fisheries management institutions based on Native beliefs and norms of behaviour (Higgs, 1982, 251). One key factor both in constraining access and effort and in facilitating the enforcement of effective property rights was that the Aboriginal salmon fishery was generally a riverine activity. Fish were caught in-river (not in the open ocean) using low-cost weirs and traps (Higgs, 1982; Schwindt, 1995; Weinstein, 2000). The evidence suggests that the Aboriginal population had the knowledge, incentives, and social organization to allow sufficient spawning fish through to replenish the stock (Higgs, 1982).

The arrival of European fishers, who were not subject to indigenous institutions, resulted in open access. They introduced a boat fishery that allowed them to leapfrog Aboriginal riverine fisheries by fishing further out to sea (Schwindt, 1995). This leapfrogging both created an open-access environment and introduced higher-cost fishing methods (Washington State, 1919, 9; quoted in Higgs, 1982, 264). One estimate is that in the 1930s traps in neighbouring Washington State were approximately two-thirds more cost-effective than the emerging small-boat fishery, and that without the interception of fish by the small-boat fishers, the traps could have been five-sixths more cost-effective (Higgs, 1982).

The early history of the BC salmon fishery has been extensively documented (Canada, Commission on Pacific Fisheries Policy, 1982; Schwindt, 1995; Schwindt, Vining, and Globerman, 2000; Weinstein, 2000). We focus here only on those policy developments that are most relevant to current economic and ecological problems, including the Sinclair Report/Davis Plan, the Pearse Commission, and the restructurings of the late 1990s.

Recognizing that the salmon fishery was in a precarious state, the federal government in 1958 commissioned a study by Sol Sinclair of ways to restrict open access. The study identified three possible policy options to resolve the problem: sole ownership (delegated by the federal government to a non-governmental corporation or to a private equity corporation), taxation of excess profits from fishers, and limited entry (Sinclair, 1960). Sinclair rejected the sole-ownership option on the grounds that it was "out of the question on many legal, political or social grounds quite apart from any possible abuses that may arise out of the monopoly position" (Sinclair, 1960, 101). He also rejected a policy of taxing the rents out of the system, believing that the tax would have to be set at too high a level to effectively curb effort in a timely manner. Instead, Sinclair opted for limited entry through licensing, and this scheme met little opposition. "Incumbent vessel owners generally approved of the plan ...

the revocation of rights provoked no public outcry ... the interest group adversely affected (potential participants) was dispersed, unorganized, and undoubtedly incapable of calculating the loss" (Schwindt, 1995, 106). It is important to note that Sinclair did not contemplate a reduction in the role of the federal government as single regulator. Indeed, the DFO would have an expanded role as a distributor of the property rights to harvest and sell the resource, no small power position in the scheme of arrangements.

In 1968 the Davis Plan introduced licence limitation.* It also introduced a voluntary buyback of some existing licences. But the buyback raised the market value of licences that were left and quickly exhausted the government's buyback budget. The Davis Plan also froze vessel types to seine, gillnet, troll, and combination gillnet-troll boats, which have very different capabilities and efficiencies. It did stop new entry and therefore eliminated open access. However, it did not stop licence holders from investing in newer boats and in equipment that enhanced their harvesting capability. The fishery thus switched to open effort as existing licensees competed for the allowable catch with ever more sophisticated and expensive equipment, a process known as "capital-stuffing" (Townsend, 1990). Between 1978 and 1983, landed values (i.e., the value of the fish before processing) dropped substantially. New fishers who had purchased licences from incumbents faced a financial crisis, as did incumbents who had participated in the capital-stuffing.

The emerging crisis led to the Commission on Pacific Fisheries Policy, known as the Pearse Commission, in 1982. Commissioner Peter H. Pearse found that restrictions on fishing times and allowable gear, habitat protection, and salmon enhancement investments (e.g., hatcheries) were generally successful in protecting the viability of the major stocks (Canada, Commission on Pacific Fisheries Policy, 1982). However, substantial overcapacity resulted in high harvesting costs and difficulty in managing smaller, more vulnerable stocks. He found that previous efforts to limit boat length and tonnage alone had not successfully

---

* It is important to note that from the outset of the commercial salmon fishery, possession of a licence did not vest de jure ownership, even though it conveyed significant de facto property rights, including the right to sell the licence (Huestis, 1992; Schwindt, 1995, 134). Thus if comprehensive ownership rights have never been transferred to a specific, fixed group of incumbents, there is no formal "common property" ownership of the resource (Ostrom, 1990), as will be described below in relation to the exclusive ownership rights alternative for the Fraser River.

restricted capital-stuffing. The Pearse Commission proposed to curb excess harvesting capacity by imposing a royalty tax on the gross value of the harvest, reducing the fleet by one-half, and auctioning licences (for details, see Schwindt, Vining and Weimer, 2003). But none of the commission recommendations were implemented because of their unpopularity with incumbents and because the financial state of the fishery improved in the mid-1980s. Consequently, at the end of 1995, the size of the fleet was approximately the same as it had been in 1982. However, capital-stuffing continued to increase fishing power, inevitably leading to ever shorter openings in order to protect the fish stocks. While short openings generally protected the viability of the major stocks, for many river runs there was little margin for error. This situation, in turn, put tremendous pressure on DFO scientists to get their estimates of specific run sizes right. The federal government seemed to think that good technical calculations of fishery migrations could solve the political problem of too many effective fishing vessels.

By the mid-1990s the fishery was once again in crisis, and in 1996 the federal government introduced the Pacific Salmon Revitalization Strategy (PSRS). The PSRS reduced the fleet in two ways. First, $80 million was allocated to a voluntary licence buyback program. This buyback retired nearly eight hundred vessels (approximately 18 per cent of the fleet). Second, area licensing was imposed, consisting of two geographic regions for seine vessels and three for gillnet and troll vessels. Licence holders had to select one geographic area. They could, however, purchase additional licences from other licence holders. Area licensing is a further attempt to curb effort and reduce what economists like to call congestion externalities and what the layperson would call overcrowding.*

Despite the buybacks and licence consolidation, the fleet was still much larger than required to bring in the harvest. Recognizing this problem, the federal government committed an additional $400 million in 1998 to the Pacific Fisheries Adjustment and Restructuring Program (PFARP). About half the funds were allocated to fleet and gear reductions. Between 1998 and 1999 the federal government spent $195 million to retire 1409 licences. This program, in combination with the PSRS buyback of 1996 and licence consolidation, resulted in a dramatic

---

* Congestion externalities refer to the effects that result from multiple users trying to use a resource simultaneously, such as traffic gridlock. The massing of vessels at specific openings made it very difficult, sometimes impossible, for resource managers to control the harvest. Sometimes the allowable catch was taken within the first minutes of the opening.

57 per cent reduction in the size of the fleet and more than achieved the Pearse Commission's recommendation of halving the fleet.[*]

Alarmed at the state of chinook and coho stocks, the PFARP also put substantial emphasis on (and money into) selective fishing techniques. Regulators sought to encourage fishing methods that more effectively discriminated between strong and weak stocks. To that end, the federal government financially supported the introduction and testing of new technologies and the modification of existing gear to achieve selective fishing. Note again how the DFO remained the single regulator and responded (selectively) to the interests of incumbent fishers.

RECENT INSTITUTIONAL REFORMS, THE RISE OF AQUACULTURE, AND THE CURRENT STATE OF THE FISHERY

The late 1990s certainly saw a major effort by the federal government to reform the fishery. Did it succeed? Regardless of whether the stocks recover, the DFO's policy of precautionary management raises harvesting costs. Selective fishing and the live release of non-target species and stocks lower productivity (narrowly defined) and thereby raise costs. If stocks do recover, there will still be private rents (excess profits) for the fishers who remain. It is important to note that private rents will be very high if landed values recover and, while less, would still be significant under a limited recovery scenario. The sector is likely to hold and attract harvesting capacity (see Schwindt, Vining, and Weimer, 2003, for a detailed explanation).

Ideally, commercial salmon fishing licence values should reflect the value that fishermen attach to participation in the fishery. The 1994 market value of licences (in private transactions) was nearly half the buyback price paid in the 1996 program. In other words, based upon an anticipated smaller fleet and therefore anticipated increased rents accruing to each remaining vessel, the value of licences nearly doubled (see table 11.1).[†] Between the PSRS program (1996) and the second round of the PFARP program (1998), licence prices increased modestly. The fact that they even held their value between 1996 and 1998 is telling, given

---

[*]   These figures understate the extent of vessel retirement. Approximately 345 Aboriginal licences are not assigned to a specific vessel. It is known that a number of these are used on vessels with conventional licences.

[†]   Gislason et al. (1998, 3–2) state that licence prices doubled between December 1995 and the conclusion of the 1996 buyback program.

Table 11.1
British Columbia salmon licence values, 1994–2007

	Seine	Gillnet	Troll
1994 license values	$225,000	$35,700	$35,700
Mifflin buyback (1996)	$413,900	$79,200	$77,100
PFARP round 1 (Dec. 1998)	$420,152	$77,880	$77,532
PFARP round 2 (Feb. 1999)	$432,115	$80,830	$82,150
PFARP round 3 (Dec. 1999)	$435,578	$84,231	$85,872
PRIVATE sales (c. March 2007)	$327,500	$77,700	$148,300

SOURCES: 1994 values from Canada, DFO, 1995; 1996 buyback prices from Gislason et al., 1998; PFARP prices from Canada, DFO, 2000a; 2007 prices from private communications with licence brokers.
NOTE: 2007 prices are averages across areas (licences now specify a gear type and a fishing area).

both the low landing values (see figure 11.1) and widespread pessimism over the state of the salmon stocks. What is more remarkable is the value of licences in early 2007, given the decline in both value and volume of landings in the first years of the twenty-first century. Seine licence values have declined slightly from 1999 levels, while both gillnet and troll licences have increased in value, and in the case of troll gear, the value has gone up dramatically. It is clear that incumbents anticipate the availability of future rents in the fishery and will therefore likely engage in a new round of capital-stuffing.

In summary, it is unlikely that the recent, costly restructuring of the BC salmon fishery will lead to a cost-efficient industry. Also, fishers have no more incentive to practise conservation now than they did before the restructuring. All that has changed is that they are easier to manage because there are fewer of them on the fishing grounds. If the emergence of substantial private rents leads to new capital investments in lethal harvesting capacity, effective management will once again be compromised.

Historically, the salmon fishery has been characterized by "boom and bust" cycles. Figure 11.1 shows the dramatic fluctuations in the value of the harvest over the past thirty years, ranging from a high of nearly $440 million to a low of $27 million (in constant 2002 dollars). Arguably, the promise of boom years has exacerbated the reluctance of fishers to leave the industry. However, regardless of whether the stocks recover, it is unlikely that harvest values will ever approach their historical highs, because the dramatic increase in the worldwide supply of farmed salmon will continue to dampen prices for both farmed and wild-stock product.

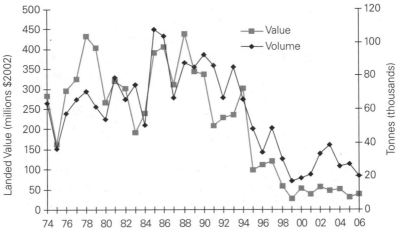

Figure 11.1 British Columbia wild-stock salmon landings, value, and volume.

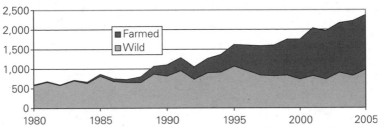

Figure 11.2 World production of wild and farmed salmon, 1980–2005.
SOURCE: United Nations, Food and Agriculture Organization, 2007.

Competition from farm salmon, or aquaculture, now dominates the world supply of salmon (see figure 11.2). Indeed, over the period 1980–2005, farmed salmon supply increased from 10 thousand to 1.4 million metric tonnes, while the world harvest of wild salmon rose from 587 000 to approximately 965 000 tonnes. Total world supply of salmon increased over the period by nearly 300 per cent. The ratio of farmed to wild has changed even more dramatically in British Columbia (see figure 11.3) The harvest of wild salmon declined over the 1986–2005 period, while the production of farmed product increased from negligible volumes to approximately 63 thousand tonnes. In 2005, farmed volumes were more than double the wild salmon harvest volumes. Not surprisingly, given this shift in supply, there has been a significant decline in the

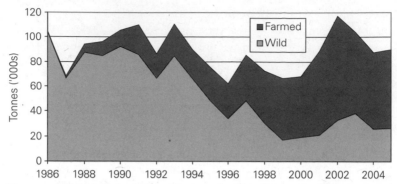

Figure 11.3 British Columbia production of wild and farmed salmon, 1986–2004.
SOURCE: British Columbia, Ministry of Agricultue, Food and Fisheries, various years.

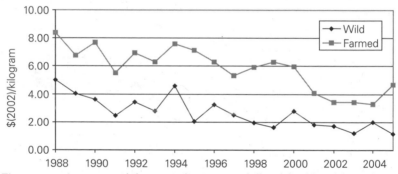

Figure 11.4 Average per kilogram value in 2002 dollars of wild and farmed BC salmon, 1988–2005.
SOURCE: British Columbia, Ministry of Agriculture, Food and Fisheries, various years.

average per kilogram value of both farmed and wild product in British Columbia (see figure 11.4). For the most part, these price declines have been a global phenomenon (Knapp, Roheim, and Anderson, 2007).

Most observers predict that the supply of farmed salmon will continue to expand (both globally and in British Columbia), with a continued concomitant downward pressure on prices for all salmon. Aquaculture is not subject to either major open-access or open-effort problems that plague the wild salmon fishery. Given the projected growth of aquaculture, Schwindt, Vining, and Weimer (2003) assumed that the value of wild salmon landings would not return to their 1988–94 levels in the fore-seeable future, and they argue that the growth in farmed salmon will make the wild salmon industry increasingly less viable from an economic perspective.

Not only has the rapid growth of salmon aquaculture put a downward pressure on prices, but it has raised environmental concerns and, as a result, created friction between fishers, aquaculturists, and the DFO and provincial fisheries authorities. Arguably, controversy over potential, deleterious environmental impacts of salmon farming is the principal source of conflict over coastal water use in the province of British Columbia today. Salmon fishers, supported by a number of environmental organizations, believe that salmon farming creates significant environmental risks for the wild stocks (Leggatt, 2001). They have identified two main threats: the transmission of diseases and parasites from farms to the wild stocks and the displacement of wild stocks from their natal spawning grounds by escaped Atlantic salmon, the preferred species of the farms. Most research dealing with the interaction of farmed and wild salmon stocks has focused on major European aquaculture regions, particularly Scotland and Norway. In both jurisdictions, farmed salmon production is much greater than in British Columbia, and in both, native wild stocks are weak and of limited economic importance. Evidence from these regions indicates that salmon farming can pose an ecological threat to wild stocks. Escaped farmed fish can displace wild stocks in spawning areas (Sægrov et al., 1997). There is evidence that escaped Atlantic salmon have successfully spawned in a number of BC rivers (Volpe et al., 2000). Sea lice infestations and other diseases on farms can contribute to infections in wild stocks (McVicar, 1997). In 2001 unusually high levels of lice were found on out-migrating wild salmon smolts as they passed through an area of very high farm concentration (the Broughton Archipelago), and the following year a significant drop in returning wild spawners was observed (Naylor, Eagle, and Smith, 2003). While a causal link between the infestation and the decline in spawners was not proven, the provincial government required fallowing of a number of farms to protect the out-migration in 2003. It should be noted that in Alaska, where the wild stock salmon fishery is of greater absolute and relative economic importance than in British Columbia, fishers have adamantly opposed salmon farming and, assisted by conservation groups, have succeeded in convincing the state government to maintain an outright prohibition of salmon aquaculture (Leggatt, 2001). The federal government (DFO) and the province of British Columbia share responsibility for regulating aquaculture under the Canada–British Columbia Memorandum of Understanding on Aquaculture Development, signed on 6 September 1988 (Canada, DFO, 2005).

In summary, the BC commercial salmon fishery faces a number of serious problems that threaten its viability. First, when both private and governmental costs are considered, the fishery extinguishes wealth rather than creates it (Schwindt, Vining, and Globerman, 2000). One indicator of the economic crisis that faces the sector (although by no means the whole story) is that between 1996 and 2001 the Canadian government spent nearly $500 million in total on the BC salmon fishery, mostly to buy back salmon fishing licences (Schwindt, Vining, and Weimer, 2003). Second, there is evidence that a substantial number of salmon stocks and subspecies are in a precarious state of survival (Walters and Cahoon, 1985). And third, the small-boat salmon fishery faces significant competition in the marketplace from the rapid growth of salmon aquaculture, both globally and locally. The former NDP government placed a moratorium on new aquaculture licences, but the current Liberal government has changed this policy. Even in the absence of intense competition from local farmed salmon, however, the small-boat fishery faces rapidly increasing competition from foreign aquaculture.

Almost all of these problems engender conflict. The economic and fiscal crisis places the industry squarely in conflict with the federal government over regulation, allocation, and subsidy levels. The rise of salmon aquaculture puts the industry in conflict with the provincial government (aquaculture is largely under provincial jurisdiction) and with commercial interest groups associated with salmon aquaculture. The looming environmental crisis puts the industry in conflict with environmentalists, environmental agencies of the federal government, and other interest groups that have exacerbated the crisis by degrading freshwater and saltwater salmon habitat. Any resolution of these problems will be complicated by three new emerging pressures on resource managers (McRae and Pearse, 2004, 25). First, the DFO has adopted a precautionary approach to management that involves more conservative harvesting rates. Second, passage of the Species at Risk Act in 2003 now explicitly requires federal authorities to protect endangered species, including specific salmon runs. And third, allocation of rights to salmon is a contentious issue in treaty-making with Aboriginal groups, and as treaty-making progresses, reallocation of some fishery property rights is inevitable. Even if treaty-making is not the major impetus, there is increasing recognition that the current situation is not sustainable vis-à-vis Aboriginal fishery issues. Given this pessimism over the prospects for the newly restructured small-boat fishery and the poor prognosis on prices, what are the options for the wild salmon fishery?

THE INSTITUTIONAL STATUS QUO, POLICY OPTIONS, AND THE FUTURE OF THE FISHERY

The analysis begins with an identification of appropriate policy goals. The preceding discussion of problems inherent in the status quo immediately suggests three important policy goals. First, although the salmon fishery is a potentially valuable resource, it is currently a net drain on society because of too much fishing effort in a limited common-pool resource. A primary policy goal, therefore, should be economically efficient use of the fishery.

Second, the current policy poses a risk to the preservation of salmon runs. While there are only five species of salmon, there are more than 8000 genetically distinct stocks (Walters, 1995; Sprott, 1997). Most Canadians place a positive value on preserving the fishery and its genetic diversity for multiple uses and future generations (Pearce and Turner, 1990; Vining and Weimer, 1998). It should be noted that there are two main threats to sustainability of salmon stocks – overharvesting and degradation of freshwater salmon habitat (both the freshwater migratory "paths" and the spawning grounds themselves). Overharvesting, or non-selective harvesting, is largely the result of open effort. Freshwater habitat degradation results in part from the imbalance in interests between those responsible for and benefiting from upstream resource use (e.g., population centres, industrial facilities, and logging operations) and downstream victims (e.g., fishers) (Wu et al., 2003). Upstream users have a clear interest in the use (or misuse) of specific watersheds. Fishers, because they target multiple stocks from a multitude of freshwater habitats, have limited interest in the protection of any specific stream or spawning ground. Various agencies of different levels of government share legal responsibilities for these concerns.

The advent and growth of salmon farming in British Columbia's coastal waters has raised serious concerns over potential threats posed by aquaculture to the wild salmon stocks. Public policy toward the wild-stock fishery cannot directly mitigate these concerns. However, it can give stakeholders in the wild-stock fishery greater incentives to monitor these potential threats and to ensure that regulations bearing directly on aquaculture are adequate and that they are enforced. This process can mean cooperative management by stakeholders, co-management by stakeholders and the BC agencies, or even horizontal management by the two levels of government. In any case, rules for conflict resolution will need to be devised and enforced, which is not an easy task in any common pool. It is clear that preservation of the native wild salmon stocks should be a policy goal. The primary criterion for measuring progress toward this goal is the maximization of the number of viable runs. This, in turn, depends upon adequate escapements and successful freshwater migration and spawning.

The third goal is that the costs and benefits of the fishery be fairly distributed among important stakeholders. These include incumbent fishers, Aboriginal bands, and the taxpayers who have subsidized the fishers of the wild stocks. The legal status of Aboriginal rights to salmon is in flux for several reasons. For example, the Supreme Court has held (in *Sparrow*) that Aboriginals have a right to salmon for "food, ceremonial and social purposes," which, after conservation, take priority over all other uses. However, the courts have not precisely defined these "purposes"; nor have they quantified the allocation required to satisfy them. Furthermore, fishing rights are an integral part of many of the as-yet-unresolved Aboriginal land claims in British Columbia. Resolution of many of these claims will involve the allocation of harvesting rights.

In short, fisheries management policy can simultaneously seek to achieve the main goals of economic efficiency, stock preservation, and social equity. To various extents, these are also the goals that the governments of British Columbia and Canada have tried to achieve in past fisheries policies, though with limited success. One reason for this is the fact that these goals sometimes conflict. For example, while allowing small salmon runs to be extinguished might be consistent with economic efficiency, it would conflict with the goal of preserving species diversity. Selecting the most socially desirable policy involves making trade-offs among the goals.

More extensive changes would include revising the rules under which federal and provincial resource agencies operate, such as by new legislation of parliaments and legislatures. Only the courts seem prepared to rejig the rules, and then only so far as they impinge on traditional Aboriginal rights. If we project into the future, four options for managing British Columbia's wild salmon fishery are possible. First, the status quo option, which we have reviewed at length, seems to fail on all three evaluation goals: it seems unlikely to limit fishing effort, it rests on ineffective informational premises about salmon migrations, and it is inequitable to all but the incumbent licence-holders. Second, the recommendations of the Pearse Commission would make some improvements in efficiencies but would still favour a small-boat over weir fishing. They would make no new improvements to preservation, and they would also lock into supremacy the incumbent fishers and the Aboriginal fishers. There are, however, two options that merit fuller discussion: exclusive ownership rights on a river and the "individual transferable quota" system.

River-Specific Exclusive Ownership Rights (with Joint Ownership Rights on the Fraser)

Under this option, the right to catch all salmon entering a river system would be allocated for a period of twenty-five years to a single owner (this could be a cooperative of incumbent fishers, a cooperative of all stakeholders including aquaculture owners and Aboriginals, or a government agency or private for-profit business). During the last five years an incumbent would only be allowed to catch the same average number of fish as in the first five years of the tenure. The salmon fleet would be significantly reduced, and the residual would become appurtenant to specific river fisheries; that is, rights owners could choose to target "their" returning spawners before entry into the river system.* Rights holders would almost certainly adopt fish traps and weirs, the lowest-cost method of catching salmon, to take most of their harvest. However, quality considerations would lead to some harvesting offshore.† Fish hatcheries would be included in the allocation: holders would have the right to continue using them or closing them down. The only river system in British Columbia where it will be impossible from a practical standpoint to sell rights to a single private or government monopolist is the Fraser. There are too many other potential users of both the resource and the river itself, and specific Aboriginal bands on the Fraser River have constitutionally protected ownership rights.

---

* This right would be limited to runs whose river of origin could be clearly identified. Moreover, some boats would have to be maintained both for test fishing and, given international disagreements over fishing rights, to maintain the ability to intercept fish that do not originate in BC watersheds.
† There is deterioration in fish quality as salmon approach their spawning grounds. This varies by species.

The advantage of this option is that it is the lowest-cost fish-catching regime and therefore offers the potential of being the most efficient – at least 50 per cent lower-cost than the small-boat fishery option. As owners would have a monopoly, they would have the correct efficiency incentives for avoiding the dissipation of rents (Agnello and Donnelley, 1975; Grafton, Squires, and Fox, 2000). Under this option, the small-boat fishery is retired; on the face of it, this approach does not look good for incumbent fishers. However, because this option is so efficient, it offers the potential for considerable rent. Some of this rent could be used to compensate existing fishers.

This policy option allocates a fixed percentage of river-specific rights to Aboriginals. It is therefore equitable to them relative to the status quo. The option would also enhance government revenues considerably, especially once small-boat licence holders have been reimbursed. Indeed, it would probably generate the largest benefit to taxpayers. The reason is that such rights would be extremely valuable resources because they offer a low-cost regime for catching the fish. Licences should therefore be auctioned for high prices; the total revenue from all river auctions should considerably exceed the total revenue from auctions of small-boat fishery licences as proposed by Pearse.[*]

Individual Transferable Quota Scheme

One widely recommended fisheries regime is individual transferable quotas (ITQs). Under this system, fishers are allocated a share of the allowable catch prior to the fishing season. The intent is to stop the "race for the fish," which in turn reduces the cost and increases the value of the harvest. Costs are reduced because fishers, confident of taking their allocations, seek to do so in the least costly manner. The incentives for capital-stuffing in order to out-fish rivals are extinguished. Commonly, ITQ systems also result in higher landed values because fishers focus on value not volume. The catch is handled more carefully and taken at times to exploit market demand. A dramatic example of this effect has been observed in the BC halibut fishery (Grafton, Squires, and Fox, 2000). In 1990, prior to the introduction of ITQs, the allowable catch was taken in six days, and the fishery was characterized by unsafe

---

[*]   The government could also take "payment in kind." For example, allocation of river-specific ownership rights could help to settle land claims and to reduce public transfer payments to economically distressed Aboriginal and non-Aboriginal coastal communities.

fishing conditions, substantial by-catch waste, poor product quality, and low landed prices (mainly because the fish had to be frozen rather than being shipped to more profitable fresh markets). With the introduction of ITQs, the season now extends for eight months, prices have increased markedly as supply matches fresh demand, the number of vessels has declined, and efficiency has improved (Macgillivray, 1997; Grafton, Squires, and Fox, 2000).

Several studies in Jones (2003b) evaluated a number of Pacific fisheries that have moved from open access or open effort to management regimes based on institutionalized property rights (primarily ITQs) in terms of impacts on resource conservation, economic viability, and working conditions. It was found that in most cases the establishment of property rights slowed or stopped the "race to the resource," and this outcome in turn resulted in more effective stock management (i.e., a more effective setting and enforcement of the allowable catch), better economic viability (i.e., lower-cost harvesting of higher-value product), and better working conditions (i.e., a safer work environment as fishers avoided risks associated with racing to harvest the resource). In six (geoduck, sablefish, halibut, green sea urchin, red sea urchin, and sea cucumber) of the nine fisheries where property rights–based management was introduced, performance improved on all dimensions; in two (groundfish trawl and roe herring) performance likely improved on all dimensions, but results were preliminary; and in one (abalone), performance was unchanged (Jones, 2003b, 106). ITQs are now widely used in New Zealand, Iceland, Australia, South Africa, the United States, and Canada (Grafton, 1996). A tremendous amount has been learned over the last decade from the experiences in New Zealand and Iceland as to the appropriate structure of ITQs in fisheries with high stock variability (Annala, 1996; Arnason, 1996).

On the other hand, the biology of salmon leads some analysts to conclude that ITQs are inappropriate for this fishery (Copes, 1998). Because salmon are migratory, management focuses on ensuring optimal escapements, as opposed to taking a sustainable portion of a relatively static biomass. The idea is to allow just enough fish through to fully utilize (but not crowd) spawning beds. Unfortunately, the size of returning runs is highly variable from year to year and is difficult to predict. The complexity in allocating property rights to fixed amounts of the resource to commercial harvesters is exacerbated by the hierarchy of rights to the returning fish. Table 11.2 sets out that hierarchy for Fraser River sockeye. The first priority is conservation, and so adequate

Table 11.2
Hierarchy of rights to Fraser River sockeye

Escapement required for spawning

US allocation

Aboriginal food, social, and ceremonial fishery

Recreational and commercial fishery

Allocation between commercial gear types

Other water uses

---

escapement for spawning dominates all other claims. However, actual escapement is not fully known until the fish reach the spawning grounds. Required escapements are deduced from estimates of the returning runs in order to produce estimates of "harvestable" volumes. These are reduced by the US share. The first claim to the Canadian harvestable volume is for the Aboriginal food, social, and ceremonial fishery, which largely takes place in-river. The remaining harvestable volume is then allocated between recreational and commercial fishers, and then the commercial fishers' share is divided between gear types (i.e., seine, gillnet, and troll). In effect, rights to the fish are largely opposite to the actual physical movement of the salmon (McRae and Pearse, 2004, 24). For example, troll fishers, who often range far off the coast, might be the first to take their share, although their rights are subordinate to conservation, Aboriginal, and foreign claims and parallel to the claims of other gear types and recreational fishers.

Management requires ongoing monitoring of the size of the run as the fish move toward the mouths of their rivers of origin and continual revision of the allowable catch as more information is collected. These in-season adjustments would make it difficult to provide fishers with secure access to the resource, notwithstanding their possession of an ITQ. Given this uncertainty, fishermen would be motivated to race for the fish to ensure that they captured their quotas, an outcome that would, of course, frustrate achievement of the main benefits of an ITQ system (Sprott, 1997).

Yet it might be possible to allocate ITQs on the basis of a percentage share of the salmon total allowable catch (TAC). This is in fact the recommendation of the Federal-Provincial/Post Treaty Fishery Joint Task Group (McRae and Pearse, 2004). Government biologists would continue to predict the TAC and would have the power to adjust it throughout the harvesting season. Fixed quotas offer more certainty, and therefore value, to fishers, but allocation of shares rather than a number or weight of fish ensures that fishers bear the risks associated with the large temporal fluctuations in the salmon harvest (Walters and Pearse, 1996). The fishery would remain a small-boat activity. Once allocated, quotas would be transferable to other incumbents or to potential new entrants. The Pearse-McRae report recommends that allocation of the shares of individual fishers "should be determined by the fishers themselves" and could be based on equal shares, catch histories, or any other reasonable basis (McRae and Pearse, 2004, 41). Provided that fishers are reasonably certain that they can "make" their quota using current levels of inputs, ITQs should reduce incremental overcapitalization incentives, although not congestion externalities at specific locations.

Reviews of both the New Zealand and Icelandic experiences with ITQs conclude that efficiency has improved: the economic performance of participants has improved, total catches have increased, and invested capital has been reduced (Annala, 1996: Arnason, 1996). Copes (1998) also concedes that ITQs have often brought short-term efficiency gains by removing excess capacity. The evidence suggests, however, that ITQ regimes have a mixed record with respect to the preservation of marine resources. Resource conservation problems have occurred when TACs have been set too high. Copes (1998), for example, notes that the introduction of ITQs contributed to the virtual destruction of the abalone resource in British Columbia. Jones (2003b) acknowledges continued conservation problems in this fishery but argues that the situation is not worse than under the pre-ITQ regime.

One advantage that ITQs would have in the BC salmon fishery is that the TAC under the new regime would not be very different from the current catch. In many other fisheries ITQs have been introduced in open-access contexts where the resource was seriously threatened, and TACs needed to be set considerably lower than current catch levels (Francis, Gilbert, and Annala, 1993). Finally, ITQs would not provide strong incentives for freshwater habitat protection or enhancement.

The ITQ system proposed in the Pearse-McRae report allocates ITQs to incumbents and therefore would be generous to those currently in the fishery. However, as noted earlier, the report recommends leaving the allocation of specific quotas up to the fishers themselves. We suspect that no matter what scheme is adopted, some fishers would claim inequity. While ITQs appear to favour incumbents, current licence holders still dislike them (Toy, 1998). This option also does nothing for Aboriginal fishers, except to the extent that they hold commercial fishing licences. Additionally, it does relatively less for taxpayers than other options. It is not clear that current government expenditures would be reduced either, because of the potential for high administrative costs.

CONCLUSION: INSTITUTIONAL DESIGN OF THE BC SALMON FISHERY AND ITS IMPACT ON WIDER CONFLICTS

Of course, one's preferred option depends on how one weights the goals described above. It is clear that all three options are superior to the status quo in terms of almost all the goals and criteria. The river-specific exclusive ownership rights model is the highest-ranked option in terms of reversing and eliminating rent dissipation because it would eliminate the small-boat fishery and utilize the lowest-cost fishing technology. The Pearse Commission proposal and ITQs probably do equally well in preserving economic profits since they would encourage licence utilization by those who could exploit the resource most efficiently.

All four options appear to give advantages to incumbent fishers (as well as the Aboriginal fishery). On balance, policy-makers should give very serious consideration to the river-specific exclusive ownership rights option. It scores well in terms of efficiency and preservation, two principal policy goals. It also has the potential to score well with respect to equity. Certainly, a cooperative organization amongst stakeholders offers the best choice of ameliorating conflicts in the long run. There would still be disputes over "fair shares to the resource," but such a cooperative might be better positioned to establish a disputes-settling mechanism than a single private or public monopolist. A more traditional monopoly solution with a single public or private organization could possibly work, depending on how current licence holders are compensated when losing their rights, how Aboriginals fare in the allocation of rights (and, importantly, how benefits are distributed between Aboriginals), and how the proceeds of the allocation are garnered, whether through payment in money (i.e., through auctions) or through payment in kind (i.e., through allocations based upon broader social policy goals). Unfortunately, this latter option may be strongly resisted by incumbents, notwithstanding compensation for their extant rights.

We believe that a reorganized riverine-based fishery would reduce dysfunctional conflict between a wide range of actors: between fishers in the wild fishery, between wild fishers and aquaculturalists, between the fishing industry and environmentalists, and between the fisheries stakeholders and governmental regulators. It would do so because it would allocate and clarify property rights to specific salmon. We should emphasize that it would not eliminate conflict per se, especially in the short run. The actors would have the incentive to protect their property right against anyone degrading it (Demsetz, 1967). Also, all parties to the water, including wild salmon harvesters, would know that they were in for the long run. In game theory terms, the water-use game would move from a "one-shot" iteration to that of an "infinitely repeated" game (Klein, 1985; Messick, 1999). To take one example, the owner of a specific riverine salmon right would have a clearer incentive to challenge polluters of a river that are threatening salmon stocks. Similarly, the owner of a river right would have an incentive to challenge deleterious aquaculture practices that spilled over to that particular adjacent river. This form of "conflict" could be played out through private negotiation, through the courts, or through reform of governmental rules for regulations and their enforcement (Ellickson, 1991).

Without fairly radical institutional reform to the Pacific commercial salmon fishery, it is unlikely that a stable economic future can be created for all participants that use the coastal waters. The current regime of an inefficient, ineffective, and inequitable common-pool resource is now contested by newer aquaculture processes and by foreign farmed stocks of salmon. Some policy options have been assessed for the current regime. More radical changes in institutions may be necessary. It remains to be seen if the proposed new Fisheries Act will initiate this type of institutional reform.

Conclusion:

Institutions and Water Governance in Canada

B. TIMOTHY HEINMILLER, CAROLYN JOHNS,

AND MARK SPROULE-JONES

Our case studies reveal the endemic nature of conflict between the various users of rivers, coasts, lakes, and aquifers. Rarely is a water body given over to a single class of water uses or so abundant as to accommodate all actual and potential users. Sharing a water body can bring conflict, then agreement or arbitration by regulation, then change, and then often cycling back through these phases. What is remarkable about the case evidence is how successful water user groups in one part of this cyclical process remain winners in subsequent parts, including new cycles and new uses. The winners include incumbent holders of commercial fishing vessel licences on the two coasts, irrigation farmers in Alberta, the waste disposal "industry" on the Great Lakes, including farmers disposing of animal wastes on shoreline properties, and the commercial shipping industry that uses the St Lawrence. Only in the case of the conflict between conservationists and commercial interests over the export of Great Lakes water is there a continuous search for some kind of equilibrium, perhaps because this issue emerged later than the others, after the environmentalist movement had been well established.

The stability of the pattern of winners and losers in the sharing of a water body could perhaps be attributed to an inherent conservatism in the Canadian culture and politics. More likely, however, it is due to the "rig of the political game" or the way our institutions are structured and respond to conflicts among users. We will review some of these basic factors in part one of this chapter. Part two will delve deeper by revisiting the analytical framework provided in the introduction in the broader context of the case-study findings and the literature on the governance of common pools and of water resources more generally. In so doing, it will develop some more fundamental conclusions about future governance challenges and lines of inquiry. Thus we first turn to review our case-study findings about how political institutions seem to work, and then, second, we analyze the explanatory findings implied in our study.

GENERAL FINDINGS

First, all of the case studies illustrate that collective action is more likely to be successful where the use of water resources is mono-functional, where there are fewer users, and where those user groups are more homogeneous, with shared norms and possibly a history of collaboration. The cases also all show that across the country and over time, this reality is long gone, and increasingly, multiple, conflicting users of water at various scales place increased pressure on existing institutional arrangements, which are based on historical uses and user rights.

A second and somewhat obvious finding is that governments are at or near the centre of water resource disputes, most typically as regulators. Notably, they are often government departments or ministries, such as the Department of Fisheries and Oceans (DFO) or provincial ministries, or sometimes arm's-length agencies such as the St Lawrence Seaway Development Corporation. These bureaucratic institutions have been granted broad discretionary powers by legislation and report to ministers and cabinets and legislatures in varying degrees of frequency and detail. These substantial discretionary powers allow them to act like owners and proprietors to manage, lease, and include and exclude users. Provincial water licensing departments enjoy this kind of status relative to water takings and permissible pollution. At other times they may just be regulators operating under broad legislative mandates. The fisheries cases clearly illustrate that the DFO acts in this way. The important point to note is that discretionary powers can be used for good or ill. So the DFO can regulate the access and the efforts of fishers to harvest any species on the Atlantic and Pacific coasts. In so doing, it may limit fishing and create profits for the "lucky" licensees or, alternatively, establish lax rules on access and efforts that ultimately lead to the possible exhaustion of the common pool. Much conflict and politics occurs in disputes about the access and efforts of current and future users, and government agencies play a key role.

Third, these agencies and departments increasingly find that their powers are contested. The cases illustrate that sometimes the institutional challenge comes from within the state itself –from the Supreme Court, royal commissions, or intergovernmental sources. In many of the cases discussed in this volume, existing institutional arrangements were challenged by new water users or organized interest groups.

A fourth finding is that international (Canada–United States) boundaries sometimes place limits on the discretionary powers of Canadian agencies, whether federal or provincial. This is especially evident on the Great Lakes, where some waters fall under provincial jurisdiction, some are under exclusive US jurisdiction (for example, Lake Michigan), and some are classified as international waters. Eight US states, two Canadian provinces, and two national governments develop ways to work together to limit or resolve disputes, with the number of government bodies varying, depending on the scale of the resource dispute. Such collaborations have had only modest impacts in terms of water quality in the regulation of the waste disposers such as industries and municipalities, but they have had greater impact on commercial interests anxious to divert or extract raw water from the basin.

Finally, our major finding from the case studies relates to the slowness of institutional change in management and regulation. Ironically, even though some agencies have discretionary powers to alter their management instruments or their regulations and though serious crises and conflicts occurred in most of the cases, agencies seem reluctant to alter existing patterns. There may be different reasons for this torpor. In some cases it may be due to the abundance of the water resource, as in the Great Lakes. In others, incumbent winners have entrenched relationships with regulators, as in the Hamilton Harbour case. In further instances, there may be few institutional contests, such as with provincial water-extraction regimes. Parliaments and legislatures also seem to lack the interest and capacity to reform governance arrangements without the spur of a severe crisis. It is notable that, in most instances, legislatures were not the initiators of institutional change or redesign, only weighing in after existing institutional arrangements were challenged or stressed by some form of crisis or conflict. In recent years even the crises of Walkerton, of the northern cod, of proposed water diversions to the arid southwest United States, and of major climate change seem to elicit modest political interest and change at best.

In sum, we need to take our understandings deeper and develop enriched explanations of how governance institutions work. We now return to an examination of the cases in the broader contexts of the analytical framework and factors we outlined in the introduction and of common pool theory.

EXPLANATORY FINDINGS
ON INSTITUTIONS AND WATER

First and foremost, as outlined in chapter 1, the challenges involved in governing water resources stem from the properties of water as a natural resource. Water is distinct from most other public policy goods and most other natural resources in that it has three distinct natural principles or dimensions: its non-substitutability, its tendency toward multiple use, and its fugitive and cross-medium nature. Those who rely on water for various purposes depend specifically on water and can not substitute it for some other good if it becomes scarce or unavailable. When freshwater resources are degraded for fish habitat or human consumption and overused or depleted in ways that prevent their use, conflict is inherent. There is no readily available substitute for fresh water from local sources, short of cloud seeding or the desalination of sea water, neither of which is yet economical or practical on a large scale. The more likely options are migration in search of more water or the importation of water from other areas via pipeline, diversion, or motorized transport. Any of these options can create severe water-use conflicts and considerable ecological and socio-economic dislocation.

The second major dimension of water that creates governance challenges is its multi-use nature. To a certain extent, all natural resources serve multiple purposes both in their natural state and in their harvest and production as economic goods. Some of these purposes are complementary, but many are not, and it is the tension and competition between various uses of a resource that often lead to intractable resource governance challenges. In areas such as the St Lawrence River and Hamilton Harbour, where the multiplicity of uses is particularly intense, conflicts between different types of users are almost inevitable, and a considerable amount of time and effort must be directed toward finding effective trade-offs and accommodations between them. Furthermore, the aesthetic value of water and Canadians' affective and cultural (almost nationalistic) attachment to their water resources can complicate water-use conflicts by injecting emotional sentiments into otherwise rational debates between water users. Few other resources touch as many socio-economic, environmental, and cultural interests as water does.

The fugitive and cross-medium nature of water resources also presents significant governance challenges. Consider the cautionary example of the Walkerton E. coli contamination, in which the interdependence of domestic town water users and rural farmers sharing a single groundwater source was suddenly and tragically highlighted. The movement of water through the hydrological cycle and across vast expanses of time and space creates complex interdependencies that are not as evident in the governance of more stationary resources (such as lands, forests, minerals, and fossil fuels), and these interdependencies create coordination problems that are quite specific to water as a policy good.

Ultimately, water is a resource unlike most others, and scholars and analysts must exercise considerable caution in applying the policies used and the lessons learned in the governance of other natural resources and other common pools to the governance of water. The multiple-use character of water is only going to intensify in the future. When this issue is combined with the enduring impact of property rights and the political economy of water, to which we now turn, the importance of significant institutional innovation and redesign to reflect more balance between the various users and uses will be evident.

PROPERTY RIGHTS, POLITICAL ECONOMY, AND THE IMPORTANCE OF LAYING CLAIM

As many of the cases discussed in this volume have suggested, property rights are very important in shaping water governance in Canada. They are so because they significantly influence the power dynamics of any water-use situation. Those with recognized water rights enjoy a privileged legal position in relation to those without similar rights, and they can use this advantage to fend off challenges or encroachments to their water use. This conflict between rights holders and non-rights holders, as well as conflicts between those with varying bundles of rights, underlies many of the water-use controversies outlined in this book, particularly those between economic users with entrenched water rights and environmentalists without entrenched rights. Accordingly, it is important to examine the historical and social roots of this conflict.

Fundamentally, the creation of water property rights is about laying claim. Claiming access to and use of water, together with the recognition of these claims, is important to water users because it increases the security of their water use. In turn, this security provides incentives for water users to invest their time and capital in water-related enterprises, which are crucial in any economy. So, from a development perspective, the creation and implementation of water property rights is a key factor in economic stability and growth.

In the process of laying claim, though, it is inevitable that some potential water users will be privileged over others, and the privileged users will generally be those whose claims are recognized first. The recognized claimants have their claims entrenched as property rights, and all potential users who emerge in the future must either challenge or compensate these early rights holders before they can have any kind of secure water use themselves. In other words, those user groups that lay claim early on and have their property rights recognized in the primary stages of resource exploitation put themselves in a strong position long into the future, and they will fight any challenges to their rights from the legal high ground. Thus the main power dynamic of many water-use conflicts is defined by the fortuitous circumstance of which water users were first to have their water rights recognized in law.

The most obvious example of this process is found in the prior-allocation water-rights regime of Alberta, described by Keith Brownsey in chapter 5. This regime is designed around the principle of "first in time, first in right," so that those water users, usually irrigators, who have the earliest water-use licences have the first chance to access and divert available water. This gives early licence holders a greater degree of water-use security than those with more recent licences and a much greater degree of security than those without licences. It also means that irrigators, who hold most of the early licences and consume the bulk of the water in southern Alberta, have been able to resist more recent claims for water by urban communities and oil producers. Although the Albertan prior-allocation regime is a good example of the importance of laying claim, it is also somewhat unusual because it is a regime that has been purposefully designed to assign priority to the earliest claims. In other cases, the power of early water claimants is simply an incidental outcome to the creation of water rights and may not have been intended at all.

For a different example, consider the water rights that were entrenched in the IJC Order of Approval for the operation of the St Lawrence River dams, as described in chapter 9. The existing claims on the St Lawrence from riparians, shippers, and hydroelectricity generators were all recognized in the Order of Approval and protected in the regulation plan for the maintenance of water levels in Lake Ontario and the St Lawrence. Whether intended or not, the recognition and institutionalization of these rights has made it quite difficult for subsequent users of the St Lawrence, especially recreational boaters and environmentalists, to have their interests in the river recognized on a par with the entrenched economic uses. Quite simply, because the economic uses laid claim first, before the environmentalist movement was born, they occupy the legal high ground, and environmentalists are forced to challenge them on these terms. This is a dynamic that is common in many water and resource governance issues in Canada, and it seems that entrenched economic uses consistently have this advantage over more recently developed environmental concerns.

Yet in Canada's current constitutional context, it can not be taken for granted that economic users are always the earliest recognized claimant of the country's water resources. Increasingly, Aboriginal peoples are making claims that predate any economic use in Canada, and when these have been recognized, they have considerably altered the power dynamics of some water-use conflicts, as outlined in the fisheries cases in this book. The Aboriginal claims for water and fishing rights are distinct because they are being recognized retroactively, often in the courts and sometimes by politicians, as a result of the enforcement of neglected treaties from the past and the affirmation of Aboriginal resource rights stemming from section 35 of the Constitution Act, 1982. The retroactive nature of these Aboriginal rights means that existing economic uses which were allowed to develop in the absence of recognized Aboriginal rights are significantly threatened, creating serious potential for conflict and even violence. Conflicts of this sort are evident in various places in this book, but most vividly in the hostilities over fishing rights in Burnt Church, described in chapter 10.

The disproportionate power of early claimants stems not only from their privileged legal position but also from the private, social, and political investments stemming from these early claims. Once claimants have succeeded in having their water rights recognized, large amounts of capital are invested in water-use activities, communities and cultures develop around these activities, and public money is allocated in support of these sectors and communities. Any potential water user that emerges in the future is confronted not only with legally entrenched property rights but with an almost overwhelming amount of investment that is not easily abandoned. This investment can make many established water uses almost self-perpetuating, even if the potential uses that later emerge are more efficient, beneficial, or sustainable.

The importance of investment in perpetuating early water uses is evident in both the Alberta and St Lawrence cases. In southern Alberta, irrigators were the first recognized water claimants under the North-west Irrigation Act, and millions of public and private dollars were invested in the development of irrigated agriculture, to the point that many communities in this region are essentially based on irrigation. Other water users, particularly in urban areas, have subsequently emerged and claimed that they could make better use of this water, but the irrigation sector is already firmly in place and could not be abandoned without substantial social upheaval and dislocation in rural areas. Similarly, in the St Lawrence, early investments in navigation and the development of a Canadian staples economy dependent on these navigation routes have made it extremely unlikely that environmentalists will succeed in restoring the seaway to a pristine, natural river. There is simply too much investment and too many vested interests in the St Lawrence Seaway to make this possible.

The case of Aboriginal resource rights also shows the importance of early investments in water-based activities, but in a somewhat different way. Conflicts pitting Aboriginal resource rights against established non-Aboriginal economic activities are, in part, a confrontation between the Aboriginals' recently designated legal priority and the non-Aboriginals' long-standing socio-economic investment (and recently trumped property rights). In these cases, both sides feel that they have valid and strong claims of priority and access to the same resource, one side basing its claim on ancestral occupation and the courts' recognition of this claim, and the other side basing its claim on the substantial investments made in livelihoods and communities. Because the claims on both sides are justifiable, the potential for conflict and violence is high, and finding a way for these claims to coexist is a very delicate political exercise – an exercise in which Canadian governments are increasingly involved.

Overall, it is important to understand the implications of laying claim because early claimants gain power that has implications far into the future. Once water rights are distributed, rights holders have a legal advantage in subsequent water-use conflicts, forcing would-be water users who later emerge to challenge their established position. Furthermore, early water uses generally attract significant private, social, and political investment, helping to perpetuate them far into the future. All of this speaks to the durability of established institutions and the significant obstacles that exist to institutional change, particularly the adaptation of water management institutions to changing water uses and water management goals.

INSTITUTIONAL DESIGN: BEYOND THE
MANAGERIALIST AND COMMUNITY-BASED DEBATE

The relative merits of centralized, managerialist governance by the state versus localized, community-based governance constitute a central question that has long shaped research agendas in common-pool, natural resource management, and water policy scholarship. In recent years, a general understanding has emerged that aspects of both governance models can contribute to effective resource governance, and the question is no longer framed as an either/or proposition but as finding an effective balance between two ideal types. Determining this balance can be quite difficult though, and researchers are still investigating various institutional designs in an effort to find institutions that combine the best aspects of state managerialism with those of community involvement (Ostrom, 2004). As some of the cases in this volume suggest, most Canadian water governance institutions have yet to attain this balance, as long-standing traditions of state managerialism still tend to predominate over more recent efforts to expand processes of community involvement.

As is now well-known, the Canadian economy was developed, in large part, on the basis of a staples trade that relied on the harvest and export of a variety of natural resources. The staples-based economy did not develop spontaneously, however. It was assisted and cultivated by interventionist Canadian governments that developed a strong managerialist tradition for both resources and resource-based industries (Hodgetts, 1964). Contemporary advocates of state managerialism continue to argue that most resource management problems stem from rivalries among resource users and that the state is the only social actor with the legitimate coercive authority to regulate and settle such rivalries and protect the public interest. Furthermore, modern public bureaucracies are a centre of considerable knowledge and expertise, and these experts should be given a central role in managing our natural resources on a scientific basis. The cases analyzed in this book illustrate the central role of bureaucratic institutions in water politics in Canada, but at the same time they demonstrate that state managerialism has been somewhat curtailed in recent years by new governance philosophies such as the "new public management" and challenges from other users with significant knowledge, expertise, and rights related to water.

In contrast, significant community involvement is a more recent development in Canadian resource governance, having arrived since the advent of the environmentalist movement in the 1960s (Dorcey and McDaniels, 2001). Advocates of community-based governance on the left and right of the political spectrum object to paternalistic state managerialism on a number of grounds. First, they argue that the state is inherently political and that politicians support policies which help them to secure votes and protect vested interests, not policies which are necessarily in the public interest. Second, those communities that live with and depend on a resource have the most intimate knowledge of the resource, not remote bureaucrats, and local communities are quite capable of grasping the public interest and devising rules to restrain resource rivalries (Ostrom, 1990). Canada's past utilization of state managerialism has been far from impressive, as a number of our cases related to fisheries and water quantity and quality illustrate.

Despite their divergent approaches, the issue in Canada is not so much a matter of choosing between these models, as both have apparent weaknesses, but of finding an effective synthesis between them. The essence of this synthesis is the realization that government managers and community participants can act as a check on each other's excesses and a complement to each other's knowledge bases, if both are provided with sufficiently influential roles in resource governance. What is still being worked out by many scholars, however, is how to design institutions that can put this ideal into action. The tension between state managerialism and community involvement was evident in many of the cases documented in this volume, but particularly in the Hamilton Harbour and water export cases. These cases are also instructive because they provide contrasting examples of the ways in which the interested public can become engaged in water governance issues, and they illustrate the relative predominance that state managerialism continues to hold over community involvement in Canadian political culture.

The Hamilton Harbour case is an example of community involvement designed along the lines of participatory democracy. In this approach, community representatives are directly involved in decision-making processes and should, ideally, be able to convey community concerns to government regulators and ensure that they are considered in the making of policy decisions. In Hamilton Harbour, though, it was abundantly clear that, although provision had been made for community stakeholders to be involved in the remediation processes, their influence in these processes was slight, and governmental actors felt little compunction about manipulating these processes to serve their own ends. As already indicated, state managerialism has a long history in Canadian resource management, and the community involvement processes for Hamilton Harbour were ultimately little more than an "add-on" to the traditional managerialist approach. Accordingly, community participants were shut out of important decisions and left with little recourse but to challenge these decisions once they had already been made, leaving them with little effective role in the remediation policy process.

The water export case was different in a number of ways, but primarily because community involvement in this instance occurred through representative democracy. In the representative model, community concerns are conveyed to the elected representatives involved in decision-making processes, who should be responsive to these concerns if they wish to secure future electoral support. In the case of water exports, for example, the Canadian public let their elected representatives know that they were against the harvesting of Canadian water for bulk export purposes, and almost every province has responded with regulations to prohibit this water use within its jurisdiction. Even in Ontario, where permission had been granted to commence water exports by tanker from Lake Superior in early 1999, intense public pressure on the Harris government eventually persuaded it to reverse course within just a few months and ban bulk water exports. In this instance at least, community influence seemed to be a decisive factor in shaping water policy.

The Hamilton Harbour and water export cases are instructive, but they should not be taken to mean that participatory democracy always fails and that representative democracy always succeeds in facilitating community involvement in Canadian water governance. A crucial difference between these cases was the existence of powerful vested interests in Hamilton Harbour and an almost complete absence of vested interests in water export. The companies that use and pollute Hamilton Harbour are major contributors to the local economy, with considerable financial and human resources at their disposal and a network of personal and professional linkages with actors at all levels of government. In contrast, the nascent bulk water export industry has none of these. Thus it is little wonder that governments were much less willing to respond to community concerns in the former case than in the latter.

It is probably fair to conclude from this comparison, however, that community involvement through representative democracy coexists with Canada's traditional state managerialism much more easily than does participatory democracy. Representative democracy assumes that centralized decision-making within government by elected representatives is necessary and acceptable, while participatory democracy challenges the very legitimacy of this centralized decision-making. Yet the trend in Canada is toward the participatory model, as many community groups demand to be directly involved in pressing water governance issues. Clearly, the cases highlight the need for innovative institutional designs that can effectively integrate and balance state managerialism with the participatory model, so that community participation is no longer regarded as a mere afterthought to traditional state managerialism. Beyond this factor is the need to recognize the reality and challenge of institutional interplay in addressing multiple-use water resource management issues and conflicts in the future.

INSTITUTIONAL INTERPLAY

Given the unique nature of water and the range of interdependencies involved in its use, it is clear from the case studies that multiple institutions, differentiated according to jurisdiction, type of use, and social scale, are often involved in its governance. Each of the cases confirmed the theoretical and analytical necessity of examining a range of water conflicts across the country and the numerous institutions involved in trying to manage all the multiple uses outlined in chapter 1. The Atlantic fisheries case clearly shows that even within one broad use such as fisheries, multiple users and different institutional arrangements are layered in the broader context of multiple uses of coastal waters. This institutional interplay is central to furthering theory and institutional design to improve water politics and policy.

In recent work, one of the most prominent scholars in this area, Oran Young, has distinguished between a number of different types of institutional interplay. One of the most important distinctions he draws is between horizontal and vertical interplay. While horizontal interplay refers to interactions between institutions that exist at a comparable social scale, vertical interplay refers to interactions between institutions that exist at different scales (Young, 2002, 23). Classic examples of horizontal and vertical interplay are found in Canadian federalism. The provincial and federal governments exist at different social scales, the provinces obviously operating at a smaller scale than their federal counterpart. Accordingly, interactions between two provincial institutions constitute horizontal interplay, and interactions between a federal institution and a provincial institution constitute vertical interplay. Instances of horizontal and vertical interplay are common in Canadian federalism but are evident at other scales as well.

Beyond horizontal and vertical interplay, Young also makes a crucial distinction between two origins or causes of institutional interplay. These causes are referred to as functional interdependence, on one hand, and the politics of design and management, on the other. "Functional interdependence is a fact of life. It occurs – whether we like it or not – when substantive problems that two or more institutions address are linked in biogeophysical or socioeconomic terms. The politics of institutional design and management, in contrast, comes into play when actors forge links between issues and institutions intentionally in the interests of pursuing individual or collective goals" (Young, 2002, 23).

In the case of water, functional interdependence is prevalent because of the multi-use nature of this resource. Thus, for instance, water policy and energy policy are functionally linked because of water's hydro-electricity-generating potential, and water policy and transportation policy are functionally linked because of water's use as a transportation link. The politics of institutional design and management is also important in water governance, given the fragmentation of authority in many water issues and the need to link these centres of authority to pursue common policy goals. So when, for example, governments become party to an agreement to reduce water pollution or improve water conservation, they are making purposive institutional linkages, a process that is the essence of the politics of institutional design and management. Overall, both causes of institutional interplay produce institutional interactive effects, but one is more implicit and the other more explicit. When the two key dimensions of institutional interplay identified by Young are considered together, a two-by-two matrix emerges that portrays four clearly distinct types of institutional interplay (as illustrated in table C.1). Examples of each type are described in further detail below, in an effort to provide a clearer idea of the institutional design challenges involved in each.

As suggested above, the Walkerton E. coli contamination demonstrates in stark terms the inherent interdependence of the users sharing a water resource. Viewed from the perspective of institutional interplay, the tragedy can be even more specifically described as an instance of horizontal-functional interplay. The functional aspect of this case relates to the intersection of domestic water supply management and agricultural nutrient management, a linkage that is more inherent than intentionally constructed. The institutions regulating both aspects of this linkage exist predominantly at the provincial level, giving them a

Table C.1
A typology of institutional interplay

Scales involved in interplay	Origins of interplay	
	Functional	Designed
Vertical	Vertical–functional (e.g., interplay between international trade rules, federal export control rules, and provincial water-taking rules)	Vertical–designed (e.g., interplay between water allocations rules in the MAA, Alberta water policy, and the irrigation districts)
Horizontal	Horizontal–functional (e.g., interplay between agricultural land use and municipal water provision in the Walkerton tragedy)	Horizontal–designed (e.g., the IJC and its 1956 Order of Approval for Lake Ontario– St Lawrence River levels)

MAA = Master Agreement on Apportionment.
IJC = International Joint Commission.

horizontal relationship, though it is also obvious that there was vertical interplay between these provincial institutions and the local institutions that substantially mismanaged the Walkerton water system itself.

Horizontal-functional interplay, such as that between water and agriculture, presents great challenges for water governance because it runs contrary to the vertically oriented departmental structure of Canadian governments. Horizontal management institutions can be created within cabinets, across departments, and between governments, but the vast number of potential horizontal-functional linkages involving water make it quite difficult to actively manage them all. Accordingly, many horizontal-functional linkages tend to remain politically latent and are only specifically addressed when they become politically salient. This was the case with Walkerton, as outlined in chapter 8. Prior to Walkerton, the linkage between water policy and agricultural policy was of little immediate concern, but since Walkerton and the public outcry following the tragedy, the linkage between water and agriculture has been specifically addressed in a round of new legislation and institutional development. As Sproule-Jones (2000) has shown, horizontal management institutions can be designed in a number of different ways, and it is important to consider these design options in any effort to manage horizontal-functional linkages, with the ultimate aim of recognizing and avoiding latent tragedies such as the Walkerton contamination.

The governance of St Lawrence River levels is also an example of institutional interplay, but in this case of horizontal-designed interplay. The headwaters of the St Lawrence are an international boundary water, shared by Canada and the United States; so some type of horizontal interplay between the water management institutions of these governments is virtually inevitable. The International Boundary Waters Treaty of 1909 and the International Joint Commission (IJC) were created to help manage this horizontal interplay, and when the St Lawrence Seaway was undertaken in the 1950s, the US and Canadian governments used these institutions accordingly. A set of rules was designed for the management of St Lawrence water levels in an IJC order of approval and regulation plan, and the horizontal interplay between the US and Canadian governments was effectively managed.

The St Lawrence case is illustrative of horizontal-designed interplay, but not all instances of this type of interplay are as cooperative and peaceable as this one. A vast literature by international relations scholars documents many failures and conflicts in the governance of international water resources, and an equally vast literature documents similar problems within federal states. It is not possible to describe all of these problems here, but most of them relate either to the difficulties involved in achieving cooperative agreements to manage interplay or to the problems involved with implementing and enforcing these agreements once they are achieved. Given the vast number of water resources that are shared between Canadian municipalities and provinces and the multitude of boundary waters that are shared with the United States, horizontal-designed interplay is a very important aspect of Canadian water governance. In many cases, cooperative institutions have been developed to address this interplay, but managing these horizontal relationships remains a continuous challenge.

The third type of institutional interplay of interest is the vertical-functional variety, and this was particularly evident in the water export case outlined in chapter 6. Water exports lie at the intersection of water policy and trade policy, and in Canada these two policy areas are assigned to different levels of government. While the provinces have regulatory authority over most water-taking activities within their borders, the federal government has regulatory authority over international trade. After the negotiation of the NAFTA and WTO agreements in the early 1990s, these institutions also became relevant to the regulation of water exports, and a distinct vertical interplay situation was created. In total, four institutional levels at four different social scales (provincial, national, continental, and global) contained rules pertaining to the regulation of Canadian water exports, creating a very complex situation of vertical interplay. Rather than an intended institutional design, though, this was more a result of the functional, and somewhat obscure, linkage between water and international trade.

As the water export case suggests, vertical-functional interplay creates situations in which developments at remote scales can significantly impact policy decisions at other levels. For instance, with the introduction of the NAFTA and WTO, the federal and provincial governments found their water export policy options constrained by new international trade rules. The federal government could not institute a water export ban without violating these rules, and any provincial restrictions had to be framed in terms of water-taking, rather than water export. Faced with these constraints, British Columbia and some other provinces developed an innovative policy design that restricted water-takings based on the size of the containers used but was still substantially in compliance with international trade rules. Once the other provinces realized that this approach allowed them to effectively prohibit bulk water exports, it was quickly adopted across the country. Clearly, the water export policies developed by the provinces were more than just the product of provincial politics alone; they were undertaken and shaped by the linkage between water and international trade in the 1990s and the constraints created by the vertical-functional interplay of these institutions.

The last type of interplay to be considered is vertical-designed interplay, and this is most evident in the case of Alberta water management. Southern Alberta is one of the most water-scarce areas in Canada, and institutions at a number of scales have been designed to manage this scarcity: the 1969 Master Agreement on Apportionment (MAA) allocates water between the Prairie provinces at the basin level, the Alberta Water Act and other regulations allocate water to irrigation districts and municipalities at the provincial level, and the irrigation districts and municipalities allocate water to individuals at the community level. The interplay between these various institutions is clearly vertical, and the whole institutional complex has been intentionally designed to manage water scarcity, notwithstanding doubts about its effectiveness or fairness. In times of severe drought, provincial allocations under the MAA are reduced, triggering a prioritization of water allocations between urban municipalities and irrigation districts (and among irrigation districts) and also triggering changes in allocations between individuals. In

short, when scarcity develops at one level, the institutions are intentionally linked to ensure that scarcity management efforts are put in place at
other levels as well.

In most instances, vertical-designed interplay is used to coordinate
multiple institutions at different social scales toward common policy
goals. However, vertical linkages between institutions can be forged in
various ways, and at least some consideration must be given to this matter of institutional architecture. In the governance of Alberta water, the
vertical linkages are primarily "top-down," with developments at higher
levels prompting adjustments at lower levels. In other cases, though, the
vertical linkages may be "bottom-up," with developments at lower levels prompting adjustments at higher levels. The difference between top-
down and bottom-up vertical linkages is very important because most of
the problems associated with top-down arrangements involve the principle-
agent dynamic, and most of the problems associated with bottom-up arrangements involve the collective action dynamic. Thus depending on
how the vertical linkages have been designed, the social dynamics of
vertical-designed interplay can vary considerably. This is a very important fact that both scholars and architects of Canadian water governance
institutions must take into account in their institutional design and evaluation efforts.

Ultimately, this protracted discussion of institutional interplay suggests
that many Canadian water governance issues can only be accurately and
fully understood if the multiple institutions involved and the interplay between these institutions are adequately taken into account. Various types
of institutional interplay and the social dynamics associated with them
have been described here, and in some cases, there may be more than one
type of institutional interplay involved. For example, Johns's account of
the Walkerton E. coli contamination in chapter 8 focuses on the horizontal-
functional interplay that was evident between water and agricultural
policy, but it also addresses the vertical-designed interplay between the
provincial and municipal governments, which was also undoubtedly
important. As well, the Alberta water governance example analyzes
the vertical-designed interplay between interprovincial, provincial, and
community-level institutions but does not elaborate on the horizontal-
functional interplay between the Prairie provinces in their shared river
basin, which is institutionalized in the MAA.

In sum, the concept of institutional interplay reveals that it is not just
the existing institutional rules but the lasting interactive effects of existing
institutional rules that are important in water management. Any effort at
institutional design must give adequate consideration to the implications

of institutional interplay of various sorts if it is to have any hope of success. This concern may add to the difficulties faced by those tasked with institutional design, but it also reveals a serious potential pitfall and may explain why various past institutional designs ended in failure.

LEARNING PROCESSES AND POLICY PROCESSES

A final theme touched upon in many of the chapters in this volume is the importance of knowledge, science, and learning in Canadian water policy. Extensive knowledge and good science are important elements in the development of both fisheries and water management policy because it is impossible to make good rules for the management of a resource without some understanding of the size of the available resource, the level of use it can sustain, its interactions with other resources, and the processes by which it naturally renews itself. Nevertheless, despite best efforts, it is not possible to gain full knowledge of a resource because natural and social conditions are continually changing on various scales and at different temporal speeds, in ways that are not fully explicable. So, although we are a long way from having full knowledge of most water resources, it is very unlikely that water resource management will ever be reduced to a predictive science with ironclad laws of effective management. Instead, the best we can do is to continuously learn about our water resources, accumulate this knowledge, and apply it to the development of policy (Lee, 1993; Wilson, 2002). Effective learning, then, is one of the most important aspects of water resource governance.

The fundamental challenge to effective learning is that it occurs simultaneously with the development and implementation of policy. Ideally, learning processes and policy processes should be mutually reinforcing, so that learning processes improve the design of policies and policy processes contribute to learning. C.S. Holling (1995) has termed this ideal "adaptive management," but it is much easier to describe in the abstract than it is to achieve in practice. Learning processes and policy processes are not inherently compatible. While the former have the goal of accumulating and improving knowledge, the latter are more about social and political accommodation. Forging an effective link between learning processes and policy processes can be quite difficult, given their divergent ends, and either group of processes can be easily distorted by the presence of the other. Each side of this potentially dysfunctional relationship is explored here, drawing examples from the Canadian fisheries management experiences outlined in chapters 10 and 11.

In many resource management cases, the locus of both learning processes and policy processes is found in public bureaucracies, particularly those line departments with specific resource management responsibilities, such as the federal Department of Fisheries and Oceans, Environment Canada, and Natural Resources Canada. This is especially true of countries that have strong traditions of state managerialism, such as Canada. Departments such as these have dual responsibilities both to implement existing policies and to undertake research and evaluations in order to facilitate the development of future policies. For example, both chapters 10 and 11 remark on how the annual determination of total allowable catches (TACs) for many fish species in Canada rely heavily on estimates and models of fish populations developed by DFO scientists. The important link between learning and policy is clear, but these divergent processes coexist uneasily within many public bureaucracies, and more often than not, learning processes are the ones most adversely affected.

While policy processes are almost inherently political, effective learning processes should be apolitical because they are about the improvement and expansion of knowledge, rather than the setting of social priorities. There is no getting away from the reality, though, that learning processes within public bureaucracies are situated within an overtly political context, and it is extremely difficult to build effective organizational and cultural firewalls between political policy processes and apolitical learning processes. Some political influence is bound to penetrate the learning processes and, potentially, distort them. Furthermore, political considerations are almost always likely to trump apolitical learning objectives because the politicians who direct and oversee public bureaucracies respond primarily to political incentives, and they usually have the decisive input on policy. Take, for example, the political distortions involved in the setting of cod TACs that were evident during the 1980s and early 1990s, prior to the collapse of the Atlantic cod stocks. Based on their own measurements and scientific studies, some DFO scientists became concerned with the state of the cod and recommended to their political masters that the cod TAC be cut by as much as 50 per cent in order to preserve the stock. Without evidence disproving the DFO's concerns, federal fisheries ministers ignored this advice and reduced TACs by much smaller margins, allowing overfishing to continue because of political concerns about how significant TAC cuts would hurt the government's popularity in eastern Canada. Political considerations overrode bureaucratic learning, and a resource management disaster was the result.

While political interference is a major source of distortion in bureaucratic learning processes, there are other sources of distortion as well. In most public bureaucracies, learning processes are overwhelmingly dominated by scientists trained in various specialized fields, and most of the learning that takes place occurs according to the rigours of the scientific method. As a way of learning, the scientific method has become almost hegemonic and acts as a cognitive filter that tends to block out other potential sources of knowledge, such as experiential knowledge gained through resource use and stewardship. This is why, when cod fishers complained of dwindling stocks and smaller fish, these claims were ignored by DFO scientists until they could be scientifically verified. It should also be remembered that most government scientists work within hierarchical organizations in which promotion and advancement are controlled from above, by actors who are quite sensitive to or directly involved in political concerns. This milieu creates incentives and reinforcements for career-minded scientists to produce results that support the prevailing political line, and it may explain, in part, why DFO scientists have been slow to report on the decline of many fish species, while politicians, not coincidentally, were hoping to maintain relatively high TACs (Schrecker, 2001, 36–8).

Even with minimal political interference and objective knowledge generation, distortions in learning can still occur as experts attempt to transmit their knowledge to actors in policy processes. Most knowledge, particularly that obtained through the scientific method, is tentative, because it is circumscribed according to various levels of uncertainty and is subject to revision in light of new evidence (Lee, 1993; Wilson, 2002). Actors involved in policy formation, however, prefer to deal with facts and certainties because these allow them to make safe promises to constituent groups and to predict the outcomes of proposed policy measures. This difference in perspective means that expert recommendations are sometimes misunderstood or misused by politicians who fail to grasp the disclaimers of uncertainty attached to them or are simply disregarded by politicians who do. The effects of aquaculture on wild salmon stocks provide an interesting example of this phenomenon. A considerable degree of uncertainty still remains concerning the deleterious effects of farmed salmon on wild salmon, but politicians in different jurisdictions have dealt with this uncertainty in varying ways. While British Columbia has greatly expanded its aquaculture industry over the past decade, Alaska has banned farmed salmon, both governments basing their decisions on substantially the same knowledge set. Though there are other forces at work in the establishment of these policies, the contrast between British Columbia and Alaska provides a telling example of how politicians differentially interpret the knowledge presented to them by scientific experts.

So far, the discussion in this chapter has focused on how the policy process can distort effective learning, but an undue preoccupation with learning can also have a negative impact on policy. While learning should inform the development of new policy, a preoccupation with it can lead to a situation of continual policy change in which policies are repeatedly adjusted on the basis of the most recent lessons learned. From the perspective of those subject to these policies, the outcome is instability because the rules to which they must adhere are constantly in flux. This situation makes it very difficult for them to plan and invest in resource use activities, and a stable, predictable, "bad" policy would be preferable to a series of continually changing "good" policies. Furthermore, constantly changing rules tend to have little legitimacy, because what is policy today may not be tomorrow, and policy compliance can become increasingly problematic. One could argue that the salmon fishery in British Columbia is an example of this problem, since fishers in this sector have had to adjust to a series of federal policy initiatives that have attempted to protect habitat and preserve salmon stocks as new lessons have been learned about the state of the fishery and the environment. Perhaps it is this instability and not just poor policy design, which has contributed to what Schwindt and Vining have shown to be a poorly managed fishery. In short, when policy becomes hypersensitive to learning, instability can be the unintended and unfortunate result.

Creating an effective linkage between learning processes and policy processes is a difficult institutional problem, as the above examples suggest, and the cases in this book do not provide a clear indication of how this dilemma can be resolved. Other scholars, however, have looked at the issue and made a number of suggestions. One is to create effective organizational firewalls between learning processes and policy processes, mostly to avoid problems of political interference with learning. Another suggestion is to encourage greater transparency and public debate about the knowledge and research methods utilized by policymakers, in an effort to ensure that all relevant knowledge sources have been utilized and properly understood (Schrecker, 2001, 49–51). Suggestions such as these seem quite sensible, but in the absence of further work to verify them, they remain propositions rather than prescriptions about the learning-policy nexus.

FUTURE WATER GOVERNANCE
CHALLENGES IN CANADA

As outlined in this chapter, this book has yielded a variety of important findings about Canadian water-use conflicts and the operation of the various institutions created to manage these conflicts. These propositions and principles are relevant both in a practical sense, in the actual design and operation of water management institutions, and in a theoretical sense, as social scientists seek to advance theories of resource and common-pool governance beyond their current state. In closing, however, one can not help but speculate on some of the challenges that Canadians and their water management institutions are likely to encounter in the near future. A number of significant challenges seem to be looming on the horizon, and the future politics of Canadian water may centre on how well the current water management institutions are able to adapt to meet these changes.

One challenge that immediately springs to mind is global climate change and the implications it may have for the distribution of water in Canada and around the world. While the effects of future climate change are still contested, it seems most likely that it will result in higher water variability, both across regions and over time. This change means that Canadians may be subjected to greater variances in water scarcity and abundance, a climatic feature that is alien to most parts of Canada, the southern prairies and the far north being notable exceptions. Most Canadian water management institutions are not designed to handle such variability, and significant adaptation of property rights and government policies may be necessary. In addition, increased water variability is likely to increase demands for water redistribution projects – pipelines, diversions, and exports – and Canadians may be forced to make difficult allocation decisions about many of their water resources.

Another important challenge that has its own history of institutional concerns is transboundary water governance. Although as chapters 6 and 9 illustrate, transboundary water issues have faced policy-makers in Canada and the United States for decades and have ebbed and flowed from the agendas of federal and sub-national governments, there is a pressing sense that emerging challenges will require new approaches in the North American and global contexts. Approximately 40 per cent of the 8000-kilometre boundary between Canada and the United States is water (Gray, 2005), and this reality presents a number of institutional challenges for policy-makers (Johns, 2005; Bakker et al., 2007).

Within Canada, the continuing trend of urbanization also promises to present significant challenges to water management institutions in the near future. As Canadian cities and suburbs continue to grow and push further into traditionally rural areas, the interplay between agricultural land use and municipal water provision, so tragically evident in Walkerton, is likely to remain important. There is also a danger that urban land developers will continue to reclaim and pave over many of Canada's natural wetland areas and that municipal and industrial waste from urban centres will increasingly pollute the aquifers, rivers, and lakes on which they and many others rely. In some urban areas, such as Kitchener-Waterloo, where the only available water source is groundwater, and London, where water is brought to the city via pipelines from Lake Ontario and Lake Erie, there is an even more basic problem of simply finding enough water to support burgeoning populations. Thus far, many local water management institutions have struggled to address these issues, and it is likely that some institutional adaptation will be necessary in the face of even further urbanization. This adaptation could take the form of an increased federal role in urban water provision, a new institutional relationship between local and provincial governments, or increased reliance on user-pays policy instruments, but urban water issues promise to be a locus of increased political debate in the future.

Groundwater and groundwater management also promise to be a matter of growing concern. Although many communities and industries in Canada rely heavily or exclusively on groundwater resources, most are not even aware of how much groundwater is actually available and whether their usage is sustainable over the long term. Some governments have recently embarked on programs to map underground aquifers and their interconnections with surface water sources, but scarcity and pollution issues are already becoming evident. In southern Ontario alone, farmers in Grey County are locked in conflict with a local water-bottling plant that is alleged to be depleting groundwater supplies, and the residents of Walkerton in neighbouring Bruce County are still recovering from the groundwater contamination that devastated their town in 2000. Unfortunately, neither the science nor the institutions exist to deal with groundwater issues in most parts of the country, yet groundwater is becoming an increasingly important resource for Canadians.

Finally, an issue that has already emerged as a significant challenge for Canadian governments is the provision of safe drinking water on First Nations reserves. Though Aboriginal groups have argued for some time that their water infrastructure and drinking-water quality is well below accepted Canadian standards, it was not until the Kashechewan crisis in late 2005 that the issue was given priority on government agendas. Now, governments are confronted with the challenges of resolving jurisdictional ambiguities between three levels of government, finding the money necessary to substantially build or rebuild water-treatment facilities on many First Nations reserves, and establishing the local capacity necessary to ensure that the provision of quality drinking water can be sustained over the long term. It remains to be seen whether Canadian governments will continue to be committed to resolving these challenges once the media spotlight has dimmed, but the current problems in Aboriginal water provision will continue until they are properly addressed.

Ultimately, water is a policy area that has grown in importance in recent years and is likely to continue to grow into the future. The United Nations General Assembly in December 2003 proclaimed the years 2005 to 2015 "Water for Life, the International Decade for Action." While Canadians have enjoyed all the benefits of being a water-rich country, we are confronted with many of the same water governance challenges and user conflicts that face other peoples around the world. The distribution of our water resources, our history as a predominantly staples economy, and our distinct institutions all make the Canadian experience distinctive in its own right. Though we can learn from others and others can learn from us, the physical, socio-economic and institutional imperatives of the Canadian situation must not be underestimated.

Bibliography

Agnello, R., and L. Donnelley. 1975. "Property Rights and Efficiency in the Oyster Industry." *Journal of Law and Economics* 18, no. 2: 521–33.

Alberta. 1998. *Water Act.* Water (Ministerial) Regulation 205/1998, sec. 37. Edmonton: Queen's Printer.

– 2000a. *Irrigation Districts Act.* Edmonton: Queen's Printer.

– 2000b. *Water Act. Revised Statutes of Alberta 2000.* Edmonton: Queen's Printer.

Alberta. Alberta Environment. 2002. *Water for Life: Facts and Information on Water in Alberta 2002.* Edmonton: Alberta Environment. http://www.waterforlife.gov.ab.ca/docs/infobook.pdf (accessed 1 August 2005).

– 2003a. *Water for Life: Alberta's Strategy for Sustainability.* Edmonton: Alberta Environment. http://www.waterforlife.gov.ab.ca/docs/strategyNov03.pdf (accessed 1 August 2005).

– 2003b. *Water Use for Injection Purposes in Alberta.* Report prepared for Alberta Environment. Calgary: Geowa Information Technologies. http: www.waterforlife.gov.ab.ca/docs/geowa_report.pdf (accessed 1 August 2005).

Allen, R. 1991. "The Two English Agricultural Revolutions, 1450–1850." In *Land, Labour and Livestock: Historical Studies in European Agricultural Productivity,* ed. Bruce M.S. Campbell and Mark Overton. Manchester: Manchester University Press.

Anderson, David. 2000. "The Environmental Challenge in the 21st Century." Address to Globe 2000, Vancouver, 23 March.

Anderson, L.G. 1994. "Highgrading in ITQ Fisheries." *Marine Resource Economics* 9, no. 3: 209–26.

Anderson, Terry L., ed. 1994. *Continental Water Marketing.* San Francisco: Pacific Research Institute for Public Policy.

Annala, J.H. 1996. "New Zealand's ITQ System: Have the First Eight Years Been a Success or Failure?" *Reviews in Fish Biology and Fisheries* 6, no. 1: 43–62.

Arai, A.B. 1994. "Policy and Practice in the Atlantic Fisheries: Problems of Regulatory Enforcement." *Canadian Public Policy* 40, no. 4: 353–64.

Arnason, R. 1996. "On the ITQ Fisheries Management System in Iceland." *Reviews in Fish Biology and Fisheries* 6, no. 1: 63–90.

Arora, Seema. 1999. "Green and Competitive: Evidence from the Stock Market." Paper presented at the Western Economic Association Annual Meeting, San Diego, CA, 6–10 July.

Attridge, Ian C. 1997. *Conservation Easement Valuation and Taxation in Canada*. Report no. 97–01. Prepared for the North American Wetlands Conservation Council and Environment Canada, Canadian Wildlife Service, Habitat Conservation Division. Ottawa: Environment Canada.

Averill, N., and A. Whelan, eds. 2000. *Water Management in Canada: Proceedings of the Government's Roundtable on Water*. Ottawa: Public Policy Forum.

Bakker, Karen, et al. 2007. *Eau Canada: The Future of Canada's Water*. Vancouver: UBC Press.

Baldwin, John H. 1985. *Environmental Planning and Management*. London: Westview Press.

Barlow, Maude, and Tony Clark. 2002. *Blue Gold: The Fight to Stop the Corporate Theft of the World's Water*. Toronto: New Press.

Barnes, R.S.K., and K.H. Mann. 1991. *Fundamentals of Aquatic Ecology*. Oxford: Blackwell Scientific.

Barsh, Russel Lawrence. 2002. "Netukulimk Past and Present: Mikmaw Ethics and the Atlantic Fishery." *Journal of Canadian Studies* 37, no. 1: 15–42.

Bartlett, Richard. 1986. *Aboriginal Water Rights in Canada*. Calgary: Canadian Institute of Resources Law.

– 1988. *Aboriginal Water Rights in Canada: A Study of Aboriginal Title to Water and Indian Water Rights*. Calgary: Canadian Institute of Resources Law.

Barton, Barry. 1986. "Cooperative Management of Interprovincial Water Resources." In *Managing Natural Resources in a Federal State*, ed. J. Owen Saunders. Toronto: Carswell.

Becker, N., and K.W. Easter. 1999. "Conflict and Cooperation in Managing International Water Resources such as the Great Lakes." *Land Economics* 75, no. 2: 233–45.

Bemelmans-Videc, Marie-Louise, Ray C. Rist, and Evert Vedung, eds. 1998. *Carrots, Sticks and Sermons: Policy Instruments and Their Evaluation*. London: Transaction Publishers.

Benidickson, Jamie. 2002. *The Development of Water Supply and Sewage Infrastructure in Ontario 1880–1990's: Legal and Institutional Aspects of*

Public Health and Environmental History. The Walkerton Inquiry commissioned paper, 1. Toronto: Queen's Printer for Ontario.

Bennett, W.A.C. n.d. Quoted by A.G.L. McNaughton in address to the Royal Society of Canada; Sherbrooke, QC, 8 June 1966. In *The Dictionary of Canadian Quotations and Phrases*, ed. R.M. Hamilton and Dorothy Shields, 949. Toronto: McClelland & Stewart, 1979.

Biro, Andrew. 2002. "Wet Dreams: Ideology and the Debates over Canadian Water Exports." *Capitalism, Nature, Socialism* 13, no. 4: 29–50.

Bjorndal, T. 1990. *The Economics of Salmon Aquaculture.* Oxford: Blackwell.

Blackstock, Michael. 2001. "Water: A First Nation's Spiritual and Ecological Perspective." BC *Journal of Ecosystems and Management* 1, no. 1. http://www.forrex.org/publications/jem/jem.asp?issue=1 (accessed 22 August 2006).

Blomquist, W., and E. Ostrom. 1985. "Institutional Capacity and the Resolution of a Commons Dilemma." *Policy Studies Review* 5, no. 2: 283–93.

Bloomfield, L.M., and Gerald F. Fitzgerald. 1958. *Boundary Waters Problems of Canada and the United States.* Toronto: Carswell.

Boardman, Robert, ed. 1992. *Canadian Environmental Policy: Ecosystems, Politics, and Process.* Toronto: Oxford University Press.

Booth, L., and F. Quinn. 1995. "Twenty-five Years of the *Canada Water Act.*" *Canadian Water Resources Journal* 20, no. 2: 65–90.

Botts, L., and P. Muldoon. 1997. *The Great Lakes Water Quality Agreement: Its Past Successes and Uncertain Future.* Hanover, NH: The Institute on International Environmental Governance.

Bow River Basin Council. 2002. *Guidebook for Water Management: Background Information on Organizations, Policies, Legislation, Programs and Projects in the Bow River Basin.* Edmonton: Alberta Environment. http://www.brbc.ab.ca/pdfs/Guidebook.pdf' (accessed 1 August 2005).

Boyd, D.R. 2001. *Canada vs. the OECD: An Environmental Comparison.* Victoria, BC: University of Victoria. http://www.environmentalindicators.com/htdocs/PDF/CanadavsOECD.pdf (accessed 25 July 2005).

– 2003. *Unnatural Law: Rethinking Canadian Environmental Law and Policy.* Vancouver: UBC Press.

Boyd, R.O., and C.M. Dewees. 1992. "Putting Theory into Practice: Individual Transferable Quotas in New Zealand's Fisheries." *Society and Natural Resources* 5, no. 2: 179–98.

Bressers, Hans T.A., and Laurence J. O'Toole. 1998. "The Selection of Policy Instruments: A Network Based Perspective." *Journal of Public Policy* 18, no. 3: 213–39.

Bressers, Hans, Laurence J. O'Toole, and Jeremy Richardson, eds. 1995. *Networks for Water Policy: A Comparative Perspective.* London: Frank Cass.

British Columbia. Ministry of Agriculture, Food and Fisheries. various years. *Fisheries Production Statistics of British Columbia.* Victoria: Ministry of Agriculture, Food and Fisheries. http://www.agf.gov.bc.ca/fish_stats/pub-list.htm (accessed 28 July 2005).

British Columbia. Ministry of Environment, Lands and Parks. 1999. *Non-Point Source Action Plan.* Victoria: Ministry of Environment, Lands and Parks. Previously available at http://www.env.gov.bc.ca/wat/ (accessed March 1999).

– 2000. *A Freshwater Strategy for British Columbia: A Progress Report.* Victoria: Ministry of Environment, Lands and Parks. http://wlapwww.gov.bc.ca/wat/fws/fws_2000_03_update.html (accessed 1 August 2005).

British Columbia. Ministry of Water, Land, and Air Protection. 1999a. *Tackling Non-Point Source Water Pollution in British Columbia: An Action Plan.* Victoria: Ministry of Water, Land, and Air Protection. http://wlapwww.gov.bc.ca/wat/wq/bmps/npsaction.html (accessed 1 August 2005).

– 1999b. *Water Use Efficiency Catalogue for British Columbia.* Victoria: Ministry of Water, Land, and Air Protection. http://wlapwww.gov.bc.ca/wat/wtr_use_eff_cat_bc/toc.html (accessed 1 August 2005).

Bromley, D.W., D. Feeney, M. McKean, P. Peters, J. Gilles, R. Oakerson, C. Ford Runge, and James Thompson, eds. 1992. *Making the Commons Work: Theory, Practice, and Policy.* San Francisco: ICS Press.

Brooks, Stephen. 2003. "Water Policy." In *Public Policy in Canada: An Introduction,* ed. Stephen Brooks and Lydia Miljan. 4th ed. Toronto: Oxford University Press.

Brown, F.L. 1997. "Adaptive Solutions to Increasing Problems of International Water Shortages." *Water Supply* 15, no. 4: 173–81.

Brown, L.R. 2001. "How Water Scarcity Will Shape the New Century." *Water Science and Technology* 43, no. 4: 17–22.

Bruce, James, and Bruce Mitchell. 1995. *Broadening Perspectives on Water Issues.* Incidental Report no. IR95-1. Ottawa: Royal Society of Canada.

Buchanan, J.M., and G. Tullock. 1962. *The Calculus of Consent.* Ann Arbor: University of Michigan Press.

Burke, Brenda Lee. 2001. *Don't Drink the Water: The Walkerton Tragedy.* Victoria, BC: Trafford Books.

Calhoun, Sue. 1991. *A Word to Say: The Story of the Maritime Fishermen's Union.* Halifax: Nimbus Publishing.

Campbell, R., A.D. Scott, and P. Pearse. 1974. "Water Management in Ontario." *Osgoode Hall Law Journal* 12: 475–526.

Canada. 1992a. *North American Free Trade Agreement: Tariff Schedule of Canada.* Ottawa: Canada Communications Group, 1992.

– 1992b. *Nunavut Final Agreement*. Ottawa: Supply and Services Canada.

– 1993. NAFTA *Supplemental Agreements: North American Agreement on En-vironmental Co-Operation*. Washington, DC: United States Government Printing Office.

– 2002. "The Canadian Forest Industry: Innovation Profile Series [online]." Ottawa. http://www.innovation.gc.ca/gol/innovation/site.nsf/en/in02576.html (accessed 29 July 2003).

Canada. Agriculture and Agri-Food Canada. 1996. "Backgrounder on the En-vironmental Farm Plans. Ottawa: Agriculture and Agri-Food Canada." http://res2.agr.ca/london/gp/efp/efp_back.html (accessed October 1999).

– 2001. "National Water Supply Expansion Program." Ottawa: Agriculture and Agri-Food Canada. http://www.agr.gc.ca/env/index_e.php?section= h2o &page=h2o.

Canada. Canadian Food Inspection Agency and Health Canada. 2002. "Mak-ing It Clear: Renewing the Federal Regulations on Bottled Water." Ottawa: Canadian Food Inspection Agency and Health Canada. http://www.hc-sc. gc.ca/food-aliment/friia-raaii/frp-pra/water-eau/e_rfr_bottle_water_tofc.php (accessed 29 July 2005).

Canada. Commission on Pacific Fisheries Policy. 1982. *Turning the Tide: A New Policy for Canada's Pacific Fisheries: The Commission on Pacific Fisheries Pol-icy Final Report*. Peter H. Pearse, commissioner. Vancouver: The Commission.

Canada. Department of Fisheries and Oceans (DFO). 1995. *An Analysis of Cur-rent Fishing License and Vessel Values: West Coast Fishing Fleet*. Ottawa: Department of Fisheries and Oceans.

– 1998. *A New Direction of Canada's Pacific Salmon Fisheries*. Vancouver: De-partment of Fisheries and Oceans. http://www-comm.pac.dfo-mpo.gc.ca/ publications/allocation/st9808e.htm (accessed 29 July 2005).

– 1999a. "Freshwater Initiative: Department of Fisheries and Oceans Discussion Document." Ottawa: Fisheries and Oceans Canada, 1999. http://www.dfo-mpo.gc.ca/regions/central/pub/initiative/index_e.htm (accessed 29 July 2005).

– 1999b. *Integrated Fisheries Management Plan, Herring – Area 16*. Moncton: Department of Fisheries and Oceans, Gulf Fisheries Management Region.

– 1999c. *Pacific Fisheries Adjustment and Restructuring Program: A Plan to Revitalize Canada's Pacific Fisheries, Progress Report for Year One – June 1998 to July 1999*. Vancouver: Department of Fisheries and Oceans. http:// www-comm.pac.dfo-mpo.gc.ca/english/restruct/oneyear.htm.

– 2000a. "Backgrounder: Restructuring the Commercial Salmon Fleet." Vancouver: Department of Fisheries and Oceans. http://www-comm.pac. dfo-mpo.gc.ca/pages/release/bckgrnd/2000/bg04restructuring.PDF (accessed 29 July 2005).

– 2000b. *Estimates, 1999–2000.* Ottawa: Department of Fisheries and Oceans, 2000.

– 2001a. "Independent Panel on Access Criteria (IPAC): Mandate and Objectives." Backgrounder B-HQ-01–66(176). Ottawa: Department of Fisheries and Oceans.

– 2001b. "Independent Panel on Access Criteria (IPAC): Membership." Backgrounder B-HQ-01–66(177). Ottawa: Department of Fisheries and Oceans, 2001.

– 2001c. "Pacific Fisheries Adjustment and Restructuring Program: Year Three Progress Report." Vancouver: Department of Fisheries and Oceans. http://www-comm.pac.dfo-mpo.gc.ca/pages/release/bckgrnd/2001/bg022_e.htm (accessed 29 July 2005).

– 2002a. *Canada's Oceans Strategy.* Ottawa: Department of Fisheries and Oceans.

– 2002b. *Policy and Operational Framework for Integrated Management of Estuarine, Coastal and Marine Environments in Canada.* Ottawa: Department of Fisheries and Oceans.

– 2003a. *Atlantic Seal Hunt 2003–2005 Management Plan.* Ottawa: Department of Fisheries and Oceans.

– 2003b. *Preserving the Independence of the Inshore Fleet in Canada's Atlantic Fisheries.* Ottawa: Atlantic Fisheries Policy Review, Department of Fisheries and Oceans.

– 2003c. *Southern Gulf of St. Lawrence (4T) Herring: Stock Status Report 2003/05.* Dartmouth, NS: Department of Fisheries and Oceans Science, Gulf Region.

– 2003d. *Strengthening Our Relationship: The Aboriginal Fisheries Strategy and Beyond.* Ottawa: Department of Fisheries and Oceans.

– 2004a. *Accomplishments under the Marshall Response Initiative: Backgrounder.* Ottawa: Department of Fisheries and Oceans.

– 2004b. "Atlantic Fisheries Policy Review: Frequently Asked Questions." Ottawa: Department of Fisheries and Oceans. http://www.dfo-mpo.gc.ca/afpr-rppa/FAQs_e.htm.

– 2004c. "Commercial Catch Statistics." Vancouver: Department of Fisheries and Oceans. http://www-sci.pac.dfo-mpo.gc.ca/sa/Commercial/default_e.htm (accessed 28 July 2005).

– 2004d. *A Policy Framework for the Management of Fisheries on Canada's Atlantic Coast.* Ottawa: Department of Fisheries and Oceans.

– 2004e. "Regan Announces Management Measures for Herring Seiners Fishing off PEI." Press release. Ottawa: Department of Fisheries and Oceans, 24 September.

– 2004f. "Regan Releases Atlantic Fisheries Policy Framework and Stabilizes Sharing Arrangements for 2004." Press release. Ottawa: Department of Fisheries and Oceans, 25 March.

– 2004g. "Southern Gulf of St. Lawrence Herring Quotas Increase Significantly for 2004." Press release. Ottawa: Department of Fisheries and Oceans, 20 April.

– 2005. *2005–2010 Strategic Plan: Our Waters, Our Future.* Ottawa: Department of Fisheries and Oceans. http://www.dfo-mpo.gc.ca/dfo-mpo/plan_e. htm#2d.

– 2006. *2006–2010 Atlantic Seal management Plan Highlights: Backgrounder.* Ottawa: Department of Fisheries and Oceans.

– 2007. "Minister Hearn Announces 2007 Management Measures for Atlantic Seal Hunt." Press release. Ottawa: Department of Fisheries and Oceans, 29 March.

Canada. Department of Justice. 2001. *International Boundary Waters Treaty Act.* Rev. ed. Ottawa: Department of Justice. http//:www.laws.justice.gc.ca/ en/I-17/77063.html (accessed 18 December 2003).

Canada. Department of the Environment. 1998. "Federal-Provincial State-of-the-Environment Team." In *Fluctuating Water Levels in the St. Lawrence River,* researched and written by A. Robichaud and R. Drolet. State of the St. Lawrence River Series. Montreal: St. Lawrence Vision 2000, Department of the Environment.

– Interdepartmental Committee on Water. 1990. *Federal Water Policy: A Progress Report.* Ottawa: Minister of Supply and Services.

– 1994. *Federal Water Policy: Progress Report No. 2.* Ottawa: Minister of Supply and Services.

Canada. Environment Canada. n.d. *Water Survey Canada: Hydrology of Canada.* Ottawa: Environment Canada. http://www.wsc.ec.gc.ca/hydrology/ main_e.cfm?cname=hydro_e.cfm (accessed 27 July 2005).

– 1975. *The Legal Framework for Public Participation in Canadian Water Management.* Ottawa: Environment Canada.

– 1985. *Currents of Change: Final Report of the Enquiry on Federal Water Policy.* Ottawa: Minister of Supply and Services, 1985.

– 1987. Freshwater Web site. Ottawa: Environment Canada. http:// www.ec.gc.ca/water (accessed 27 July 2005).

– 1992. *Water Conservation – Every Drops Counts.* Ottawa: Environment Canada.

– 1994a. *A Primer on Freshwater.* Ottawa: Supply and Services Canada.

– 1994b. *Reviewing CEPA: The Issues – Economic Incentives.* Ottawa.

– 1995. *Canada's Ecological Gifts Program.* Ottawa: Environment Canada. http://www.cws-scf.ec.gc.ca/ecogifts/intro_e.cfm.

– 1996. *Survey on the Importance of Nature to Canadians: A Federal-Provincial-Territorial Initiative.* Ottawa: Environment Canada. http://www.ec.gc.ca/nature/index_e.htm (accessed 22 May 2003).

– 1997a. *Canada Water Act: Annual Report, 1995–1996.* Ottawa: Minister of Supply and Services.

– 1997b. *Ecological Gifts: Implementing Provisions of the Income Tax Act of Canada.* Ottawa: Canadian Wildlife Service, Environment Canada.

– 1998a. *Canada and Freshwater: Experience and Practices.* Sustainable Development in Canada monograph series, no. 6. Ottawa: Public Works and Government Services Canada. http://www.sdinfo.gc.ca/reports/en/monograph6/splash.cfm (accessed 29 July 2005).

– 1998b. *Ecological Gifts: Implementing Provisions of the Income Tax Act of Canada.* Rev. ed. Ottawa: Canadian Wildlife Service, Environment Canada.

– 2000a. "Eco-gifts Are Good for Nature and for Taxpayers." News release. Ottawa: Environment Canada, 4 October.

– 2000b. *1999–2000 Estimates: A Report on Plans and Priorities.* Ottawa: Environment Canada, 2000. http://www.ec.gc.ca/rpp/1999/rpp_e.pdf (accessed 29 July 2005).

– 2000c. *A Primer on Fresh Water: Questions and Answers.* 5th ed. Ottawa: Environment Canada. http://www.ec.gc.ca/water/en/info/pubs/primer/e_primer09.htm (accessed 27 January 2006).

– 2001a. *Policy Framework for Environmental Performance Agreements.* Ottawa: Environment Canada.

– 2001b. *The State of Municipal Wastewater Effluents in Canada.* Ottawa: Environment Canada.

– 2001c. *Sustainable Development Strategy 2001–2003.* Ottawa: Environment Canada. http://www.ec.gc.ca/sd-dd_consult/index_e.cfm.

– 2002a. Freshwater Web site: "The Management of Water." Ottawa: Environment Canada. http://www.ec.gc.ca/water/en/manage/e_manag.htm (accessed 29 July 2005).

– 2002b. "Propur: Reduction in Volume of Drinking Water Used to Wash Potatoes." Enviroclub Project information sheet. Ottawa: Environment Canada. http://www.enviroclub.ca/pdf/en/proPur_en.pdf.

– 2003a. Freshwater Web site: "The Nature of Water." Ottawa: Environment Canada, 2003. http://www.ec.gc.ca/water/en/nature/e_nature.htm (accessed 29 July 2003).

– 2003b. *Implementation Progress Report 2002.* Ottawa: Environment Canada. http://www.ec.gc.ca/sd-dd_consult/DPR2002Table_e.html.

– 2003c. *Water and Canada: Preserving a Legacy for People and the Environment.* Ottawa: Environment Canada.

- 2004a. Freshwater Web site: "Quickfacts." Ottawa: Environment Canada, 2004. http://www.ec.gc.ca/water/en/e_quickfacts.htm (accessed 7 January 2005).
- 2004b. *Implementation Progress Report 2003*. Ottawa: Environment Canada. http://www.ec.gc.ca/sd-dd_consult/DPR2003Table_e.html.
- 2004c. *National Overview: Summary of 2002 Data*. Ottawa: Environment Canada.
- 2004d. "The Nature of Water Page." http://www.ec.gc.ca/water/en/nature/prop/e_cycle.htm
- 2004e. *Species at Risk – Beluga Whales*. Ottawa: Environment Canada. http://www.speciesatrisk.gc.ca/search/speciesDetails_e.cfm?SpeciesID=102 (accessed 16 February 2005).
- 2005a. *Canada and Freshwater – Experiences and Practices: Sustainable Water Management*. Ottawa: Environment Canada. http://www.sdinfo.gc.ca/reports/en/monograph6/suswtmgt.cfm (accessed 27 July 2005).
- 2005b. Freshwater Web site: "Freshwater Facts for Canada and the World." Ottawa: Environment Canada. http://www.ec.gc.ca/water/en/info/facts (accessed 27 January 2006).
- 2005c. Freshwater Web site: "Water – Forever on the Move." Ottawa: Environment Canada. http://www.ec.gc.ca/water/en/info/pubs/primer/e_prim01.htm (accessed 29 July 2005).
- 2006a. *The Management of Water: Background Information on Bulk Water Removal and Water Exports*. Ottawa: Environment Canada. http://www.ec.gc.ca/water/en/manage/removal/e_backgr.htm (accessed 4 February 2006).
- 2006b. *Water and Canadian Identity*. Ottawa: Environment Canada. http://www.ec.gc.ca/Water/en/culture/ident/e_ident.htm (accessed 22 August 2006).
- 2008a. "The Ecological Gifts Program: History." http://www.cws-scf.ec.gc.ca/egp-pde/default.asp?lang=En&n=3DA6734-1 (accessed 4 May 2008).
- 2008b. *Water and Climate*. http://www.ec.gc.ca/water/en/nature/clim/e_clim.htm.
- SOLEC. 1995–2007. State of the Lakes Ecosystem Conference: SOLEC Reports. Ottawa: Environment Canada. Available at http://www.on.ec.gc.ca/solec/.
Canada. Environment Canada and the US Environmental Protection Agency. 1995. *Environmental Atlas and Resource Book: The Great Lakes*. Ottawa: Environment Canada.
- 2001. *State of the Great Lakes, 2001*. http://binational.net/sogl2001/download.html.
- 2003. *State of the Great Lakes, 2003*. http://www.binational.net/sogl2003/scglo3eng.pdf.

Canada. Federal Court of Canada. 2004. *Ecology Action Centre v. Canada (Attorney General)*, FC 1087.

Canada. House of Commons. Standing Committee on Fisheries and Oceans. 1998a. *Central Canada's Freshwater Fisheries Report*. Ottawa: House of Commons, Standing Committee on Fisheries and Oceans, November.

– 1998b. *The East Coast Report*. Ottawa: House of Commons, Standing Committee on Fisheries and Oceans, Spring.

– 1998c. *The Nunavut Report*. Ottawa: House of Commons, Standing Committee on Fisheries and Oceans, December.

– 1998d. *The PEI Report*. Ottawa: House of Commons, Standing Committee on Fisheries and Oceans, December.

– 1998e. *The West Coast Report*. Ottawa: House of Commons, Standing Committee on Fisheries and Oceans, October.

– 1999. *The Seal Report*. Ottawa: House of Commons, Standing Committee on Fisheries and Oceans, June.

– 2002. *Foreign Overfishing: Its Impacts and Solutions*. Ottawa: House of Commons, Standing Committee on Fisheries and Oceans, June.

– 2004. *Safe, Secure, Sovereign: Reinventing the Canadian Coast Guard*. Ottawa: House of Commons, Standing Committee on Fisheries and Oceans.

Canada. Indian and Northern Affairs Canada (INAC). 2001. *Safe Drinking Water on First Nations Reserves: Roles and Responsibilities*. Ottawa: Indian and Northern Affairs Canada. http://epe.lac-bac.gc.ca/100/200/301/inac-ainc/safe_drinking_water-e/wqr_e.pdf (accessed 27 July 2005).

– 2003. *National Assessment of Water and Wastewater Systems in First Nations Communities: Summary Report*. Ottawa: Indian and Northern Affairs Canada. http://epe.lac-bac.gc.ca/100/200/301/inac-ainc/national_assessment-e/watw_e.pdf (accessed 27 July 2005).

– 2007. "Water Management in Northwest Territories and Nunavut." www.ainc-inac.gc.ca/ps/nap/wat/watmannwt_e.html (accessed July 2007).

Canada. Industry Canada. 2002. "A Synopsis of the Bottled Water Market in Canada." http://strategis.ic.gc.ca/searchstrategis.

Canada. Inquiry on Federal Water Policy. 1985. *Currents of Change: Final Report, Inquiry on Federal Water Policy*. P.H. Pearse et al. Ottawa: Environment Canada.

Canada. Interdepartmental Committee on Water. 1990. *Federal Water Policy: A Progress Report*. Ottawa: Interdepartmental Committee on Water.

Canada. International Trade Canada. 2004. "Dispute Settlement [Web page]." Ottawa: International Trade Canada. http://www.dfait-maeci.gc.ca/tna-nac/sunbelt-en.asp (accessed 9 February 2005).

Canada. Library of Parliament. 2007. "Legislative Summary: Bill C-45: An Act respecting the sustainable development of Canada's seacoast and inland fisheries." Ottawa: Library of Parliament.

Canada. National Round Table on the Environment and the Economy(NRTEE). 2002. *Toward a Canadian Agenda for Ecological Fiscal Reform: First Steps.* Ottawa: National Round Table on the Environment and the Economy. http://www.nrtee-trnee.ca/Publications/PDF/Report_EFR-First-Steps_E.pdf (accessed 1 August 2005).

Canada. National Water Research Institute. 1998. *Non-Point Sources of Pollution Project.* Ottawa: National Water Research Institute, Aquatic Ecosystem Protection Branch. http://www.cciw.ca/nwri-e/aepb/non-point (accessed 5 December 1998).

Canada. Natural Resources Canada. 1997. *Electric Power in Canada.* Ottawa: Natural Resources Canada.

– 2003. *The Atlas of Canada.* Ottawa: Natural Resources Canada. http://atlas.gc.ca/site/english/index.html (accessed 2 October 2003).

– 2004. *Climate Change Impacts and Adaptation: A Canadian Perspective.* www.adaptation.nrcan.gc.ca/perspective/index_e.php (accessed 21 April 2008).

Canada. Office of the Auditor General. 1999. *Report of the Commissioner of the Environment and Sustainable Development to the House of Commons.* Ottawa: Office of the Auditor General.

– 2005. *Report of the Commissioner of the Environment and Sustainable Development.* Ottawa: Office of the Auditor General.

Canada. Policy Research Initiative (PRI). 2006a. *Can Water Quality Trading Help to Address Agricultural Sources of Pollution in Canada?* Ottawa: Policy Research Initiative. http://policyresearch.gc.ca/doclib/PR_SD_WQT_200605_e.pdf.

– 2006b. *Freshwater for the Future: Policies for Sustainable Water Management in Canada, Conference Proceedings.* Ottawa: Policy Research Initiative.

– 2007. *Is Water a Tradable Commodity?* Ottawa: Policy Research Initiative, 2007. http://policyresearch.gc.ca/doclib/SD_BN_Water%20Tradable_e.pdf.

Canada. Royal Commission on Aboriginal Peoples. 1996. *Report.* Ottawa: The Commission.

Canada. Royal Commission on Seals and Sealing. 1985. *Report.* 3 vols. Ottawa: The Commission.

Canada. Statistics Canada. 2000. *Human Activity and the Environment 2000.* Ottawa: Statistics Canada.

– 2002. *Human Activity and the Environment*. www.statcan.ca/english/ads/11-509-XPE/ecozones.htm (assessed 1 May 2008).

– 2003. "Freshwater Resources in Canada." In *Human Activity and the Environment: Annual Statistics*. http://www.statcan.ca/bsolc/english/bsolc?catno=16-201-X20030006667.

Canada. Supreme Court of Canada. 1990. *R. v. Sparrow* [1990] 1 S.C.R..

– 1999a. *R. v. Marshall* [1999] 3 S.C.R., 17 September.

– 1999b. *R. v. Marshall*, (Motion for Rehearing and Stay) [1999] 3 S.C.R, 5 November.

– 2002. *Ward v. Canada (Attorney General)* [2002] 1 S.C.R.

Canada-Alberta Environmentally Sustainable Agriculture Water Quality Committee. 1998. *Agricultural Impacts on Water Quality in Alberta*. Edmonton: Queen's Printer, 1998.

Canada and the United States. n.d. "Great Lakes St. Lawrence Seaway System: About Us: Competitiveness [Web page]." The St Lawrence Seaway Management Corporation and St Lawrence Seaway Development Corporation. http://www.greatlakes-seaway.com/en/aboutus/competitiveness.html (accessed 12 July 2004).

Canada Official Report (Hansard). 1999. 135S, no. 177S (1st Session S, 36th Parliament, Tuesday, 9 February), 11616. Previously available at www.parl.gc.ca/PDF/36/1/parlbus/chambus/house/debates/han177-e.pdf (accessed 12 February 2005).

The Canadian Atlas Online. Royal Geographical Society of Canada. http://www.canadiangeographic.ca/atlas/intro.aspx?lang=En (accessed 19 January 2006).

Canadian Chemical Producers Association (CCPA). 2002. *Reducing Emissions: 2002 Emissions Inventory and 5-Year Projections: A Responsible Care Initiative*. Ottawa: Canadian Chemical Producers Association.

– 2005. *Canada's Chemical Producers: Responsible Care Program*. Ottawa: Canadian Chemical Producers Association. http://www.ccpa.ca/Responsible Care/.

Canadian Council of Ministers of the Environment (CCME). 1999a. *Accord for the Prohibition of Bulk Water Removal from Drainage Basins*. http://www.ccme.ca/about/mediacentre/1999.html?item=13 (accessed 30 April 2003).

– 1999b. *Water Accord Backgrounder*. Kananaskis, AB: Canadian Council of Ministers of the Environment. http://www.ccme.ca/about/communiques/1999.html?item=13 (accessed 29 July 2005).

– 2003. *Water Quality Guidelines*. Winnipeg: Canadian Council of Ministers of the Environment. http://www.ccme.ca/assets/pdf/e1_062.pdf.

– 2004a. *Canada Wide Accord on Environmental Harmonization*. Canadian Council of Ministers of the Environment. http://www.ccme.ca/assets/pdf/accord_harmonization_e.pdf (accessed 29 July 2005).

– 2004b. *From Source to Tap: Guidance on the Multi Barrier Approach to Safe Drinking Water*. Winnipeg: Canadian Council of Ministers of the Environment. http://www.ccme.ca/assets/pdf/mba_guidance_doc_e.pdf (accessed 29 July 2005).

Canadian Environmental Advisory Council. 1987. *Canada and Sustainable Development*. Ottawa: Canadian Environmental Advisory Council.

Canadian Environmental Law Association. 1999. "Federal Government Ban on Bulk Water Renewals Only Partially Closes off Exports Threat, Says CELA." Toronto: Canadian Environmental Law Association. http://www.web.net/cela/mr99126.htm (accessed 26 November 1999).

– 2004. *Safeguarding Ontario's Drinking Water Sources: Essential Elements of Source Protection Legislation*. CELA Publication no. 478. Toronto: Canadian Environmental Law Association. http://62.44.8.131/uploads/f8e04c51a8e0404 1f6f7faa046b03a7c/478_sodws.pdf (accessed 29 July 2005).

– 2006. "Press Release: A Step in the Right Direction for Great Lakes Protection." http://www.cela.ca/newsevents/detail.shtml?x=2430 (accessed 29 March 2006).

Canadian Institute for Environmental Law and Policy (CIELP). 2002. *Sixth Annual Report on Ontario's Environment*. http://cielp.org/pdf/sixthannual.pdf.

Canadian Water and Wastewater Association. 2000–01. *Brief [to the] Walkerton Inquiry*. Ottawa: Canadian Water and Wastewater Association. http://www.cwwa.ca/pdf_files/walkertonbrief.pdf (accessed 25 July 2005).

Canadian Water Resources Association. 1998. *Water News Profile* 17. http://www.cwra.org/news/arts/fwsumrec.html.

Cavanagh, N., T. McDaniels, L. Axelrod, and P. Slovic. 2000. "Perceived Ecological Risks from Selected Forest Industry Activities." *Forest Science* 46, no. 3: 344–55.

CBC News. 2006. "Martin Announces $1 Billion Water Cleanup." 7 January. http://www.cbc.story/canadavotes2006/national/2006/01/07/elnx-water 060107.html.

Chandler, M. 1985. "The Resource Amendment (92A) and the Political Economy of Canadian Federalism" *Osgood Hall Law Journal* 23: 253–74.

Chandran, Carol. 2003. "First Nations and Natural Resources – The Canadian Context [Web page]." Fredericksburg, VA: First Peoples Worldwide. http://www.firstpeoples.org/land_rights/canada/summary_of_land_rights/fnnr_2001.htm (accessed 21 May 2003).

Chepel, L.I. 2000. *Northwest Atlantic: Fisheries, Science, Regulation.* Dartmouth NS: North Atlantic Fisheries Organization.

Christy, F.T. 2000. "Common Property Rights: An Alternative to ITQs." In *Use of Property Rights in Fisheries Management,* ed. R. Shotton. Rome: Food and Agriculture Organization.

Cicin-Sain, Biliana, and Robert W. Knecht. 1998. *Integrated Coastal and Ocean Management: Concepts and Practices.* Washington, DC: Island Press.

– 2000. *The Future of US Ocean Policy: Choices for a New Century.* Washington, DC: Island Press.

Clancy, Peter. 1999. "The Politics and Administration of Aboriginal Claims Settlements." In *Public Administration and Policy,* ed. Martin W. Westmacott and Hugh P. Mellon. Scarborough, ON: Prentice Hall Allyn and Bacon.

– 2000. "The H$_2$ Woes of the DFO." In *How Ottawa Spends, 2000–2001: Past Imperfect, Future Tense,* ed. Leslie A. Pal. Don Mills, ON: Oxford University Press.

Clarke, R. 2003. "Water Crisis?" *OECD Observer* 236: 8–11.

Clarke, Tony. 2007. *Inside the Bottle: Exposing the Bottled Water Industry.* Ottawa: Canadian Centre for Policy Alternatives and Polaris Institute.

Clement, Wallace. 1986. *The Struggle to Organize: Resistance in Canada's Fishery.* Toronto: McClelland and Stewart.

Coates, Ken. 2000. *The Marshall Decision and Native Rights.* Montreal: McGill-Queen's University Press.

Colborn, Theodora, et al. 1990. *Great Lakes, Great Legacy?* Washington, DC: Conservation Foundation; Ottawa: Institute for Research on Public Policy.

Commission for Environmental Cooperation. 1998. *Voluntary Measures to Ensure Environmental Compliance: A Review and Analysis of North American Initiatives.* Montreal: CEC.

Commons, J.R. 1924. *The Legal Foundations of Capitalism.* Madison: University of Wisconsin Press.

Conference Board of Canada. 2000. *The Optimal Policy Mix: Matching Ends and Means in Environmental Policy Making.* Ottawa: Conference Board of Canada.

– 2007. *Navigating the Shoals: Assessing Water Governance and Management in Canada* Ottawa: Conference Board of Canada. http://www.conference-board.ca/documents.asp?rnext=1993 (accessed 1 May 2007).

Conservation Council of Ontario. 2001. *Protecting the Environment.* Toronto: Conservation Council of Ontario. http://www.greenontario.org/cco/protect.pdf (accessed 1 August 2005).

Conservation Ontario. 2003. *Watershed Economic Incentives through Phosphorus Trading and Water Quality.* Newmarket: Conservation Ontario. http://conservation-ontario.on.ca/projects/pdf/watershed_PP/WaterQualityReport2003.pdf (accessed 1 August 2005).

- 2005. "Conservation Authorities of Ontario [map]." http://www.conservation-ontario.on.ca/profile/ca_map.pdf.

Coote, D.R., and L.J. Gingerich. 2000. *The Health of Our Water: Toward Sustainable Agriculture in Canada*. Ottawa: Agriculture and Agri-Food Canada.

Copes, P. 1998. *Coping with the Coho Crisis: A Conservation-Minded, Stakeholder-Sensitive and Community-Oriented Strategy*. Report commissioned by the British Columbia Ministry of Fisheries. Victoria: Ministry of Fisheries.

Cordon, Sandra. 2000. "Ottawa Worried for a Decade about Water Exports, Documents Show." Canadian Press Newswire. 4 January.

Council of Canadians. n.d.(a). *Campaigns*. Ottawa: Council of Canadians. http://www.canadians.org/campaigns/ (accessed 11 January 2000).

- n.d.(b). *You Have No Mandate to Trade Away Our Water*. Ottawa: Council of Canadians. http://www.canadians.org/documents/NM_Water.pdf (accessed 7 January 2005).

- 2000. *A Water Policy for Canada*. Ottawa: Council of Canadians. http://www.canadians.org/display_document.htm?COC_token=024F024&id=238&isdoc=1(accessed 26 July 2005).

- 2006. *New Agreement Will Weaken Canadian Control and Protection of Great Lakes*. http://www.Canadians.org/display_document.htm?COC_token=COC_token&id+1290&is (accessed 29 March 2006).

Council of Great Lakes Governors. n.d. *The Great Lakes Charter*. Chicago: Council of Great Lakes Governors. http://www.cglg.org/pub/charter (accessed 1 October 2002).

- 2001. *The Great Lakes Charter Annex*. Chicago: Council of Great Lakes Governors. http://www.cglg.org/projects/water/annex2001.pdf (accessed 7 October 2002).

- 2006. *Great Lakes–St. Lawrence River Basin Sustainable Water Resources Agreement*. Available at http://www.cglg.org/projects/water/annex2001 Implementing.asp (accessed 29 March 2006).

Coutlee, Charles B. 1910. "The Water Wealth of Canada." Speech delivered before the first annual meeting of the Commission of Conservation, Ottawa, 18–21 January. In Canada, Commission of Conservation, *Report of the Annual Meeting*. Ottawa: Commission of Conservation.

Crane, T., and M. Ratliff. 1997. "Water Use Approaches Trillion Gallons Per Day." *Advisor* 10, no. 3: 9.

Creighton, Donald G. 1956. *The Empire of the St. Lawrence*. Toronto: Macmillan Co. of Canada.

- 1958. *Empire of the St. Lawrence*. 2nd ed. Boston: Houghton Miflin Company.

Day, J.C., and F. Quinn. 1992. *Water Diversion and Export: Learning from Canadian Experience*. Waterloo: Department of Geography, University of Waterloo.

de Loe, R. 1999. "Dam the News: Newspapers and the Oldman River Dam Project in Alberta." *Journal of Environmental Management* 55: 219–37.

de Loe, R., R. Kreutzwiser, and J. Ivey. 2001. "Agricultural Water Use in Ontario." *Canadian Water Resources Journal* 26, no. 1: 17–42.

Demsetz, H. 1967. "Towards a Theory of Property Rights." *American Economic Review Papers and Proceedings* 57, no. 2: 347–60.

Denhez, M. 1992. *You Can't Give It Away: Tax Aspects of Ecologically Sensitive Lands*. Ottawa: North American Wetlands Conservation Council.

de Soto, H. 2000. *The Mystery of Capital: Why Capitalism Triumphs in the West and Fails Everywhere Else*. New York: Basic Books.

DeVoretz, D., and R. Schwindt. 1985. "Harvesting Canadian Fish and Rents: A Partial Review of the Report of the Commission on Canadian Pacific Fisheries Policy." *Marine Resource Economics* 1, no. 4: 347–67.

Dietz, Thomas, and Paul Stern, eds. 2002. *New Tools for Environmental Protection: Education, Information, and Voluntary Measures*. Washington, DC: National Academy Press.

Diof, J. 2003. "Agriculture, Food Security, and Water: Towards a Blue Revolution." *OECD Observer* 236: 21–2.

Dobson, Mike, and Chris Frid. 1998. *Ecology of Aquatic Systems*. Harlow, UK: Addison, Wesley Longman.

Doerkson, Harvey. 1978. "Water, Politics, and Ideology: An Overview of Water Resources Management." In *Policy Studies Review Annual*, vol. 2, ed. H. Freeman. Beverly Hills: Sage Publications.

Doern, G. Bruce, and Thomas Conway. 1994. *The Greening of Canada: Federal Institutions and Decisions*. Toronto: University of Toronto Press.

Doern, Bruce G., and Richard W. Phidd. 1992. *Canadian Public Policy: Ideas, Structure, Process*. 2nd ed. Scarborough, ON: Nelson Canada.

Dofasco. 2003. *Environmental Management Agreement: Annual Progress Report 2002*. Hamilton: Dofasco. Previously available at http://www. dofasco.ca (accessed May 2005).

D'Ombrain, N. 1997. "Public Inquiries in Canada." *Canadian Public Administration* 40, no. 1: 86–107.

Dorcey, A.H.J., and T. McDaniels. 2001. "Great Expectations, Mixed Results: Trends in Citizen Involvement in Canadian Environmental Governance." In *Governing the Environment: Persistent Challenges, Uncertain Innovations*, ed. E.A. Parson. Toronto: University of Toronto Press.

Dorcey, A.H.J. and C.L. Riek. 1987. "Negotiation-Based Approaches to the Settlement of Environmental Disputes in Canada." In *The Place of Negotiation in Environmental Assessment*. Ottawa: Canadian Environment Research Council.

Dryzek, J. 1997. *The Politics of the Earth*. Toronto: Oxford University Press.

Dubin, J.A. 1974. *Jackson v. Doury Construction Co. Ltd*. In *Revised Statutes of Canada*.

Dupont, D.P. 1990. "Rent Dissipation in Restricted Access Fisheries." *Journal of Environmental Economics and Management* 19, no. 1: 26–44.

Eckerberg, K. 1997. "Comparing the Local Use of Environmental Policy Instruments in the Nordic and Baltic Countries: The Issue of Diffuse Water Pollution." *Environmental Politics* 6, no. 2: 24–47.

Eckert, Claude. 2004. Interview. Calgary, 17 February.

Edmonton Journal. 2003. "Alberta's Drought Officially Over." 5 June, A3.

Elidias, Pearl, Margaret M. Hill and Michael Howlett, eds. 2005. *Designing Government: From Instruments to Governance*. Montreal: McGill-Queen's University Press.

Ellickson, R.C. 1991. *Order without Law: How Neighbors Settle Disputes*. Cambridge, MA: Harvard University Press.

Elwell, Christine, and the Sierra Club of Canada. 2001. "NAFTA Effects on Water: Testing for NAFTA Effects in the Great Lakes Basin." *Toledo Journal of Great Lakes Law, Science and Policy* 3, no. 2: 151–212.

Estrin, David, and John Swaigen. 1993. *Environment on Trial: A Guide to Ontario Environmental Law and Policy*. 3rd ed. Toronto: Emond Montgomery Publications.

European Environment Agency. 1997. *Environmental Agreements: Environmental Effectiveness*. Environmental Issue series, no. 3, vol. 1. Copenhagen: European Environment Agency. http://reports.eea.eu.int/92-9167-052-9/en (accessed 1 August 2005).

Fafard, Patrick C., and Kathryn Harrison. 2000. *Managing the Environmental Union: Intergovernmental Relations and Environmental Policy in Canada*. Kingston: McGill-Queen's University Press.

Farid, C., J. Jackson, and K. Clark. 1997. *The Fate of the Great Lakes: Sustaining or Draining the Sweetwater Seas?* Montreal and Buffalo, NY: Great Lakes United. http://www.glu.org/english/index.html (accessed 29 July 2005).

Fernandez, R., and D. Rodrik. 1991. "Resistance to Reform: Status Quo Bias in the Presence of Individual-Specific Uncertainty." *American Economic Review* 81, no. 5: 1146–56.

Fife, Robert. 1999. "Liberals Set Aside $500M to Settle Native Fishing Crisis." *Globe and Mail*, 30 October.

Fife, Robert, and Graham Hamilton. 1999. "Judges Rule Natives Not Immune to Fishing Laws." *National Post*, 18 November.

Filyk, G., and R. Cote. 1992. "Pressures from Inside: Advisory Groups and the Environmental Policy Community." In *Canadian Environmental Policy: Ecosystems, Politics, and Processes*, ed. Robert Boardman. Toronto: Oxford University Press.

Finlayson, Alan Christopher. 1994. *Fishing for Truth*. St John's: Institute for Social and Economic Research.

Fishermen and Scientists Research Society. 2003. Fishermen and Scientists Research Society Web page. Halifax: FSRS. http://www.fsrs.ns.ca.

Fitzgibon, J., et al. 2000. *Environmental Farm Plan Indicator Survey*. Guelph: Ontario Farm Coalition.

Flanagan, Cathleen, and Melinda Laituri, 2004. "Local Cultural Knowledge and Water Resource Management: The Wind River Indian Reservation." *Environmental Management* 33, no. 2: 262–70.

Francis, R.D., D.J. Gilbert, and J.H. Annala. 1993. "Rejoinder – Fishery Management by Individual Quotas: Theory and Practice." *Marine Policy* 17, no. 1: 64–6.

Francoeur, L.G. 2000. "Ecosystem in Peril – the St. Lawrence River." In *Voices for the Watershed: Environmental Issues in the Great Lakes–St Lawrence Drainage Basin*, ed. Gregor Gilpin-Beck and Bruce Littlejohn. Montreal and Kingston: McGill-Queen's University Press.

Freeman, Neil. 1996. *The Politics of Power: Ontario Hydro and Its Government, 1906–1995*. Toronto: University of Toronto Press.

Frerichs, S., and K.W. Easter. 1990. "Regulation of Interbasin Transfers and Consumptive Uses from the Great Lakes." *Natural Resources Journal* 30, no. 3: 561–79.

Fritz, G., and M.J. McKinney. 1994. "Canadian Water-Export Policy and Continental Water Marketing." In *Continental Water Marketing*, ed. Terry L. Anderson. San Francisco: Pacific Research Institute for Public Policy.

Gallon, Gary. 1997. *Voluntary Environmental Measures: The Canadian Experience*. Toronto and Montreal: Canadian Institute for Business and the Environment.

Galloway, Gerald, and Ralph Pentland. 2003. *Managing Groundwater in the Great Lakes Basin: Securing Our Future*. Working paper for the Program on Water Issues. Toronto: University of Toronto.

Gardner, B.D. 1985. "Institutional Impediments to Efficient Water Allocation." *Policy Studies Review*. 5, no. 2: 353–63.

Gibson, C., et al. 2000. "The Concept of Scale and the Human Dimensions of Global Change." *Ecological Economics* 32: 217–39.

Gibson, Robert, ed. 1999. *Voluntary Initiatives and the New Corporate Greening*. Peterborough, ON: Broadview Press.

Gislason, Gordon, et al. 1998. "Fishing for Money, Challenges and Opportunities in the BC Salmon Industry." Report prepared by G.S. Gislason and Associates for the British Columbia Job Protection Commission, 10 June.

Gleick, P.H. 1993. *Water Crisis: A Guide to the World's Fresh Water Resources*. New York: Oxford University Press.

– 2000. *The World's Water, 2000–2001: The Biennial Report on Freshwater Resources*. Washington, DC: Island Press.

Glenn, J. 1999. *Once Upon an Oldman. Special Interest Politics and the Oldman River Dam*. Vancouver: University of British Columbia Press.

Goodstein, E.S. 2001. *Economics and the Environment*. 3rd ed. New York: John Wiley and Sons.

Graedel, T.E., and B.R. Allenby. 1995. *Industrial Ecology*. Englewood Cliffs, NJ: Prentice Hall.

Grafton, R.Q. 1996. "Individual Transferable Quotas: Theory and Practice." *Reviews in Fish Biology and Fisheries* 6, no. 1: 5–20.

Grafton, R.Q., D. Squires, and K. Fox. 2000. "Private Property and Economic Efficiency: A Study of a Common-Pool Resource." *Journal of Law and Economics* 43, no. 2: 679–713.

Grafton, R.Q., D. Squires, and J.E. Kirkley. 1996. "Private Property Rights and Crises in World Fisheries: Turning the Tide?" *Contemporary Economic Policy*. 14, no. 4: 90–9.

Graham, Jennifer, Stephen Eagle, and Maria Recchia. 2002. *Local Knowledge and Local Stocks: An Atlas of Groundfish Spawning in the Bay of Fundy*. Antigonish, NS: Centre for Community-Based Management.

Gray, Herb. 2005. "Transboundary Issues in Water Governance" Address by the Canadian chair, International Joint Commission, Hamilton, Ontario, 4 November.

Gray, J.H. 1996. *Men against the Desert*. Saskatoon: Fifth House Publishers.

Great Canadian Rivers. 2003. "The St. Lawrence River Ecosystem [Web page]." Toronto: Good Earth Productions. http://www.greatcanadianrivers.com/rivers/stlawer/species-home.html (accessed 16 February 2005).

Great Lakes Commission. 2000a. "Great Lakes Regional Water Use Database [Web page]." Ann Arbor, MI: Great Lakes Commission. http://www.glc.org/wateruse/database/ (accessed 23 September 2004).

– 2000b. "Human Health and the Great Lakes: Recreational Water in the Great Lakes [Web page]." Ann Arbor, MI: Great Lakes Commission. http://www.great-lakes.net/humanhealth/rec/ (accessed 22 May 2003).

Great Lakes National Program Office. 2000. *Recreational Water in the Great Lakes*. www.great-lakes.net/humanhealth/rec/ (accessed 22 May 2003).

Great Lakes Science Advisory Board et al. 2003. *Priorities 2001–2003: Priorities and Progress under the Great Lakes Water Quality Agreement*. Report to the International Joint Commission. Windsor, ON: The International Joint Commission.

Griffiths, Mary, et al. 2006. *Troubled Waters, Troubling Trends: Technology and Policy Options to Reduce Water Use in Oil and Oil Sands Development in Alberta*. Calgary:Pembina Institute. http://pubs.pembina.org/reports/TroubledW_Full.pdf (accessed May 2007).

Gunningham, Neil. 2005. "Reconfiguring Environmental Regulation." In *Designing Government: From Instruments to Governance*, ed. Pearl Elidias, Margaret M. Hill and Michael Howlett. Montreal: McGill-Queen's University Press.

Guy, Ray. 2000. "Seal Wars." *Canadian Geographic,* January-February, 37–48.

Hamilton, Graeme. 1999. "N.S. Mi'kmaq Risk Scuttling Deal by Setting Unlicensed Traps." *National Post,* 30 November.

Hamilton, James T. 1995. "Pollution as News: Media and Stock Market Reactions to the Toxics Release Inventory Data." *Journal of Environmental Economics and Management* 28: 98–113.

Hanner, J. 1981. "Government Response to the Buffalo Hide Trade, 1871–1883." *Journal of Law and Economics* 24, no. 2: 239–71.

Hardin, Garrett. 1968. "The Tragedy of the Commons." *Science* 162, no. 3859: 1243–9.

Harris, Michael. 1998. *Lament for an Ocean: The Collapse of the Atlantic Cod Fishery*. Toronto: McClelland and Stewart.

Harrison, Kathryn. 1995. "Federalism, Environmental Protection and Blame Avoidance." In *New Trends in Canadian Federalism*, ed. François Rocher and Miriam Smith. Toronto: Broadview Press.

– 1996. *Passing the Buck: Federalism and Canadian Environmental Policy*. Vancouver: University of British Columbia Press.

– 1998. "Talking with the Donkey: Cooperative Approaches to Environmental Protection." Paper presented at the Canadian Political Science Association annual meeting, Ottawa, June.

– 2000. "The Origins of National Standards: Comparing Federal Government Involvement in Environmental Policy in Canada and the United States." In *Managing the Environmental Union: Intergovernmental Relations and Environmental Policy in Canada,* ed. Patrick C. Fafard and Kathryn Harrison. Montreal and Kingston: McGill-Queen's University Press.

Healy, M.C., and R.R. Wallace. 1987. *Canadian Aquatic Resources*. Ottawa: Department of Fisheries and Oceans.

Heinmiller, B. Timothy. 2003. "Harmonization through Emulation: Canadian Federalism and Water Export Policy." *Canadian Public Administration* 46, no. 4: 495–513.

Henderson, Sakej, and Adrian Tanner. 1992. "Atlantic Treaty Rights." In *Aboriginal Land Claims in Canada,* ed. Ken Coates and William Morrison. Mississauga: Copp Clark Pitman.

Henke, Janice Scott. 1985. *Seal Wars! An American Viewpoint.* St John's: Breakwater Books.

Herscovici, Alan. 1985. *Second Nature: The Animal Rights Controversy.* Toronto: CBC Enterprises.

Hertlein, L. 1999. *Lake Winnipeg Regulation: Churchill–Nelson River Diversion Project in the Crees of Northern Manitoba, Canada.* Report prepared for the World Commission on Dams. Cape Town: World Commission on Dams. http://www.damsreport.org/docs/kbase/contrib/soc205.pdf (accessed 27 July 2005).

Hessing, M., M. Howlett, and T. Summerville. 2005. *Canadian Natural Resource and Environmental Policy: Political Economy and Public Policy.* 2nd ed. Vancouver: University of British Columbia Press.

Hessing, Melody, and Michael Howlett. 1997. *Canadian Natural Resource and Environmental Policy: Political Economy and Public Policy.* Vancouver: University of British Columbia Press.

Higgs, R. 1982. "Legally Induced Technical Regress in the Washington Salmon Fishery." *Research in Economic History* 7: 55–86.

Hoberg, George. 1992. "Comparing Canadian Performance in Environmental Policy." In *Canadian Environmental Policy: Ecosystems, Politics, and Process,* ed. Robert Boardman. Toronto: Oxford University Press.

Hoberg, George, and Kathryn Harrison. 1994. "It's Not Easy Being Green: The Politics of Canada's Green Plan." *Canadian Public Policy* 20, no. 2: 119–37.

Hodgetts, J.E. 1964. "Challenge and Response: A Retrospective View of the Public Service of Canada." *Canadian Public Administration* 7: 409–21.

– 1995. *From Arm's-Length to Hands-On: The Formative Years of Ontario's Public Service, 1867–1940.* Toronto: University of Toronto Press.

Hohfield, W. 1919. *Fundamental Legal Conceptions.* New Haven, CT: Yale University Press.

Holland, D.S. 2000. "Fencing the Fisheries Commons: Regulatory Barbed Wire in the Alaskan Groundfish Fisheries." *Marine Resource Economics* 15, no. 2: 141–9.

Holling, C. 1995. "What Barriers, What Bridges?" In *Barriers and Bridges to the Renewal of Ecosystems and Institutions,* ed. L.H. Gunderson, C. Holling, and S.S. Light. New York: Columbia University Press.

Howell, T.A. 2001. "Enhancing Water Use Efficiency in Irrigated Agriculture."
    Agronomy Journal 93: 281–9.

Howlett, Michael. 1991. "Policy Instruments, Policy Styles, and Policy Imple-
    mentation: National Approaches to Theories of Instrument Choice." *Policy
    Studies Journal* 19, no. 2: 1–21.

– 2003. "Canadian Environmental Policy and the Natural Resources Sector:
    Paradoxical Aspects of the Transition to a Post-staples Political Economy."
    In *The Integrity Gap: Canada's Environmental Policy and Institutions,* ed.
    Eugene Lee and Anthony Perl. Vancouver: University of British Columbia
    Press.

Howlett, Michael, and M. Ramesh. 1993. "Patterns of Policy Instrument
    Choice: Policy Styles, Policy Learning, and the Privatization Experience."
    Policy Studies Review 12, no. 1: 3–24.

– 1995. *Studying Public Policy: Policy Cycles and Policy Subsystems.* Toronto:
    Oxford University Press.

Huang, G.H., and J. Xia. 2001. "Barriers to Sustainable Water-Quality Man-
    agement." *Journal of Environmental Management* 61: 1–23.

Huestis, L.B. 1992. "The Legal Basis for Compensation for the Taking of Fish-
    eries Resource Interests." In *Compensation Valuation Study: A Study Com-
    pleted for the Commercial Industry Council of Issues Related to
    Compensation to the Commercial Fishing Industry for Reallocation to the
    Aboriginal Fishery,* ed. Edwin Blewett. Vancouver: EB Economics, 1992.

Hutchings, Jeffrey A., Carl Walters, and Richard L. Haedrich. 1997. "Is Scien-
    tific Inquiry Incompatible with Government Information Control?" *Cana-
    dian Journal of Aquatic Science* 54: 1198–210.

Innis, Harold A. 1930. *The Fur Trade in Canada: An Introduction to Canadian
    Economic History.* New Haven, CT: Yale University Press; London: H. Mil-
    ford, Oxford University Press.

– 1954. *The Cod Fisheries: The History of an International Economy.* To-
    ronto: University of Toronto Press.

International Joint Commission (IJC). 1956. *Order of Approval – In the Matter
    of the Applications of the Government of Canada and the Government of the
    United States of America for an Order of Approval of the Construction of
    Certain Works for Development of Power in the International Rapids Section
    of the St. Lawrence River.* Washington, DC, and Ottawa: IJC.

– 2000. *Protection of the Waters of the Great Lakes: Final Report to the Govern-
    ment of Canada and the United States.* Washington, DC, and Ottawa: Interna-
    tional Joint Commission. http://www.ijc.org/php/publications/html/finalreport.
    html (accessed 29 July 2005).

International Lake Ontario–St Lawrence River Study Board. 2004. "About Us [Web page]." Buffalo, NY, and Ottawa: The Board. http://www.losl.org/about/about-e.html (accessed 15 July 2004).

– 2006. *Final Report of the International Lake Ontario-St. Lawrence River Study Board to the International Joint Commission.* Buffalo, NY, and Ottawa: The Board. http://www.losl.org/PDF/report-main-e.pdf (accessed 2 November 2007).

International Water Levels Coalition. 2004. "IWLC Goals [Web page]." Clayton, NY, and Brockville, ON: International Water Levels Coalition. www.iwlc.org/goals.html (accessed 12 July 2004).

Ipsos Reid. 2004. "Canadians Agree Canada Should Adopt a Comprehensive National Water Policy that Recognizes Clean Drinking Water as a Basic Human Right." 29 April. http://www.ipsos-na.com/news/pressreleases/m?id= 2193# (accessed 21 April 2008).

Jacquez, A.S. 2002a. "Charting the Most Feasible Course." *Great Lakes/Seaway Review* 30: 49–50.

– 2002b. "The Future of Commercial Navigation in the Great Lakes St. Lawrence System." Paper presented at the International Association of the Great Lakes and St Lawrence Mayors, Salaberry-de-Valleyfield, QC, 14 June.

Johannes, R.E. 1981. *Words of the Lagoon: Fishing and Marine Lore in the Palau District of Micronesia.* Berkeley: University of California Press.

Johansen, David. 1990. *Water Exports (Issue Review).* Ottawa: Canada Communications Group.

– 1999. "Water Exports and the NAFTA." *Government of Canada, Law and Government Branch.* http://dsppsd/ pwgsc.gc.ca/collection-R/LoPBdP/BP/prb995e. htm.

– 2001. "Bulk Water Removals, Water Exports and the NAFTA." Parliamentary Research Branch, Library of Parliament, PRB 00-41E, 20 February. http://dsp-psd.communication.gc.ca/Collection-RL/LoPBdP/BP/prb0041-e.htm (accessed 6 March 2003)

Johns, Carolyn. 2000. "Non–Point Source Water Pollution Management in Canada and the United States: A Comparative Analysis of Institutional Arrangements and Policy Instruments." PhD dissertation, McMaster University.

– 2002. *Policy Instruments to Manage Non-Point Source Water Pollution: Comparison of US States and Ontario.* Walkerton Inquiry commissioned paper. Toronto: Ministry of the Attorney General, Queen's Printer for Ontario.

– 2005. "Transboundary Water Governance: Future Challenges." *Optimum On-line: The Journal of Public Sector Management* 35, no. 4.

Johnson, N., C. Revenga, and Jaime Echeverria. 2001. "Managing Water for People and Nature." *Science* 292, no. 5519: 1071–2.

Johnston, Kenneth. 1977. *The Aquatic Explorers: A History of the Fisheries Research Board of Canada.* Toronto: University of Toronto Press.

Jones, Laura. 2003. "Custodians, not Miners." AIMS presentation, Halifax, 18 June. http://www.aims.ca/library/ep_atlanticfisheries.pdf (accessed 28 July 2005).

– 2003. *Managing Fish: Ten Case Studies from Canada's Pacific Coast.* Vancouver: The Fraser Institute.

Jones, Laura, and Michael Walker, eds. 1997. *Fish or Cut Bait: The Case for Individual Transferable Quotas in the Salmon Fishery of British Columbia.* Vancouver: The Fraser Institute.

Karvinen, William O., and Mary Louise McAllister. 1994. *Rising to the Surface: Emerging Groundwater Policy Trends in Canada.* Kingston: Centre for Resource Studies, Queen's University.

Kearney, John, Anthony Davis, et al. 1999. "Common Groundfish." *Sunday Herald,* 31 October, sec. B2.

Keating, Michael. 1986. *To the Last Drop: Canada and the World's Water Crisis.* Toronto: Macmillan Canada.

Kennett, Steven A. 1991. *Managing Interjurisdictional Waters in Canada: A Constitutional Analysis.* Calgary: Canadian Institute for Resources Law.

– 1992. *The Design of Federalism and Water Resources Management in Canada.* Kingston: Institute of Intergovernmental Relations and Queen's University Press.

Kerry, Alison, et al. 1998. *Alternative Service Delivery Study: Water Issues Case Study, Final Report, March 1998.* Ottawa: Canadian Meteorological Centre, Environment Canada. Previously available at http://www.msc-smc.ec.gc.ca/asd-dmps/water_case1_eng.htm.

Khanna, M., and L. Damon. 1999. "EPA's Voluntary 33/50 Program: Impact on Toxic Releases and Economic Performance of Firms." *Journal of Environmental Economics and Management* 37: 1–25.

Kinnie, Sarah. 2001. *Southern Gulf of St. Lawrence Herring Fishery.* Social Research for Sustainable Fisheries Project, Fact Sheet 5. Antigonish, NS: St. Francis Xavier University.

Klein, B. 1985. "Self-Enforcing Contracts." *Journal of Theoretical and Institutional Economics* 141: 594–600.

Knapp, G., C. Roheim, and J. Anderson. 2007. *The Great Salmon Run: Competition between Wild and Farmed Salmon.* Washington DC: World Wildlife Fund.

Krajnc, Anita. 2000. "Wither Ontario's Environment? Neo-conservatism and the Decline of the Environment Ministry." *Canadian Public Policy,* March, 111–27.

Kramer, R.A., W.T. McSweeny, W.R. Kerns, and R.W. Stavros. 1984. "An Evaluation of Alternative Policies for Controlling Agricultural Non Point Source Pollution." *Water Resources Bulletin* 20: 841–6.

Krutilla, John V. 1967. *The Columbia River Treaty: The Economics of an International River Basin Development.* Baltimore: The Johns Hopkins Press.

La Forest, Gerard V. 1969. *Natural Resources and Public Property under the Canadian Constitution.* Toronto: University of Toronto Press.

Lambden, Daniel W., and Izzak de Rijcke. 1985. "Boundaries and Surveys, Title 19." In *Canadian Encyclopedic Digest.* Toronto: Carswell.

Lamson, Cynthia, ed. 1994. *The Sea Has Many Voices: Oceans Policy for a Complex World.* Montreal: McGill-Queen's University Press.

Lamson, Cynthia, and Arthur Hanson. 1984. *Atlantic Fisheries and Coastal Communities: Fisheries Decision Making Case Studies.* Halifax: Dalhousie Ocean Studies Program.

Larkin, Peter. 1974. *Freshwater Pollution, Canadian Style.* Montreal: McGill–Queen's University Press.

Laycock, A.H. 1987. "The Amount of Canadian Water and Its Distribution." In "Canadian Aquatic Resources," ed. M.C. Healey and R.R. Wallace. *Canadian Bulletin of Fisheries and Aquatic Sciences* 215: 13–42.

Leal, D. 1996."Community-Run Fisheries: Preventing the Tragedy of the Commons." In *Taking Ownership: Property Rights and Fishery Management on the Atlantic Coast,* ed. B.L. Crowley. Halifax: Atlantic Institute for Market Studies.

Lee, Eugene, and Anthony Perl, eds. 2003. *The Integrity Gap: Canadian Environmental Policy and Institutions.* Vancouver: UBC Press.

Lee, K.N. 1993. *Compass and Gyroscope: Integrating Science and Politics for the Environment.* Washington, DC: Island Press.

Leggatt, S. 2001. *Clear Choices, Clean Water: The Leggatt Inquiry into Salmon Farming in British Columbia.* Vancouver: David Suzuki Foundation Publishers. Previously available at: www.leggattinquiry.com/files/Leggatt_reportfinal.pdf.

Lester, James P. 1986. "New Federalism and Environmental Policy." *Publius* 16 no. 1: 149–65.

– 1990. "A New Federalism? Environmental Policy in the States." In *Environmental Policy in the 1990s,* ed. Norman J. Vig and Michael E. Kraft. Washington, DC: Congressional Quarterly Press.

– ed. 1989. *Environmental Politics and Policy: Theories and Evidence.* Durham, NC: Duke University Press.

Levi, Margaret. 1988. *Of Rule and Revenue*. Berkeley: University of California Press.

Lewis, G.D., D. Milburn, and A. Smart. 1991. "The Challenge of Interjurisdictional Water Management in the MacKenzie River Basin." *Canadian Water Resources Journal* 16, no. 4: 381–90.

Libecap, G.B. 1986. "Property Rights in Economic History: Explanation." *Economic History* 23: 227–52.

Lilley, J., and C. Labatiuk. 2001. "Edmonton's Draft Guidelines for Constructed Stormwater Wetlands." *Canadian Water Resources Journa.* 26, no. 2: 195–210.

Linder, S.H., and B.G. Peters. 1989. "Instruments of Government: Perceptions and Context." *Journal of Public Policy* 9, no. 1: 35–58.

Lindholm, Goran. 2000. "Consumption of Water in the Pulp and Paper Industry." *Paper Technology*, May, 57–60.

Linton, Jamie. 1997. *Beneath the Surface: The State of Water in Canada*. Ottawa: Canadian Wildlife Federation.

Livernois, J. 2002. *The Economic Costs of the Walkerton Water Crisis*. Walkerton Inquiry commissioned paper, 14. Toronto: Queen's Printer for Ontario.

Lotspeich, Richard. 1996. "Comparative Environmental Policy: Market Type Instruments in Industrialized Capitalist Countries." *Policy Studies Journal* 20, no. 1: 85–102.

Lucas, Alistair R. 1986. "Harmonization of Federal and Provincial Environmental Policies: The Changing Legal and Policy Framework." In *Managing Natural Resources in a Federal State,* ed. J.O. Saunders. Toronto: Carswell.

Macdonald, Douglas. 2001. "Coerciveness and the Selection of Environmental Policy Instruments." *Canadian Public Administration* 44: 161–87.

Macgillivray, P. 1997. "Individual Vessel Quotas in the Halibut Fishery of British Columbia." In *Fish or Cut Bait: The Case for Individual Transferable Quotas in the Salmon Fishery of British Columbia,* ed. Laura Jones and Michael Walker. Vancouver: The Fraser Institute.

MacKenzie, Debbie. 2004. *The Starving Ocean* [Web site]. www.fisherycrisis. com (accessed December 2004).

MacLaren, Ian, Solange Brault, John Harwood, and David Vardy. 2001. *Report of the Eminent Panel on Seal Management*. Ottawa: Fisheries and Oceans Canada. www.dfo-mpo.gc.ca/seal-phoque/reports-rapports/mgtplan-plangestoo1/EPSM-GEGP_e.pdf (accessed 1 August 2005).

Mancl, K. 1996. "Wastewater Treatment Principles and Regulations." Ohio State University Extension fact sheet. Columbus: Ohio State University. ohioline.osu.edu/aex-fact/0768.html (accessed 22 May 2003).

Mann Borgese, Elizabeth. 1996. *The Oceanic Circle: Governing the Seas as a Global Resource.* Tokyo: United Nations University.

Marsalak, J., K. Schaefer, K. Exall, L. Brannen, and B. Aidun. 2002. *Water Reuse and Recycling.* CCME Linking Water Science to Policy Workshop Series, report no. 3. Winnipeg: Canadian Council of Ministers of the Environment.

Matthews, Ralph. 1993. *Controlling Common Property: Regulating Canada's East Coast Fishery.* Toronto: University of Toronto Press.

May, A. 1996. *Altering Course: A Report to the Minister of Fisheries and Oceans on Intersectoral Allocations of Salmon in British Columbia.* St John's: Memorial University of Newfoundland.

McCay, Bonnie J., and James M. Acheson. 1987. *The Question of the Commons: The Culture and Ecology of Communal Resources.* Tucson: University of Arizona Press.

McCulloch, P., and P. Muldoon. 1999. *A Sustainable Water Strategy for Ontario.* Toronto: Canadian Environmental Law Association. cela.ca/uploads/f8e04c51a8e04041f6f7faa046b03a7c/367water.pdf (accessed 1 August 2005).

McGinnis, M.D., ed. 1999. *Polycentric Governance and Development.* Ann Arbor: University of Michigan Press.

McIroy, Anne, and Heather Scoffield. 1999. "Big Buyout of Atlantic Fishermen Proposed." *Globe and Mail,* 27 November.

McKenzie, Judith I. 2004. "Walkerton: Requiem for the New Public Management in Ontario." *International Journal of Environment and Pollution* 21: 309–24.

McMillan, Tom. 1990. "Water Resource Planning in Canada." *Journal of Soil and Water Conservation* 45, no. 6: 614.

McRae, Donald M., and Peter H. Pearse. 2004. *Treaties and Transition: Towards a Sustainable Fishery on Canada's Pacific Coast.* Vancouver: Department of Fisheries and Oceans.

McVicar, A.H. 1997. "Disease and Parasite Implications of the Coexistence of Wild and Cultured Atlantic Salmon Populations." *ICES Journal of Marine Science* 54, no. 6: 1093–103.

Merendino, M.T., G.B. McCullough, and N.R. North. 1995. "Wetland Availability and Use by Breeding Waterfowl in Southern Ontario." *Journal of Wildlife Management* 59, no. 3: 527–32.

Merritt, James, and Christopher Gore. 2002. *Drinking Water Services: A Functional Review of the Ontario Ministry of the Environment.* Walkerton Inquiry Commissioned Paper no. 5. Toronto: Ontario Ministry of the Attorney General.

Messick, R.E. 1999. "Judicial Reform and Economic Development: A Survey of the Issues." *World Bank Research Observer* 14, no. 1: 117–36.

Michigan. Department of Environmental Quality. n.d. "Background Information on Great Lakes Diversions [Web page]." Previously available at www.michigan.gov/deq (accessed 10 March 2003).

Miller, G. Tyler, Jr. 2004. *Living in the Environment: Principles, Connections, and Solutions.* 13th ed. Pacific Grove, CA: Brooks/Cole-Thompson Learning.

Mitchell, B., and R. de Loe. 1997. *Reflections on Water: Canadian Water Resources Association 1947–1997.* Cambridge, ON: Canadian Water Resources Association.

Mitchell, B., and D. Shrubsole. 1994. "Reorienting to Achieve Sustainability in Canadian Water Management." *Canadian Water Resources Journal* 19, no. 4: 335–47.

Mitchell, Michael E. 2000. "OMB Decision: Municipalities Can Use Zoning By-laws to Restrict Intensive Livestock Operations." *Municipal World,* October, 19.

Molot, Lewis, et al. 2001. *Liquid Assets: Monitoring Water Quality in Ontario.* Toronto: Canadian Institute of Environmental Law and Policy, Faculty of Environmental Studies, York University.

Monahan, P. 2002. *Essentials of Canadian Law – Constitutional Law.* 2nd ed. Toronto: Irwin Law.

Montpetit, E. 2002. "Sound Science and Moral Suasion, not Regulation: Facing Difficult Decisions on Agricultural Non–point Source Pollution." In *Canadian Environmental Policy: Context and Cases,* ed. Deborah L. VanNijnatten and Robert Boardman. 2nd ed. Toronto: Oxford University Press.

Montpetit, E., and W. Coleman. 1999. "Policy Communities and Policy Divergence in Canada: Agro-environmental Policy Development in Quebec and Ontario." *Canadian Journal of Political Science* 32: 4.

Muldoon, Paul. 2000. "The Case against Water Exports." *Canadian Environmental Law Association Newsletter* 25, no. 2. www.cela.ca/newsletter/detail_art.shtml?x=1436 (accessed 14 January 2005).

Mullan, D.J. 1996. *Administrative Law.* 3rd ed. Toronto: Carswell.

Munk Centre for International Studies, University of Toronto. Program on Water Issues. 2004. *Political Diversions: Annex 2001 and the Future of the Great Lakes.* Trans. Andrew Nikiforuk. Toronto: Munk Centre for International Studies.

Naylor, R., J. Eagle, and W. Smith. 2003. "Salmon Aquaculture in the Pacific Northwest, a Global Industry." *Environment* 45, no. 6: 18–39.

Neis, Barbara, and Lawrence Felt. 2000. *Finding Our Sea Legs: Linking Fishery People and Their Knowledge with Science and Management.* St John's: Institute for Social and Economic Research.

New Brunswick. Department of the Environment and Local Government. n.d. "An Overview of Legislation [Web page]." Fredericton: Department of the Environment and Local Government. http://www.gnb.ca/0009/0355/0005/0029-e.asp (accessed 29 July 2005).

Newfoundland and Labrador. 2001. *Export of Bulk Water from Newfoundland and Labrador: A Report of the Ministerial Committee Examining the Export of Bulk Water.* St John's: Government of Newfoundland and Labrador. http://www.gov.nf.ca/publicat/ReportoftheMinisterailCommitteeExaminingtheExportofBulkWater.pdf (accessed 30 April 2003).

New Zealand. Ministry of Agriculture and Forestry. 2003. *Policy Strategies for Natural Resource Management.* MAF Technical Paper 2003/1. Wellington: Ministry of Agriculture and Forestry. http://www.maf.govt.nz/mafnet/rural-nz/sustainable-resource-use/resource-management/policy-strategies-natural-resource-management/index.htm (accessed 1 August 2003).

Nikiforuk, A. 2003. "Water Takings – the Enduring Need for Regulation." Presentation at Calgary Regional Group, Institute of Public Administration of Canada, 6 June 6.

Nolan, Linda. 2007. "Out of Sight, Out of Mind? Taking Canada's Groundwater for Granted." In *Eau Canada: The Future of Canada's Water*, ed. Karen Bakker. Vancouver: UBC Press.

Nottawasaga Valley Conservation Authority. 1999. "Nottawasaga Valley Conservation Authority: Healthy Waters Program [Web page]." Utopia, ON: Nottawasaga Valley Conservation Authority. www.nvca.on.ca/healthy_waters/index.htm (accessed 1 August 2005).

Nova Scotia. 2004. *Environmental Management Systems and ISO 14000.* Pollution Prevention Fact Sheet. http://www.gov.ns.ca/enla/pollutionprevention/docs/EMS_factsheet.pdf.

Nova Scotia. Department of Agriculture and Fisheries. 2002. *What You Should Know about Irrigation Water Quality Safety.* Fact Sheet. Truro: Department of Agriculture and Fisheries. http://www.nsac.ns.ca/eng/outreach/Irrigation%20water%20quality.pdf (accessed 13 March 2003).

Nowlan, Linda. 2005. *Buried Treasure: Groundwater Permitting and Pricing in Canada.* For the Walter and Duncan Gordon Foundation; with case studies by Geological Survey of Canada, West Coast Environmental Law, and Sierra Legal Defence Fund. Toronto: Walter and Duncan Gordon Foundation.

Oates, W.E., and P. Portney. 1992. "Economic Incentives and the Containment of Global Warming." *Eastern Economic Journal* 18, no. 1: 85–98.

O'Connor, D.R. 2002. *Report of the Walkerton Inquiry.* 2 vols. Toronto: Ontario Ministry of the Attorney General.

O'Grady, Dennis, and Mary Ann Wilson. n.d. *Phosphorus Trading in the South Nation River Watershed, Ontario, Canada.* Previously available at www.envtn.org/wqt/programs/ontario.pdf (accessed May 2005).

Ontario. 2002. *Ontario Sustainable Water and Sewage Systems Act.* 2002, amended 2007. http://www.canlii.org/on/laws/sta/2002c.29/20070516/whole.html.

Ontario. Ministry of Agriculture, Food and Rural Affairs. 2003. "Nutrient Management Protocol [Web page]." Toronto: Ministry of Agriculture, Food and Rural Affairs. http://www.gov.on.ca/OMAFRA/english/nm/regs/nmpro/nmpro11.htm (accessed 29 July 2005).

– 2004. *Certification and Training for Large Farm Operators Who Wish to Prepare Their Own Nutrient Management Strategy/Plan.* Toronto: Ministry of Agriculture, Food and Rural Affairs. http://www.gov.on.ca/omafra/english/nm/cert/lfcert.htm (accessed 29 July 2005).

Ontario. Ministry of Environment and Energy. 1992. *1992 Status Report on Ontario's Air, Water and Waste.* Toronto: Ministry of Environment and Energy.

– 1994. *Water Management: Policy, Guidelines, Provincial Water Quality Objectives of the Ministry of Environment and Energy.* Toronto: Queen's Printer for Ontario. http://www.ene.gov.on.ca/envision/gp/3303e.pdf (accessed 27 July 2005).

Ontario. Ministry of Natural Resources. 1984. *Water Quantity Resources of Ontario.* Fort Erie: Ministry of Natural Resources.

– 1999. *Guide to Conservation Land Tax Incentive Program.* Toronto: Ministry of Natural Resources.

– 2006. *Protecting Great Lakes–St. Lawrence River Basin Waters.* Available at http://www.mnr.gov.on.ca/mnr/water/greatlakes/ (accessed 31 March 2006).

Ontario. Ministry of Natural Resources. Lands and Natural Heritage Branch. 1999. Presentation at the annual conference of the Ontario Nature Trust Alliance, 13 November.

Ontario. Office of Privatization. 1998. *The Ontario Clean Water Agency.* Fact Sheet. March. Previously available at http://www.ene.gov.on.ca/envision/news/fact.htm (accessed 2001).

Ontario. Ministry of the Environment (MOE). 1986. *Municipal-Industrial Strategy for Abatement: A Policy and Program Statement.* Toronto: Ministry of the Environment.

– 1994. *Guideline F-15 (formerly 02–03). Financial assurance.* Toronto: Ministry of the Environment.

– 1998. *City of Barrie's Water Conservation Program: Huge Success.* Green Industry series. Toronto: Ministry of the Environment.

– "Business Plan [Web page]." Toronto: Ministry of the Environment. http://www.gov.on.ca/MBS/english/press/plans99/env.html#allocations.

– 2000. *Drinking Water in Ontario: A Summary Report 1993–1997*. Toronto: Queen's Printer.

– 2001. *Ontario Initiatives in Pollution Prevention: Progress Report 2001*. Toronto: Ministry of the Environment.

– 2002a. *Nutrient Management Act 2002*. Nutrient Management Protocol, Regulation 267/03, S.O. 2002. Toronto: Ministry of the Environment.

– 2002b. *Ontario's Lake Partner Program*. Toronto: Ministry of the Environment.

– 2002c. "Safe Drinking Water Act 2002 Passed by Legislature." Media backgrounder, 11 December. www.ene.gov.on.ca/envision/news/2002/12/10/mb.htm (accessed 17 November 2003)

– 2003a. *Drinking Water Surveillance Program Summary Report for 2000–2002*. Toronto: Ministry of the Environment.

– 2003b. "Eves Government Implements Another Water Commitment." Press release. Toronto: Drinking Water Management Division, Ministry of the Environment.

– 2004a. *Notice of Proposal for Drinking Water Source Protection Act*. Toronto: Ministry of the Environment. http://www.ene.gov.on.ca/envregistry/023184ea.htm (accessed 29 July 2005).

– 2004b. *White Paper on Watershed-based Source Protection Planning*. Toronto: Ministry of the Environment. http://www.ene.gov.on.ca/programs/3585e01.pdf (accessed 29 July 2005).

– 2005a. *Environmental Bill of Rights Registry*. Toronto: Ministry of the Environment.

– 2005b. *The Nutrient Management Act*. Toronto: Ministry of the Environment. http://www.ene.gov.on.ca/envision/land/nutrient_management.htm (accessed 29 July 2005).

– 2007. "Ontario Charging Commercial, Industrial Users for Water: Water Charge Will Help Fund Water Resource Management; Encourage Conservation." News release. Toronto: Ministry of the Environment, 14 August. http://www.ene.gov.on.ca/en/news/2007/081401.php.

Ontario and Canada. 1998a. "Water Management." In *Best Management Practices: Nutrient Management Practice*. Toronto: Ministry of Agriculture, Food and Rural Affairs and Canada Department of Agriculture and Agri-food.

– 1998b. "Water Wells." In: *Best Management Practices: Nutrient Management Practice*. Toronto: Ministry of Agriculture, Food and Rural Affairs and Canada Department of Agriculture and Agri-food.

Ontario Environmental Farm Coalition. 1997. *Our Farm Environmental Agenda: What's Been Achieved 1992–1995*. Guelph: Ontario Soil and Crop Improvement Association.

"Ontario's Bottled Water Rules Are Changing." 2003. *H₂O* [electronic mailing list]. http://www.H2infO.org (accessed 7 January 2003).

Ontario Soil and Crop Improvement Association. 1997. *EFP Closes in on Milestone.* Guelph: Ontario Soil and Crop Improvement Association.

Organisation for Economic Co-operation and Development (OECD). 1996. *Environmental Performance Reviews: Progress in the 1990s.* Paris: OECD.

– 1999. *Voluntary Approaches for Environmental Policy: An Assessment.* Paris: OECD.

– 2000. *Economic Survey of Canada.* Paris: OECD.

– 2001. *OECD Environmental Outlook.* Paris: OECD.

– 2002. *OECD Environmental Outlook.* Paris: OECD.

Ostrom, Elinor. 1990. *Governing the Commons: The Evolution of Institutions for Collective Action.* Cambridge: Cambridge University Press, 1990.

– 2001. "Reformulating the Commons." In *Protecting the Commons: A Framework for Resource Management in the Americas,* ed. Joanna Burger et al. Washington, DC: Island Press.

– 2004. "Rules without Enforcement Are but Words on Paper." *IHDP Update* 2: 8–10.

Ostrom, Elinor, and Roy Gardner. 1993. "Coping with Asymmetries in the Commons: Self-Governing Irrigation Systems Can Work." *Journal of Economic Perspectives* 7, no. 4: 93–112.

Ostrom, Elinor, Roy Gardner, and James Walker, eds. 1994. *Rules, Games and Common-Pool Resources.* Ann Arbor: The University of Michigan Press.

Ostrom, Elinor, et al., eds. 2002. *The Drama of the Commons.* Washington, DC: National Academy Press.

O'Toole, Laurence, et al. 1997. "Reducing Toxic Chemical Releases and Transfers: Explaining Outcomes for a Voluntary Program." *Policy Studies Journal* 25, no. 1: 11–26.

Overcash, Michael R., and James M. Davidson, eds. 1980. *Environmental Impact of Nonpoint Source Pollution.* Ann Arbor, MI: Ann Arbor Science.

Parenteau, Bill. 1998. "Care, Control and Supervision: Native People in the Canadian Atlantic Fishery, 1867–1900." *Canadian Historical Review* 79, no. 1: 1–35.

Parson, Edward A., ed. 2001a. *Governing the Environment: Persistent Challenge, Uncertain Innovations.* Toronto: University of Toronto Press.

Parson, Edward A. 2001b. "Persistent Challenges, Uncertain Innovations: A Synthesis." In *Governing the Environment: Persistent Challenge, Uncertain Innovations,* ed. E.A. Parson. Toronto: University of Toronto Press.

Parsons, L.S. 1993. *Management of Marine Fisheries in Canada.* Ottawa: National Research Council.

Pearce, D.W., and R.K. Turner. 1990. *Economics, Natural Resources and the Environment.* Baltimore: John Hopkins University Press.

Pearse, Peter H. 1996. *Allocating the Catch among Fishermen.* Halifax: AIMS Research Report.

– 1998. "Water Management in Canada: The Continuing Search for the Federal Role." Keynote address at the 51st Annual Conference of the Canadian Water Resources Association, Victoria, BC, 10–12 June.

Pearse, Peter H., and Frank Quinn. 1996. "Recent Developments in Federal Water Policy: One Step Forward, Two Steps Back." *Canadian Water Resources Journal* 21, no. 4: 329–40.

Percy, D.R. 1988. *The Framework of Water Rights Legislation in Canada.* Calgary: Canadian Institute of Resource Law.

– 1996. "Seventy-five Years of Alberta Water Law: Maturity, Demise and Rebirth." *Alberta Law Review* 35, no. 1: 221–41.

– 2005. "Responding to Water Scarcity in Western Canada." *Texas Law Review* 83: 2090–107.

Peterson, H.G. 1998. "Use of Constructed Wetlands to Process Agricultural Wastewater." *Canadian Journal of Plant Science* 78: 199–210.

Phyper, John David, and Brett Ibbotson. 1996. "Regulatory Framework." In *Environmental Management in Canada,* ed. John David Phyper and Brett Ibbotson. Toronto: McGraw-Hill Ryerson.

Pollution Probe. 2003. *A Taxonomy of Canadian Environmental Standards.* Toronto: Pollution Probe. Available at: www.pollutionprobe.org/Reports/taxstandards.pdf (accessed 1 August 2005).

– 2004a. *Exploring Applications of the Net Gain Principle.* Toronto: Pollution Probe. Available at: www.pollutionprobe.org/reports/netgain.pdf (accessed 29 July 2005).

– 2004b. *The Source Water Protection Primer.* Toronto: Pollution Probe. www.pollutionprobe.org/Reports/swpprimer.pdf (accessed cited 1 August 2005).

Postel, S.L. 2000. "Entering an Era of Water Scarcity: The Challenges Ahead." *Ecological Applications* 10, no. 4: 941–8.

Potter, B. 2003. "Transaction Costs and Host-Group Rivalry in Foreign Economic Policy: Evidence from Five North American Fisheries." *Canadian Journal of Political Science* 36, no. 4: 741–64.

Prins, Harald E.L. 1996. *The Mi'kmaq: Resistance, Accommodation and Cultural Survival.* Orlando: Holt, Rinehart Winston.

Pross, A. Paul, and Susan McCorquodale. 1987. *Economic Resurgence and the Constitutional Agenda: The Case of the East Coast Fisheries.* Kingston: Queen's University.

Prowse, T., et al. 2003. "Dams, Reservoirs and Flow Regulation." National Water Research Institute. http://www.nwri.ca/threats2full/ch2-1-e.html.

Prudham, Scott. 2004. "Poisoning the Well: Neoliberalism and the Contamination of Municipal Water in Walkerton, Ontario." *Geoforum* 35: 343–59.

Quebec. 2002. *History of the Action Plan*. Previously available at www.v2000.qc.ca/plan_action (accessed 14 July 2004).

Quinn, F., and J. Edstrom. 2000. "Great Lakes Diversions and Other Removals." *Canadian Water Resources Journal* 25, no. 2: 125–51.

Rabe, Barry G. 1999. "Federalism and Entrepreneurship: Explaining American and Canadian Innovation in Pollution Prevention and Regulatory Integration." *Policy Studies Journal* 27, no. 2: 288–306.

Rabe, Barry G., and J.B. Zimmerman. 1995. "Beyond Environmental Regulatory Fragmentation: Signs of Integration in the Case of the Great Lakes Basin." *Governance* 8, no. 1: 58–77.

Rettig, R.B. 1984. "License Limitation in the United States and Canada: An Assessment." *North American Journal of Fisheries Management* 4, no. 3: 231–48.

Ribaudo, Mark, Richard D. Horan, and Mark E. Smith. 1999. *Economics of Water Quality Protection from Nonpoint Sources: Theory and Practice*. Publication 782. Washington, DC: United States Department of Agriculture, Economic Research Service. www.ers.usda.gov/publications/aer782/ (accessed 1 August 2005).

Ringquist, Evan J. 1993. *Environmental Protection at the State Level: Politics and Progress in Controlling Pollution*. New York: M.E. Sharpe.

– 1994. "Policy Influence and Policy Responsiveness in State Pollution Control." *Policy Studies Journal* 22, no. 1: 25–43.

Rist, Ray. 1998. "Choosing the Right Policy Instrument at the Right Time: The Contextual Challenges of Selection and Implementation." In *Carrots, Sticks, and Sermons: Policy Instruments and Their Evaluation*, ed. Marie-Louise Bemelmans-Videc, Ray C. Rist, and Evert Vedung. Princeton, NJ: Transaction Publishers.

Roe S., S.W. Bond, and V. Mercier. 2005. "Water Quality Index: Coming Soon to a Water Body Near You." Paper presented at the 40th Central Canadian Symposium on Water Quality Research, Burlington, ON, 14–15 February.

Rogers, D., and K. Ritchie. 2003. "OMYA gets Approval to Triple Water Take from Tay River: 4.5m Liters a Day 'Will Not Cause Harm' Minister Says." *Ottawa Citizen*, 15 February.

Rollins, K., J. Frehs, D. Tate, and O. Zachariah. 1997. "Resource Valuation and Public Policy: Consumers' Willingness to Pay for Improving Water Servicing Infrastructure." *Canadian Water Resources Journal* 22, no. 2: 185–96.

Rubin, Seymour J., and Dean C. Alexander, eds. 1996. *NAFTA and the Environment*. Boston: Kluwer Law International.

Russell, C.S., and J.F. Shogren, eds. 1993. *Theory, Modeling and Experience in the Management of Non-Point Source Pollution*. Boston: Kluwer Academic Publishers.

Rutherford, S. 2005. *Groundwater Use in Canada*. Vancouver: West Coast Environmental Law.

Ryan, Shannon. 1994. *The Ice Hunters: A History of Newfoundland Sealing to 1914*. St John's: Breakwater Books.

Rydin, Yvonne, and Eva Falleth, eds. 2006. *Networks and Institutions in Natural Resource Management*. Cheltenham, UK, and Northampton, MA: Edward Elgar.

Sægrov, H., K. Hindar, S. Kålås, and H. Lura. 1997. "Escaped Farmed Atlantic Salmon Replace the Original Salmon Stock in the River Vosso, Western Norway." *ICES Journal of Marine Science* 54, no. 6: 1166–72.

St Lawrence Seaway Management Corporation. 2003. *The Montreal/Lake Ontario Section of the Seaway*. [n.p.] St Lawrence Seaway Management Corporation.

Sancton, A. 1985. *Governing the Island of Montreal: Language Differences and Metropolitan Politics*. Berkeley: University of California Press.

Saskatchewan. 2002. *The North Battleford Water Inquiry: Submission of he Government of Saskatchewan*. Regina: Environment and Resource Management. www.northbattlefordwaterinquiry.ca/pdf/finalsubmission-governmentofsask.pdf (accessed 29 July 2005).

Saunders, J. Owen. 1988. *Interjurisdictional Issues in Canadian Water Management*. Calgary: Canadian Institute of Resources Law.

– ed. 1986. *Managing Natural Resources in a Federal State*. Toronto: Carswell.

Schaefer, K.A., and J.M. Hurst. 1997. "Municipal Water Use and Pricing in Ontario, 1983–1994." *Canadian Water Resources Journal* 22, no. 4: 417–31.

Schlager, Edella, and Elinor Ostrom. 1992. "Property Rights Regimes and Natural Resources." *Land Economics* 68: 246–62.

Schlindler, D.W., and Adele Hurley. 2004. "Rising Tensions: Canada/U.S. Cross-Border Water Issues in the 21st Century." Notes for remarks to the Centre for Global Studies Conference on Canada/US Relations, University of Victoria, Victoria, November. Toronto: Program on Water Issues, Munk Centre for International Studies, University of Toronto.

Schmid, A.A. 2004. *Conflict and Cooperation*. Oxford: Blackwell.

Schmidt, L. 2003. "Charge Oilpatch for Water: Report." *Calgary Herald*, 11 April, D1.

Schott, Stephan. 2004. "New Fishery Management in Atlantic Canada: Communities, Governments, and Alternative Targets." In *How Ottawa Spends, 2004–05: Mandate Change in the Paul Martin Era,* ed. G. Bruce Doern. Montreal: McGill-Queen's University Press.

Schrecker, T. 2001. "Using Science in Environmental Policy: Can Canada Do Better?" In *Governing the Environment: Persistent Challenges, Uncertain Innovations,* ed. E.A. Parson. Toronto: University of Toronto Press.

Schwindt, Richard. 1995. "The Case for an Expanded Indian Fishery: Efficiency, Fairness, and History." In *Market Solutions for Native Poverty: Social Policy for the Third Solitude,* ed. Helmar Drost, Brian Lee Crowley, and Richard Schwindt. Toronto: C.D. Howe Institute.

Schwindt, Richard, A.R. Vining, and S. Globerman. 2000. "Net Loss: A Cost-Benefit Analysis of the Canadian Pacific Salmon Fishery." *Journal of Policy Analysis and Management* 19, no. 1: 23–45.

Schwindt, Richard, A.R. Vining, and D.L. Weimer. 2003. "A Policy Analysis of the BC Salmon Fishery." *Canadian Public Policy* 29, no. 1: 73–93.

Science Council of Canada. 1988. *Water 2020 – Sustainable Use for Water in the 21st Century.* Ottawa: Science Council of Canada.

Scott, A., J. Olynyk, and S. Renzetti. 1986. "The Design of Water-Export Policy." In *Canada's Resource Industries and Water Export Policy,* ed. John Whalley. Toronto: University of Toronto Press and the Royal Commission on the Economic Union and Development Prospects for Canada.

Scott, James C. 1998. *Seeing like a State.* New Haven: Yale University Press.

Segerson, Kathleen. 1988. "Uncertainty and Incentives for Non-point Pollution Control." *Journal of Environmental Economics and Management* 15: 87–98.

– Kathleen. 1990. "Liability for Groundwater Contamination from Pesticides." *Journal of Environmental Economics and Management* 19: 227–43.

Sharma, Parmesh. 1998. *Aboriginal Fishing Rights.* Halifax: Fernwood.

Shortle, James S., and David G. Abler. 1997. "Non-point pollution." In *The International Yearbook of Environmental and Resource Economics, 1997–98.* Lyme, NH: Edward Elgar Publishing.

Shrybman, Steven. 1999. "A Legal Opinion Concerning Water Export Controls and Canadian Obligations under NAFTA and the WTO." *West Coast Environmental Law.* www.wcel.org/wcelpub/1999/12926.html (accessed 29 July 2005).

Sierra Club. n.d. *Ecoregions:* "Mississippi Basin Ecoregion [Web page]." San Francisco: Sierra Club. www.sierraclub.org/ecoregions/missbasin.asp (accessed 22 May 2003).

Sierra Legal Defence Fund. 2006. "Waterproof 2: Canada's Drinking Water Report Card." http://www.ecojustice.ca/publications/reports/waterproof-2-canadas-drinking-water-report-card/attachment

Silver, T.M., I.C. Attridge, M. MacRae, and K.W. Cox. 1995. *Canadian Legislation for Conservation Covenants, Easements and Servitudes: The Current Situation*. Ottawa: North American Wetlands Conservation Council.

Sinclair, William F. 1990. *Controlling Pollution from Canadian Pulp and Paper Manufacturers: A Federal Perspective*. Ottawa: Environment Canada, Conservation and Protection.

Singer, S.N., Cheng, C.K., and M.G. Scafe. 2003. *The Hydrology of Southern Ontario*. 2nd ed. Toronto: Environmental Monitoring and Reporting Branch, Ministry of the Environment.

Skogstad, Grace. 1996. "Intergovernmental Relations and the Politics of Environmental Protection in Canada." In *Federalism and the Environment: Environmental Policymaking in Australia, Canada, and the United States,* ed. Kenneth M. Holland, F.L. Morton, and Brian Galligan. Westport, CT: Greenwood.

Skogstad, Grace, and Paul Kopas. 1992. "Environmental Policy in a Federal System: Ottawa and the Provinces." In *Canadian Environmental Policy: Ecosystems, Politics, and Process,* ed. Robert Boardman. Toronto: Oxford University Press.

Söllner, Fritz. 1994. "The Role of Common Law in Environmental Policy." *Public Choice* 80: 69–82.

Sporer, C. 2006. *2005 Licence Area F, ITQ Demonstration Fishery – a Review*. Vancouver: Department of Fisheries and Oceans.

Sprott, P. 1997. "Management Issues and Quotas in the Salmon Fishery of British Columbia." In *Fish or Cut Bait: The Case for Individual Transferable Quotas in the Salmon Fishery of British Columbia,* ed. Laura Jones and Michael Walker. Vancouver: The Fraser Institute.

Sproule-Jones, Mark H. 1974. "Towards a Dynamic Analysis of Collective Action." *Western Political Quarterly* 26: 414–26.

– 1981. *The Real World of Pollution Control*. Vancouver: Westwater Research Centre.

– 1993. *Governments at Work: Canadian Parliamentary Federalism and Its Public Policy Effects*. Toronto: University of Toronto Press.

– 1999. "Restoring the Great Lakes: Institutional Analysis and Design." *Coastal Management* 27: 291–316.

– 2000. "Horizontal Management: Implementing Programs across Interdependent Organizations." *Canadian Public Administration* 43, no. 1: 93–109.

– 2002. *Restoration of the Great Lakes: Promises, Practices, Performances*. Vancouver: University of British Columbia Press.

Stamp, Judith, ed. 1999. *Water Resources Management Reader*. Toronto: University of Toronto at Mississauga.

Stiefelmeyer, K. 2003. "The Pathogen Abatement Effects of Nutrient Management Policies in Agriculture." MSc thesis, Ryerson University.

Strategic Alternatives et al. 2002. "The Costs of Clean Water: Estimates of Costs Arising from the Recommendations of the Walkerton Inquiry." Walkerton Inquiry commissioned paper 25.

Stuip, M.A.M., C.J. Baker, and W. Oosterberg. 2002. *The Socio-Economic Impacts of Wetlands*. The Netherlands: Wetlands International and RIZA.

Surette, Allister. 2004. "Conflict between Mobile and Fixed Gear Herring Fishers in the Southern Gulf of St. Lawrence." Open letter to the Minister of the Department of Fisheries and Oceans, February. www.dfo-mpo.gc.ca/surette/a_e.htm (accessed 29 July 2005).

Surette, Ralph. 2004. "Is Marine Life Starving? And Other Pointed Queries." *Chronicle-Herald*, 15 January.

Swainson, Neil A. 1979. *Conflict over the Columbia: The Canadian Background to an Historic Treaty*. Montreal: McGill-Queen's University Press.

Taylor, B. 2003. *Irrigation Districts: Alberta Irrigation Information for the Year 2002*. Lethbridge: Irrigation Branch, Alberta Agriculture, Food and Rural Development.

Tietenberg, T. 2001. "The Tradable Permits Approach to Protecting the Commons." In *The Drama of the Commons*, ed. Elinor Ostrom et al. Washington, DC: National Academic Press.

Toronto. 2000. *Protecting Water Quality: Sewer-Use Bylaw*. www.city.toronto.on.ca/water/protecting_quality/sewer_bylaw/index.htm (accessed cited May 2005).

Townsend, R.E. 1990. "Entry Restrictions in the Fishery: A Survey of the Evidence." *Land Economics* 66, no. 4: 359–78.

Toy, S. 1998. *Recommendations for Policy Changes Implementing Several Recommendations of Dr. A.W. May's Report "Altering Course" on Intersectoral Allocations of Salmon in British Columbia*. Report prepared for the minister of Fisheries and Oceans.

TRW Inc. n.d. "NASA's Observatorium: Hydrologic Cycle [Web page]." observe.arc.nasa.gov/nasa/earth/hydrocycle/hydro1.html (accessed 14 May 2003).

Tullock, Gordon. 1980. "The Transitional Gains Trap." In *Toward a Theory of the Rent-Seeking Society*, ed. James M. Buchanan, Robert D. Tollison, and Gordon Tullock. College Station: Texas A&M University Press.

Tuohy, Carolyn. 1992. *Policy and Politics in Canada: Institutionalized Ambivalence*. Philadelphia: Temple University Press.

Underhill, Brian, and Lois Legge. 1999. "Mi'kmaq Rights Upheld." *Chronicle-Herald*, 18 September.

United Nations. 2003. *The UN World Water Development Report: Water for People, Water for Life*. World Water Assessment Program, 2003.

United Nations. Food and Agriculture Organization. 2007. "FishStat Plus." http://www.fao.org/fi/website/FIRetrieveAction.do?dom=topic&fid=16073 (accessed 20 March 2007).

United States. Department of Agriculture and Environmental Protection Agency. 1999. *Unified National Strategy for Animal Feeding Operations.* Washington, DC: Department of Agriculture–Environmental Protection Agency, March.

United States. Environmental Protection Agency. 1995. *Progress Report.* Washington, DC: Environmental Protection Agency.

– 2000. *Non–point Source Management Program.* Washington, DC: Environmental Protection Agency, Office of Water. www.epa.gov/OWOW/NPS/index.html (accessed 29 July 2005).

– 2003. *Water Quality Trading Policy.* Washington, DC: Environmental Protection Agency, Office of Water.

United States. Office of Technology Assessment. 1995. *Environmental Policy Tools: A User's Guide.* Washington, DC: Office of Technology Assessment.

Vaillancourt, M., et al. 2003. *St. Lawrence Vision 2000 – Five-Year Report (1998–2003).* Report to the Government of Canada and Government of Quebec.

VanderZwaag, David L. 1983. *The Fish Feud: The U.S. and Canada Boundary Dispute.* Lexington, MA: Lexington Books.

VanderZwaag, David L., and L. Duncan. 1992. "Canada and Environmental Protection: Confident Political Faces, Uncertain Legal Hands." In *Canadian Environmental Policy: Ecosystems, Politics, and Process,* ed. Robert Boardman. Toronto: Oxford University Press.

van Herk, Aritha. 2001. *Mavericks: An Incorrigible History of Alberta.* Toronto: Penguin.

Varela, Jorge Luis. 1996. "Regional Trends in International Law and Domestic Environmental Law: The Inter-American Hemisphere." In *NAFTA and the Environment,* ed. S.J. Rubin and D.C. Alexander. Boston: Kluwer Law International.

Vining, A.R., and D.L. Weimer. 1998. "Passive Use Benefits: Existence, Option, and Quasi-option Value." In *Handbook in Public Finance,* ed, F. Thompson and M. Green. New York: Marcel Dekker.

Volpe J., E. Taylor, B. Rimmer, and B. Glickman. 2000. "Evidence of Natural Reproduction of Aquaculture-Escaped Atlantic Salmon in a Coastal British Columbia River." *Conservation Biology* 14, no. 3: 899–903.

Vonhof, J.A. 1985. *Groundwater Issues: An Overview.* Research paper no. 4 for the Inquiry on Federal Water Policy. Toronto: University of Toronto.

Waite, Thomas D. 1984. *Principles of Water Quality.* New York: Academic Press.

Walters, Carl. 1995. *Fish on the Line: The Future of Pacific Fisheries.* Vancouver: David Suzuki Foundation.

Walters, Carl, and Peter Cahoon. 1985. "Evidence for Decreasing Spatial Diversity in British Columbia Salmon Stocks." *Canadian Journal of Fisheries and Aquatic Sciences* 42, no. 5: 1033–7.

Walters, Carl, and Peter H. Pearse. 1996. "Stock Information Requirements for Quota Management Systems in Commercial Fisheries." *Reviews in Fish Biology and Fisheries* 6, no. 1: 21–42.

Ward, James, and Lloyd Augustine. 2000. *Draft for EFN Management Plan.* Waterford: New Brunswick Environmental Network. www.nben.ca/aboutus/caucus/archived_caucuses/ffa_archive/00/mplan.htm (accessed December 2004).

Washington State. 1919. *Annual Report of the State Fish Commissioner.* Report 28–29. Olympia.

Waterfield, Donald. 1970. *Continental Waterboy: The Columbia River Controversy.* Toronto: Clark, Irwin and Company.

Waterloo, Region of. 2003. *Business Water Quality Program.* Previously available at www.oceta.on.ca/programs/bwqp_brochure/business%20water%20quality.htm (accessed November 2003).

"Water Policy: There's Plenty Up North." 1999. *Economist* 350, no. 8103: 26–9.

Watson, Paul. 2002. *Seal Wars: Twenty-five Years on the Front Lines with the Harp Seals.* Toronto: Key Porter Books.

Webb, Kernaghan. 2005. "Sustainable Governance in the Twenty First Century: Moving beyond Instrument Choice." In *Designing Government: From Instruments to Governance*, ed. Pearl Eliadis, Margaret M. Hill, and Michael Howlett. Montreal: McGill-Queen's University Press.

Weersink, Alfons, John Livernois, Jason Shogren, and James Shortle. 1998. "Economic Instruments and Environmental Policy in Agriculture." *Canadian Public Policy* 24, no. 3: 309–27.

Weinstein, M. 2000. "Pieces of the Puzzle: Solutions for Community-Based Fisheries Management from Native Canadians, Japanese Cooperatives, and Common Property Researchers." *Georgetown International Law Review* 12, no. 2: 375–412.

Wenar, Leif. 1997. "Private Property: Conceptual and Normative Analyses." PhD dissertation, Harvard University.

Whorley, D., and M. Winfield. 2002. "Competing Narratives and the Walkerton Inquiry: Institutional Factors in Tragic Choices." Paper presented at the Canadian Political Science Association annual meeting, University of Toronto, Toronto, 30 May.

Whylynko, B. 1999. "Beyond Command and Control: A New Environmental Strategy Links Voluntarism and Government Initiative." In *Voluntary Initia-*

tives and the New Politics of Corporate Greening, ed. Robert Gibson. Peterborough, ON: Broadview Press.

Wicken, William C. 2002. *Mi'kmaq Treaties on Trial: History, Land and Donald Marshall Junior.* Toronto: University of Toronto Press.

Willis, Nancy. 2003. "Fishermen Gather to Decide Next Steps in Herring Protest." *Guardian,* 11 November.

Wilson, J. 2002. "Scientific Uncertainty, Complex Systems, and the Design of Common-Pool Institutions." In *The Drama of the Commons,* ed. Elinor Ostrom et al. Washington, DC: National Academy Press.

Windsor, J.F., ed. 1992. *Water Export: Should Canada's Water Be for Sale?* Cambridge, ON: Canadian Water Resources Association.

Winfield, M. 1994. "The Ultimate Horizontal Issue." *Canadian Journal of Political Science* 27: 1.

Wood, Owen. 2002. *Water Facts and Figures.* CBC News online. Previously available at cbc.ca/news/indepth/background/groundwater2.html (accessed 1 July 2003).

World Commission on Dams. 2000. *Dams and Development: A New Framework for Decision Making: The Report of the World Commission on Dams.* London: Earthscan Publications.

World Commission on Environment and Development. 1987. *Our Common Future.* Oxford: Oxford University Press.

Wu, J., K. Skelton-Groth, W.G. Boggess, and R.M. Adams. 2003. "Pacific Salmon Restoration: Trade-offs between Economic Efficiency and Political Acceptance." *Contemporary Economic Policy* 21, no. 1: 78–89.

Yee, P., R. Edgett, and A. Eberhardt. 1990. *Great Lakes–St. Lawrence River Regulation: What It Means and How It Works.* Environment Canada and U.S. Army Corps of Engineers.

Young, Oran R. 2002. *The Institutional Dimensions of Environmental Change: Fit, Interplay, and Scale.* Cambridge: MIT Press.

Index